Eclipse For Dumm...

Sheet

Getting Stuff Done

Create a project: Choose File⇨New⇨Project. In the New Project dialog, select Java Project, and click Next. In the New Java Project Wizard, fill in the Project Name field, and click Finish.

Create a package: Right-click a project in the Package Explorer's tree. In the resulting context menu, choose New⇨Package. In the New Java Package dialog, fill in the Name field (with a name like `com.allmycode.mypackage`) and click Finish.

Create a Java class: Right-click a package in the Package Explorer's tree. In the resulting context menu, choose New⇨Class. In the New Java Class Wizard, fill in the Name field. Then click Finish.

Create a main method: Place the cursor in the editor at the point where the main method belongs. Type **main**, and press Ctrl+Space. In the resulting pop-up list, select `main - main method`.

Quickly correct a compiler error: Right-click the red error marker in the editor's marker bar (to the left of the code). In the resulting context menu, choose Quick Fix. A list of possible fixes appears. Select an item in the list to find out how that item's fix modified your code. When you find an item that you like, double-click the item, or simply press Enter.

Format your code: Select one or more Java classes. Then, on the main menu, choose Source⇨Format. Eclipse doesn't automatically save the code after formatting, so finish up by choosing File⇨Save.

Locate text in one file: Select a file in an editor. Then, on the main menu, choose Edit⇨Find/Replace. The Find/Replace dialog appears. In the dialog's Find field, type the text that you want to locate. If you intend to replace text, type the replacement text in the Replace With field. Then click Find, Replace/Find, Replace, or Replace All.

Locate text in a collection of files (without regard to the meaning of the text in a Java program): Select the files that you want to search. (Select them in the Package Explorer or the Navigator view.) Then, on the main menu, choose Search⇨File. The Search dialog appears. (The Search dialog displays its File Search tab.) Type the text that you want to locate in the Containing Text field. Choose Selected Resources in the lower half of the File Search tab. Then click Search.

Locate text in a collection of files (taking into account the meaning of the text in a Java program): Select the files that you want to search. (Select them in the Package Explorer or the Navigator view.) Then, on the main menu, choose Search⇨Java. The Search dialog appears. (The Search dialog displays its Java Search tab.) Type the text that you want to locate in the Search String field. Narrow your search with the Search For and Limit To radio buttons. Choose Selected Resources in the lower half of the File Search tab. Then click Search.

Add a Javadoc comment: Place the cursor in the editor at the point where the new Javadoc comment belongs. Then choose Source⇨Add Javadoc Comment from the main menu bar.

Eclipse For Dummies®

Cheat Sheet

Getting Stuff Done (continued)

Create Javadoc pages from existing Javadoc comments: Select the projects or source files whose Javadoc pages you want to create. (Select them in the Package Explorer, the Navigator view, the Outline view, or in an editor.) Then, on the main menu bar, choose Project⇨Generate Javadoc.

See an existing Javadoc page: Select the element whose Javadoc page you want to see. (Select it in the Package Explorer, the Outline view, or in an editor.) Then, on the main menu bar, choose Navigate⇨Open External Javadoc.

Run a class that contains a main method: Select a class. (Select it in the Package Explorer, the Navigator view, the Outline view, or in an editor.) Then, on the main menu bar, choose Run⇨Run⇨Java Application.

Run a class with main method arguments: Select a class. (Select it in the Package Explorer, the Navigator view, the Outline view, or in an editor.) Then, on the main menu bar, choose Run⇨Run. A Run dialog appears. If the class that you selected doesn't appear as a branch in the Run dialog's tree, then double-click the tree's Java Application branch. In the body of the Run dialog, select the Arguments tab. In the Arguments tab's Program Arguments field, type the string values that you want to give to the main method's arguments array. (Use blank spaces to separate the string values from one another. Don't surround the string values with quotation marks.) Finally, click Apply, and then click Run.

Allow one project to refer to other projects' names: Right-click a project's branch in the Package Explorer. On the resulting context menu, choose Properties. A Properties dialog appears. In the dialog's left pane, select Java Build Path. Then, on the right side of the Run dialog, select the Projects tab. In the Projects tab's list, put check marks next to projects that contain targeted names.

For context-sensitive help: In Windows, press F1. In Linux, press Ctrl+F1. On a Mac, press Help.

For help that's not context-sensitive: On the main menu bar, choose Help⇨Help Contents. The Help view appears. In the Help view's Search field, type the words that you need help understanding. Press GO, and wait for the `To search the documentation, type a query. . .` message to disappear. When at last the Search Results tab displays a list of pages, select a page. The page opens in the Help view's browser pane.

Close Eclipse, and then reopen Eclipse using another workspace: On the main menu bar, choose File⇨Switch Workspace. Then in the Workspace Launcher dialog, type the name of the folder that contains the new workspace. Finally, click OK.

Copyright © 2005 Wiley Publishing, Inc.
All rights reserved.

Item 7470-1.

For more information about Wiley Publishing, call 1-800-762-2974.

For Dummies: Bestselling Book Series for Beginners

by Barry Burd

Wiley Publishing, Inc.

Eclipse For Dummies®

Published by
Wiley Publishing, Inc.
111 River Street
Hoboken, NJ 07030-5774

Copyright © 2005 by Wiley Publishing, Inc., Indianapolis, Indiana

Published by Wiley Publishing, Inc., Indianapolis, Indiana

Published simultaneously in Canada

WILEY

About the Author

Dr. Barry Burd received an M.S. degree in Computer Science at Rutgers University and a Ph.D. in Mathematics at the University of Illinois. As a teaching assistant in Champaign-Urbana, Illinois, he was elected five times to the university-wide List of Teachers Ranked as Excellent by their Students.

Since 1980, Dr. Burd has been a professor in the Department of Mathematics and Computer Science at Drew University in Madison, New Jersey. When he's not lecturing at Drew University, Dr. Burd leads training courses for professional programmers in business and industry. He has lectured at conferences in the United States, Europe, Australia, and Asia. He is the author of several articles and books, including *JSP: JavaServer Pages,* published by Wiley Publishing, Inc.

Dr. Burd lives in Madison, New Jersey, with his wife and two children. In his spare time, he enjoys being a workaholic.

Dedication

For

Abram and Katie, Benjamin and Jennie, Sam and Ruth, Harriet, Sam, and Jennie,

Author's Acknowledgments

	Tasks ⊠	
11 items		
·	Description	
	THANK YOU to Paul Levesque, winner of this year's award for the Classiest and Most Patient Project Editor	
	THANK YOU to Katie Feltman, for her unrelenting belief in this project (and in my ability to finish it)	
	THANKS to Rebecca Senninger for untangling the tightly drawn knots that I call sentences and paragraphs	
	THANKS to tech editor John Purdum for finding my mistakes before this book goes to print	
	THANKS to Laura Lewin and the people at Studio B for tending to business matters (which I always hate doing)	
	A BIG THANK YOU to Faizan Ahmed for introducing me to Eclipse	
	THANKS to the members of the Central Jersey Java Users' Group, the Java Users Group of the	
	. Amateur Computer Group of New Jersey, and the New York Java Special Interest Group	
	AND SPECIAL THANKS (AS USUAL) to Jennie, Sam, and Harriet who put up with me day in and day out	
	. (with almost minimal complaining, except when I deserve it, which is more often than I'd like to admit)	

Publisher's Acknowledgments

We're proud of this book; please send us your comments through our online registration form located at `www.dummies.com/register/`.

Some of the people who helped bring this book to market include the following:

Acquisitions, Editorial, and Media Development

Project Editor: Paul Levesque

Acquisitions Editor: Katie Feltman

Copy Editor: Rebecca Senninger

Technical Editor: John Purdum

Editorial Manager: Kevin Kirschner

Media Development Manager: Laura VanWinkle

Media Development Supervisor: Richard Graves

Editorial Assistant: Amanda Foxworth

Cartoons: Rich Tennant (`www.the5thwave.com`)

Composition Services

Project Coordinator: Maridee Ennis

Layout and Graphics: Andrea Dahl, Lauren Goddard, Joyce Haughey, Barry Offringa, Lynsey Osborn, Jacque Roth, Heather Ryan, Julie Trippetti, Mary Gillot Virgin

Proofreaders: Leeann Harney, Joe Niesen, TECHBOOKS Production Services

Indexer: TECHBOOKS Production Services

Publishing and Editorial for Technology Dummies

Richard Swadley, Vice President and Executive Group Publisher

Andy Cummings, Vice President and Publisher

Mary Bednarek, Executive Acquisitions Director

Mary C. Corder, Editorial Director

Publishing for Consumer Dummies

Diane Graves Steele, Vice President and Publisher

Joyce Pepple, Acquisitions Director

Composition Services

Gerry Fahey, Vice President of Production Services

Debbie Stailey, Director of Composition Services

Contents at a Glance

Table of Contents

Introduction

∙ ∙

"There's no such thing as a free lunch."

That's what New York City Mayor Fiorello LaGuardia said back in 1934. Not many people understood the meaning or the impact of Mayor LaGuardia's statement, because he said it in Latin. ("E finita la cuccagna," said the mayor.) But today, most people agree with the spirit of LaGuardia's proclamation.

Well, they're all wrong. I have two stunning examples to prove that there is such a thing as a free lunch.

- ✔ I'm the faculty representative to the Dining Service Committee at Drew University. During the regular academic year, the committee meets once every two weeks. We meet in the university commons to evaluate and discuss the dining facilities. As a courtesy to all committee members, lunch is free.

- ✔ Open source software doesn't cost a dime. You can download it, use it, modify it, and reuse it. If you have questions about the software, you can post your questions for free in online forums. Usually someone answers your question quickly (and for free).

Many people shy away from open source software. They think open source software is unreliable. They believe that software created by a community of volunteers is less robust than software created by organized business. Again, they're wrong. The open source Linux project shows that a community of volunteers can rival the effectiveness of a commercial software vendor. And some of my favorite Windows utilities are free for download on the Web.*

This harangue about open source software brings me to one of my favorite subjects: namely, Eclipse. When you download Eclipse, you pay nothing, nada, zip, bupkis, goose egg, diddly-squat. And what you get is a robust, powerful, extensible Java development environment.

The free CatFish program from Equi4 software does a better job cataloging CD-ROMs than any commercial software that I've tried. Mike Lin's Startup Control Panel and MCL utilities beat the competition without costing any money. You can find CatFish at www.equi4.com, and Mike Lin's programs live at www.mlin.net.

In a recent survey conducted by QA Systems, Eclipse has a 45 percent share in the Java IDE market.* That's nearly three times the market share of the highest-ranking competitor — Borland JBuilder. In June 2003, the editors of the *Java Developer's Journal* gave two Editors' Choice awards to Eclipse. As one editor wrote, "After being anti-IDE for so long I've finally caved in. It (Eclipse) has nice CVS utils, project frameworks, code refactoring and 'sensible' code generation (especially for beans). Add industry backing and a very fired up user base and you have one winning product."**

Conventions Used in This Book

Almost every technical book starts with a little typeface legend, and *Eclipse For Dummies* is no exception. What follows is a brief explanation of the typefaces used in this book.

- ✔ New terms are set in *italics*.

- ✔ If you need to type something that's mixed in with the regular text, the characters you type appear in bold. For example: "Type **MyNewProject** in the text field."

- ✔ You also see this `computerese` font. I use computerese for Java code, filenames, Web page addresses (URLs), on-screen messages, and other such things. Also, if something you need to type is really long, it appears in computerese font on its own line (or lines).

- ✔ You need to change certain things when you type them on your own computer keyboard. For instance, I may ask you to type

```
public class Anyname
```

which means that you type **public class** and then some name that you make up on your own. Words that you need to replace with your own words are set in *italicized computerese*.

What You Don't Have to Read

Eclipse For Dummies is a reference manual, not a tutorial guide. You can read this book from the middle forward, from the middle backward, from the inside out, upside down, or any way you want to read it.

* *For more information, visit* `www.qa-systems.com/products/qstudio forjava/ide_marketshare.html`.

** *For details, visit* `www.eclipse.org/org/press-release/ jun92003jdjadv.html`.

Naturally, some parts of the book use terms that I describe in other parts of the book. But I don't throw around terminology unless I absolutely must. And at many points in the book I include Cross Reference icons. A Cross Reference icon reminds you that the confusion you may feel is normal. Refer to *such-and-such* chapter to rid yourself of that confused feeling.

The sidebars and Technical Stuff icons are extra material — stuff that you can skip without getting into any trouble at all. So if you want to ignore a sidebar or a Technical Stuff icon, please do. In fact, if you want to skip anything at all, feel free.

Foolish Assumptions

In this book, I make a few assumptions about you, the reader. If one of these assumptions is incorrect, you're probably okay. If all these assumptions are incorrect . . . well, buy the book anyway.

- ✔ **I assume that you have access to a computer.** You need a 330 MHz computer with 256MB RAM and 300MB of free hard drive space. If you have a faster computer with more RAM or more free hard drive space, then you're in very good shape. The computer doesn't have to run Windows. It can run Windows, UNIX, Linux, or Mac OS X 10.2 or higher.

- ✔ **I assume that you can navigate through your computer's common menus and dialogs.** You don't have to be a Windows, UNIX, or Macintosh power user, but you should be able to start a program, find a file, put a file into a certain directory . . . that sort of thing. Most of the time, when you practice the stuff in this book, you're typing code on your keyboard, not pointing and clicking your mouse.

  On those rare occasions when you need to drag and drop, cut and paste, or plug and play, I guide you carefully through the steps. But your computer may be configured in any of several billion ways, and my instructions may not quite fit your special situation. So, when you reach one of these platform-specific tasks, try following the steps in this book. If the steps don't quite fit, consult a book with instructions tailored to your system.

- ✔ **I assume that you can write Java programs, or that you're learning Java from some other source while you read *Eclipse For Dummies*.** In Chapter 1, I make a big fuss about Eclipse's use with many different programming languages. "Eclipse is . . . a Java development environment, a C++ development environment, or even a COBOL development environment."

  But from Chapter 2 on, I say "Java *this*," and "Java *that*." Heck, the beginning of Chapter 2 tells you to download the Java Runtime Environment. Well, what do you expect? I wrote *Java 2 For Dummies*. Of course I'm partial to Java.

In fact, Eclipse as it's currently implemented is very biased toward Java. So most of this book's examples refer to Java programs of one kind or another. Besides, if you don't know much about Java, then many of Eclipse's menu items (items such as Add Javadoc Comment and Convert Local Variable to Field) won't make much sense to you.

As you read this book, you may not know Java from the get-go. You may be using *Eclipse For Dummies* as a supplement while you learn Java programming. That's just fine. Pick and choose what you read and what you don't read.

If a section in this book uses unfamiliar Java terminology, then skip that section. And if you can't skip a section, then postpone reading the section until you've slurped a little more Java. And . . . if you can't postpone your reading, then try reading the Eclipse section without dwelling on the section's example. You have plenty of alternatives. One way or another, you can get what you need from this book.

How This Book Is Organized

This book is divided into subsections, which are grouped into sections, which come together to make chapters, which are lumped finally into four parts. (When you write a book, you get to know your book's structure pretty well. After months of writing, you find yourself dreaming in sections and chapters when you go to bed at night.)

Part I: The Eclipse Landscape

To a novice, the look and feel of Eclipse can be intimidating. The big Eclipse window contains many smaller windows, and some of the smaller windows have dozens of menus and buttons. When you first see all this, you may experience "Eclipse shock."

Part I helps you overcome Eclipse shock. This part guides you through each piece of Eclipse's user interface, and explains how each piece works.

Part II: Using the Eclipse Environment

Part II shows you what to do with Eclipse's vast system of menus. Edit Java source files, use refactoring to improve your code, search for elements within your Java projects. Everything you can think of doing with a Java program lies somewhere within these menus. (In fact, everything that everyone ever thought of doing with anything lies somewhere within these menus.)

Part III: Doing More with Eclipse

What more is there to do? Lots more. Part III describes ways to customize a Java project and the run of a Java program. This part also tells you how to find help on Eclipse's murkier features.

Part IV: The Part of Tens

The Part of Tens is a little Eclipse candy store. In The Part of Tens, you can find lots of useful tips.

Additional Web Sources!

One of my favorite things is writing code. But if your idea of a good time isn't writing code, I include every code listing in this book on a companion Web site at `www.dummies.com/go/eclipse_fd`. Feel free to download any code listings into Eclipse to follow along with my examples in this book or for any of your own projects.

And be sure to visit my Web site, `www.BurdBrain.com`, for any updates to *Eclipse For Dummies* and my additional ramblings about Eclipse.

Icons Used in This Book

If you could watch me write this book, you'd see me sitting at my computer, talking to myself. I say each sentence in my head. Most of the sentences I mutter several times. When I have an extra thought, a side comment, something that doesn't belong in the regular stream, I twist my head a little bit. That way, whoever's listening to me (usually nobody) knows that I'm off on a momentary tangent.

Of course, in print, you can't see me twisting my head. I need some other way of setting a side thought in a corner by itself. I do it with icons. When you see a Tip icon or a Remember icon, you know that I'm taking a quick detour.

Here's a list of icons that I use in this book.

A tip is an extra piece of information — something helpful that the other books may forget to tell you.

Everyone makes mistakes. Heaven knows that I've made a few in my time. Anyway, when I think people are especially prone to make a mistake, I mark it with a Warning icon.

Sometimes I want to hire a skywriting airplane crew. "Barry," says the white smoky cloud, "if you want to rename a Java element, start by selecting that element in the Package Explorer. Please don't forget to do this." Because I can't afford skywriting, I have to settle for something more modest. I create a Remember icon.

"If you don't remember what *such-and-such* means, see *blah-blah-blah*," or "For more information, read *blahbity-blah-blah.*"

This icon calls attention to useful material that you can find online. (You don't have to wait long to see one of these icons. I use one at the end of this introduction!)

Occasionally I run across a technical tidbit. The tidbit may help you understand what the people behind the scenes (the people who developed Java) were thinking. You don't have to read it, but you may find it useful. You may also find the tidbit helpful if you plan to read other (more geeky) books about Eclipse.

Where to Go from Here

If you've gotten this far, you're ready to start reading about Eclipse. Think of me (the author) as your guide, your host, your personal assistant. I do everything I can to keep things interesting and, most importantly, help you understand.

If you like what you read, send me a note. My e-mail address, which I created just for comments and questions about this book, is Eclipse@BurdBrain.com. And don't forget you can get the latest *Eclipse For Dummies* information at www.BurdBrain.com.

Part I
The Eclipse Landscape

The 5th Wave — By Rich Tennant

"Why, of course. I'd be very interested in seeing this new milestone in the project."

In this part . . .

I'll be the first to admit it. When I started working with Eclipse, I was confused. I saw an editor here, tabs and panes everywhere, and dozens upon dozens of menu options. Eclipse is more complicated than your run-of-the-mill programming environment. So your first taste of Eclipse can be intimidating.

But if you calm down and take things step by step, then Eclipse's options make sense. Eventually you become comfortable to the point of using Eclipse on autopilot.

So this part of *Eclipse For Dummies* contains the "calm down" chapters. This part describes Eclipse's user interface and tells you how to get the most out of Eclipse's grand user interface.

Chapter 1

Reader, Meet Eclipse; Eclipse, Meet the Reader

In This Chapter

▶ How I learned to love Eclipse

▶ How the Eclipse project is organized

▶ How Eclipse puts widgets on your screen

*T*he little hamlet of Somerset, New Jersey, is home to an official Sun Microsystems sales office. Once a month, that office hosts a meeting of the world-renowned Central Jersey Java Users' Group.

At one month's meeting, group members were discussing their favorite Java development environments. "I prefer JBlipper," said one of the members. "My favorite is Javoorta Pro," said another. Then one fellow (Faizan was his name) turned to the group and said, "What about Eclipse? It's pretty sweet."

Of course, Faizan's remark touched off an argument. Everyone in the group is attached to his or her favorite Java development tools. "Does Javoorta do refactoring?" "Does JBlipper support Enterprise JavaBeans?" "Does Eclipse run on a Mac?" "How can you say that your development environment is better?" "And what about good old UNIX vi?"

Then someone asked Faizan to demonstrate Eclipse at the next users' group meeting. Faizan agreed, so I ended the discussion by suggesting that we go out for a beer. "I don't drink," said one of the group members. "I don't either," I said. So we went out for pizza.

At the next meeting, Faizan demonstrated the Eclipse development environment. After Faizan's presentation, peoples' objections to Eclipse were more muted. "Are you sure that Eclipse runs well under Linux?" "Can you really extend Eclipse so easily?" "How does the open source community create such good software for free?"

A few months later, I ran into a group member at a local Linux conference. "Does Javoorta Pro run under Linux?" I asked. "I don't use Javoorta Pro anymore. I've switched to Eclipse," he said. "That's interesting," I said. "Hey, let's go out for a beer."

An Integrated Development Environment

An *integrated development environment* (IDE) is an all-in-one tool for writing, editing, compiling, and running computer programs. And Eclipse is an excellent integrated development environment. In a sense, that's all ye need to know.

Of course, what you absolutely need to know and what's good for you to know may be two different things. You can learn all kinds of things about Java and Eclipse, and still benefit by learning more. So with that in mind, I've put together this chapter full of facts. I call it my "useful things to know about Eclipse" (my "uttkaE") chapter.

A Little Bit of History (Not Too Much)

In November 2001, IBM released $40 million worth of software tools into the public domain. Starting with this collection of tools, several organizations created a consortium of IDE providers. They called this consortium the Eclipse Foundation, Inc. Eclipse was to be "a universal tool platform — an open extensible IDE for anything and nothing in particular."* (I know, it sounds a little like Seinfeld's "nothing." But don't be lead astray. Eclipse and Seinfeld have very little in common.)

This talk about "anything and nothing in particular" reflects Eclipse's ingenious plug-in architecture. At its heart, Eclipse isn't really a Java development environment. Eclipse is just a vessel — a holder for a bunch of add-ons that form a kick-butt Java, C++, or even a COBOL development environment. Each add-on is called a *plug-in,* and the Eclipse that you normally use is composed of more than 80 useful plug-ins.

While the Eclipse Foundation was shifting into high gear, several other things were happening in the world of integrated development environments. IBM was building WebSphere Studio Application Developer (WSAD) — a big Java development environment based on Eclipse. And Sun Microsystems was

Quoted from the eclipse.org Web site: www.eclipse.org.

promoting NetBeans. Like Eclipse, NetBeans is a set of building blocks for creating Java development environments. But unlike Eclipse, NetBeans is pure Java. So a few years ago, war broke out between Eclipse people and NetBeans people. And the war continues to this day.

In 2004, the Eclipse Foundation turned itself from an industry consortium to an independent not-for-profit organization. Among other things, this meant having an Executive Director — Mike Milinkovich, formerly of Oracle Corporation. Apparently, Milinkovich is the Eclipse Foundation's only paid employee. Everybody else donates his or her time to create Eclipse — the world's most popular Java development environment.

The Grand Scheme of Things in Eclipse

The Eclipse Foundation divides its work into projects and subprojects. The projects you may hear about the most are the Eclipse project, the Eclipse Tools project, and the Eclipse Technology project.

Sure, these project names can be confusing. The "Eclipse project" is only one part of the Eclipse Foundation's work, and the "Eclipse project" is different from the "Eclipse Tools project." But bear with me. This section gives you some background on all these different projects.

And why would you ever want to know about the Eclipse Foundation's projects? Why should I bother you with details about the Foundation's administrative organization? Well, when you read about the Foundation's projects, you get a sense of the way the Eclipse software is organized. You have a better understanding of where you are and what you're doing when you use Eclipse.

The Eclipse project

The *Eclipse project* is the Eclipse Foundation's major backbone. This big Eclipse project has three subprojects — the Platform subproject, the Java Development Tools subproject, and the Plug-in Development subproject.

The Platform subproject

The *Platform subproject* deals with things that are common to all aspects of Eclipse — things such as text editing, searching, help pages, debugging, and versioning.

At the very center of the Platform subproject is the platform *core*. The core consists of the barebones necessities — the code for starting and running Eclipse, the creation and management of plug-ins, and the management of other basic program resources.

In addition, the Platform subproject defines the general look and feel of Eclipse's user interface. This user interface is based on two technologies — one that's controversial, and another that's not so controversial. The controversial technology is called SWT — the *Standard Widget Toolkit*. The not-so-controversial technology is called *JFace*.

✔ The Standard Widget Toolkit is a collection of basic graphical interface classes and methods, including things such as buttons, menus, labels, and events.

For more chitchat about the Standard Widget Toolkit (and to find out why the Toolkit is so controversial), see the second half of this chapter.

✔ JFace is a set of higher-level graphical interface tools, including things such as wizards, viewers, and text formatters. JFace builds on the work that the Standard Widget Toolkit starts.

The Java Development Tools (JDT) subproject

The word "Java" appears more than 700 times in this book. (Yes, I counted.) In many people's minds, Eclipse is nothing more than an integrated development environment for Java. Heck, if you start running Eclipse you see the Java perspective, Java projects, Java search tools, and a bunch of other Java-specific things.

But Java is only part of the Eclipse picture. In reality, Eclipse is a language-neutral platform that happens to house a mature Java development environment. That Java development environment is a separate subproject. It's called the *Java Development Tools* (JDT) subproject. The subproject includes things like the Java compiler, Java editor enhancements, an integrated debugger, and more.

When Eclipse documentation refers to the "core," it can be referring to a number of different things. The Platform subproject has a core, and the JDT subproject has a core of its own. Before you jump to one core or another in search of information, check to see what the word "core" means in context.

The Plug-in Development Environment (PDE) subproject

Eclipse is very modular. Eclipse is nothing but a bony frame on which dozens of plug-ins have been added. Each plug-in creates a bit of functionality, and together the plug-ins make a very rich integrated development environment.

But wait! A plug-in is a piece of code, and the people who create plug-ins use development environments, too. For these plug-in creators, Eclipse is both a tool and a target. These people use Eclipse in order to write plug-ins for Eclipse.

So wouldn't it be nice to have some specialized tools for creating Eclipse plug-ins? That way, a programmer can seamlessly use Eclipse while writing code for Eclipse.

Well, whadaya' know? Someone's already thought up this specialized tools idea. They call it PDE — the *Plug-in Development Environment* — and they have an entire subproject devoted to this Plug-in Development Environment.

The Eclipse Tools project

Compared with the main Eclipse project, the *Eclipse Tools* project houses subprojects that are a bit farther from Eclipse's center. Here are some examples.

The Visual Editor subproject

If you're familiar with products like Visual Basic, then you've seen some handy drag-and-drop tools. With these tools you drag buttons, text fields, and other goodies from a palette onto a user form. To create an application's user interface, you don't describe the interface with cryptic code. Instead you draw the interface with your mouse.

In Eclipse 3.0, these drag-and-drop capabilities still aren't integrated into the main Eclipse bundle. Instead, they're a separate download. They're housed in the *Visual Editor* (VE) — a subproject of the Eclipse Tools Project.

The CDT and COBOL IDE subprojects

The *C/C++ Development Tools* (CDT) subproject develops an IDE for the C/C++ family of languages. So after downloading a plug-in, you can use Eclipse to write C++ programs.

As if the CDT isn't far enough from Java, the *COBOL IDE* subproject has its own Eclipse-based integrated development environment. (COBOL programs don't look anything like Java programs. After using Eclipse for a few years to develop Java programs, I feel really strange staring at a COBOL program in Eclipse's editor.)

The UML2 subproject

The *Unified Modeling Language* (UML) is a very popular methodology for modeling software processes. With UML diagrams, you can plan a large programming endeavor, and work your way thoughtfully from the plan to the actual code. The tricks for any integrated development environment are to help you create models, and to provide automated pathways between the models and the code. That's what *UML2* (another subproject of the Eclipse Tools project) is all about.

The Eclipse Technology project

The *Eclipse Technology project* is all about outreach — helping the rest of the world become involved in Eclipse and its endeavors. The Technology project fosters research, educates the masses, and acts as a home for ideas that are on their way to becoming major subprojects.

As of 2004, this project's emerging technologies include *Voice Tools* — tools to work effectively with speech recognition, pronunciation, and the control of voice-driven user interfaces.

Another cool item in the Eclipse Technology project is *AspectJ.* The name AspectJ comes from two terms — aspect-oriented programming and Java. In AspectJ, you can connect similar parts of a programming project even though the parts live in separate regions of your code. AspectJ is an up-and-coming extension to the Java programming language.

What's the Best Way to Create a Window?

According to Sun Microsystems, Java is a "Write Once, Run Anywhere" programming language. This means that a Java program written on a Macintosh runs effortlessly on a Microsoft Windows or UNIX computer. That's fine for programs that deal exclusively with text, but what about windows, buttons, text fields, and all that good stuff? When it comes to using graphical interfaces, the "Write Once, Run Anywhere" philosophy comes up against some serious obstacles.

Each operating system (Windows, UNIX, or whatever) has its own idiosyncratic way of creating graphical components. A call to select text in one operating system's text field may not work at all on another operating system's text field. And when you try to translate one operating system's calls to another operating system's calls, you run into trouble. There's no good English translation for the Yiddish word *schlemiel,* and there's no good Linux translation for Microsoft's object linking and embedding calls.

When Java was first created, it came with only one set of graphical interface classes. This set of classes is called the *Abstract Windowing Toolkit* (AWT). With the AWT, you can create windows, buttons, text fields, and other nice looking things. Like any of Java's "Write Once, Run Anywhere" libraries, the AWT runs on any operating system. But the AWT has an awkward relationship with each operating system's code.

The AWT uses something called *peers.* You don't have to know exactly how peers work. All you have to know is that a peer is an extra layer of code. It's an extra layer between the AWT and a particular operating system's graphical interface code. On one computer, a peer lives between the AWT code and the UNIX code. On another computer, the peer lives between the AWT code and the Microsoft Windows code.

The AWT with its peer architecture has at least one big disadvantage. The AWT can't do anything that's not similar across all operating systems. If two operating systems do radically different things to display trees, then the AWT simply cannot display trees. Each of the AWT's capabilities belongs to the least common denominator — the set of things that every popular operating system can do.

Here comes Swing

Somewhere along the way, the people at Sun Microsystems agreed that the AWT isn't an ideal graphical interface library. So they created *Swing* — a newer alternative that doesn't rely on peers. In fact, Swing relies on almost nothing.

With the AWT, you write code that says "Microsoft Windows, please display a button for me." But with Swing you don't do this. With Swing you say "draw some lines, then fill in a rectangle, then put some text in the rectangle." Eventually you have all the lines and colors that make up a button. But Microsoft Windows doesn't know (or care) that you've drawn a button.

To use the official slogan, Swing is "pure Java." Swing draws everything on your screen from scratch. Sure, a Swing button may look like a UNIX button, a Macintosh button, or a Microsoft Windows button. But that's just because the Swing developers work hard to replicate each operating system's look and feel.

Here's the problem with Swing: Drawing windows and buttons from scratch can be very time consuming. In my experience, Swing applications tend to run slowly.* That's why people who develop Eclipse plug-ins don't use Java's Swing classes. Instead, they use classes from the Standard Widget Toolkit (SWT).

The Standard Widget Toolkit

The word "widget" comes from the play "Beggar on Horseback," written in the early 1920s by George Kaufman and Marc Connelly. (I first heard of widgets when I saw the 1963 James Garner movie *The Wheeler Dealers*.) In ordinary usage, the word "widget" means a vaguely described gadget —

My friends at Sun Microsystems claim that Swing applications are lightning fast, but I can't tackle that debate in this book.

a hypothetical product whose use and design is unimportant compared to its marketing potential.

In computing, the word "widget" represents a component in a graphical user interface — a button, a text field, a window, or whatever. That's why a group of developers coined the phrase *Standard Widget Toolkit* (SWT). These developers were people from Object Technology International and IBM. At first they created widgets for the language SmallTalk. Later they moved from SmallTalk to Java.

In contrast to Swing, Eclipse's SWT is very fast and efficient. When I run Eclipse under Linux, I don't wait and watch as my buttons appear on the screen. My SWT buttons appear very quickly — as quickly as my plain, old Linux buttons.

To achieve this speed, the SWT ignores Java's "Write Once, Run Anywhere" philosophy. Like the AWT, the SWT isn't pure Java. But unlike the AWT, the SWT has no peer layer.

The SWT isn't nearly as portable as Swing's pure Java code, and this lack of portability drives the "pure Java" advocates crazy. So the big debate is between Swing and the SWT. Sun's NetBeans IDE calls Swing classes to display its dialogs and editors, and Eclipse calls SWT classes. This difference between NetBeans and Eclipse has several important consequences.

- ✔ **Eclipse runs noticeably faster than NetBeans (unless you run NetBeans on a very powerful computer).**

- ✔ **Eclipse's graphical interface isn't merely an imitation of your computer's interface.**

  The button on a NetBeans panel may look like a Linux button or like a Microsoft Windows button, but it's not really one of these buttons. A NetBeans button is a drawing that's made to look like a Microsoft Windows button.

  In contrast, the button on an Eclipse panel is the real McCoy. When you run Eclipse on a Macintosh, you see real Macintosh buttons. When you run Eclipse in Windows, you see Bill Gates's own buttons.

  Do you want real buttons or simulated buttons? Believe it or not, you can see the difference.

- ✔ **Eclipse can use tools that are specific to each operating system.**

  If you run Eclipse under Microsoft Windows, you can take advantage of the functionality provided by Windows ActiveX components. But if you run Eclipse under Linux, then you can't use ActiveX components. That's why certain features of the Eclipse IDE are available in Windows, but not in Linux.

In stark contrast to the situation with Eclipse, NetBeans doesn't use ActiveX components. (Even on a computer that runs Microsoft Windows, NetBeans doesn't take advantage of any ActiveX functionality.)

✔ **In theory, Eclipse isn't as portable as NetBeans.**

At www.eclipse.org you can download versions of Eclipse for Microsoft Windows, Linux, Solaris, QNX, UNIX, and Mac OS X. But if someone creates the MyNewOS operating system, then the NetBeans/Swing camp has a slight advantage over the Eclipse/SWT people.

All in all, I prefer Eclipse to NetBeans. And I'm not saying this only because I have a contract to write *Eclipse For Dummies.* For my money, the Eclipse development environment is simply a better tool than NetBeans.

Relax and Enjoy the Ride

As an Eclipse user, you wade through lots of written material about the SWT. That's why you want to know about the "SWT versus Swing" issue. But "knowing" doesn't mean "worrying." The war between the SWT and Swing has the greatest impact on people who write code for the Eclipse Foundation. The "SWT versus Swing" controversy comes alive when you try to enhance the Eclipse development environment. But as a plain, old Eclipse user, you can just sit back and watch other people argue.

Using Eclipse, you can write Swing, SWT, AWT, and text-based applications. You can just go about your business and write whatever Java code you're accustomed to writing. So don't be upset by this chapter's "SWT versus Swing" harangue. Just remember some of the issues whenever you read other peoples' stories about Eclipse.

Chapter 2

Installing Eclipse

In This Chapter

▶ Downloading Eclipse

▶ Installing the software

▶ Testing your Eclipse installation

. . . .

Several months ago, my wife noticed a warm, musty odor coming from the clothes dryer. For me, it was a comforting odor. But my wife pointed out that a defective dryer vent hose is a safety hazard. So I went out and purchased a brand new vent hose.

When I returned home, I got right to work. Instead of fussing over every detail (the way I usually do), I just attached the hose and went back to my writing. I felt so proud. "I must be getting good at this sort of thing," I said to myself.

Several hours later, I went out to get some groceries. When I returned, I heard a curious humming noise coming from the basement. I guessed that my household computer-driven caller ID speaker system was misbehaving. I went down to the basement to have a look.

Lo, and behold! Everything in my basement office was wet, including my main Windows computer, my Linux box, my Solaris machine, and my beloved caller ID computer. I had removed my washer's drain hose, and forgotten to reattach it. Of course, my first instinct was to get on the phone and call my publisher. I wanted to milk this incident as an excuse for missing a deadline.

So that's the story. I can't be trusted to install household appliance parts. Fortunately for everyone, I'm much better at installing computer software.

Setting Up Eclipse on Your Computer

In this chapter, I make a doubtful assumption. I assume that you know very little about installing software on your computer's operating system. Chances are, this assumption is wrong, wrong, wrong. But that's okay. You can skip any material that's too elementary for your tastes. (Unfortunately, I can't reimburse you for the price of the pages that you don't read.)

Installing Eclipse is like installing almost any other software. First you make sure you have the prerequisite tools, then you download the software, and finally you deposit the software in a reasonable place on your computer's hard drive.

Having enough hardware

No one can tell you exactly how much hardware is enough. The amount of hardware you need depends upon several factors, such as the kinds of Java programs you want to run, the amount of time you're willing to watch Eclipse work, and so on. The hardware also involves tradeoffs. For instance, if you have a little more memory, you can get away with a little less processing power. I've installed Eclipse on a Pentium II running at 330 MHz with 256MB RAM. With this configuration, I wait about a minute for Eclipse to start up, but it's worth the wait. When the program runs, the performance is acceptable.

How much hard drive space do you need? Again, it depends on what you're doing, but here's the general idea:

- ✔ **You need more than 100MB of disk space for the Eclipse code.**
- ✔ **You need another 70MB for the Java Runtime Environment.**
- ✔ **You need space to store whatever code you plan to develop using Eclipse.**

    If you're just tinkering to learn to use Eclipse, the additional space for this item is negligible. But if you're creating an industrial-strength application, you need gigabytes (or even terabytes).

- ✔ **You need wiggle room for all the other things your computer has to do.**

    I become nervous when I have less than 100MB of free disk space. But that's a very personal preference.

Taking all four items into consideration, I like to start with at least 300MB of free disk space. If I don't have 300MB, then I don't install Eclipse. (If I don't have 300MB, I install a disk-cleaning program whether I plan to install Eclipse or not.)

Getting and installing the Java Runtime Environment

Eclipse comes with *almost* everything you need to write and run Java programs. I emphasize "almost" because Eclipse doesn't come with everything. In addition to Eclipse, you need the *Java Runtime Environment* (JRE). You may already have it on your computer. You need JRE version 1.4.1 or higher.

Java's alphabet soup

What you normally call "Java" is really a combination of several things:

✔ A *compiler,* to turn the *source code* that you write into *bytecode* that your computer can run.

✔ A *Java Virtual Machine* (JVM), to carry out the bytecode's instructions when the computer runs your program.

✔ An *Application Programming Interface* (API) containing thousands of pre-written programs for use by your newly created Java code.

Of course, the proliferation of terminology doesn't end with these three items. If you visit java.sun.com/j2se, you can download either the *Java Development Kit* (JDK) or the *Java Runtime Environment* (JRE).

✔ When you download the JRE, you get the Java Virtual Machine and the Application Programming Interface.

✔ When you download the JDK, you get the compiler and the Application Programming Interface. As a separate installation, you get the JRE, which includes the JVM and another copy of the API.

The JRE includes everything you need in order to run existing Java programs. When I say "existing" Java programs, I mean Java programs that have already been compiled. The JRE doesn't include a compiler. But that's okay because in this book, you don't need the JDK's compiler. Throughout most of this book, you use another compiler — the compiler that comes with Eclipse.

For more details on compilers, bytecode, and things like that, pick up a copy of *Java 2 For Dummies,* 2nd Edition. (It's a good book. I wrote it.)

Java's version numbering can be really confusing. After version 1.4.1 comes version 1.4.2 (with intermediate stops at versions like 1.4.1_02). Then, after 1.4.2, the next version is version 5.0. (That's no misprint. In Javaville, 5.0 comes immediately after 1.4.2.) To make matters worse, versions numbered 1.2 onward have an extra "2" in their names. So the formal name for version 5.0 is "Java 2 Platform, Standard Edition 5.0." And to make matters even worse, the people at Sun Microsystems are thinking about removing the extra "2." So after "Java 2, 5.1" you may see plain old "Java, 5.2."

Do you already have the Java Runtime Environment?

Chances are, your computer already has an up-to-date Java Runtime Environment (in which case, you don't have to download another one). Here's how you check for the presence of the JRE.

1. **Choose Start⇨Run (Windows only).**

   The Run dialog makes an on-screen appearance.

2. **Call up the command prompt:**

   In Windows, type cmd, **and click OK in the Run dialog's text field.**

If your computer tells you that it can't find cmd, you have an older version of Microsoft Windows. With older Windows versions, type **command** instead of **cmd**.

With Red Hat Fedora with Gnome, right-click a blank area on the desktop and choose Open Terminal.

With Mac OS X, choose Applications⇨Utilities⇨Terminal.

3. **In the command prompt window, type** java -version, **and press Enter.**

What happens next depends on your computer's response to the java -version command:

- If you see an error message such as 'java' is not recognized as an internal or external command or Bad command or file name, then your computer probably doesn't have an installed JRE.

  Skip to the instructions for downloading and installing the JRE (later in this chapter).

- If you see a message that includes text like the following

  ```
  Java(TM) 2 Runtime Environment (build 5.0)
  ```

  then your computer has an installed JRE. Check the version number (a.k.a. the build number) to make sure that the number is at least 1.4.1.

  If the number is at least 1.4.1 (including numbers like 5.0 or 5.0.1), then your computer has a usable JRE. You can skip this chapter's instructions for downloading the JRE.

  If the number is lower than 1.4.1 (including numbers like 1.3 or 1.4.0), then follow the instructions for downloading and installing the JRE (later in this chapter).

Finding the JRE on the Web

If your computer doesn't already have the JRE, you can get the JRE by visiting java.sun.com/j2se.

If you're a Macintosh user and you need to download the JRE, don't bother visiting java.sun.com. Instead, visit developer.apple.com/java.

When I want the weather to be sunny, I bring an umbrella to work. Bringing an umbrella tells the weather gods to do the opposite of whatever Barry anticipates. The same kind of thing happens with the Java Web site. If I want someone to redesign the Web site, I just write an article describing exactly how to navigate the site. Sometime between the time of my writing and the date of the article's publication, the people at Sun Microsystems reorganize the entire Web site. It's as dependable as the tides.

Anyway, the Java Web site is in a constant state of flux. That's why I don't put detailed instructions for downloading the JRE in this book. Instead, I offer some timeless tips.

To find detailed, up-to-date instructions for downloading the JRE from `java.sun.com`, visit this book's Web site.

1. **Visit** `java.sun.com/j2se`.

2. **Look for a <u>Download J2SE</u> link (or something like that).**

    The page may have several J2SE version numbers for you to choose from. You may see links to J2SE 1.4.2, J2SE 5.0, and beyond. If you're not sure which version you want, choosing the highest version number is probably safe, even if that version number is labeled "Beta." (The Java beta releases are fairly sturdy.)

    While you wander around, you may notice links labeled *J2EE* or *J2ME*. If you know what these are, and you know you need them, then by all means, download these goodies. But if you're not sure, then bypass both the J2EE and the J2ME. Instead, follow the *J2SE* (Java 2 *Standard* Edition) links.

    The abbreviation J2EE stands for Java 2 Enterprise Edition and J2ME stands for Java 2 Micro Edition. You don't need the J2EE or the J2ME to run any of the examples in this book.

3. **On the J2SE download page, look for an appropriate download link.**

    A download link is "appropriate" as long as the link refers to J2SE (Java 2 Platform, Standard Edition), to JRE (Java Runtime Environment), and to your particular operating system (such as Windows, Linux, or Solaris). From all possible links, you may have to choose between links labeled for 32-bit systems and links labeled for 64-bit systems. If you don't know which to choose, and you're running Windows, then you probably have a 32-bit system.

    Another choice you may have to make is between an offline and online installation:

    • With the offline installation, you begin by downloading a 15MB setup file. The file takes up space on your hard drive, but if you ever need to install the JRE again, you have the file on your own computer. Until you update your version of the JRE, you don't need to download the JRE again.

    • With the online installation, you don't download a big setup file. Instead, you download a teeny little setup file. Then you download (and discard) pieces of the big 15MB file as you need them. Using online installation saves you 15MB of hard drive space. But, if you want to install the same version of the JRE a second time, you have to redo the whole surf/click/download process.

Why would anyone want to install the same version of the JRE a second time? Typically, I have two reasons. Either I want to install the software on a second computer, or I mess something up and have to uninstall (and then reinstall) the software.

4. **Download whichever file you chose in Step 3.**

5. **Execute the file that you've downloaded.**

   With offline or online installation you download an executable file onto your computer's hard drive. Execute this file to complete the JRE installation.

At some point in all this clicking and linking, you're probably asked to accept a software license agreement. I've accepted this agreement several hundred times, and nothing bad has ever happened to me. (Well, nothing bad having anything to do with Java license agreements has ever happened to me.) Of course, you should accept the software license agreement only if you intend to abide by the agreement's terms. That goes without saying.

Downloading Eclipse

To download Eclipse, visit www.eclipse.org. As with all Web sites, this site's structure is likely to change between my writing and your reading *Eclipse For Dummies*. Anyway, the last time I looked, this Web site's home page had plenty of links to the Eclipse download page. The download page lists a zillion mirror sites, and each mirror site contains (more or less) the latest release-for-the-public version of Eclipse.

Many software providers use a main-site/mirror-site scheme. The *main site* contains the official versions of all files. Each *mirror site* contains copies of the *main site's* files. A typical mirror site updates its copies every few hours, or every few days. When you download from a mirror site, you do a good deed. (You avoid placing a burden on the main site's server.)

Some mirror sites have visitor-friendly Web pages; others don't. If you reach a site whose interface isn't comfortable for you, then backtrack and try another site. Eventually, you'll find a site that you can navigate reasonably well.

Yes, this is another warning! Eclipse is hot stuff. Many Eclipse download sites are overloaded with traffic. If you get no response when you click links, please don't be discouraged. Try a different mirror site, try a different time of day, or try clicking the same link a second time. Take comfort in the fact that you're in good company. Everybody, everywhere wants to download Eclipse.

After picking a mirror site, you may have a choice of several things to download. You can get release builds, stable builds, nightly builds, legacy versions, and so on. Because you're reading *Eclipse For Dummies* (and not *Eclipse For*

People Who Already Know Everything about Eclipse), I assume that you don't want last night's hot-off-the-press, still-full-of-bugs build. Instead, you want the latest "regular" release.

So click the link leading to the latest Eclipse release. After clicking the link, you may see a list of operating systems (Windows, Linux, Mac OS X, and so on). You may also see alternative download links (http versus ftp). You may even see md5 checksum links, and links to various other things (things like the RCP Runtime Binary and the Platform SDK — things that don't concern a new Eclipse user).

Click the http or ftp link corresponding to your computer's operating system. Clicking either link starts up the usual download process on your computer. Save the file that you download to a safe place on your hard drive, and then proceed to this book's next fun-filled section.

Installing Eclipse

Unlike many other pieces of software, Eclipse doesn't come with a fancy installation routine. That's actually a good thing. Eclipse doesn't need to have a fancy installation routine. Eclipse doesn't tangle itself up with the rest of your system. Eclipse is just an innocent bunch of files, sitting harmlessly on your hard drive. If you're used to things such as Windows DLLs, registry changes, VB runtime libraries, and other unpleasant debris, then installing Eclipse is a breath of fresh air.

To "install" Eclipse, you just unzip the downloaded file. That's all you do. You can use WinZip, unzip, the Windows XP extraction wizard, or anything else that sucks material from ZIP files. One way or another, the extracted stuff ends up in a directory named (lowercase letter e) `eclipse`. The new `eclipse` directory contains everything you need to start running the Eclipse program.

Here are some specific tips for your operating system:

- ✔ **Microsoft Windows:** If you're a Windows user, you may be tempted to extract Eclipse into the `Program Files` directory. While that's not a terrible idea, it may eventually lead to trouble. Some Java tools don't work in directories whose names contain blank spaces.

- ✔ **UNIX or Linux:** After unzipping the Eclipse download, I normally don't change any file permissions. The `eclipse` executable comes with permissions `rwxr-xr-x`. With all these `x`s, anyone logged on to the computer can run Eclipse. If you're familiar with UNIX or Linux, and you know all about permissions, you may want to change these permission settings. But if you don't know what `rwxr-xr-x` means, it doesn't matter. You're probably okay with things as they are.

> ✔ **Macintosh:** If you use a Mac with OS X, you don't even have to unzip the downloaded file. The file comes to you as a `tar.gz` archive. The Mac unpacks the archive automatically, and puts a new Eclipse program icon on your desktop.

Running Eclipse

The first time around, starting Eclipse is a two-part process. First, you get the program running; then, you work through a few initial screens and dialogs.

Turning the ignition key

Here's how you get Eclipse to start running.

With Microsoft Windows

1. **Choose Start⇨Run.**

   A Run dialog appears.

2. **In the Run dialog, click the Browse button.**

   A Browse dialog appears.

3. **In the Browse dialog, navigate to the directory in which you installed Eclipse. (See Figure 2-1.)**

4. **Double-click the eclipse (or eclipse.exe) icon.**

   Eclipse is the blue icon with a picture of something eclipsing something else. (See Figure 2-1.)

You can also put a shortcut to Eclipse on your Windows desktop. Here's how:

1. **Find a more-or-less vacant area on the desktop, and right-click your mouse.**

   A context menu appears.

Figure 2-1:
The direc-
tory that
contains
Eclipse.

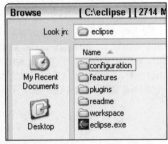

2. **On the context menu, choose New➪Shortcut.**

   A Create Shortcut Wizard appears.

3. **In the Create Shortcut Wizard, click the Browse button.**

   A Browse dialog appears.

4. **In the Browse dialog, navigate to the directory in which you installed Eclipse. (See Figure 2-2.)**

5. **Select the eclipse (or eclipse.exe) icon.**

   Once again, Eclipse is the blue icon with a picture of something eclipsing something else. (See Figure 2-2.)

6. **Click OK.**

   The Create Shortcut Wizard reappears. Now the wizard's text field contains something like `C:\eclipse\eclipse.exe` — the location of the Eclipse program on your computer's hard drive.

7. **Click Next.**

   Another wizard page appears. This page wants you to assign a friendly name to your new shortcut. The default name (`eclipse.exe`) is just fine. Any other name that reminds you of Eclipse is also fine.

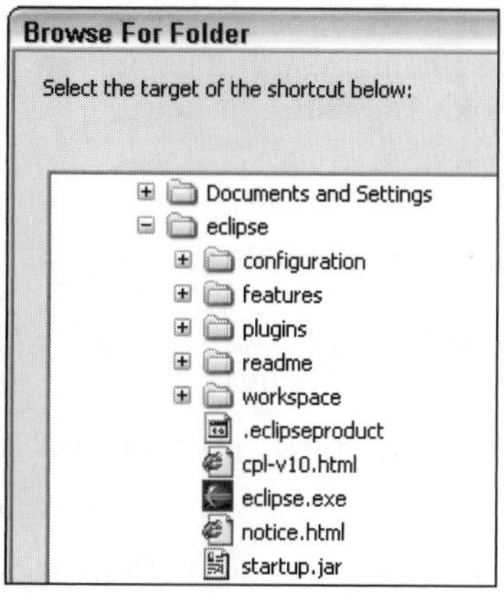

Figure 2-2:
Browsing
for Eclipse.

8. **Click Finish.**

   The new shortcut appears on your Windows desktop. To start Eclipse, just double-click the new shortcut.

With UNIX or Linux

Almost every UNIX/Linux environment has a Run box. If your environment has such a box, then follow the steps in the previous section, making changes here and there to suit your particular system. If your environment doesn't have a Run box, follow these steps:

1. **Do whatever you normally do to get a command prompt (a.k.a. shell prompt) on your system.**

   For instance, on Red Hat Fedora with Gnome, right-click a blank area on the desktop and then select Open Terminal. In the Solaris 10 Common Desktop Environment, right-click a blank area on the desktop and then choose Tools⇨Terminal.

2. **Navigate to the directory in which you installed Eclipse.**

   For example, if you unpacked the `eclipse-3.0-linux.zip` file into the `/usr/local` directory, then you created a directory named `/usr/local/eclipse`. So in the command prompt window, type **cd /usr/local/eclipse**. When you do, the command prompt window displays the new directory's name. You see

   ```
   [/usr/local/eclipse]$
   ```

   (or something like that) in the command prompt window.

3. **Type ./eclipse in the command prompt window to start a run of the Eclipse program.**

 If typing **./eclipse** gives you a `Permission denied` or a `cannot execute` message, try changing the file's permissions. Type **chmod u+x**, and then press Enter. Then try typing **./eclipse** again. If you still get a `Permission denied` message, scream (to this book's Web site) for help.

On a Mac with OS X

1. **Double-click the Eclipse icon on your system's desktop.**

   Eclipse starts running.

2. **There's no Step 2!**

   Starting Eclipse on a Mac is really easy. But if you have trouble, consult this book's Web site.

After performing the necessary clicks and keystrokes, Eclipse begins its first run. You see a blue splash screen that displays a picture of some heavenly body behind another.*

---

*Which two heavenly bodies appear in the big blue splash screen? What's doing the eclipsing, and what's being eclipsed? I searched high and low on the Web, but I couldn't find an authoritative answer. Oddly enough, this issue is important. If the blue splash screen illustrates a lunar eclipse, then everything is okay. But if the blue splash screen illustrates a solar eclipse, the folks at Sun Microsystems are offended.

This splash screen stays on your screen an uncomfortably long time while Eclipse loads its wares. Even with a fast processor, you can watch the pretty dark-blue splash screen for several seconds. (On a slower machine, I can wait more than a minute.) If you're not used to watching Eclipse start, it may seem as if the program is hung. But most likely, the program is running just fine. Eclipse is getting ready to rumble, winding up in the bullpen, building up a good head of steam.

Revving up before you leave the driveway

Sure, you may have gotten Eclipse running. But that doesn't mean you can start writing code. Before you create code, you have to do a little housekeeping. This section guides you through the housekeeping.

1. **Perform the keystrokes and mouse clicks for starting Eclipse on your computer.**

   For the specifics see the previous section.

2. **Wait patiently while the Eclipse program loads.**

   Eventually, you see a Workspace Launcher, as shown in Figure 2-3. A *workspace* is a directory in which Eclipse stores your work. You can choose one directory or another each time you launch Eclipse. You enter your choice in this Workspace Launcher.

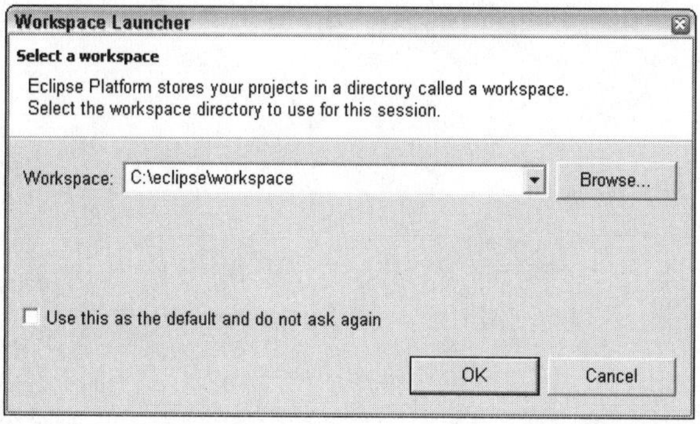

Workspace Launcher

Select a workspace

Eclipse Platform stores your projects in a directory called a workspace.
Select the workspace directory to use for this session.

Workspace: | C:\eclipse\workspace | ▼ | Browse...

☐ Use this as the default and do not ask again

| OK | Cancel |

Figure 2-3:
The
Workspace
Launcher.

Don't fuss over your choice in the Workspace Launcher. You can move from one workspace to another long after Eclipse starts running. Just choose File➪Switch Workspace on Eclipse's main menu bar.

3. **In the Workspace Launcher, click OK.**

   In this section, you accept the default directory shown in the Workspace Launcher's text field.

   After clicking OK, you see a Welcome screen like the one in Figure 2-4.

   By default, this Welcome screen is a one-time thing. The second time you run Eclipse, you don't automatically get welcomed.

   If you come to miss the Eclipse Welcome screen, don't fret. You see the Welcome screen whenever you create a new workspace. And in an existing workspace, you can still conjure up the Welcome screen. Just choose Help⇨Welcome on Eclipse's main menu bar.

4. **Click the Workbench icon — the icon in the upper right-hand corner of the Welcome screen.**

   Clicking this Workbench icon takes you to the main Eclipse screen, known formally as the Eclipse *workbench*. (See Figure 2-5.) The workbench is divided into several sections. Each section is called an *area*.

   You're ready to create your first Java project.

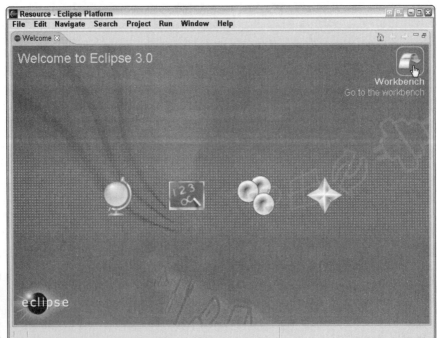

Figure 2-4:
Welcome to
Eclipse!

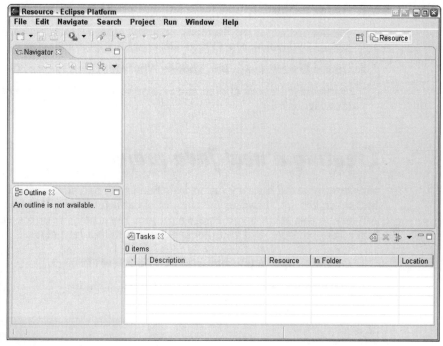

Figure 2-5:
The Eclipse
workbench.

Hello World, and Goodbye Moon

What's the first thing you do after you install a new piece of software? You run the software and do something simple with it. This first test drive confirms that you properly installed the software, and gives you a feel for the software's interface.

This section contains step-by-step instructions for testing your new Eclipse installation. As you work through each instruction, I prefer that you know why you're doing whatever it is that you're doing. So I break the instructions into smaller sets, and put each set in its own little section.

Getting started

In this tiny section, you change from one perspective to another. Sure, you may not yet know what an Eclipse "perspective" is, but that's okay. Changing from the Resource perspective to the Java perspective is easy. Besides, you can read all about perspectives in Chapters 3 through 5.

1. **Follow the instructions for starting Eclipse.**

   See the section titled "Running Eclipse." After several mouse clicks and/or keystrokes, the Eclipse workbench appears.

2. **On the Eclipse menu bar, choose Window⇨Open Perspective⇨Java.**

   In response to your choice, the Eclipse workbench rearranges itself. (See Figure 2-6.)

Creating a new Java project

How does that old nursery rhyme go? "Each sack had seven cats. Each cat had seven kittens." Imagine the amount of cat litter the woman had to have! Anyway, in this section you create a project. Eventually, your project will contain a Java package, and your package will contain a Java class.

1. **On the Eclipse menu bar, choose File⇨New⇨Project.**

   You see the New Project dialog, as shown in Figure 2-7.

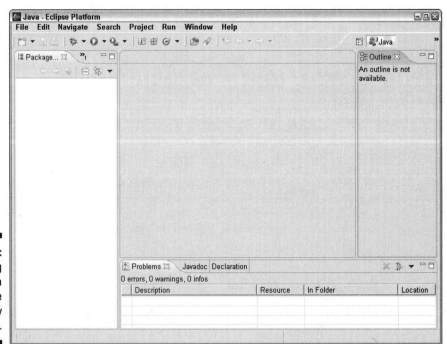

Figure 2-6:
Opening the Java perspective for the very first time.

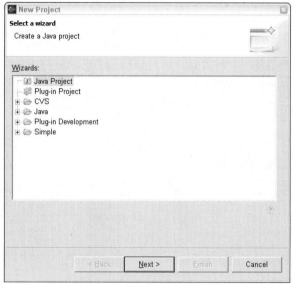

Figure 2-7:
The New
Project
dialog.

- Formally, a *project* is a collection of files and folders.

- Intuitively, a *project* is a basic work unit. For instance, a self-contained collection of Java program files to manage your CD collection (along with the files containing the data) may constitute a single Eclipse project.

2. In the New Project dialog, select Java Project, and then click Next.

You see the New Java Project Wizard, as shown in Figure 2-8.

3. In the Project Name field, type a name for your new project.

In Figure 2-8, I typed **FirstProject**. In the steps that follow, I assume that you also type **FirstProject**. Of course, you can type all kinds of things in the Project Name field. I'm an old stick in the mud so I avoid putting blank spaces in my project names. But if you insist, you can use dashes, blank spaces, and other troublesome characters.

You have to type a name for your new project. Aside from typing a name, you can accept the defaults (the Location and Project Layout stuff) in the New Java Project Wizard.

4. Click Finish.

When you click Finish, the Eclipse workbench reappears. The leftmost area contains the *Package Explorer view.* The view's list contains your new FirstProject. (See Figure 2-9.)

Figure 2-8:
The New
Java Project
Wizard.

In Eclipse, a *view* is one of the things that can fill up an area. A view illustrates information. When you read the word "view," think of it as a "point of view." Eclipse can illustrate the same information in many different ways. So Eclipse has many different kinds of views. The Package Explorer view is just one way of envisioning your Java programming projects.

Figure 2-9:
The `First
Project` in
the Package
Explorer
view.

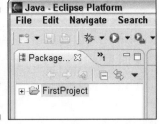

Creating a package

In the previous section, you create a project to hold your code. The next thing to do is add a package to your project.

1. **In the Package Explorer, right-click the** `FirstProject` **branch. Then, in the resulting context menu, choose New➪Package.**

   The New Java Package Wizard appears, as shown in Figure 2-10.

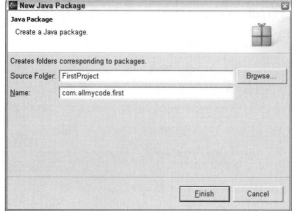

Figure 2-10:
The New
Java
Package
Wizard.

2. **In the New Java Package Wizard, type the name of your new package in the Name text field.**

In Figure 2-10, I typed the name **com.allmycode.first**.

For the package name, you're supposed to reverse your domain name and then add a descriptive word. In this example I use **com.allmycode.first** because I've registered **allmycode.com**, and this is my **first** example. If you follow this naming convention, other Java programmers will like you. But if you don't follow this convention, nothing breaks. For your own use, a package name like **almost.anything.atall** (or even a one-part **mypack** name with no dots) is just fine.

3. **Click Finish to close the New Java Package Wizard.**

Your new package (along with some other stuff) appears in the Package Explorer's tree, as shown in Figure 2-11.

Figure 2-11:
Look!
There's a
package in
the Package
Explorer!

Creating and running a Java class

Drumroll, please! It's time to write some code.

1. **In the Package Explorer, right-click your newly created package. Then, in the resulting context menu, choose New⇨Class.**

   The New Java Class Wizard miraculously appears, as shown in Figure 2-12.

2. **In the New Java Class Wizard, fill in the Name field.**

   In Figure 2-12, I typed **GoodbyeMoon**. You can type whatever you darn well please (unless you want to stay in sync with these instructions).

3. **Select other options in the New Java Class Wizard.**

   For this example, put a check mark in the `public static void main(String args[])` box. Aside from that, just accept the defaults, as shown in Figure 2-12.

4. **Click Finish.**

   After some disk chirping and some hourglass turning, you see the workbench in Figure 2-13. The Package Explorer displays a new `GoodbyeMoon.java` file, and the workbench's middle area displays a *Java editor*. The Java editor contains almost all the code in a typical `Hello World` program. All you need is the proverbial `println` call.

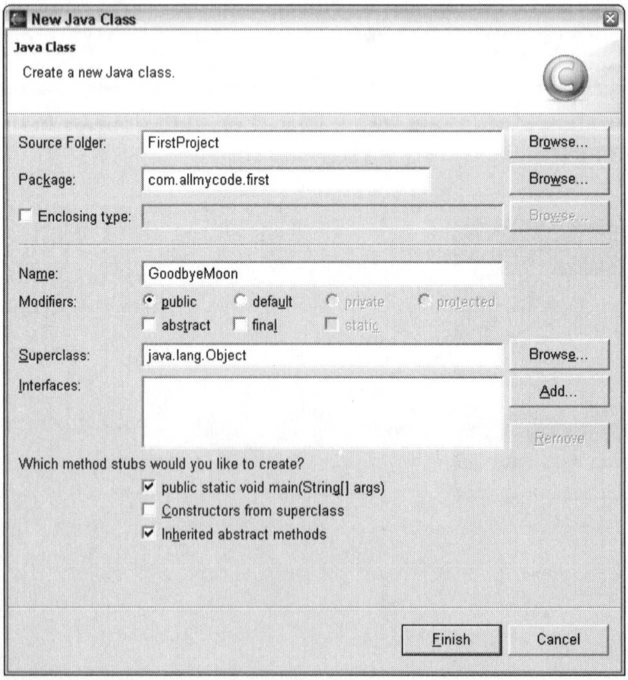

Figure 2-12: The New Java Class Wizard.

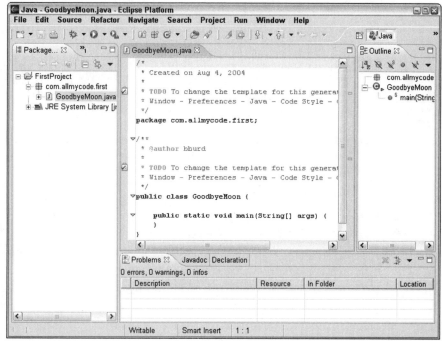

Figure 2-13:
Eclipse
creates a
skeletal
Java source
file.

5. **Add** System.out.println("Goodbye Moon!") **to the main method's body, as shown in Figure 2-14.**

   By default, Eclipse adds characters as you type. When you type the open parenthesis, Eclipse adds its own close parenthesis. When you type the quotation mark, Eclipse closes the quotation automatically.

Figure 2-14:
An addi-
tional line
of code.

```
public class GoodbyeMoon {

    public static void main(String[] args) {
        System.out.println("Goodbye Moon!");
    }
}
```

With Eclipse *templates* you can avoid doing lots of routine typing. Instead of typing **System.out.println**, you type only a letter or two. Eclipse types the rest of the code for you. For details on using templates, see Chapter 7.

6. Choose File⇨Save to save your new GoodbyeMoon.java **file.**

You don't have to tell Eclipse to compile your code. By default, Eclipse compiles as you type.

TIP

If the compile-as-you-type feature takes too much precious processor time, you can turn the feature off. On Eclipse's main menu bar, choose Project⇨Build Automatically. Choosing once turns automatic building off. Choosing again turns automatic building back on.

Of course, you want to test your new GoodbyeMoon program. Using Eclipse, you can run the program with only a few mouse clicks. Choose Run⇨Run⇨ Java Application. (See Figure 2-15.)

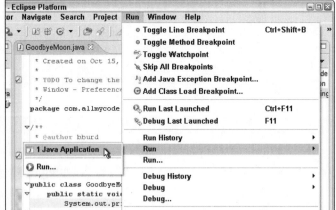

Figure 2-15:
Choosing
Run⇨
Run⇨Java
Application.

After a brief delay, a new Console view appears in the bottommost area of the Eclipse workbench. If you click the Console's tab, you see your program's output, as shown in Figure 2-16.

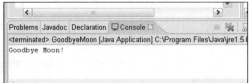

Figure 2-16:
The output
of your
Goodbye
Moon.java
program.

REMEMBER

Starting with version 3.1, Eclipse's Run menu contains two similarly labeled Run items. If you hover your mouse over one of these Run items, you see a submenu that contains a Java Application option. If you hover your mouse over the other Run item, nothing much happens. (That is, nothing happens unless you click the second Run item.) To make matters more confusing, the Java Application submenu has its own additional Run item. One way or another, the item you want to select in Step 7 is a Java Application. (Refer to Figure 2-15.)

Oops!

In the last step of the "Creating and running a Java class" instructions, you may get the following unpleasant message:

```
Errors exist in a required project. Continue launch?
```

This message probably means that your Java source code doesn't compile. Look for tiny icons on the left edge of the Java editor. (See Figure 2-17. Each icon contains an X surrounded by a red shape, and possibly a light bulb.) These icons are called *error markers,* and the whole left edge of the editor is called a *marker bar.* Besides error markers, several other kinds of markers can appear in the editor's marker bar.

Figure 2-17: Oh, no! An error marker!

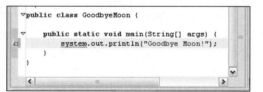

Each error marker represents a place in the code where Eclipse finds a compile-time error. The error in Figure 2-17 is the use of the word `system` (as opposed to `System`, with a capital S). If you find such an error, you can either retype the S, or you can use Eclipse's *Quick Fix* feature. Here's how:

1. **Right-click the error marker. Then, in the resulting context menu, select Quick Fix. (See Figure 2-18.)**

Figure 2-18: Invoking Quick Fix.

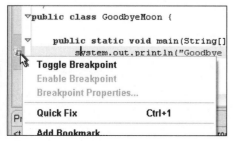

A list with one or more alternatives appears. Each alternative represents a different way of fixing the compile-time error. When you highlight an alternative, another box shows what the revised code (after applying that alternative) looks like, as shown in Figure 2-19.

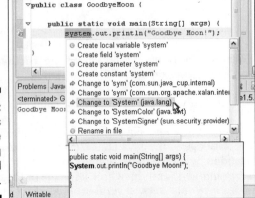

Figure 2-19:
Eclipse lets
you choose
from among
several
quick fixes.

2. **Double-click the alternative that you want to apply. Or if you like using the keyboard, you can highlight the alternative, and then press Enter.**

   Eclipse rewrites your code, and the error marker goes away. What a cool feature!

In Figures 2-18 and 2-19, the error marker contains a tiny light bulb. The light bulb reminds you that Eclipse may have some Quick Fix ideas. If you don't see the bulb, Eclipse has no ideas. But occasionally, even though you see the little bulb, Eclipse doesn't have a clue. Okay, I can live with that.

Chapter 3

Using the Eclipse Workbench

*B*elieve it or not, an editor once rejected one of my book proposals. In the margins, the editor scribbled "This is not a word" next to things like "can't," "it's," and "I've." To this day, I still do not know what this editor did not like about contractions. My own guess is that language always needs to expand. Where would we be without new words — words like *dotcom,* *infomercial,* and *vaporware?*

Even the *Oxford English Dictionary* (the last word in any argument about words) grows by more than 4,000 entries each year. That's an increase of more than 1 percent per year. It's about 11 new words per day!

The fact is, human thought is like a big high-rise building. You can't build the 50th floor until you've built at least part of the 49th. You can't talk about *spam* until you have a word like *e-mail.* With all that goes on these days, you need verbal building blocks. That's why this chapter begins with a bunch of new terms.

What's All That Stuff on the Eclipse Workbench?

The next few pages bathe you in new vocabulary. Some of this vocabulary is probably familiar old stuff. Other vocabulary is somewhat new because

Eclipse uses the vocabulary in a very specialized way. This specialization comes for two reasons:

- ✔ **As a user, you can customize many aspects of the Eclipse environment.**

  You may need to check Eclipse's Help pages for the procedure to customize some element in the environment. You can quickly find the right Help page if you know what the element is called.

- ✔ **As a programmer, you can customize even more aspects of the Eclipse environment.**

  Eclipse is open source. You can dig deeply into the code and tinker as much as you want. You can even contribute code to the official Eclipse project. Of course, you can't mess with code unless you know the exact names of things in the code.

Before you jump into the next several paragraphs, please heed my advice: Don't take my descriptions of terms too literally. These are explanations, not definitions. Yes, they're fairly precise; but no, they're not airtight. Almost every description in this section has hidden exceptions, omissions, exemptions, and exclusions. Take the paragraphs in this section to be friendly reminders, not legal contracts.

- ✔ **Workbench:** The Eclipse desktop (see Figure 3-1)

  The workbench is the environment in which you develop code.

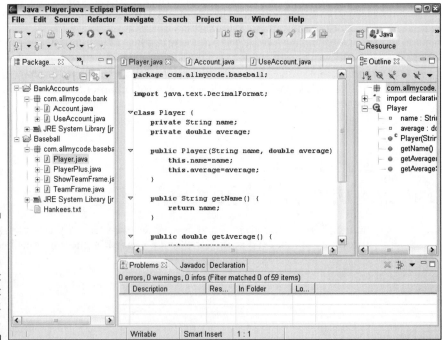

Figure 3-1:
The Eclipse workbench often (but doesn't always) look like this.

🡆 **Area:** A section of the workbench

The workbench in Figure 3-1 has four areas. (See Figure 3-2.)

🡆 **Window:** A copy of the Eclipse workbench

With Eclipse, you can have several copies of the workbench open at once. Each copy appears in its own window. (See Figure 3-3.)

To open a second window, go to the main Eclipse menu bar and choose Window➪New Window.

🡆 **Action:** A choice that's offered to you, typically when you click something

For instance, when you choose File➪New on Eclipse's main menu bar, you see a list of new things that you can create. The list usually includes Project, Folder, File, and Other but it may also include things such as Package, Class, and Interface. Each of these things (each item in the menu) is called an *action*.

You can customize the kinds of actions that Eclipse offers to you. For details, see Chapter 4.

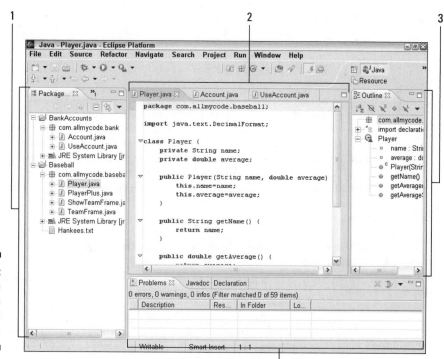

Figure 3-2:
The workbench is divided into areas.

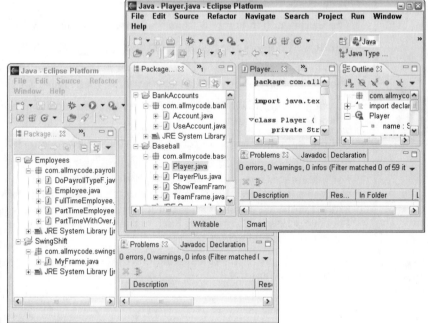

Figure 3-3:
Having two
Eclipse
windows
open at the
same time.

Views and editors

The next bunch of terms deals with things called views and editors. At first you may have difficulty understanding the difference. (A view is like an editor, which is like a view, or something like that.) If views and editors seem the same to you, and you're not sure you can tell which is which, don't be upset. As an ordinary Eclipse user, the distinction between views and editors comes naturally as you gain experience using the workbench. You rarely have to decide whether the thing you're using is a view or an editor. But if you plan to develop Eclipse plug-ins, you eventually have to figure out what's a view and what's an editor.

✔ **View:** A part of the Eclipse workbench that displays information for you to browse

In the simplest case, a view fills up an area in the workbench. For instance, in Figure 3-1, the Outline view fills up the rightmost area.

Many views display information as lists or trees. For example, in Figure 3-1, the Package Explorer and Outline views contain trees. The Problems view may contain a list such as the one shown in Figure 3-4.

You can use a view to make changes to things. For instance, to delete the Account.java file in Figure 3-1, right-click the Account.java branch in the Package Explorer view. Then, in the resulting context menu, select Delete.

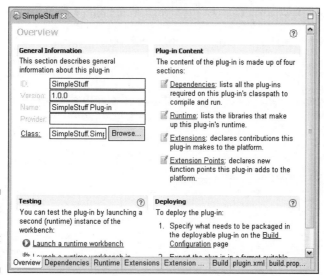

Figure 3-4:
The
Problems
view.

When you use a view to change something, the change takes place imme-diately. For example, when you select Delete on the Package Explorer's context menu, whatever file you've selected is deleted immediately. In a way, this behavior is nothing new. The same kind of thing happens when you delete a file using My Computer or Windows Explorer.

✔ **Editor:** A part of the Eclipse workbench that displays information for you to modify

A typical editor displays information in the form of text. This text can be the contents of a file. For example, an editor in the middle of Figure 3-1 displays the contents of the `Player.java` source file.

Some editors display more than just text. For instance, Figure 3-5 dis-plays part of the Plug-in manifest editor. Like many other editors, this manifest editor displays the contents of a file. But instead of showing you all the words in the file, the manifest editor displays the file's con-tents as a form on a Web page.

Figure 3-5:
The Plug-in
manifest
editor.

To find out what the Plug-in manifest editor is all about, see this book's Web site.

When you use an editor to change something, the change doesn't take place immediately. For example, look at the editor in the middle of Figure 3-1. This editor displays the contents of the Player.java source file. You can type all kinds of things in the editor pane. Nothing happens to Player.java until you choose File➪Save from the Eclipse menu bar. Of course, this behavior is nothing new. The same kind of thing happens when you work in Microsoft Word or UNIX vi.

Like other authors, I occasionally become lazy and use the word "view" when I really mean "view or editor." When you catch me doing this, just shake your head and move onward. When I'm being very careful, I use the official Eclipse terminology. I refer to views and editors as *parts* of the Eclipse workbench. Unfortunately, this "parts" terminology doesn't stick in peoples' minds very well.

✔ **Tab:** Something that's impossible to describe except by calling it a "tab"

That which we call a tab by any other name would move us as well from one view to another or from one editor to another. The important thing is, views can be *stacked* on top of one another. Eclipse displays stacked views as if they're pages in a tabbed notebook. That's why a bunch of stacked views is called a *tab group*. To bring a view in the stack to the forefront, you click that view's tab.

And, by the way, all this stuff about tabs and views holds true for tabs and editors. The only interesting thing is the way Eclipse uses the word "editor." In Eclipse, each tabbed page of the editor area is an individual editor. For example, the editor area in Figure 3-6 contains three editors (not three tabs belonging to a single editor).

✔ **Active view or active editor:** In a tab group, the view or editor that's in front

In Figure 3-6, the Player.java editor is the active editor. The Account.java and UseAccount.java editors are inactive.

Figure 3-6:
The editor
area
contains
three
editors.

Local history

You can right-click a file in the Package Explorer. Then, when you select Delete, Eclipse asks for confirmation. Are you sure you want to delete the file? If you click Yes (you *do* want to delete the file), then Eclipse removes the file from your computer's hard drive.

Okay, you deleted the file. Now what if you change your mind? Can you get the file back? Don't bother looking for the file in your system's Recycle Bin. Eclipse doesn't use the Recycle Bin. Instead, Eclipse copies the file in its own *local history*.

Eclipse's local history maintains copies of things that you modify or delete. To restore a file that you deleted, do the following:

1. Right-click a package or project branch in the Package Explorer or the Navigator view.

2. In the resulting context menu, select Restore from Local History.

   The Restore from Local History dialog appears. The dialog contains a list of deleted files, along with a check box for each file in the list.

3. Put a check mark next to the file that you want to undelete.

4. Click Restore.

   Hooray! You have your file again.

With Eclipse's local history, you can roll back small changes that you make to your Java source code. Here's an example:

1. Use the editor to modify some Java source code.

2. Choose File⇨Save.

3. Right-click the source code in the editor. In the resulting context menu, choose Replace With⇨Local History.

   The Replace from Local History dialog appears. The dialog's list contains the dates and times of any changes that you saved.

4. Select a date and time.

   The dialog shows you the changes you've made since the selected date and time.

5. Click Replace.

   Eclipse puts the file back the way it was on the selected date at the selected time.

You can decide how much stuff to save in Eclipse's local history. Choose Window⇨Preferences on Eclipse's menu bar. In the Preferences dialog's navigation tree, expand the Workbench branch. Then, in the Workbench branch, select Local History. In response, Eclipse provides Days to Keep Files, Entries per File, and Maximum File Size text fields.

What's inside a view or an editor?

The next several terms deal with individual views, individual editors, and individual areas.

- ✔ **Toolbar:** The bar of buttons (and other little things) at the top of a view (see Figure 3-7)

Tab   Close button   Minimize and Maximize buttons

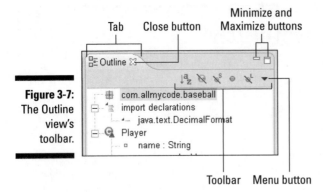

Figure 3-7:
The Outline
view's
toolbar.

Toolbar   Menu button

✔ **Menu button:** A downward-pointing arrow on the toolbar

When you click the menu button, a drop-down list of actions appears. (See Figure 3-8.) Which actions you see in the list vary from one view to another.

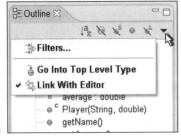

Figure 3-8:
Clicking a
view's menu
button.

✔ **Minimize and Maximize buttons:** Buttons for quickly getting an area's views out of your sight or for expanding an area to fill the entire workbench

When you minimize an area, the area's Minimize button turns into a *Restore button.* Clicking the Restore button returns the area's views to their normal size.

✔ **Close button:** A button that gets rid of a particular view or editor (refer to Figure 3-7)

✔ **Chevron:** A double arrow indicating that other tabs should appear in a particular area (but that the area isn't wide enough)

The chevron in Figure 3-9 has a little number 3 beside it. The 3 tells you that in addition to the two visible tabs, three tabs are invisible. Clicking the chevron brings up a hover tip containing the labels of all the tabs. (See Figure 3-10.)

✔ **Marker bar:** The vertical ruler on the left edge of the editor area

Eclipse displays tiny alert icons, called *markers,* inside the marker bar. For an introduction to markers and marker bars, see Chapter 2.

Figure 3-9:
The chevron indicates that three editor tabs are hidden.

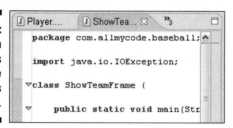

Figure 3-10:
Clicking the chevron reveals the labels of all the editors' tabs.

Understanding the big picture

The next two terms deal with Eclipse's overall look and feel.

✔ **Layout:** An arrangement of certain views

The layout in Figure 3-1 has six views, of which five are easily visible:

- At the far left, you see the Package Explorer view.

- On the far right, you have the Outline view.

- Near the bottom, you get the Problems, Javadoc, and Declaration views.

- Finally, the little chevron next to the Package Explorer tab provides access to a Hierarchy view.

Along with all these views, the layout contains a single *editor area.* Any and all open editors appear inside this editor area.

✔ **Perspective:** A very useful layout

If a particular layout is really useful, someone gives that layout a name. And if a layout has a name, you can use the layout whenever you want.

For instance, the workbench of Figure 3-1 displays the Java perspective. By default, the Java perspective contains six views, with the arrangement shown in Figure 3-1.

Along with all these views, the Java perspective contains an editor area. (Sure, the editor area has several tabs, but the number of tabs has nothing to do with the Java perspective.)

Eclipse comes with eight different perspectives, but these perspectives aren't cast in stone. You can change all kinds of things about an Eclipse perspective. You can even create new perspectives. For details, see Chapter 4.

Action sets

In reality, a perspective is more than just a layout. Each perspective determines an action set. In this chapter's first section, I call an action "A choice that's offered to you." When you switch from one perspective to another, your choices change.

For example, if you go to the Java perspective, and choose File⇨New, you see a list of choices that includes Project, Package, Class, and other items. If you switch to the Resource perspective and choose File⇨New, the list of choices includes only Project, File, Folder, and Other. Because the Resource perspective isn't specifically about Java programs, the perspective's File⇨New action set doesn't include Package and Class options.

Of course, you're not completely tied down. You can still create a package, a class, or anything else in the Resource perspective. Just select Other from the File⇨New menu. When you do, Eclipse offers you a very wide range of choices.

Juggling among perspectives

Here's something strange. . . . Look at Figure 3-1, and guess how many perspectives are open in this workbench. One? Two? More than two?

My gut tells me that only one perspective (the Java perspective) is open in the workbench. But my gut is lying to me. In a single window, you can have several perspectives open at the same time. Sure, only one perspective is *active* at a time, but several other perspectives can be lurking behind the scenes.

Look again at Figure 3-1, and notice the words Java and Resource in the upper-right corner. These Java and Resource buttons are part of the *perspective bar*. With the Java and Resource buttons showing, you know that at least two perspectives (the Java perspective and the Resource perspective) are currently open.

Figure 3-11 shows this perspective bar. When you click the Java button, nothing happens. (The Java perspective is already active.) When you click the Resource button, the workbench morphs to display the Resource perspective.

Open another
(as yet unopened)
perspective

Figure 3-11:
The
perspective
bar.

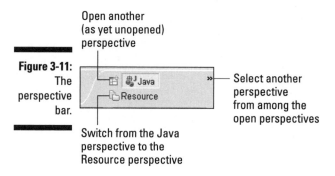

Select another
perspective
from among the
open perspectives

Switch from the Java
perspective to the
Resource perspective

Now notice the little chevron at the far right in Figure 3-11. When you click the chevron, you see the names of any other perspectives that happen to be open. (See Figure 3-12.)

Figure 3-12:
Seeing the
names of
the open
per-
spectives.

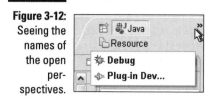

The perspective bar's leftmost (unlabeled) button is called the Open Perspective button. When you click this button, Eclipse offers you a list of some perspectives that you may want to see in the workbench. Some perspectives in the list may be open; some may not be open. (See Figure 3-13.) The list also has an option labeled Other. Selecting Other conjures up the Select Perspective dialog, shown in Figure 3-14.

Figure 3-13:
Clicking
the Open
Perspective
button.

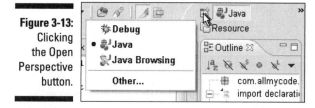

Figure 3-14:
The Select
Perspective
dialog.

That's the story on open perspectives. But wait! We just got a call from a member of our viewing audience. A "Mother from Minnesota" poses the following question: "In a single workbench window, I can see only one perspective at a time. If I can't see the Resource perspective in Figure 3-1, what difference does it make if the Resource perspective is open or not?"

Ah, yes! That's a good question. When a perspective is open, you can make changes to the perspective. You can resize areas, add and remove views, and make lots of other changes. If you do nothing special to save your changes, the changes stay in effect as long as you keep the perspective open. When you close the perspective (by choosing Window➪Close Perspective), any unsaved changes go away. At any point in time, you can have several open perspectives, each with its own temporary changes. You can switch freely among these momentarily changed perspectives by clicking the perspective bar's buttons.

And here's another thing you can do. You can open a second Eclipse window by choosing Window➪New Window on the menu bar. In one window, make the Java perspective active. In the second window, make the Resource perspective active. With this technique, you can have as many active perspectives as you want.

You can even make new perspectives open in their own windows. Choose Window➪Preferences on Eclipse's menu bar. In the Preferences dialog's navigation tree, expand the Workbench branch. Then, in the Workbench branch, select Perspectives. Select the Open a New Perspective in a New Window radio button.

With two perspectives in two separate windows, you resize each window independently, tile the windows, minimize one window at a time, or do other fancy things to conveniently display the windows.

So that's how open perspectives work. For more information on modifying perspectives, see Chapter 4.

Working with Views

Somewhere in the world, there's a Feature Density contest. The winner is the user interface that crams the largest number of features into the smallest amount of space. If the wide range of features confuses users, the interface is disqualified.

I don't know anything else about the Feature Density contest. I don't even know if the contest really exists. But if I ever find such a contest, I'll nominate Eclipse views for the top award.

Using a working set

When I first discovered Eclipse, I created a simple `Hello World` project. Then I wanted to experiment further, so I created `MySecondProject` and `MyThirdProject`. Within a few hours, I had created 17 projects, all fun (but all useless).

When I create real code in Eclipse, I do the same thing. I build small experimental projects to test concepts and try out new ideas. In addition, I normally have several projects going at once. One way or another, my Package Explorer becomes cluttered.

To remove the clutter I create *working sets.* A working set is just a bunch of things that you want to be visible. Any item that's not in the working set is out of your face and temporarily invisible.

Working sets aren't only for Java projects. Eclipse supports several different kinds of working sets. Here are three kinds:

- ✔ **Java:** A *Java working set* contains items that you see in the Package Explorer — projects, source folders, source files, packages, libraries, and other things.

- ✔ **Resource:** A *resource working set* contains items that you see in the Navigator view — files, folders, and projects.

✔ **Help:** A *help working set* contains sections from Eclipse's Help screens.

Use a help working set to narrow the collection of hits when you search for a particular topic.

To find out more about help working sets, see Chapter 15.

For a better understanding of working sets, try this experiment:

1. **Start with a few projects in the Package Explorer.**

   This experiment works well if you have at least three projects, and if at least two of those projects contain Java source code. You don't need any fancy code — just a class or two. So if you don't already have at least three projects, I suggest creating some new ones.

   Of course, if you're impatient, lazy, or both, you can still get something out of this experiment. You can try this experiment with only one project, even if that project contains no code.

   To find out how to create a Java project, see Chapter 2.

2. **Click the menu button on the Package Explorer's toolbar. In the resulting context menu, choose Select Working Set. (See Figure 3-15.)**

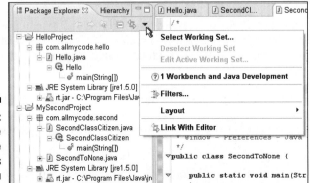

Figure 3-15:
Clicking the
Package
Explorer's
menu
button.

The Select Working Set dialog appears.

3. **In the Select Working Set dialog, click New.**

   The New Working Set Wizard appears. In the wizard's Working Set Type list you see three entries — Java, Help, and Resource, as shown in Figure 3-16.

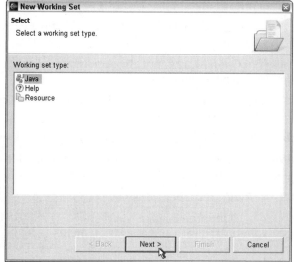

Figure 3-16:
The Select
page of
the New
Working Set
Wizard.

4. Select a working set type, and then click Next.

In this experiment, select the Java working set. When you click Next, the Java Working Set page appears, as shown in Figure 3-17.

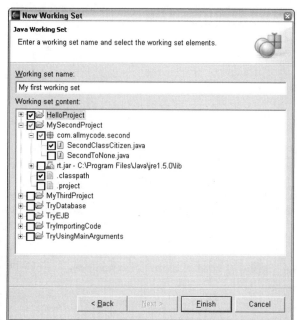

Figure 3-17:
The Java
Working
Set page.

5. **Type something informative in the Working Set Name field.**

How about typing **My first working set**? For now, that's informative enough.

6. **In the Working Set Content tree, put check marks next to the items that you want to appear in your view.**

In Figure 3-17, I select the entire `HelloProject` and portions of `MySecondProject`. I leave everything else unselected.

7. **Click Finish to dismiss the New Working Set Wizard.**

The Select Working Set dialog reappears, with the new working set you just created automatically selected.

8. **In the Select Working Set dialog, click OK.**

You get plopped back into the Eclipse workbench. Figure 3-18 shows a new Package Explorer tree with some of its branches expanded.

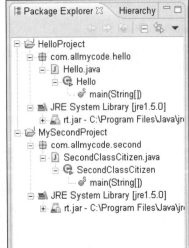

Figure 3-18:
The working set of Figure 3-17.

Figures 3-17 and 3-18 go hand in hand. When I check the boxes that I check in Figure 3-17, I get the Package Explorer shown in Figure 3-18. Comparing Figures 3-17 and 3-18, you find some expected things and some surprising things.

 ✔ **The Package Explorer contains only two projects —** `HelloProject` **and** `MySecondProject`.

That's not surprising given the check marks in Figure 3-17.

✔ **In the Package Explorer, the** `MySecondProject` **branch doesn't contain** `SecondToNone.java`.

Again, that's not surprising given the absence of a `SecondToNone.java` check mark in Figure 3-17.

✔ **The Package Explorer displays** `rt.jar` **in both the** `HelloProject` **and** `MySecondProject` **branches.**

That's surprising because, in Figure 3-17, the `rt.jar` box is unchecked.

But wait! Figure 3-17 has a nice, dark check mark next to `HelloProject`. (Compare the dark `HelloProject` check mark with the hesitant gray `MySecondProject` check mark. You may not be able to see the difference in Figure 3-17, but you can see the difference on your computer screen.)

That dark `HelloProject` check mark indicates that everything in the `HelloProject` is part of this working set. By "everything" I mean "everything including `rt.jar`." And because at least one copy of `rt.jar` is in the working set, the Package Explorer displays all the `rt.jar` branches.

✔ **No file named** `.classpath` **appears in the Package Explorer.**

That's certainly surprising. Figure 3-17 has a check mark in the `.classpath` branch. So what gives?

Like many other views, you can filter the Package Explorer. By default, the Package Explorer's filter masks files with names like `.classpath` and `.project`. For more information, see the section on "Using filters."

Each view has its own active working set. For instance, your Games working set can be active in the Package Explorer while your SmallBusiness working set is active in the Hierarchy view. Later, you can do the old switcheroo. You can make the SmallBusiness set active in the Package Explorer view while the Games set is active in the Hierarchy view.

Hey, where's my new project?

In certain circumstances, working sets can drive you crazy. Imagine that you've selected the working set shown in Figure 3-17. Then, in the Package Explorer, you create a brand new project. To your amazement, the new project does not appear in the Package Explorer's tree. Why? Because the active working set doesn't automatically add the new project. To add the new project to the active working set, follow these steps:

1. **Click the Package Explorer's menu button.**

2. **In the resulting context menu, choose Edit Active Working Set.**

   A dialog much like the one in Figure 3-17 appears.

3. **Add a check mark next to the new project's name.**

When I'm feeling really lazy, I modify Step 2 by choosing Deselect Working Set. When I do this, all the projects in my workbench suddenly reappear.

New projects aren't the only items that working sets hide. Look again at the My First Working Set group in Figure 3-17. Notice that the topmost MySecond Project branch has a gray check mark, not a black check mark. (You may not be able to see the difference between gray check marks and black check marks in Figure 3-17. But you can see the difference on your computer screen.) The gray check mark indicates that some items (not all items) from MySecond Project belong to the working set. So when you add a new class to MySecond Project, the class doesn't automatically belong to My First Working Set. If the My First Working Set group is active, the new class doesn't appear in the Package Explorer's tree.

Closing and opening projects

Tell me anything you want to do. . . . Eclipse gives you at least two ways to do it. Instead of creating a new working set, you can close some of your projects.

Figure 3-19 shows the Package Explorer with four open projects and three closed projects. (The MyThirdProject, TryEJB, and TryImportingCode projects are closed.) You can't expand a closed project's branch, so the three closed projects can't clutter up the Package Explorer. Of course, if you have dozens of closed projects, you may as well create a working set.

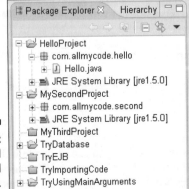

Figure 3-19:
Open and
closed
projects.

To close a project, just go to the Package Explorer and right-click the project's branch. In the resulting context menu, choose Close Project.

By default, the Package Explorer's tree contains a branch for each closed project. But with a filter you can hide the closed projects' branches. For details, see the next section.

Using filters

If you click a view's menu button, you may see a Filters item. What are these filters all about? The answer is a familiar one. Filters are about reducing clutter.

Filters and working sets complement one another. When you create a working set, you pick specific files, folders, and other things. When you use a filter, you tend not to pick specific things. Instead you specify general criteria. Eclipse checks each file, each folder, each Java element, to see if that element matches the criteria.

Each view's filtering mechanism applies uniquely to that view. From one view to another, the criteria that you use for filtering are different. This chapter emphasizes the Package Explorer and Problems filters. Other views have similar — but not identical — filtering mechanisms.

An example: Package Explorer filters

To get some practice with filters, click the menu button on the Package Explorer's toolbar. In the resulting menu, choose Filters. When you do all this, the big Java Element Filters dialog appears on-screen, as shown in Figure 3-20.

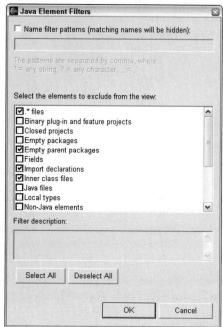

Figure 3-20:
The Java
Element
Filters
dialog.

The Java Elements Filters dialog includes a Select the Elements to Exclude from the View list. In this list, the trickiest thing is the use of check marks. A check mark indicates a filtered item. That is, anything matching a checked item does *not* appear in the Package Explorer view.

Items in the check box list can be descriptions or patterns.

✔ **Descriptions:** In Figure 3-20, most of the list's items contain descriptions of Java elements. They include Empty Packages, Fields, Import Declarations, and so on. A few items (like the Closed Projects item) contain descriptions of Eclipse-specific things.

✔ **Patterns:** The first item listed in Figure 3-20 bears a hard-to-read .* ("dot asterisk") label. In the .* pattern, the asterisk stands for any string of characters (including the empty string containing no characters). So any name that starts with a dot matches this pattern. If the .* item is checked, files with names like .classpath and .project don't appear in the Package Explorer view.

The Package Explorer's menu button keeps track of your most recent filtering behavior. You can quickly filter and unfilter some items by selecting options from the menu. For example, in Figure 3-21, I choose to hide inner class files as well as files whose names begin with a dot. I choose not to hide closed projects.

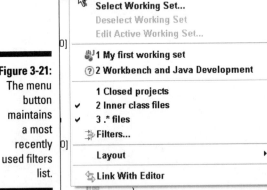

Figure 3-21:
The menu button maintains a most recently used filters list.

In addition to checking and unchecking list items, you can create your own filter patterns. For example, in Figure 3-22, I hide several kinds of things. I hide

✔ Things with Bean in their names

✔ Things whose names end in EJB.java

✔ XML files whose names include the word Account followed by one additional character

✔ Things whose names begin with a dot

✔ Closed projects

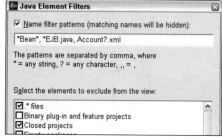

Figure 3-22:
Making
up your
own filter
patterns.

Another example: The Problems view's filters

Not all views have the same kinds of filters. For instance, the Problems view's menu button has a Filters option. With this option you can filter by project, problem severity, and type of problem. (See Figure 3-23.) If you want, you can limit the number of entries. (After all, when you have 677 problems, a little ignorance becomes bliss.)

The Filter dialog in Figure 3-23 has some useful radio buttons. With these buttons you can filter by resource, by project, or by working set.

Picture yourself glancing at the Package Explorer. You notice a red "problem" icon on the `RescueEntireCompany` project branch. You want to find all problems in the `RescueEntireCompany` project, and you want to find them fast. So you open the Problems view's Filters dialog. And you choose the On Any Resource in the Same Project radio button.

After clicking OK, you look at the list of Problems view entries. "That's not the correct list," you say to yourself. Looking again at the Package Explorer, you select a branch (any branch) in the `RescueEntireCompany` project. "Yes," you say. "Now the Problems view displays only problems in the `RescueEntire Company` project. That's great." And indeed, it is great. I'm proud of you. (Of course, I become worried when I see you talking to yourself.)

Linking views with the editors

The 1933 film *Duck Soup* features a legendary mirror scene. First Harpo crashes through a mirror, leaving an empty space behind him. Then Chico arrives, thinking that the mirror is still in place. Chico does tricks in front of the empty space while Harpo mimics Chico's every move. Chico tries some unexpected gestures and Harpo copies each one. After a while, Harpo is copying Chico, and Chico is copying Harpo. In the language of Eclipse, Chico and Harpo are *linked*.

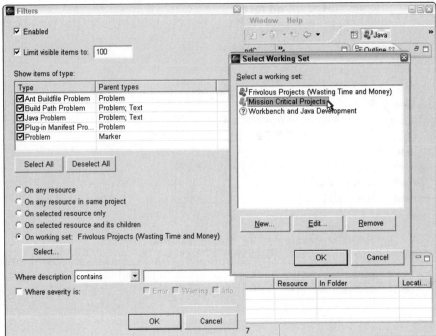

Figure 3-23:
Filtering
problems by
working set.

By default, some views are linked with the active editor, and others aren't. The Package Explorer isn't normally linked, and neither is the Navigator. But the Outline view is linked by default. To discover more about linking, try this experiment:

1. **Open two Java source files in the editor area.**

   For this experiment, any two files will do. Just be sure that these files appear in the Package Explorer view. (Oh, yes! I almost forgot. At least one of the Java source files should contain a method or a field.)

2. **Tab back and forth between the two files in the editor area.**

   In the Package Explorer, nothing happens.

3. **In the Package Explorer, select one of the two Java source files. Then select the other.**

   In the editor area, nothing happens.

4. **Click the Package Explorer's menu button. In the resulting menu, choose Link with Editor.**

   After doing this, the Package Explorer is linked with the editor. To verify this, move on to Step 5 . . .

5. **Tab back and forth between the two files in the editor area.**

   When you move from one editor to the other, the Package Explorer's display changes. Whatever file you select in the editor area is selected automatically in the Package Explorer.

6. **In the Package Explorer, select one of the two Java source files. Then select the other.**

   When you move from one file to the other, the editor area changes. Whatever file you select in the Package Explorer becomes active in the editor area.

7. **Select a method or field in the Package Explorer.**

   As long as the method or field belongs to a file you're currently editing, the editor jumps to that method or field's declaration.

8. **Select a method or field in the editor area.**

   Sorry! Nothing happens. In at least one respect, Eclipse is less effective than the Marx Brothers.

Linking does nothing if you haven't already opened files in the editor, or if you've hidden files in the Package Explorer. Imagine selecting a file in the Package Explorer — a file that's not open in the editor area. Then nothing happens. Similarly, in the editor area you may move to a file that's not visible in the Package Explorer. (Either the working set or the filters are hiding this file from the Package Explorer's display.) Once again, nothing happens.

Chapter 4

Changing Your Perspective

In This Chapter

▶ Changing the way a perspective looks

▶ Changing what a perspective does

▶ Saving perspectives

I understand. You get desensitized. I write about things you can do to change the look of an Eclipse perspective. I say you can widen an area by dragging the area's edges. You say "Big deal!"

Maybe dragging an area's edges isn't such a big deal. Nobody's surprised about dragging things with a mouse. But Eclipse is filled with surprises. This chapter covers a just few of them.

Changing the Way a Perspective Looks

Believe me — I'm not big on cosmetic features. One look at the mess in my office will convince anyone of that. But if you work with Eclipse as much as I have, you become accustomed to having things exactly the way you want them.

In this section, you move things around within an Eclipse perspective. With the right amount of moving, you make Java coding much easier.

Adding views

You can add an additional view to a perspective. For example, the lower right-hand corner of the Java perspective normally contains only three views (Problems, Javadoc, and Declaration). Figure 4-1 shows part of the Java perspective with an additional Error Log view.

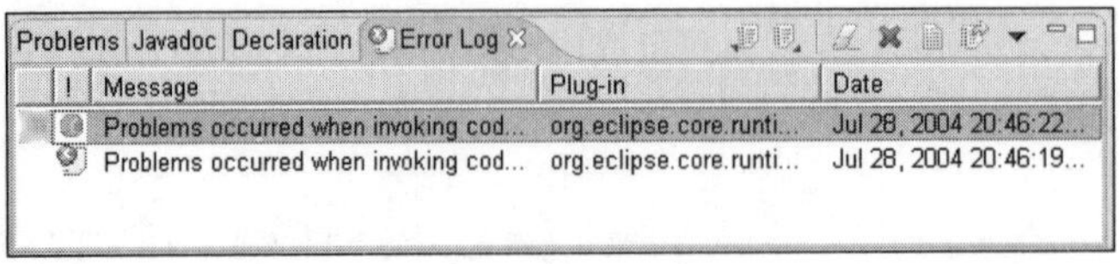

Figure 4-1:
The Error
Log view.

!	Message	Plug-in	Date
	Problems occurred when invoking cod...	org.eclipse.core.runti...	Jul 28, 2004 20:46:22...
	Problems occurred when invoking cod...	org.eclipse.core.runti...	Jul 28, 2004 20:46:19...

Problems Javadoc Declaration Error Log

The Error Log displays a list of things that have gone wrong. By default, the Error Log doesn't show up in the Java perspective. But you can make a view appear by following a few steps:

1. **On the main Eclipse menu bar, choose Window⇨Show View.**

   A submenu appears. The submenu contains the names of several views.

2. **If the view that you want to show appears on the submenu, then select the view.**

   When you work in the Java perspective, the Error Log view appears in the submenu. If you select Error Log, Eclipse displays the view in Figure 4-1.

Some of Eclipse's views don't appear on the submenu. So to dredge up certain views, you have to perform some extra steps. Here's what you do:

1. **On the main Eclipse menu bar, choose Window⇨Show View.**

   A submenu appears. In addition to the names of several views, this submenu contains an Other option.

2. **Select Other.**

   When you select Other, a Show View dialog appears. (See Figure 4-2.)

3. **Expand the Show View page's navigation tree to find the view that you want to add to the workbench.**

4. **Select the view and then click OK.**

In many cases, Eclipse opens views automatically. For instance, if you run a program that calls `System.out.println("Hello")`, the Console view appears. The word `Hello` shows up in the Console view.

For more info about the Console view, see Chapter 5.

Here's another interesting trick:

1. **Find a method name somewhere in the workbench.**

   Feel free to track down a method name in an editor, in the Package Explorer, or in some other view.

2. **Select the method name with your mouse.**

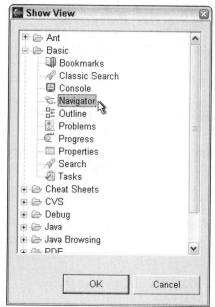

Figure 4-2:
The Show
View dialog.

3. **Right-click the selected name. Then, on the resulting context menu, select Open Call Hierarchy.**

   A view like the one in Figure 4-3 appears. The Call Hierarchy tree shows you the methods that, directly or indirectly, call your selected method. That's really cool!

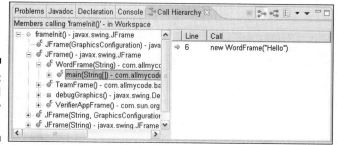

Figure 4-3:
The Call
Hierarchy
view.

In the steps for opening the Call Hierarchy, Step 2 involves your "ordinary" mouse button (for most people, the left button). At this point, the view-versus-editor distinction is important. When you poke around on a tree inside a view, Step 2 is optional. But when you rummage through text inside an editor, Step 2 is necessary. Sure, Step 2 is an extra mouse click. But sometimes, an extra mouse click is really important.

Repositioning views and editors

You can change the positions of views and editors. Here's how:

- ✔ Grab a view by its tab. Drag the view from place to place within the Eclipse window.

- ✔ Grab an editor by its tab. Drag the editor from place to place within the editor area.

- ✔ Grab a group of stacked views using some empty space to the right of all the tabs. Drag the entire group from place to place within the Eclipse window.

Views and editors are like oil and water. They generally don't mix. You can't drag a view into the editor area, and you can't drag an editor out of the editor area. (You can drag a view into what *was once* part of the editor area, but that's a different story.)

As you drag items across the workbench, you see two things:

- ✔ You see a rectangle, indicating roughly where you can drop the item.

- ✔ You see a *drop cursor*, indicating the way in which you can drop the item.

Figures 4-4 and 4-5 show you what can happen when you drag the Package Explorer near the top of the Eclipse workbench. In Figure 4-4, a big rectangle outlines the place where the dropped view is about to land. The fat arrow (the drop cursor) points downward to the landing place. When the drop cursor looks like a fat arrow, Eclipse shoves things around to make room for the item that you drop.

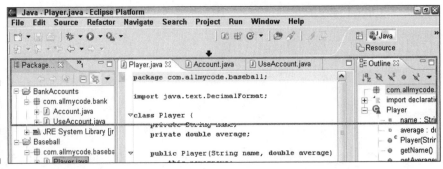

Figure 4-4:
The drop
cursor is a
fat arrow.

Indeed, in Figure 4-5, the Package Explorer lands in the place indicated in Figure 4-4. Eclipse shoves things downward to make room for the Package Explorer. After being dropped, the Package Explorer takes up a big area on its own.

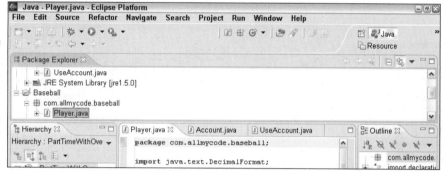

Figure 4-5: The Package Explorer shoves other parts downward.

By dragging views to certain places, you can achieve specific effects. In Figure 4-6, the rectangle covers part of the editor area. So when you release the mouse button, you get the tiling shown in Figure 4-7. The Package Explorer takes up space that was once part of the editor area. The editor area shrinks as the top of the editor area moves downward.

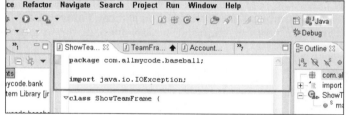

Figure 4-6: The rectangle covers part of the editor area.

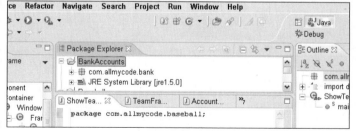

Figure 4-7: The Package Explorer shoves the editors downward.

Figures 4-8 and 4-9 tell a slightly different story. In Figure 4-8, the drop cursor looks like a stack of tabbed pages. This cursor tells you that, if you drop the view at this spot, the view joins the tab group indicated by the big rectangle. And, in Figure 4-9, the Package Explorer is playing happily with its newfound tab group friends.

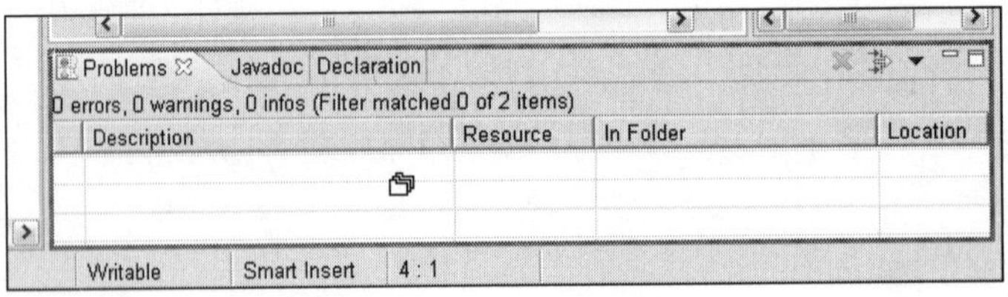

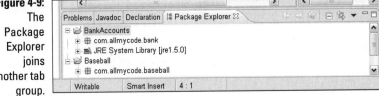

Figure 4-8:
The stack
drop cursor.

Figure 4-9:
The
Package
Explorer
joins
another tab
group.

You can move editors as well as views. Figure 4-10 shows an arrangement of editors in the workbench's editor area. You just can't move an editor outside of the editor area. Editors are cliquish. They always hang out with other editors.

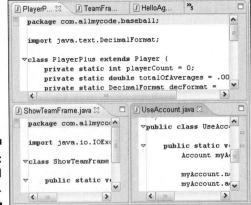

Figure 4-10:
Stacked and
tiled editors.

Detaching a view

You can drag a view off of the main window. Try this experiment:

1. **Check to make sure that the Eclipse window is *not* maximized.**

   Don't be fooled if the Eclipse window covers the whole computer screen. Eclipse sometimes takes up the whole screen without being maximized. The window is just stretched to cover every available pixel.

2. **Make sure that the Eclipse window doesn't cover the entire screen.**

   If necessary, drag one of the window's edges.

3. **Choose a view in the Eclipse window. Drag the view's tab away from the Eclipse window.**

   In Figure 4-11 the Package Explorer is detached from the main window. You can make this happen by dragging the Package Explorer's tab.

   You can drag a view off of the main Eclipse window, but you can't drag an editor off of the window. Too bad!

4. **To continue the experiment, choose another view in the main Eclipse window. Drag that view's tab away from the main Eclipse window (and away from the view that you dragged in Step 3).**

   Now you have a main window and two detached windows, as shown in Figure 4-12.

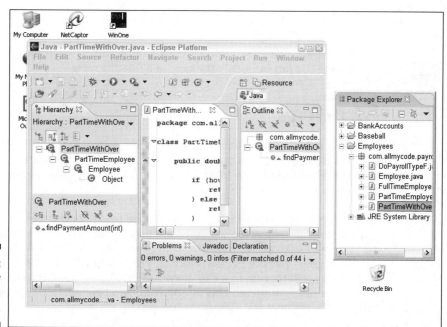

Figure 4-11:
A view
floats on
its own.

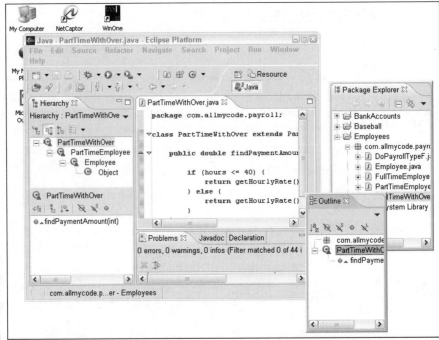

Figure 4-12:
Two views
float on
their own.

5. **Choose yet another view in the main Eclipse window. Drag that view's tab to the tab of a floating view.**

In Figure 4-13, the Hierarchy and Outline views live together in the same detached window.

To achieve this effect, release your mouse button when the drop cursor covers the tab (and only the tab) of a floating view.

Fast views

Chapter 3 tells you how to minimize and restore a view. The problem is, minimizing a view isn't always very useful. Sure, the view disappears, but what's left in the view's place can be empty space. The clutter is gone, but the waste of space is shameful.

As an alternative to minimizing views, Eclipse provides *fast views*. In some ways, a fast view is like the window minimizing that you see on your operating system's desktop. For instance, when you reduce a view to a fast view, you get a handy restore button on a *Fast View toolbar*. All the reduced views' buttons live together on this Fast View toolbar. Taken together, these buttons act like the application buttons on the Windows taskbar. Clicking a button temporarily restores the view to its full size.

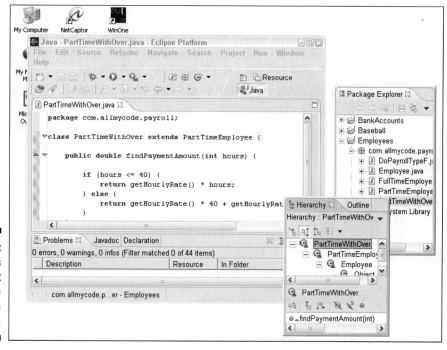

Figure 4-13:
Three views
float apart
from the
main
window.

 In the previous sentence, notice that word "temporarily." When you're finished using a restored fast view, the view re-minimizes itself automatically.
(The view goes back to being a mere button on the Fast View toolbar.) And
how does Eclipse know when you're finished using a view? To find out, see
the section titled "Temporarily restoring a view."

Creating a fast view the cool way

To get started using fast views, try the following experiment.

1. **Look for a tiny gray box in the workbench's lower-left corner.**

   By default, the box appears on the window's status bar. This box is
   called the *Fast View toolbar.* (See Figure 4-14.)

Figure 4-14:
The Fast
View toolbar
is currently
empty.

The Fast View toolbar

TIP

If you can't find the Fast View toolbar on the Eclipse status bar, don't fret. The toolbar may not be there! The toolbar may be living along the left edge or the right edge of the Eclipse window. In either case, the toolbar is difficult to find. Skip immediately to the next section to move a button onto the bar, even if you can't find the bar.

2. **Drag an open view's tab to the Fast View toolbar.**

   A small rectangle appears in the Eclipse window's status bar. The drop cursor looks like a box with an arrow inside it. (See Figure 4-15.)

Figure 4-15:
Dragging a
view to the
Fast View
toolbar.

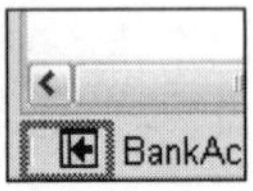

3. **Release your mouse button.**

   The view that you dragged becomes *hidden*. An icon representing the hidden view appears on the Fast View toolbar, as shown in Figure 4-16.

You can have several buttons on the Fast View toolbar. Each button represents a hidden view.

TIP

Eclipse doesn't label the buttons on the Fast View toolbar. To determine which view a button represents, let your mouse hover over the button. Alternatively, you can try to recognize the icon on the face of the button. It's the same as the icon that normally appears on the view's tab. (Go ahead. Try to remember what each view's icon looks like. I can't do it.)

Creating a fast view the lukewarm way

Occasionally, you can't create a fast view by dragging and dropping. When this happens, follow two simple steps:

1. **Right-click any view's tab.**

   A context menu appears.

2. **In the context menu, select Fast View.**

   The view becomes hidden. An icon representing the hidden view appears on the Fast View toolbar. (See Figure 4-16.)

Look Ma! No Package Explorer!

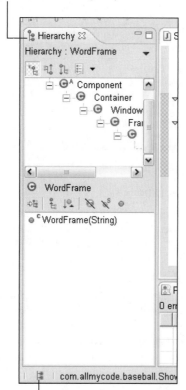

Figure 4-16:
The
Package
Explorer in
fast view
mode.

The Package Explorer's Fast View button

Temporarily restoring a view

Creating a fast view gets the view out of site quickly. But "out of sight" doesn't have to mean "out of mind." You can restore a fast view very easily. Here's how:

1. Click one of the buttons on the Fast View toolbar.

Figure 4-17 shows what happens when you click a Fast View button. (In Figure 4-17, I click the Problems view's button.) The view blossoms to its normal size, but the view doesn't appear in its usual place. The view isn't even inside a traditional workbench area. (In Figure 4-17, the Problems view covers the Package Explorer's area, and partly covers the editor area.)

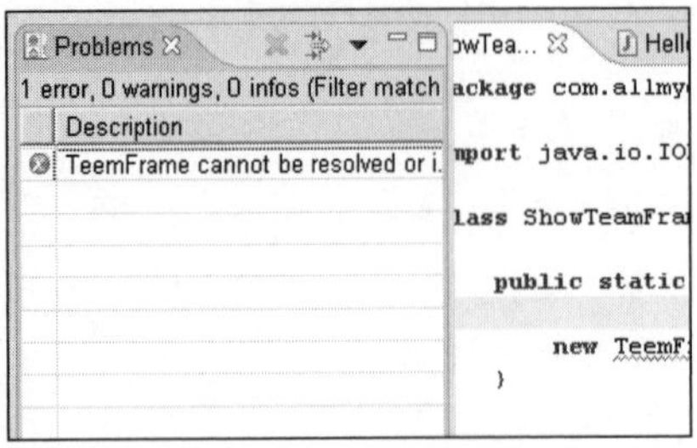

Figure 4-17:
The
Problems
view,
temporarily
unhidden.

2. **Do some clicking and other stuff inside the view.**

   Use the view as you normally would.

3. **Click anywhere else in the workbench.**

   For example, in Figure 4-17, click a visible portion of the editor area. When you do this, the view goes back to its hidden state. In other words, the view goes back to being a mere button on the Fast View toolbar.

Turning a fast view back into a slow view

You can get rid of a Fast View button and put a view "un-temporarily" back onto an area of the workbench. Just drag the Fast View button to an area on the workbench. All the drop cursor ideas (from the section titled "Repositioning views and editors") apply to dragging Fast View buttons.

Changing the Way a Perspective Behaves

You can change the actions available in an Eclipse perspective. Start by choosing Window⇨Customize Perspective on Eclipse's main menu bar. The Customize Perspective dialog has two pages — a Shortcuts page and a Commands page.

The Shortcuts page

Life is tough. To begin a new Java project, I have to click at least four times. First, I choose File⇨New⇨Project. That's three clicks. If Java Project is already selected in the New Project dialog, I have to confirm that choice by clicking Next. That's four clicks. Of course if Java Project isn't already selected, then selecting Java Project is an additional click.

Yes, life is tough. But with the Customize Perspective dialog's Shortcuts page, I can reduce the work to just three clicks. What? You say I'm spoiled? Well, maybe I am. But if you work with the same user interface day after day, month after month, you get tired of performing the same old sequence of steps. So here's what you do:

1. **Open the Java perspective.**

   For details, see Chapter 2.

2. **Choose Window⇨Customize Perspective to open the Customize Perspective dialog.**

3. **In the Customize Perspective dialog, select the Shortcuts tab.**

   The Shortcuts page has three sections — Submenus, Shortcut Categories, and Shortcuts. (See Figure 4-18.)

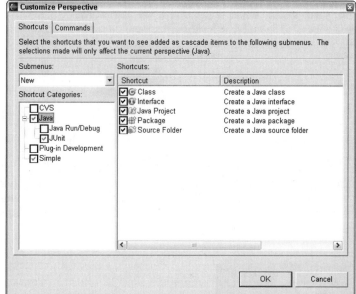

Figure 4-18:
The
Shortcuts
page of the
Customize
Perspective
dialog.

4. **Select an item in the Submenus list box.**

   With the Submenus list box, you choose New, Open Perspective, or Show View. In this example, you plan to add an item to the Java Perspective's New menu, so select New in the Submenus list box. (Refer to Figure 4-18.)

5. **Select an item in the Shortcut Categories tree.**

   The list of available shortcuts is divided into categories and subcategories. These categories and subcategories appear in the Shortcut Categories tree. I happen to know that the Java Project item (the item that you add in this example) is part of the Java category. So in this example, go to the Shortcut Categories navigation tree and select Java. (Again, refer to Figure 4-18.)

6. Check or uncheck items in the Shortcuts list.

In this example, you want to add Java Project to the New menu. So put a check mark next to the Java Project item.

7. Click OK.

You knew you'd have to click OK eventually, didn't you? When you click OK, the Customize Perspective dialog disappears.

Meanwhile, back at the workbench . . .

8. Check Eclipse's menu bar for the added or deleted items.

In this example, choose File⇨New. If all goes well, the New menu contains the Java Project option. (See Figure 4-19.)

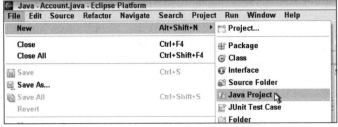

Figure 4-19: Checking for the Java Project menu option.

9. Check Eclipse's toolbar for the added or deleted items.

I'm not a fan of the Eclipse window's toolbars, but it's nice to know that you can customize these things. Figure 4-20 shows what I found when I poked around aimlessly for the New toolbar button. I found the right button, clicked it, and saw the Java Project option. Hooray!

Figure 4-20: Checking for the Java Project toolbar option.

The Commands page

The Commands page does some of the things you can't do with the Shortcuts page. For example, imagine using Eclipse to teach an introductory computer programming course. Having too many options scares students. The students become intimidated when they see 19 items on Eclipse's Run menu. Instead of 19 scary items, they'd rather see 8 not-so-scary items. So to make students happy, to get better course evaluations, to reduce tuition hikes, and ultimately, to raise the nation's standard of education, you decide to trim Eclipse's Run menu. This section's instructions show you how to do it.

1. **Open the Java perspective.**

   For details, see Chapter 2.

2. **Choose Window⇨Customize Perspective to open the Customize Perspective dialog.**

3. **In the Customize Perspective dialog, select the Commands tab.**

   The Commands page makes an appearance, as shown in Figure 4-21.

4. **Check or uncheck things in the Available Command Groups list.**

   In this example, you want to remove items from the Run menu. To find out if a particular group contains Run menu items, select that group in the Available Command Groups list. Then look at the items in the Menubar Details list.

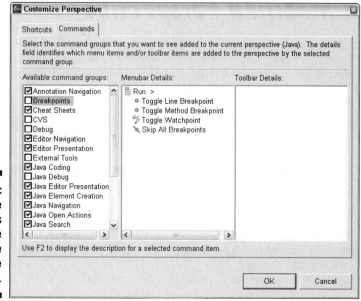

Figure 4-21: The Commands page of the Customize Perspective dialog.

According to Figure 4-21, all items in the Breakpoints group are Run menu items. So uncheck the Breakpoints group. To trim the Run menu further, uncheck the External Tools and Java Debug groups. (The Debug and Profile groups contain Run menu items but, in the Java perspective, these two groups are unchecked by default.)

5. Click OK.

At this point, what else would you expect to do?

6. Check Eclipse's menu bar and toolbar for the added or deleted items.

The Run menu in Figure 4-22 has only eight items. In a world where less is more, I call that "progress."

Figure 4-22:
A simplified
Run menu.

Saving a Modified Perspective

Most of this chapter tells you how to change a perspective. That's very nice but, if you can't save your changes, the whole business is almost useless. Fortunately, Eclipse makes it easy to save a perspective's changes.

1. Make changes to a perspective.

Add views, resize areas, change actions, do all kinds of things.

2. On Eclipse's main menu bar, choose Window⇨Save Perspective As.

The Save Perspective As dialog appears, as shown in Figure 4-23.

3. Make up a new name for your modified perspective.

In Figure 4-23, I make up the name My New Perspective.

Avoid using an existing name for your modified perspective. If you accidentally save changes to an existing perspective, you may have trouble undoing the changes.

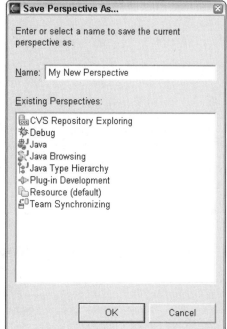

Figure 4-23:
The Save
Perspective
As dialog.

4. **Click OK.**

Your new perspective is a first-class Eclipse citizen. The perspective has a name. The perspective appears in your Select Perspective dialog. The perspective appears in the Eclipse's perspective bar. If you close Eclipse, and restart Eclipse tomorrow, the perspective is still ready and willing to serve you.

Some things about Eclipse's workbench aren't part of a perspective. For instance, the collection of open projects and open editors isn't defined as part of a perspective. Similarly, the choice of the active view in a tab group (whether the Package Explorer or the Hierarchy view is in front) isn't cast in stone as part of a perspective. Working sets and filters aren't wedded to the perspective. Furthermore, the editor area is shared by all perspectives, so things like editor tiling aren't affected when you save a perspective.

Sometimes, after I change a perspective, I don't like the changes. I move this, add that, and tweak something else. Finally I decide that the perspective was better before I messed with it. That's not a problem. Before saving the changes I choose Window➪Reset Perspective on Eclipse's main menu bar. After a brief encounter with an "are you sure" dialog, the perspective is back to the way it was before my changes. Whew!

Chapter 5

Some Useful Perspectives and Views

*I*magine yourself writing a report for tomorrow's newspaper. As you type on your computer keyboard, you look back and forth between the computer monitor and a little spiral notepad. The monitor displays your favorite word processing program, and the notepad has scribbles from a busy day on the beat.

This combination of paper notepad and word processing program is like an Eclipse perspective. You have two areas, side by side, each representing a different aspect of your work. The paper notepad is your On the Scene Facts view, and the word processor is your Written Article view. You can give this combination of views a name. Call it the Reporter's perspective.

After finishing the article, you send it to a copy editor. The Copy Editor's perspective has two views. One view, the Written Article view, is exactly the same as the reporter's Written Article view. (In fact, the reporter and the copy editor share this Written Article view.) Another view, the Dictionary view, is a dusty old book on the editor's desk. This Dictionary view lists all the words in the English language, along with their meanings, their origins, and other strange things.

After mercilessly slashing up your work, the copy editor sends it to a fact checker. The fact checker verifies the accuracy of your reporting. The Fact Checker's perspective has two views — the old Written Article view and a new Web Browser view. Using a Web browser and some fancy databases, the fact checker researches each claim in your article, looking for incorrect or incomplete information. Unlike the other two perspectives, this Fact Checker's perspective has an area that displays two different views. Both the

Written Article and the Web Browser views appear on the fact checker's computer monitor. In Eclipse terminology, the Written Article and Web Browser views are stacked.

The analogy between writing news articles and using Eclipse isn't perfect. But the analogy illustrates some important points. First, a perspective is an arrangement of views. Some of these views are shared with other perspectives. Also, as you work within Eclipse, you play many roles. Like the reporter, the copy editor, and the fact checker, you function in various perspectives as the analyst, the programmer, the tester, the debugger, and other important people.

Some Useful Perspectives

Eclipse comes bundled with eight perspectives. In this section, I describe five of them. (I describe the perspectives that are helpful to new Eclipse users.)

To switch from one perspective to another, choose Window➪Open Perspective on Eclipse's main menu bar.

Resource perspective

The *Resource perspective* displays resources in a language-independent way — a way that has nothing to do with Java, nothing to do with C++, nothing to do with any programming language in particular.

Eclipse has three kinds of *resources* — files, folders, and projects. Anything that falls into one of these three categories is a resource. None of these three categories is specific to the Java programming language. (You can find projects in every programming language, and you can find files and folders in every computer-related situation.) So, for the most part, the Resource perspective is language-neutral. The Resource perspective is good for managing things on your computer's hard drive.

The first time you open Eclipse, you see the Resource perspective. You can develop Java programs in the Resource perspective, but to use Eclipse's convenient Java-specific features, you're better off switching to the Java perspective. (For a closer look at the Resource perspective — including a lovely figure — see Chapter 2.)

Java perspective

The *Java perspective* displays things in a way that's handy for writing Java code. This is, of course, my favorite perspective. With the Java perspective

I have an editor, the Package Explorer, Outline and Console views, and lots of other goodies.

Java Browsing perspective

The *Java Browsing perspective* helps you visualize all the pieces of a chunk of Java code — packages, types, members, you name it. I use this perspective in two different ways. First, I keep track of my own code. (See Figure 5-1.) Second, I probe the code in other peoples' Java archive files. (See Figure 5-2.)

The ability to probe Java archive (JAR) files is especially handy. A JAR file is a zip file with a bunch of Java `.class` files inside it. From time immemorial, Java programmers have been frustrated by the cumbersome task of exploring JAR files' contents. But now, with Eclipse's Java Browsing perspective, the task is no longer cumbersome. At times, it can be fun.

Figure 5-1:
Examining
my code
with the
Java
Browsing
perspective.

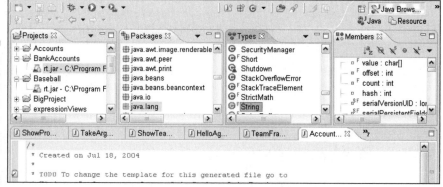

Figure 5-2:
Examining
the standard
Java API
with the
Java
Browsing
perspective.

Java Type Hierarchy perspective

The *Java Type Hierarchy perspective* shows you chains of parent classes and subclasses. This perspective provides a comfortable home for the Hierarchy view. To find out more about the Hierarchy view, see the "Hierarchy view" section (farther along in this chapter).

Debug perspective

The *Debug perspective* displays everything you need in order to step carefully and thoughtfully through a Java program's run.

For more information on debugging, see Chapter 16.

Some Useful Views

Eclipse comes stocked with about 40 different views. For your convenience, I describe about a dozen of them in this chapter.

To display a view that's not already visible, choose Window⇨Show View on Eclipse's main menu bar.

Navigator view

The *Navigator view* displays resources in a language-independent way (a way that has nothing to do with Java or any other programming language). Figure 5-3 shows the `Accounts` project's file structure in Navigator view.

In Figure 5-3, you see things that you don't normally see in a Java-specific view. You see the Eclipse `.classpath` and `.project` housekeeping files. You also see the `bin` directory, which is of little interest when you work at the Java source code level.

Notice the lack of any Java-specific information in Figure 5-3. The `Account.java` file contains methods, fields, and other interesting doodads, but the Navigator view shows none of them.

Package Explorer view

For me, the Package Explorer view is Eclipse's real workhorse. The *Package Explorer* displays things in a Java-specific way. Unlike the wimpy Navigator

view, the Package Explorer displays things such as methods and fields —
things that live inside a Java source file.

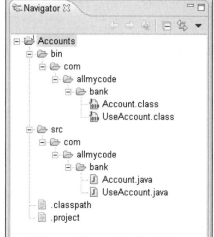

Figure 5-3:
The
Navigator
view.

Contrast the trees in Figures 5-3 and 5-4. The Package Explorer in Figure 5-4
has no Eclipse housekeeping files. Instead, the Package Explorer digs down
inside the `Account.java` and `UseAccount.java` source files. The Package
Explorer can also dig inside JAR files, and display classes in the Java runtime
library.

Outline view

The *Outline view* displays a tree or list of whatever is in the active editor. In
my mind, I liken the Outline view to the Package Explorer view.

- ✔ **If the active editor contains a Java file, then the Outline view looks
  very much like a portion of the Package Explorer view.**

  Unlike the Package Explorer, the Outline view displays only one file's
  contents at a time.

- ✔ **With the Outline view, you can drill down to see the elements inside
  many different kinds of resources.**

  The Package Explorer can drill down inside a piece of Java code. The
  Outline view looks inside Java code as well. But the Outline view is
  more versatile. For example, in Figure 5-5, the active editor displays
  an XML file. (The editor displays the file's contents as a form on a Web
  page.) The Outline view follows suit, displaying the XML file's structure
  in tree form.

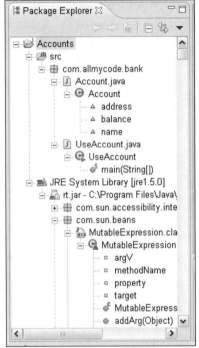

Figure 5-4:
The
Package
Explorer
view.

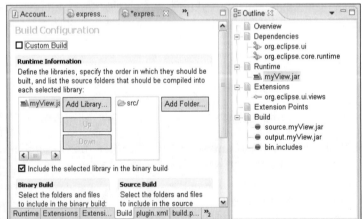

Figure 5-5:
The Outline
view
displays an
XML file's
contents.

When you display a Java class, the Outline view has some nifty toolbar buttons. In Figure 5-6, a little hover tip tells you what happens if you click a particular button. If you click the button containing a little ball, then you hide any non-public members in the Outline view's tree. (In Figure 5-6, the `name` and `average` variables are non-public members. Clicking the button makes those two branches disappear.)

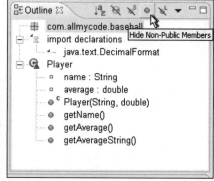

Figure 5-6: A hover tip describing the Hide Non-Public Members action.

Console view

The *Console view* displays whatever may appear in the good old-fashioned command window. I admit it. I'm a text-output junky. I like `System.out.print` and `System.err.print`. I even enjoy stack traces (when they come from other peoples' programs).

Figure 5-7 shows the Console view. For my taste, this view is very cheerful. Standard output is blue, and error output is red. Anything you type on the keyboard is green.

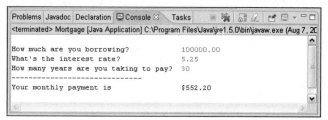

Figure 5-7: The Console view. (Love it or leave it.)

You can change the colors (and other things about the Console) by choosing Window⇨Preferences from Eclipse's main menu. In the Preferences dialog, expand the Run/Debug branch. Then, in the Run/Debug branch, select Console. In response, Eclipse shows you a page with options such as Standard Out Text Color and Displayed Tab Width.

Hierarchy view

The *Hierarchy view* displays superclasses and subclasses in a useful tree format. Figure 5-8 shows the Hierarchy view in action.

The Hierarchy view doesn't display things on its own. To display a class in the Hierarchy view, you have to put the class (somehow) into the Hierarchy view. For example, before I could see the stuff in Figure 5-8, I had to get Java's `Container` class into the Hierarchy view.

You can probably put a particular class into the Hierarchy view a million different ways. In this section, I describe two ways.

✔ Right-click the name of a class in another view, or in an editor. In the resulting context menu, choose Open Type Hierarchy.

✔ Drag the name of a class from another view to the Hierarchy view.

The Hierarchy view has lots of interesting quirks, so I devote a little extra space to this view and its uses.

Figure 5-8:
The
Hierarchy
view.

Using the Hierarchy view's toolbar buttons

You can change what the Hierarchy view displays using the view's toolbar buttons. With the Show the Type Hierarchy button selected (refer to Figure 5-8), the Hierarchy view's tree goes from `Object`, down through `Container`, and downward to the un-extended classes, such as `Box` and `CellRendererPane`.

Dragging a class to the Hierarchy view

As you drag a class into the Hierarchy view, the kind of cursor you see makes a big difference. If you use Microsoft Windows, the cursor in the figure is usually what you want to see. If you drop a class when you see that cursor, the class displays in the Hierarchy view.

The cursor in the figure contains a box with a little curvy arrow inside it. (It's like the arrow on a Windows shortcut icon.) If you don't see this curvy boxed arrow, then you may not want to drop the class. When you drop a class without seeing the curvy arrow, Eclipse offers to move the class from one part of your workspace to another (for example, from one project to another). This is probably not what you want to do. (If your goal is to display things in the Hierarchy view, then moving code around is not your first priority.)

When you drag junk to the Hierarchy view, you may also see the *restricted cursor* (a circle with a diagonal line running through it). This cursor tells you that you can't drop the class at that position in the view. In this case, releasing the mouse button does absolutely nothing.

Here's one more hint. If you don't see whatever cursor you expect to see, you may be dragging a class on top of a class that's already being displayed. Try moving your mouse to a more neutral place inside the Hierarchy view. That trick usually works for me.

Of course, all this stuff about curvy arrows applies only to Windows users. If you use UNIX, a Mac, or some other non-Windows system, the cursors don't necessarily have curvy arrows inside boxes. Do a few little experiments to find out what cursors your Hierarchy view displays.

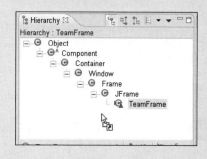

But in Figure 5-9, with the Show the Supertype Hierarchy button selected, the view's tree is upside down. Only classes from the `Container` upward display in the tree.

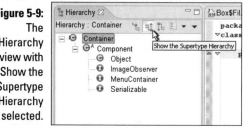

Figure 5-9: The Hierarchy view with Show the Supertype Hierarchy selected.

In Figure 5-10, the Show the Subtype Hierarchy button does almost what you see back in Figure 5-8. Of course with Show the Subtype Hierarchy, you don't see superclasses of the Container class.

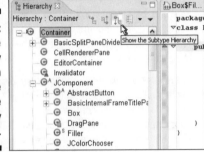

Figure 5-10:
The
Hierarchy
view with
Show the
Subtype
Hierarchy
selected.

The active working set influences what you see or don't see in the Hierarchy tree. A class that's not in the active working set may not appear at all in the Hierarchy tree. (The class may not appear, even if it's a subclass or superclass of a class that *does* appear.) In other cases, a class that's not in the active working set can appear as a grayed-out branch of the Hierarchy tree. If you want to see everything you can possibly see, deselect the working set.

For details on selecting and deselecting working sets, see Chapter 3.

Overriding methods

Imagine yourself sitting in front of your computer, staring at the Eclipse Hierarchy view. What's going through your mind? You may be thinking about all the things one class inherits from another. (Okay, I'm giving you the benefit of the doubt, but you get the point.) Maybe you're thinking that MySubclass shouldn't inherit myMethod from MyClass. Maybe you want MySubclass to override myMethod.

Here's how you override a method using the Hierarchy view:

1. **In the bottom half of the Hierarchy view, make sure that the Show All Inherited Members toolbar button is pressed. Make sure that the other toolbar buttons in the bottom half of the Hierarchy view are *not* pressed. (See Figure 5-11.)**

   If the wrong buttons are (or aren't) pressed, you may not be able to find the method that you want to override.

2. **In the top half of the Hierarchy view, select the subclass that will do the overriding.**

   I want the PartTimeEmployee class to override the getJobTitle method. So, in Figure 5-11, I selected the PartTimeEmployee class.

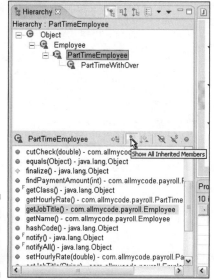

Figure 5-11:
Preparing to
override a
method.

3. **In the bottom half of the Hierarchy view, right-click the method that you want to override.**

   In Figure 5-11, I right-clicked the `getJobTitle` method.

4. **In the resulting context menu, choose Source➪Override in *(the class from Step 2)*. (See Figure 5-12.)**

   After making all these choices, a new method magically appears in the editor. Now the ball is in your court. Shuffle over to the editor and insert some real code.

Call Hierarchy view

The *Call Hierarchy view* displays methods that, directly or indirectly, call a selected method. To find out more about this view, see Chapter 4.

Declaration view

The *Declaration view* displays Java source code. When you click an identifier in an editor, the Declaration view displays the identifier's declaration. (See Figure 5-13.) If you work with a large project, this view can be very handy. After all, in a huge pile of source code, any particular use of an identifier can be very far from the identifier's declaration.

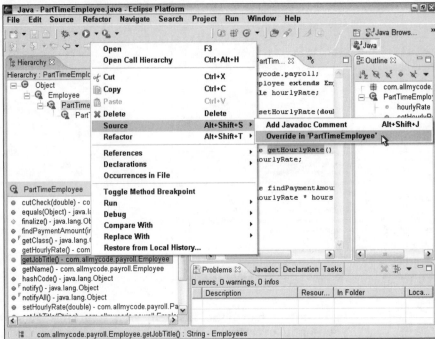

Figure 5-12:
Overriding a
method
using the
Hierarchy
view.

The Declaration view can display source code that's inside or outside of your project and your workspace. For example, with the correct settings, the view can display declarations in the Java API code.

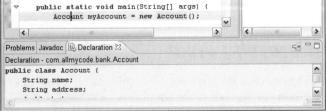

Figure 5-13:
The
Declaration
view.

The instructions that follow don't work unless your computer contains a copy of the Java API source code. As far as I know, the only reliable way to get a copy is to download and install the entire Java SDK. The SDK takes up at least 90MB on your computer's hard drive, and of that 90MB you need as little as 11MB for the source code. If you really need to save space, you can install the entire SDK and then delete everything except the SDK's `src.zip` file. To download the SDK, visit `java.sun.com/j2se/downloads`.

Here's how you get the Declaration view to display Java API source code:

1. **In the Package Explorer, expand a** JRE System Library **branch.**

   If you installed the standard JRE in Chapter 2, the JRE System Library branch contains an rt.jar branch. The letters "rt" stand for "run time." This JAR file contains the standard Java runtime library.

   The rt.jar file contains .class files, not .java source files. You want to associate a collection of .java source files with this rt.jar file.

   In this step, you pick a branch in one of the Package Explorer's projects. The Package Explorer's display may include many other projects. Don't be fooled into thinking that you're modifying only one project's properties. The change you make in this set of instructions affects all projects in your Eclipse workspace.

2. **Right-click the** rt.jar **branch of the Package Explorer's tree. In the resulting context menu, choose Properties.**

   A Properties dialog appears.

3. **On the left side of the Properties dialog, select Java Source Attachment.**

   In the main body of the Properties dialog, the Java Source Attachment page appears.

4. **In the Location Path field, enter the path to your Java API source files.**

   On my computer, the source files live in a directory named C:\Program Files\Java\jdk1.5.0\src. (See Figure 5-14.) This src directory has subdirectories named com, java, javax, and others.

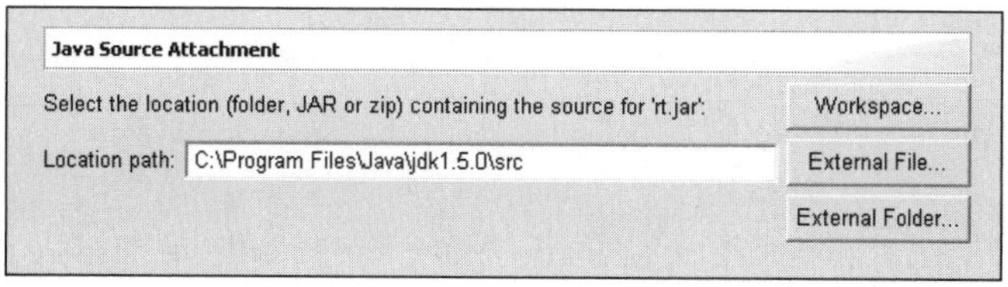

Figure 5-14:
Specifying the location of your Java API source files.

Java Source Attachment		
Select the location (folder, JAR or zip) containing the source for 'rt.jar':		Workspace...
Location path:	C:\Program Files\Java\jdk1.5.0\src	External File...
		External Folder...

5. **Click OK.**

   With this decisive click, the .class files in rt.jar become connected to a collection of Java source files. The Declaration view is ready to display Java API source code.

Using the Declaration view takes a little bit of patience. On occasion this view is sluggish. Sometimes, whatever change you make to the Java Source Attachment setting doesn't take effect right away. Of course, at times you have a right to be impatient. For instance, you select a new name in the editor and, after several seconds, you still see the previously selected name's declaration. If that keeps happening, the Declaration view probably can't find the new name's source code.

Javadoc view

The *Javadoc view* displays an "in-between" version of an item's Javadoc comment. By "in-between," I mean "better than plain text, but not as good as your Web browser's rendering of a Javadoc page." For instance, in Figure 5-15, I select String in the editor. Following along with me, the Javadoc view displays the String class's Javadoc comment.

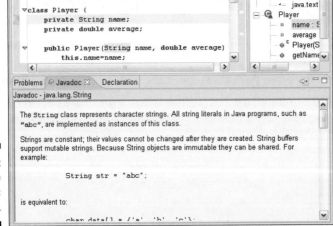

Figure 5-15: The Javadoc view.

As you see in Figure 5-15, the Javadoc view can handle things like the standard Java API files. But getting this view to work means following the steps in the "Declaration view" section. And when you get to Step 3, don't make the mistake that I often make. To get the Javadoc view working, select Java Source Attachment, and *not* Javadoc Location!

Eclipse can open your default browser and jump to an item's complete Javadoc Web page. For details, see Chapter 13.

Problems view

The *Problems view* lists things that go wrong. For instance, Figure 5-16 shows a Problems view containing messages from a failed compilation. If you click a message in the Problems view, the editor switches to the appropriate place in your Java code.

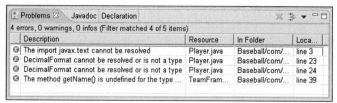

Description	Resource	In Folder	Loca...
The import javax.text cannot be resolved	Player.java	Baseball/com/...	line 3
DecimalFormat cannot be resolved or is not a type	Player.java	Baseball/com/...	line 23
DecimalFormat cannot be resolved or is not a type	Player.java	Baseball/com/...	line 24
The method getName() is undefined for the type ...	TeamFram...	Baseball/com/...	line 39

Problems ⊠ Javadoc Declaration

4 errors, 0 warnings, 0 infos (Filter matched 4 of 5 items)

You can change what you see in the Problems view. Click the view's menu button and, in the resulting context menu, choose Filters.

You can get more information about the Problems view and its filters. If you're interested, see Chapter 3.

Tasks view

The Tasks view is a big To Do list. The view displays

✔ To Do items that Eclipse generates automatically for you

✔ To Do items that you create on your own

To find out how the Tasks view works, try this experiment:

1. **Go to the Java perspective.**

   To go to the Java perspective, choose Window➪Open Perspective➪Java.

2. **Open the Tasks view.**

   For help with this, see Chapter 4. The Tasks view is on the Basic branch in the Show View dialog.

3. **Click the Task view's menu button. In the resulting context menu, choose Filters.**

   The Task view's Filters dialog appears. For more information about filters, see Chapter 3.

4. **Remove the check mark from the Enabled box in the Task view's Filters dialog.**

   With filters disabled, the Tasks view displays all your tasks. (The Tasks view doesn't censor any of the tasks.)

5. **In the active editor, add a comment containing the word** TODO **to your code.**

   Type something like

   ```
   // TODO Thank the author of Eclipse For Dummies
   ```

6. **Choose File⇨Save.**

7. **Look at the Tasks view, and scroll down until you find your new entry.**

   See Figure 5-17.

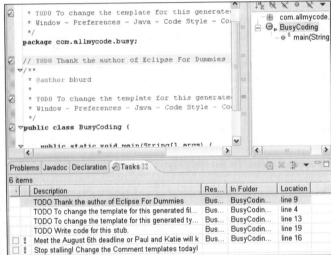

Figure 5-17:
The Tasks
view.

When you put the word TODO in a comment, Eclipse creates a new task. Eclipse associates this task with whatever line of code contains the comment. That's why, in Figure 5-17, the editor's marker bar has little icons (little clipboards with check marks in them). Each of these *task markers* indicates a point in the code that's associated with a Tasks view entry.

Eclipse automatically puts the word TODO into some of your code's comments. So, to some extent, the Tasks view becomes populated on its own.

Here's a really picky point. The Tasks view doesn't necessarily display all the text on a comment's TODO line. If the line contains * My code: TODO Describe the code here, then the new Tasks view entry contains TODO

`Describe the code here.` If a line contains `//TODO date TODO day` then you get two new Tasks view entries — one entry says `TODO date`; the other entry says `TODO day`.

Reminding yourself in more ways about the work you have to do

In the previous set of instructions, you add a `TODO` comment to your Java source code. If typing a `TODO` comment is too "manual" for your taste, don't despair. Eclipse gives you many ways to create new tasks:

- ✔ **Right-click a point in the editor's marker bar. In the resulting context menu, choose Add Task.**

  When you do this, you get a New Task dialog like the one shown in Figure 5-18. Eclipse fills in the On Resource, In Folder, and Location fields for you. All you have to do is type something in the Description field. (Type a friendly reminder to yourself. Don't make the reminder too threatening. If it's threatening, you may scare yourself away.)

  After you click OK, Eclipse adds an entry to the Tasks view and adds an icon to the appropriate place in your code's marker bar. (Eclipse does not add a comment to your Java source file. If you look at the source, you don't see a new `TODO` comment.)

- ✔ **Right-click a row of the Tasks view and, in the resulting context menu, choose Add Task.**

  When you do all this, you get a dialog very much like the one shown in Figure 5-18. In this case, the dialog's On Resource, In Folder, and Location fields are empty. When you add a task this way, Eclipse doesn't associate the task with a line of code in a file.

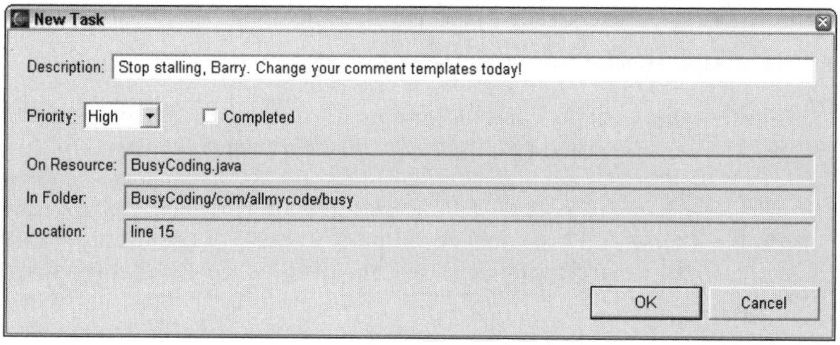

Figure 5-18:
The New
Task dialog.

When I'm given the choice, I prefer not to type `TODO` in my code's comments. Instead, I add tasks with one of the right-click/dialog techniques. With either of these techniques, I eventually get the satisfaction of filling in a little "completed task" check box. This check box is at the leftmost edge of a Tasks view entry. (Refer to Figure 5-17.)

Later, if I'm feeling happy and carefree, I remove all of my deleted tasks. I do this by right-clicking any Tasks view row, and then choosing Delete Completed Tasks.

Customizing your list of tasks

You can customize virtually everything having anything to do with the Tasks view:

✔ **You can (and should) customize the text that Eclipse automatically adds to all your comments.**

Choose Window➪Preferences. Then in the resulting Preferences dialog, expand the Java/Code Style tree branches. Select the Code Templates branch of the tree. Then, on the right side of the Preferences dialog, expand the Comments branch of the tree. Select Methods to change what Eclipse adds automatically in a method's comment. Select Types to change what Eclipse adds automatically in a class's comment. And so on.

✔ **You can add words such as TODO to the Tasks view's vocabulary.**

By default, the Tasks view creates entries for the words TODO, FIXME, and XXX in Java comments. You can modify this behavior in all kinds of ways. Start by choosing Window➪Preferences. In the resulting Preferences dialog, expand the Java tree branch. Then select the Code Task Tags branch of the tree.

✔ **You can sort and filter tasks.**

In this way, the Tasks view is very similar to the Problems view.

Projects, Packages, Types, and Members views

These four views go hand in hand as part of the Java Browsing perspective. See the section titled (what else?) "Java Browsing perspective" for more.

The *Projects view* is like a little Package Explorer, except that branches in the Projects view don't expand very much. Instead of seeing branches expand, you see things appearing and disappearing in the other three views.

For instance, back in Figure 5-2 everything ripples along from left to right. If you select an item in the Projects view, then the Packages view immediately displays all the Java packages in that item. At the same time, the Types and Members views temporarily become blank.

Later, when you select a package shown in the Packages view, the Types view immediately displays the names of classes defined inside that package. And so on.

Search view

As the name says, this view displays the results of searches. (See Figure 5-19.) It's such an important view that I can't bear to omit it from this chapter's list. But Eclipse's search mechanisms have tons of interesting options. It would be unfair for me to summarize the options here. Instead, you can find out more about searching and the Search view in Chapter 12.

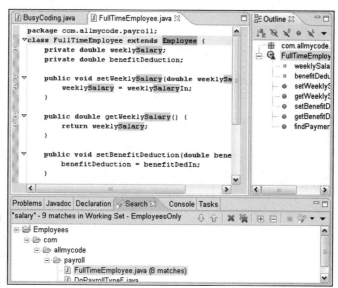

Figure 5-19:
The Search
view.

Part II
Using the Eclipse Environment

The 5th Wave   By Rich Tennant

"The funny thing is he's spent 9 hours organizing his computer desktop."

In this part . . .

*I*t's amazing. People stop me on the street with questions. They ask questions like "How do you create an interface from a class using Eclipse?" And they ask other questions — questions like "Why is your car's tire on my foot?"

The chapters in this part answer questions of the first kind — "how to" questions about Eclipse. For answers to questions about my car and its tires, don't read this part of *Eclipse For Dummies*. Instead, talk to my lawyer.

Chapter 6

Using the Java Editor

In This Chapter

▶ Making the most of the Java editor

▶ Configuring editor settings

▶ Finding relief for your tired fingers

*I*t happens at so many Java conferences and events. The speaker begins by taking a quick audience survey.

"How many of you use Borland JBuilder?" A number of people raise their hands.

"And how many use Eclipse?" Again there's a show of hands.

"And finally, how many of you use a plain old text editor, such as Windows Notepad or UNIX vi?" Suddenly, discomfort starts rippling throughout the room. A few raise their hands proudly and noisily (as if that's possible). Others raise their hands just to look tough. Some people smirk because Notepad is so primitive and vi is so old. Someone asks "what's vi?" and the rest of the crowd laughs.

Okay, I'll answer the question. Bill Joy and Chuck Haley created vi at UC Berkeley in the late 1970s. At the time, vi was a groundbreaking, full-screen text editor. Instead of typing cryptic commands, you used arrow keys. (Well, actually, you moved around on a page using the H, J, K, and L keys, but who cares? In vi, these letter keys behaved as if they were arrow keys.)

Things have changed since the 1970s. We have mice, drag and drop, and language-aware editors. By a "language-aware editor" I mean an editor that treats your code as more than just character soup. The editor knows one Java statement from another, and the editor helps you compose your code.

We've come a long way since the 1970s. This chapter is about Eclipse's Java-aware editor.

Navigating the Preferences Dialog

Have you ever spent too many hours driving on long boring highways? After a while, your brain becomes etched. You pull over to rest, but in your mind you still see the highway going by. You close your eyes and start dreaming about highway. It's terrible. You've done so much driving that you can't get the experience out of your head.

A similar thing happened when I wrote the first draft of this chapter. I spent so much time writing about Eclipse's Preferences dialog that I had dreams about preferences chasing me down long corridors. "That does it," I said. "I'm making all my paragraphs shorter."

So here's a typical scenario. In the next section, I write about visiting "the Keyboard Shortcuts tab of the Workbench⇨Keys page in the Window⇨ Preferences dialog." Here's what that long-winded instruction really means:

1. **On Eclipse's main menu bar, choose Window⇨Preferences.**

   The Preferences dialog opens.

2. **In the tree on the left side of the Preferences dialog, expand the Workbench branch. Within the Workbench branch, select the Keys branch.**

   The Keys page appears inside the Preferences dialog. The page appears immediately to the right of the Preferences dialog's tree.

3. **On the Keys page, select the Keyboard Shortcuts tab.**

   That's it! See Figure 6-1.

Using Keyboard Shortcuts

I'm not a fan of keyboard shortcuts. I remember a few shortcuts, and quickly forget all the rest. So I don't have a long list of shortcuts you can use in Eclipse's editor.

But if you need a particular shortcut, I can tell you exactly where to hunt for it. Visit the Keyboard Shortcuts tab of the Workbench⇨Keys page in the Window⇨Preferences dialog. (For details on tabs, pages, and dialogs, see my "Navigating the Preferences Dialog" section.)

Eclipse divides its shortcuts into categories like Compare, Edit, File, and Search. Each category contains several functions. For instance, the File category contains functions like New, Close, Save As, and Save.

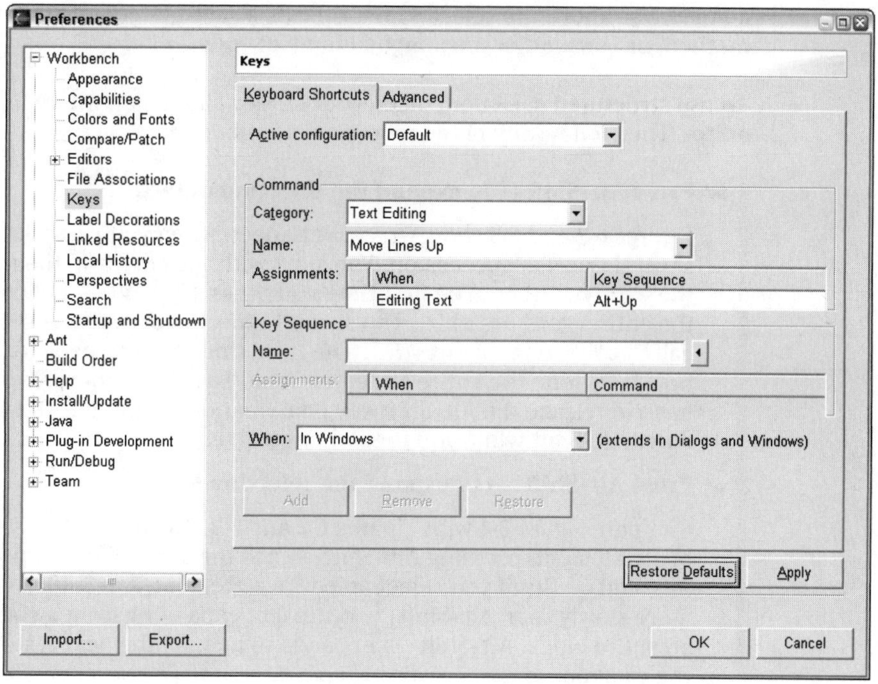

Figure 6-1:
Configuring
keyboard
shortcuts.

In some cases, you have to fish around among the categories to find a partic-
ular function. For example, the Edit category contains the Copy, Cut, and
Paste functions. The similarly named Text Editing category has functions like
Move Lines Up and To Lower Case. You can get all this information from the
Command group (refer to Figure 6-1).

After finding the function that you want, you can mess with the function's
keyboard shortcut. You can

✔ Change an existing shortcut

✔ Remove an existing shortcut

✔ Add a shortcut for a function that doesn't already have a shortcut

You do all this with the Key Sequence group, the When list box, and the
Add/Remove/Restore buttons (refer to Figure 6-1). (When I say "you do this,"
I really mean "you." Personally, I don't play with these things very much.)

Using Structured Selections

I don't remember most keyboard shortcuts, but the shortcuts that I do
remember are the ones for *structured selections*. Instead of selecting a word or

a line, these shortcuts select a method call, a Java statement, a block, a method, or some other meaningful chunk of code.

To use structured selection, place your cursor almost anywhere in the Java editor. Then follow any of the following instructions:

✔ **Press Alt+Shift+↑ to expand the selection outward.**

Figures 6-2 and 6-3 show what can happen when you press Alt+Shift+↑ several times in succession. You start with the cursor in the middle of the word println. The first time you press Alt+Shift+↑, Eclipse selects the entire word println. The second time, Eclipse selects the method call System.out.println(). The third time, Eclipse expands the selection to include the entire statement. And so on. (Of course, you don't have to release the Alt+Shift key combination each time. You can hold down Alt+Shift while you press ↑ several times.)

✔ **Press Alt+Shift+→ to expand the selection forward.**

Compare Figure 6-4 with Figures 6-2 and 6-3. If you select only part of a statement, pressing Alt+Shift+→ has the same effect as pressing Alt+Shift+↑. But if you select an entire statement, Alt+Shift+→ expands more slowly than Alt+Shift+↑. Instead of expanding from a statement to an entire block, Alt+Shift+→ expands to include the next statement in the program.

Successive pressing of Alt+Shift+→ expands the selection one statement or declaration at a time. Finally, when you reach the last statement in a block, pressing Alt+Shift+→ selects the entire block.

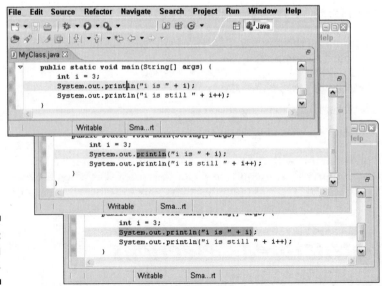

Figure 6-2:
Pressing
Alt+Shift+↑.

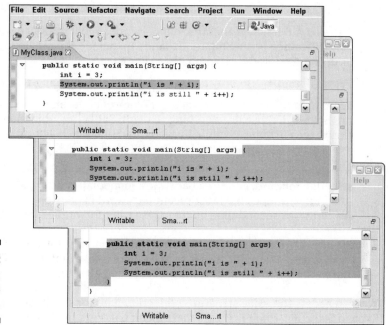

Figure 6-3:
Continuing
to press
Alt+Shift+↑.

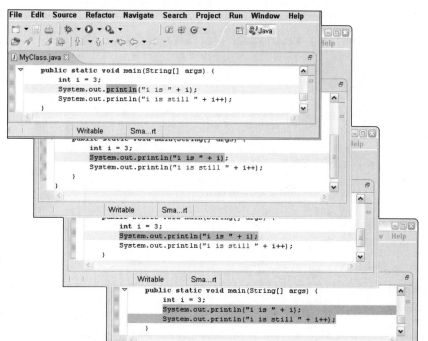

Figure 6-4:
Pressing
Alt+
Shift+→.

✔ **Press Alt+Shift+← to expand the selection backward.**

Pressing Alt+Shift+→ and Alt+Shift+← work almost the same way. The only difference is Alt+Shift+← expands to include the previous statement or declaration in the program. (See Figure 6-5.)

✔ **Press Alt+Shift+↓ to play a sequence of selection changes in reverse.**

If you drag the cursor to select a big block of code, and then press Alt+Shift+↓, Eclipse does nothing. The Alt+Shift+↓ combination doesn't shrink the current selection. Instead, Alt+Shift+↓ acts like an undo for the other Alt+Shift combinations.

For example, press Alt+Shift+→ and then Alt+Shift+← to expand the selection forward, and then backward. Immediately afterward, pressing Alt+Shift+↓ undoes the most recent backward expansion. Pressing Alt+Shift+↓ a second time undoes the earlier forward expansion.

If your code contains an error, structured selection may not work. For example, try removing the semicolon from the end of a Java statement. Then put your cursor inside that bad line of code. Pressing Alt+Shift+↑ has no effect.

You can access the same structured selection functions by choosing Edit⇨ Expand Selection To on Eclipse's main menu bar. Personally, I never use this feature. Instead of navigating a bunch of menu items, I just select text the old-fashioned way. I drag my mouse across a bunch of Java code.

Figure 6-5:
Pressing
Alt+
Shift+←.

As far as I know, Eclipse doesn't support the dragging and dropping of editor text. If I select a line, and then try to drag that line with my mouse, the line doesn't move. What a pity!

Folding Your Source Code

At some point, the Java editor becomes cluttered. You have to scroll up and down to see different parts of a file. You can do several things about this:

- ✔ (The most mundane . . .) Enlarge the Java editor by dragging its edges with your mouse.

- ✔ (The fastest . . .) Maximize the Java editor by double-clicking the editor's tab.

- ✔ (The most elaborate . . .) Jump to different parts of your source file by selecting Package Explorer branches. (For details, see the section on linking views and editors in Chapter 3.)

- ✔ (The most fun . . .) Fold parts of your code by clicking the arrows on the editor's marker bar.

You can fold method bodies, comments, and other Java elements. Figure 6-6 shows some getter and setter methods, with various parts folded and unfolded. In the figure, notice the little arrows on the editor's marker bar. A rightward-pointing arrow represents folded code, and a downward-pointing arrow represents unfolded code.

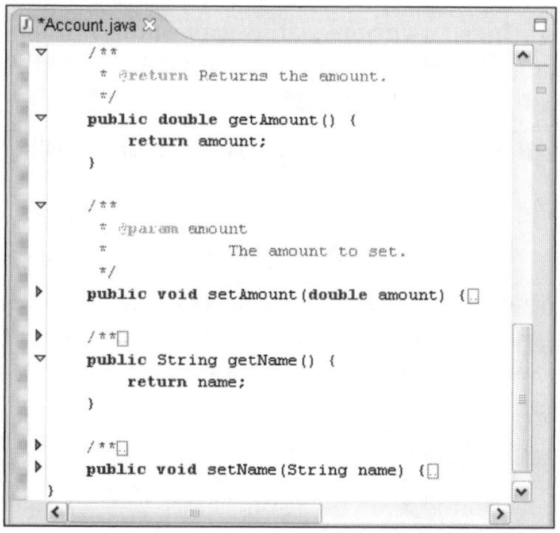

Figure 6-6:
Folded and
unfolded
code.

```
/**
 * @return Returns the amount.
 */
public double getAmount() {
    return amount;
}

/**
 * @param amount
 *                The amount to set.
 */
public void setAmount(double amount) {

/**
public String getName() {
    return name;
}

/**
public void setName(String name) {
}
```

Here's a neat trick. You can see folded code without bothering to unfold it. Hover your mouse over a rightward-pointing arrow. When you do, you see a tip containing the folded code. (If you're not convinced, see Figure 6-7.)

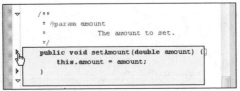

Figure 6-7:
A tip
displaying
folded code.

Letting Eclipse Do the Typing

This section is about *smart typing* — Eclipse's answer to the evils of bad punctuation. Smart typing saves you time, makes your code clearer, and keeps you from worrying about all those nasty braces and dots. It's like having a copy editor for your Java code.

Configuring the smart typing options

Before you try this chapter's smart typing tricks, I ask you to change a few of the smart typing configuration options.

1. **Select the Typing tab of the Java⇨Editor page in the Window⇨ Preferences dialog.**

   The wording in Step 1 uses my abbreviated way of describing a part of the Preferences dialog. For details, see the "Navigating the Preferences Dialog" section near the start of this chapter.

2. **Stare at the huge collection of options on this Typing tab's page.**

   Repeat after me. Say "Wow!"

3. **Add check marks next to my favorite options.**

   In case you don't know, my favorite options are Escape Text When Pasting into a String Literal, Smart Semicolon Positioning, and Smart Brace Positioning. (See Figure 6-8.) For some reason, these options are unchecked by default.

4. **Click Apply, and then click OK.**

   Goodbye, Preferences dialog! See you soon.

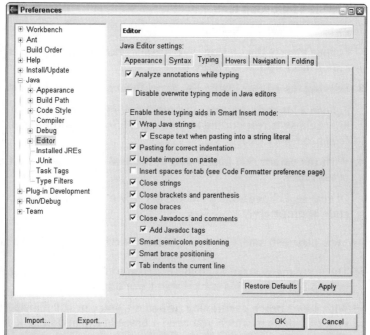

Figure 6-8:
The Smart
Typing
Preferences
page.

Using smart typing

Are you ready to experience the joy of smart typing? This section walks you through some of Eclipse's smart typing tricks.

Before you work your way through this section's experiments, follow the instructions in the "Configuring the smart typing options" section.

A few parenthetical remarks

Parentheses, brackets, and braces are very gregarious. They hate being alone. The tricks in this section ensure that things such as open parentheses never have to be alone — not even for a few seconds.

1. **Create a new Java class.**

    Some skeletal code appears in the editor.

    For help creating a Java class, see Chapter 2.

2. **Type the following text:**

```
static void myMethod(
```

Eclipse inserts the closing parenthesis. (Notice the Close Brackets and Parenthesis option in Figure 6-8.)

3. **Leaving the cursor inside the parentheses, type an open curly brace.**

Eclipse adds the curly brace where it belongs — at the end of the current line. Eclipse is responding to your Smart Brace Positioning preference (refer to Figure 6-8).

4. **With the cursor still positioned at the end of the method's header line, press Enter.**

Of course, Eclipse adds a close curly brace and indents your next line of code appropriately.

When you play with smart brace positioning, keep the following things in mind:

✔ There are many ways to confuse the smart brace positioning mechanism in Step 3. If at first this trick doesn't work, please try again.

✔ With smart brace positioning turned on, you can still manage those rare situations in which you need a brace in the middle of a line. Just type an open brace and then, immediately afterward, press Backspace. In response to the Backspace, Eclipse undoes smart positioning and returns the brace to the middle of the line.

✔ Some people prefer having the open curly brace on a brand new line of code. Eclipse's smart brace positioning always seems to put the brace at the end of the current line. But that's okay. With a few mouse clicks, you can reposition all the braces in your code. For details, see the section pertaining to automatic code formatting in Chapter 8.

Pulling strings apart

As an author and conference speaker, I'm always worried about line length. Does a line of code fit the page width? Does the line fit conveniently on a PowerPoint slide? This section's tips help you manage line length (at least, when a long string literal is involved).

1. **Type the following text:**

```
System.out.println("
```

Eclipse closes the quotation mark and the parenthesis. By now, you're probably not surprised.

2. **Type characters inside the quotation marks.**

I don't know about you, but for this experiment, I typed skdfjaldkfjl skjdfkjskf. It's my favorite thing to type.

3. **Position your cursor anywhere in the middle of the quoted string. Then press Enter.**

   This is so cool! Instead of giving you

   ```
   System.out.println("skdfjaldkfj
           lskjdfkjskf")
   ```

   which is illegal in Java, Eclipse gives you

   ```
   System.out.println("skdfjaldkfj" +
           "lskjdfkjskf")
   ```

   That's exactly what you want! This neat behavior comes from the default Wrap Java Strings preference (refer to Figure 6-8).

4. **Without moving your cursor, type a semicolon.**

   Eclipse puts the new semicolon at the end of the current line.

Getting Eclipse to Mark Occurrences

You want to see something cool? I'll show you something that's cool. An Eclipse editor can automatically *mark occurrences*. When you place your cursor on a variable name, the editor highlights all occurrences of that name in the file. (See Figure 6-9.)

Eclipse's mark occurrences mechanism is pretty smart. For instance, in Figure 6-9, I selected a constructor's jobTitle parameter. In the body of the constructor, Eclipse marks the jobTitle parameter without marking the class-wide jobTitle field.

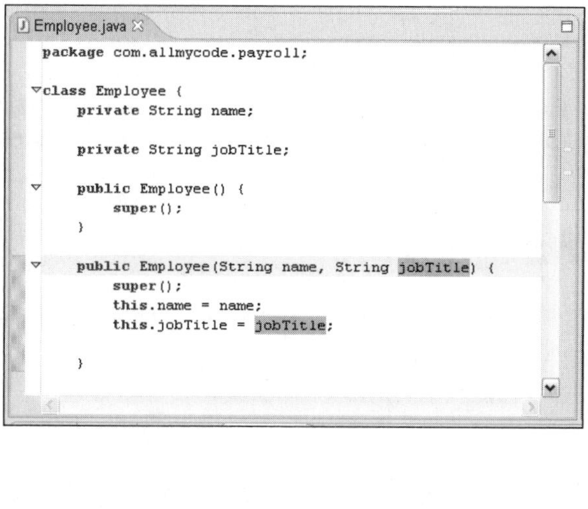

Figure 6-9: Eclipse marks occurrences of the jobTitle parameter.

```java
package com.allmycode.payroll;

class Employee {
    private String name;

    private String jobTitle;

    public Employee() {
        super();
    }

    public Employee(String name, String jobTitle) {
        super();
        this.name = name;
        this.jobTitle = jobTitle;
    }
}
```
Employee.java

By default, Eclipse highlights occurrences in yellow. But you can change the color by visiting the Workbench➪Editors➪Annotations page of the Window➪ Preferences dialog. (Just select the Occurrences item in that page's Annotation Presentation list.)

Marking and unmarking

Eclipse gives you a few ways to turn the mark occurrences mechanism on and off. For my money, none of these ways is very convenient. (But money has nothing to do with it. After all, Eclipse is free.)

- ✔ Press Alt+Shift+O to toggle between marking and not marking occurrences.

- ✔ Press the Mark Occurrences button on Eclipse's toolbar to toggle between marking and not marking occurrences. The button's icon is the picture of a yellow highlight marker. (See Figure 6-10.)

- ✔ When the Mark Occurrences feature is on, press Alt+Shift+U to temporarily remove the highlighting. The highlighting goes away until you click another name. (When you move to another name, Eclipse marks all occurrences of the new name.)

Figure 6-10:
The hard-to
find Mark
Occur-
rences
button.

You can pick the kinds of names whose occurrences you want marked. Visit the Java➪Editor➪Mark Occurrences page of the Window➪Preferences dialog.

Some marking magic

When it comes to marking occurrences, Eclipse has two really cute tricks up its virtual sleeve.

✔ Put your cursor on the return type in a method's header. Eclipse marks all exit points in the method's body. (See Figure 6-11.)

✔ Put your cursor on the name of a Java exception. Eclipse marks any method calls that throw the exception.* (See Figure 6-12.)

Figure 6-11: Eclipse marks a method's exit points.

```
String toString(int number) {
    switch (number) {
    case 0:
        return "zero";
    case 1:
        return "one";
    case 2:
        return "two";
    default:
        return "many";
    }
}
```

Figure 6-12: Eclipse marks statements that throw a particular exception.

```
try {
    while (resultSet.next()) {
        intAcct.fillFrom(resultSet);
        intAcct.addInterest();
        resultSet.updateDouble("Balance", intAcct.getBalance());
        resultSet.updateRow();
    }
} catch (SQLException e) {
    e.printStackTrace();
}
```

WARNING!

If your code doesn't compile because it contains errors, Eclipse's mark occurrences mechanism may not work.

---

* When Erich Gamma unveiled this trick at JavaOne 2004, the session's attendees applauded.

Chapter 7

Getting Eclipse to Write Your Code

In This Chapter

▶ Using code assist

▶ Using templates

▶ Creating your own templates

My wife and kids say that I never finish sentences. "Hey, Sam," I say. "What?" he asks. "I found something that'll really interest you. I found . . . " and then several seconds go by.

"You found what?" he says. "What did you find? Finish the @!&(% sentence!"

It's a simple process. In the middle of a sentence, my mind wanders and I become interested in something else. Suddenly, the external world fades to the background and my internal thoughts dance before my eyes. It's not my fault. It's an inherited trait. My mother used to do the same thing.

If I'm lucky, generations of *For Dummies* readers will analyze this aspect of my psyche. "What made Burd's works so unique was the fact that he wrote several books while suffering from disosyllabicmonohypotopia. In *Eclipse For Dummies,* Burd admits that he paused more often than he spoke."

Before you make fun of me, picture yourself sitting in front of a computer. You start typing a line of Java code, say `frame.setBackground(Color.` "What color names are available?" you ask yourself. "Can I use `Color.DARKGRAY` or do I need `Color.DARK_GRAY`? And is it `GRAY` or `GREY`? I never could spell that word. My third grade teacher . . . Hey, what was the name of that kid who used to bully me?" And so on. Your mind wanders.

If Eclipse could talk, it may say *"Color dot* what? Forget about third grade and finish typing the @!&(% statement!" But instead, Eclipse opens a hover tip containing all the static members of the `Color` class. How thoughtful of Eclipse to do such a thing!

Code Assist

Imagine staring at someone, and waiting for him to tell you what to say. I see my friend George. Then George looks back at me and says "Your choices are 'Hello, George,' or 'How are things, George?' or 'You owe me ten bucks, George.'" So I say, "You owe me ten bucks," and before I finish, he says "George."

That's what code assist is like. You may have used code assist with other programming languages and with other development environments. The idea is, you type some incomplete Java code, and then Eclipse tells you all the ways you can complete it.

Using code assist

What follows are some scenarios using code assist (also known as *content assist*). In each scenario, you start by positioning your cursor in the Java editor section of the Eclipse workbench. Then you type some incomplete code (maybe a few characters, maybe more). At that point, you want to use code assist. Here's how you do it:

1. **Press Ctrl+Space or go to Eclipse's menu bar and choose Edit➪Content Assist.**

   A list of possible code *completions* appears. (See Figure 7-1.)

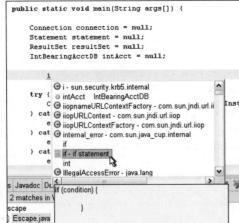

Figure 7-1: Eclipse presents a list of possible code completions.

2. **Double-click whichever completion suits you best.**

   Alternatively, use the arrow keys to select your favorite completion and then press Enter.

   Eclipse pastes the selected completion into your code, and positions your cursor at a likely place (that is, at a place where your next keystroke is likely to be).

If you're just browsing through the chapters of this book and aren't quite sure yet what all this talk of workbenches and Java editors is about, check out Chapter 3, where you can get sufficiently enlightened.

The next several paragraphs show you the kinds of things you can do with code assist. And remember:

"When in doubt, press Control+Space."

-Barry Burd, author of *Eclipse For Dummies*

Type names, statements, and other things

Between two statements inside a method body, type the letter **i**. Then press Ctrl+Space. Code assist offers to complete the line, with suggestions like `int`, the keyword `if`, an entire `if` statement, and a myriad of other choices. (Refer to Figure 7-1.)

Variable names

Declare a variable named `accountBalance`. Then between two statements inside a method, type the letter **a**, followed by Ctrl+Space. Among Eclipse's many suggestions, you find your `accountBalance` variable.

Methods declarations and calls

Declare two methods — `void myMethod(int i)` and `void myMess(String s, double d)`. Then, somewhere in the same class, type **myM** and press Ctrl+Space.

What you get depends on where you type **myM**. If you type **myM** where a method call belongs, then Eclipse offers to call `myMethod` or `myMess`. (See Figure 7-2.) But if you type **myM** outside of a method body, Eclipse doesn't offer you any choices. Instead, Eclipse declares a new `myM` method. See Figure 7-3.

By default, when code assist has only one possible suggestion, Eclipse doesn't offer you a choice. Instead Eclipse just inserts text based on that one suggestion. You can change this behavior by visiting the Java⇨Editor⇨Code Assist page of the Window⇨Preferences dialog. Near the top of the page, uncheck the Insert Single Proposals Automatically box.

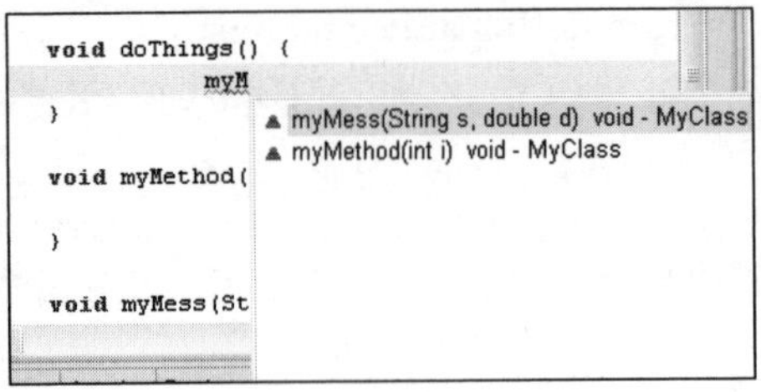

```
void doThings() {
        myM
}

void myMethod(

}

void myMess(St
```

▲ myMess(String s, double d) void - MyClass
▲ myMethod(int i) void - MyClass

Figure 7-2:
Eclipse
offers to call
a method.

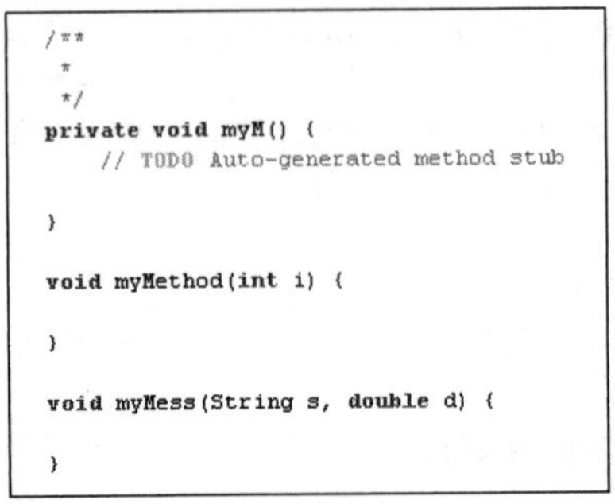

```
/**
 *
 */
private void myM() {
    // TODO Auto-generated method stub

}

void myMethod(int i) {

}

void myMess(String s, double d) {

}
```

Figure 7-3:
Eclipse
creates a
new
method.

Parameter lists

Declare two methods — myMethod(int i) and myMethod(boolean b). Then, in a place where a method call belongs, type **myMethod(**. That is, type **myMethod**, followed by an open parenthesis. Then press Ctrl+Space. Code assist offers two versions of myMethod — the int version and the boolean version.

Create constructors; override method declarations; implement interface methods

Place the cursor inside a class, but outside of any method. Without typing any visible characters, press Ctrl+Space. Code assist offers to either create a constructor, override an inherited method, or to implement an interface's method. For instance, if the class extends java.lang.Object, Eclipse offers to override clone, equals, finalize, and other Object methods. (See Figure 7-4.)

Notice the large hover tip on the left side of Figure 7-4 — the tip containing the equals method's Javadoc comment. Eclipse can show you the Javadoc comment of whatever method you highlight in the code assist list. Before you can see this hover tip for a method in the Java API, you have to tell Eclipse the location of the Java API source files. For details, see Chapter 5.

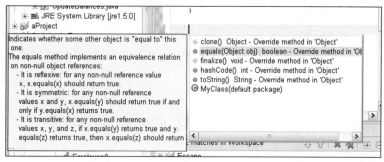

Figure 7-4:
Eclipse
offers to
override
methods or
to create a
`MyClass`
constructor.

Sometimes, when I type the letter **i**, code assist offers to insert an `if` statement even though my cursor isn't inside a method body. Of course, if I select that option, Eclipse duly creates an `if` statement and I get a syntax error. Oh, well! Nothing's perfect — not even code assist.

Generate getter and setter methods

Place the cursor inside a class, but outside of any method. Type the word **get**, followed by Ctrl+Space. Code assist offers to create a getter method for any of your class's fields. The method even includes an appropriate return statement.

In the getter method department, code assist is very smart. If a field already has a getter method, code assist doesn't suggest creating an additional getter.

Of course, everything I say about getters holds true of setters also. To create a setter method, type **set** and then press Ctrl+Space. The new setter method has its own `this.field = field` statement.

Using code assist in Javadoc comments

When you use Eclipse to write Java code, don't forget to edit the Javadoc comments (the things that start with `/**`). Eclipse automatically puts Javadoc comments in all your new classes. But these default Javadoc comments are just reminders. They contain almost no information about the code that you're writing.

You can add useful information when you edit the Javadoc comments. And as you edit Javadoc comments, Eclipse's code assist offers suggestions.

Place your cursor inside a Javadoc comment, and press Ctrl+Space. Eclipse suggests two kinds of tags — HTML tags and Javadoc tags.

- The HTML tags include things like `<b>`, `<i>`, `<code>`, and so on.
- The Javadoc tags include things like `@author`, `@deprecated`, and `@see`.

In some cases, Eclipse's suggestions include dozens of tags. In other cases, Eclipse suggests only a few tags. In a few cases, Eclipse offers no suggestions. Eclipse tries to suggest tags that are appropriate in context. So the tags that Eclipse suggests depend on where you place your cursor within the Javadoc comment.

Filtering code assist suggestions

I don't know about you, but I never use CORBA. I know what CORBA is because I hear about it occasionally at Java user group meetings. (It's a way of getting diverse applications on different kinds of computers to cooperate with one another. Isn't that nice?) Yes, I know what problem CORBA is supposed to solve. Other than that, I know nothing about CORBA.

So when I invoke code assist, I don't want to see any CORBA-related suggestions. Here's how I shield these suggestions from my view:

1. **Visit the Java⇨Type Filters page of the Window⇨Preferences dialog.**

2. **Click New.**

   The Type Filter dialog appears.

3. **In the dialog's one and only field, type *CORBA*.**

   This hides anything from any package whose name contains the uppercase letters *CORBA*. It hides things like `IDLType` from the package `org.omg.CORBA`.

4. **Click OK.**

5. **Back on the Type Filters page, make sure that the *CORBA* check box has a check mark in it.**

6. **Click OK to close the Preferences dialog.**

The previous steps take care of `org.omg.CORBA`, but what about packages like `com.sun.corba.whatever.whateverelse`? In Java, case-sensitivity is more than just a myth. You can repeat Steps 2 through 4 with the lowercase expression ***corba***, but you can also browse for package names. Here's how:

1. **Visit the Java⇨Type Filters page of the Window⇨Preferences dialog.**

2. **Click Add Packages.**

   The Package Selection dialog appears.

3. **Double-click the com.sun.corba entry.**

   After double-clicking, you're back to the Type Filters page. The page has a new com.sun.corba.* entry.

4. **Make sure that the com.sun.corba.* check box has a check mark in it.**

5. **Click OK.**

   After following these steps, nothing in any of the `com.sun.corba` pack-ages appear in your code assist lists.

   In addition to filtering code assist suggestions, the steps in this section filter Quick Fix suggestions. For information on Quick Fix, see Chapter 2.

Auto activation

Sometimes you don't want to beg Eclipse for code assistance. You want Eclipse to just "know" that you can use a little hint. And sure enough, Eclipse can pro-vide hints even when you don't press Ctrl+Space. This feature is called *auto activation*.

Position your mouse at a point where you can make a method call. Then type the word **System**, followed by a dot. After a brief pause (whose duration is customizable), Eclipse offers completions like `System.out`, `System. arraycopy`, `System.exit`, and so on. Eclipse doesn't wait for you to press Ctrl+Space.

The same thing happens with the @ sign in a Javadoc comment. Inside a Javadoc comment, type @. After a brief delay, Eclipse suggests `@author`, `@deprecated`, and so on.

You can customize the way auto activation works. Visit the Java⇨Editor⇨ Code Assist page of the Window⇨Preferences dialog.

✔ **Check or uncheck the Enable Auto Activation box.**

✔ **Change the Auto Activation Delay from 500 milliseconds (half a second) to some other duration.**

✔ **Change the triggers.**

   Notice the little dot in the Auto Activation Triggers for Java box.

   • If you insert a plus sign as in Figure 7-5, Eclipse auto activates code assist whenever you type a plus sign in the editor.

   • If you insert a blank space into the Auto Activation Triggers for Java box, Eclipse auto activates code assist whenever you type a blank space in the editor.

   For your own sanity, insert the blank space immediately before the dot in the Auto Activation Triggers for Java box. A blank space after a dot looks exactly like nothing after a dot. If you put the blank space after the dot, you may wonder later why Eclipse is being so aggres-sive with auto activation.

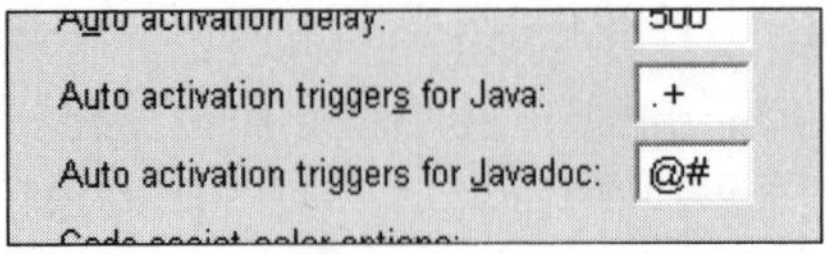

Figure 7-5:
Changing
the auto
activation
triggers.

Auto activation delay:	500
Auto activation triggers for Java:	.+
Auto activation triggers for Javadoc:	@#
Code assist color options:	

With a bit more fiddling, you can auto activate code assist for method call parameter lists. Here's how:

1. **Visit the Java⇨Editor⇨Code Assist page of the Window⇨Preferences dialog.**

2. **Add the open parenthesis character to the Auto Activation Triggers for Java box. (See Figure 7-6.)**

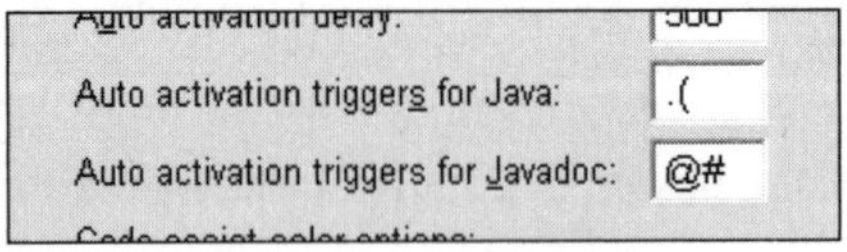

Figure 7-6:
Adding an
open
parenthesis
to the auto
activation
triggers.

Auto activation delay:	500
Auto activation triggers for Java:	.(
Auto activation triggers for Javadoc:	@#
Code assist color options:	

At this point, you may think you're done. But you're not. If you don't tweak another setting, the auto activation feature for open parenthesis doesn't work.

3. **Switch to the Typing tab of the Java⇨Editor page. In the collection of options, uncheck the Close Brackets and Parenthesis box.**

Auto activation for open parenthesis works only if Eclipse doesn't close the parenthesis for you.

Templates

I remember my first paint-by-numbers experience. How relaxing it was! I painted a cat playing with a ball of yarn. Don't tell me that I just filled in someone else's color pattern. I felt as if I'd created a work of art!

Ah, those were the good old days. Do they even make those paint-by-numbers sets anymore? I suppose I can check my local crafts store, but that's too much physical effort. Instead, I can stay at home and paint online. I visit www. segmation.com and start filling in the colors with my mouse. The Web site uses a Java applet to create point-and-click pictures. And with Java running on my computer, I can convince myself that I'm working!

So what gives? Why this sudden interest in paint by numbers? The answer is simple. I'm writing about Eclipse templates, and templates remind me of painting by numbers. With a template, you create code by filling in the blanks. Some blanks match up with other blanks (like two colored regions containing the same number).

At first, you think you're cheating. Eclipse writes most of the code for you, and then you add a few names of your own. But you're not cheating. Templates add consistency and uniformity to your code. Besides, templates relieve the programming drudgery. They help you focus your attention on things that really matter — the design and logic of your application.

Eclipse comes with about 40 of its own ready-made templates. You can change any of these ready-made templates, or add new templates to suit your needs. The next section tells you how to use templates (the templates that Eclipse provides and any templates that you create on your own).

Using templates

To activate a template, type the first few letters of the template's name, and then press Ctrl+Space. (The Ctrl+Space key combination does double-duty. This combination invokes both code assist and templates.) Here are some examples.

Adding a main method

Put your cursor at a place in your code where you can declare a new method. Type the letters **ma**, and then press Ctrl+Space.

Among other things, Eclipse offers to apply a main method template. This template adds a skeletal main method to your code. (See Figures 7-7 and 7-8.)

Figure 7-7:
Eclipse
suggests
adding a
main
method.

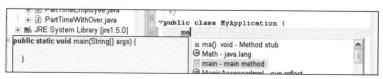

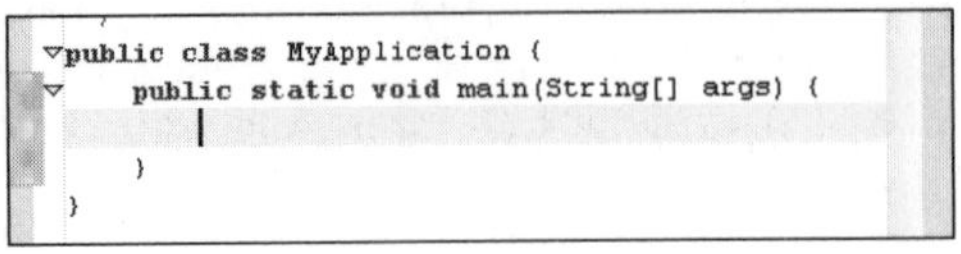

Figure 7-8:
Eclipse
creates
a main
method
from a
template.

```
▽public class MyApplication {
   ▽   public static void main(String[] args) {
            |
        }
   }
}
```

Writing to System.out

Put your cursor at a place in your code where you can call a method. Type the letters **Sys** or **sys**, and then press Ctrl+Space.

Among Eclipse's suggestions, you find `sysout - print to standard out`. If you select this suggestion, Eclipse adds a `System.out.println` call to your code.

Automatic insertions

Put the cursor at a place in your code where you can call a method. Type the letters **sysout**, and then press Ctrl+Space.

Eclipse doesn't bother to ask you what you want. There's only one template named `sysout`, so Eclipse immediately adds a call to `System.out.println` to your code.

You can suppress this automatic insertion behavior, but you have to suppress it for both templates and code assist. (You can't suppress one without suppressing the other.) Visit the Java⇨Editor⇨Code Assist page of the Window⇨Preferences dialog. Near the top of the page, uncheck the Insert Single Proposals Automatically box.

Narrowing choices as you type

Put the cursor at a place in your code where you can call a method. Type the letters **sy**, and then press Ctrl+Space.

Eclipse's suggestions include things like `symbol`, `synchronized`, and (way down on the list) `sysout`.

Instead of selecting a suggestion, type the letter **s**, and watch the list's choices suddenly narrow. The list includes words starting with `sys` — words like `System`, `syserr`, `sysout`, and so on.

Don't select a suggestion yet. Instead, type the letter **o**. Now the only suggestion is sysout — the System.out.println() template. When you press Enter, Eclipse adds System.out.println() to your code.

The narrowing-as-you-type trick works with both templates and code assist.

Using template edit mode

Put the cursor at a place in your code where you can create a for statement. Type the letters **for**, and press Ctrl+Space.

Eclipse offers several choices, with at least three choices to create for loops. In this example, choose for - iterate over collection. Eclipse pastes an elaborate bunch of text, rectangles, and boxes into your code. Congratulations! You're in *template edit mode*. (See Figure 7-9.)

Figure 7-9:
Template
edit mode.

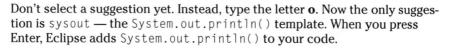

```
for (Iterator iter = collection.iterator(); iter.hasNext();) {
    type element = (type) iter.next();

}
```

In Figure 7-9, the rectangles and boxes are placeholders. Squint for a long time at Figure 7-9, and you can see that the cursor is planted firmly inside the first iter box. The word iter is a placeholder for any variable name that you type. While you type a variable name, Eclipse substitutes that name for every boxed occurrence of the word iter. That's so cool! You type the variable name once, and Eclipse populates the rest of the loop with copies of that name. It's like paint-by-numbers (except in this case, it's create-identifiers-by-placeholders).

You can click anywhere among the boxes and start editing. Eclipse copies anything you type into boxes of the same name. You can type characters, backspace, left-arrow, right-arrow, all that stuff.

You can also move among the boxes by pressing Tab and Shift+Tab. Pressing Tab moves you to the next box; pressing Shift+Tab moves you to the previous box.

You can keep tabbing and typing, tabbing and typing. Finally, you reach the element box in Figure 7-9. After filling in the element box, you press Tab one more time. In response to your Tab, the cursor jumps to the vertical line that's immediately beneath the type box. This vertical line marks the place where you add statements to the body of the for loop.

At this point, any character that you type forces Eclipse out of template edit mode. The boxes disappear. All the names in boxes turn into plain old text. (Well, as much as anything in Eclipse's editor is plain old text, these names become plain old text.)

You can bail out of template edit mode before filling in all the boxes. Just press Enter or Esc. Pressing Enter jumps your cursor to the little vertical line (the place in the text where you would normally stop being in template edit mode). Pressing Esc leaves your cursor where it is, and gets rid of all the funny-looking placeholder boxes. Alternatively, you can click your way out of template edit mode. Click anywhere outside of a rectangle or box and template edit mode is gone.

Creating your own template

If you don't like the templates that come with Eclipse, no problem. You can change any of the pre-written templates, or create templates of your own. For example, I occasionally write code that looks like this:

```
int i = 0;
while (i < 100) {
    //Do something with i
    i++;
}
```

I want a template for a `while` loop with a manual counter. When I type the word **while** and press Ctrl+Space, I want to see a `while loop with counter` choice, as in Figure 7-10.

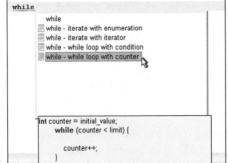

Figure 7-10:
Invoking a
user-made
template.

Then, if I select the `while loop with counter` template, I want the text and placeholders shown in Figure 7-11.

Figure 7-11:
A new
while-
loop
template.

```
int counter = initial_value;
while (counter < limit) {
    |
        counter++;
}
```

According to Eclipse's official terminology, the template in Figure 7-11 has java context. In fact, each template has one of two possible contexts — the *javadoc* or *java* context. When you're editing a source file, and you press Ctrl+Space, Eclipse examines each template's context. If you're editing a Javadoc comment, Eclipse offers to apply templates that have javadoc context. When you select one of these templates, Eclipse applies the template to your source code.

Look again at the while loop template in Figure 7-11. A while loop doesn't belong inside a Javadoc comment. So if you're editing a Javadoc comment, and you press Ctrl+Space, Eclipse doesn't offer to apply this while loop template. Eclipse knows not to suggest any while loop templates because none of the while loop templates have javadoc context. (All the while loop templates have java context.)

With all that stuff about context in mind, you're ready to create a new template. Here's what you do:

1. **Visit the Java⇨Editor⇨Templates page of the Window⇨Preferences dialog.**

2. **On the right side of the page, click New.**

   The New Template Wizard appears. (See Figure 7-12.)

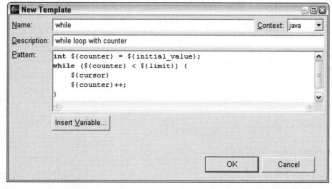

Figure 7-12:
The New
Template
Wizard.

3. **Create a name for your template.**

In Figure 7-12, I typed the name **while**. Eclipse already has other templates named `while`, but that's okay.

Eclipse uses template names to decide which templates to include in a hover tip. For example, in Figure 7-10 I typed the word **while** and then pressed Ctrl+Space. In response, Eclipse offers five suggestions. The last four suggestions represent four different templates — each with the same name *while*. (The first suggestion is part of Eclipse's plain old code assist mechanism.)

4. **Set the context for your template.**

If you do nothing in this step, the context is javadoc.

In this example, you create a `while` loop template. Because a `while` loop doesn't normally belong inside a Javadoc comment, you change the context from javadoc to java. (Refer to Figure 7-12.)

5. **Create a description for your template.**

In Figure 7-12, I typed the description **while loop with counter**. The description is important. The description shows in the hover tip. The description also distinguishes this template from any other templates with the same name. (Refer to Figure 7-10. Each of the templates named `while` has its own unique description.)

6. **Type a pattern for your template.**

In this example, type the stuff in the Pattern field of Figure 7-12. The pattern is a mini-program, telling Eclipse what to do when someone selects the template. The pattern can include *template variables* to mark important parts of the text. Each template variable is a dollar sign, followed by a word in curly braces.

When someone uses your template, many of the template variables become placeholders for plain old Java names or variables. For instance, Figure 7-12 has a template variable named `${counter}`. In Figure 7-11, when someone uses this template, the word `counter` becomes a placeholder for what eventually becomes a Java variable name.

Don't let the curly braces seduce you into using blank spaces. A template variable's name must not contain blank spaces.

7. **Click OK.**

Eclipse returns to the Preferences dialog.

8. **In the Preferences dialog, click OK.**

9. **Test your new template.**

In the Java editor, type all or part of the word **while**, and then press Ctrl+Space. Make sure that you get the behavior that's pictured in Figures 7-10 and 7-11.

Creating new template variables

The rules governing the names of template variables aren't complicated. Here's a summary:

✔ **You can make up any name on the spot, as long as the name doesn't conflict with an existing name.**

For instance, Eclipse has a pre-defined ${year} template variable. If you use the name year, Eclipse inserts 2004 (or 2005, or whatever).

✔ **You can make up a name, and use that name more than once in the same template pattern. Eclipse keeps identically named placeholders in sync during template edit mode.**

For instance, in Figure 7-11, if you type something in any of the counter boxes, then Eclipse copies what you type to the other two counter boxes.

✔ **If you make up a name, you don't have to use that name more than once in the same template pattern.**

In Figure 7-12, I make up the name ${limit}, and I use the name only once. That's just fine. In template edit mode, I can tab to the limit placeholder. (Refer to Figure 7-11.) When I type in the limit box, Eclipse doesn't copy my typing to any other boxes.

✔ **You can mix and match variables in a template pattern.**

For instance, in a particular template pattern you can use ${myFirstVar} once, use ${mySecondVar} twice, and use ${myThirdVar} ten times. When you're in template edit mode, Eclipse keeps the two mySecondVar placeholders in sync with each other, and keeps all ten myThirdVar placeholders in sync with one another.

Some special template variables

Eclipse has a bunch of predefined template variables. To see a list of these variables, type a dollar sign in the Pattern field of the New Template Wizard. (See Figure 7-13.) If, for some reason, you don't like typing dollar signs, you can get the same list by clicking the wizard's Insert Variable button.

Figure 7-13:
Get help
selecting a
predefined
template
variable.

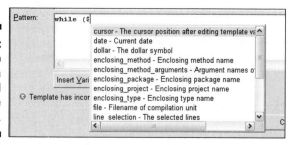

Many of Eclipse's pre-defined template variables have self-explanatory names. For instance, Eclipse substitutes the name of a package in place of the ${enclosing_package} template variable. In place of the ${date} template variable, Eclipse writes something like Aug 22, 2004.

Some other pre-defined template variables are a little more interesting. Here's a brief list:

✔ **The ${cursor} template variable marks the spot where template edit mode ends.**

For example, the do template's pattern looks like this:

```
do {
    ${line_selection}${cursor}
} while (${condition});
```

When you type **do** and then press Ctrl+Space, you see the stuff in Figure 7-14. The vertical line (above the i in while) marks the place where the ${cursor} template variable lives.

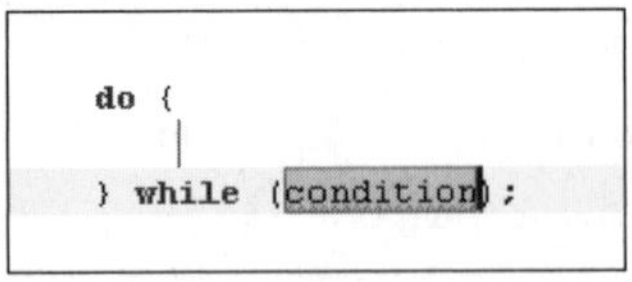

Figure 7-14:
The do
template in
action.

```
do {
   |
} while (condition);
```

At first, Eclipse positions the cursor in the condition box. You type a condition and then press Tab. With the pressing of Tab, Eclipse moves the cursor to the little vertical line and gets ready for you to type a statement or two. As soon as you start typing statements, Eclipse stops being in template edit mode.

A template's pattern can contain only one occurrence of the ${cursor} template variable.

✔ **The ${line_selection} template variable marks text that you can surround.**

Look again at the previous example's do template. If you select a bunch of statements and then press Ctrl+Space, Eclipse offers to apply the do template. (See Figure 7-15.) Eclipse makes this offer because of the ${line_selection} template variable in the do template's pattern.

If you select the do template in Figure 7-15, you get the result shown in Figure 7-16. Eclipse substitutes whatever statements you selected for the template's ${line_selection} variable.

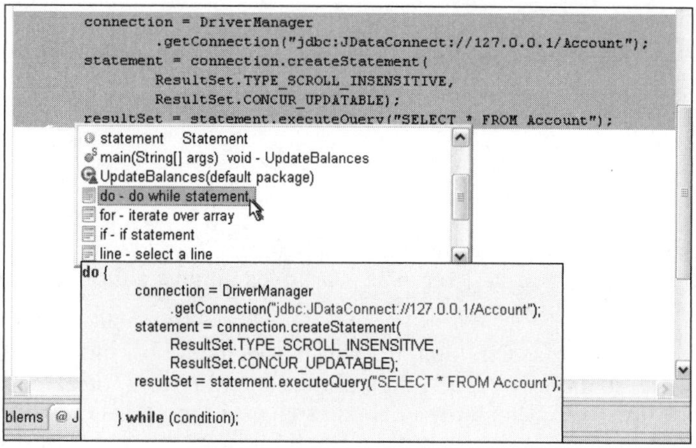
connection = DriverManager
.getConnection("jdbc:JDataConnect://127.0.0.1/Account");
statement = connection.createStatement(
ResultSet.TYPE_SCROLL_INSENSITIVE,
ResultSet.CONCUR_UPDATABLE);
resultSet = statement.executeQuery("SELECT * FROM Account");
statement Statement
main(String[] args) void - UpdateBalances
UpdateBalances(default package)
do - do while statement
for - iterate over array
if - if statement
line - select a line
do {
connection = DriverManager
.getConnection("jdbc:JDataConnect://127.0.0.1/Account");
statement = connection.createStatement(
ResultSet.TYPE_SCROLL_INSENSITIVE,
ResultSet.CONCUR_UPDATABLE);
resultSet = statement.executeQuery("SELECT * FROM Account");
} while (condition);
blems

Figure 7-15: Surrounding statements.

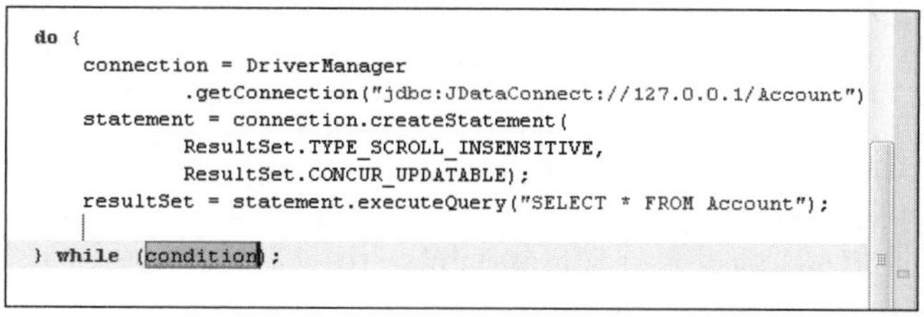
do {
connection = DriverManager
.getConnection("jdbc:JDataConnect://127.0.0.1/Account")
statement = connection.createStatement(
ResultSet.TYPE_SCROLL_INSENSITIVE,
ResultSet.CONCUR_UPDATABLE);
resultSet = statement.executeQuery("SELECT * FROM Account");
} while (condition);

Figure 7-16: Your code, after application of the do template.

- **The `${word_selection}` template variable marks text that you can surround.**

  Take, for instance, the `<b>` template:

  ```
  <b>${word_selection}${}</b>${cursor}
  ```

  If you select a part of a line and then press Ctrl+Space, Eclipse offers to apply the `<b>` template. (See Figure 7-17.) Eclipse makes this offer because of the `${word_selection}` template variable in the `<b>` template's pattern. The `<b>` template surrounds part of a line with a pair of HTML bold tags. (See Figure 7-18.)

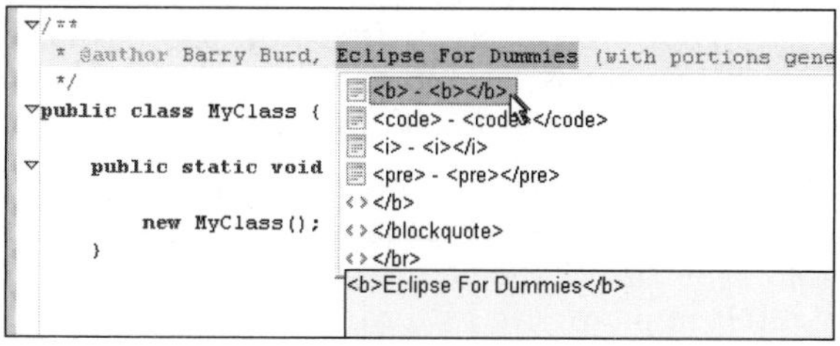
/**
* @author Barry Burd, Eclipse For Dummies (with portions gene
*/
public class MyClass {
public static void
new MyClass();
}
<b> - <b></b>
<code> - <code></code>
<i> - <i></i>
<pre> - <pre></pre>
</b>
</blockquote>
</br>
<b>Eclipse For Dummies</b>

Figure 7-17: Eclipse offers to apply the <b> template.

Figure 7-18:
Application
of the <b>
template.

But wait! Haven't you seen all this before? The ${word_selection} and ${line_selection} template variables behave almost the same way. What's the difference?

When you press Ctrl+Space, Eclipse asks itself how much text is selected. If the selected text includes an entire line (or extends from one line to another), then Eclipse suggests templates containing the ${line_selection} variable. But if the selected text is only part of a line, Eclipse suggests templates containing the ${word_selection} variable.

The ${line_selection} and ${word_selection} template variables are good for afterthoughts — things you think of adding after you've already written a piece of code. I generally know when I'm about to create a loop, so I seldom select statements and apply the do template. But I often realize after the fact that I need to enclose statements in a try block. In such situations, I apply the try template with its ${line_selection} variable.

✔ **The empty ${} template variable stands for a placeholder that initially contains no text.**

Compare the pattern for the <b> template with the result in Figure 7-18. The figure has two vertical lines:

> • **One line marks the place where the cursor lands immediately after you select the template.**
>
> That's where the <b> template's empty variable lives.
>
> • **The other line marks the place where Eclipse ends template edit mode.**
>
> That's where the <b> template's ${cursor} variable lives.

When you use the <b> template, the empty variable positions the cursor immediately after your text selection. That way, you can easily add to whatever text is between the <b> and </b> tags. Then, when you press Tab, the ${cursor} template variable takes you past the </b> tag.

What happens if a template contains more than one empty template variable? Then any text that you type in one of the empty placeholders copies automatically into all the other empty placeholders. For example, after applying the template with pattern 1.${} 2.${} 3.${}, you see the text 1. 2. 3.. Then, if you type the letters **abc**, Eclipse turns it into 1.abc 2.abc 3.abc.

Chapter 8

Straight from the Source's Mouse

*I*f you watch enough science fiction, you see people controlling things by grabbing holographic images. People design space ships by moving parts of wire-frames in three-dimensional, virtual-reality rooms. Other people control the space ships by moving transparent images on a glossy panel. It reminds me of the kinds of things you do with Eclipse's Source menu. Instead of touching your own code, you move imaginary code fragments by choosing Source menu actions. It's very high tech (and it makes Java coding a lot easier).

Eclipse's Source menu contains about 20 different actions. Each action is useful in one situation or another. This chapter covers about half of the Source menu's actions. (Chapter 9 covers most of the remaining Source menu actions.)

Coping with Comments

I'm a self-proclaimed pack rat. I never throw anything out until I'm absolutely sure that I'll never need it again. (At home, it's a wonder that I ever take trash to the curb for pickup.) So when I find some troubling code, I don't delete it right away. Instead, I comment out the code.

This section shows you how to comment and uncomment code easily.

Slash that line

If you've ever tried to comment out code using a plain old text editor, you know how cumbersome the job can be. If you use two slashes to create a // style comment, then the slashes apply to only one line of code. To create several // style comments, you have to type // on each line. How tedious!

As an alternative to Java's // style comment, you can create block comments (comments that begin with /* and end with */). But once again, you can be in for a long, difficult ride. Block comments don't nest inside one another very easily. So when block comments shrink and grow, you have to micromanage the placement of /* characters and */ characters. It's really annoying.

Thank goodness! You no longer use a plain old text editor. Instead, you use Eclipse. To turn an existing line of code into a // style comment, place your cursor anywhere on the line and choose Source⇨Toggle Comment. Do the same to remove the // characters from the start of a line of code.

To change several lines of code at once, select a bunch of lines and then choose Source⇨Toggle Comment.

No matter where you place your cursor, choosing Toggle Comment changes an entire line of code. If you start with

```
// for (int i = 0; i < myArray.length; i++) {
```

and then apply Toggle Comment, you end up with

```
for (int i = 0; i < myArray.length; i++) {
```

But if you start with

```
for (int i = 0; i < myArray.length; i++) { //main loop
```

and then apply Toggle Comment, you end up with

```
// for (int i = 0; i < myArray.length; i++) { //main loop
```

Block those lines

To surround any text with /* and */ characters, select the text and then choose Source⇨Add Block Comment. This trick operates on characters, not on lines or statements — which can lead to problems. For example, if you select just the characters ut.prin in the line

```
System.out.println();
```

and then choose Source⇨Add Block Comment, you get

```
System.o/*ut.prin*/tln();
```

Of course, such a nasty commenting job is easy to fix. Just select all the System.o/*ut.prin*/tln(); text, and choose Source⇨Add Block Comment once again. (Eclipse removes the original /* and */ characters before creating a properly placed block comment.)

To get rid of an existing block comment, position your cursor anywhere inside the comment, and then choose Source⇨Remove Block Comment.

Formatting Code

Nothing is more difficult to read than poorly formatted code. (No, not even Thomas Pynchon's *Gravity's Rainbow* is that difficult to read.) Compared with poorly formatted code, well-formatted code feels like light, bedtime reading. When formatting is consistent, your eyes know immediately where to look. You can see program blocks at a glance. You take in the logical landscape with one grand pass.

Consistent code formatting is an ideal that some programmers never achieve. When I write code by hand, my rules tend to drift. One hour I'm using blank spaces; the next hour I'm not. I try to remember, but I have other things on my mind. (With any luck, program logic is one of the important things on my mind.)

So here's how I use Eclipse. I write code in a reasonably consistent style without being obsessive about it. I try to keep things organized so that I know where I am in the general flow, but I don't worry too much about spacing and other things. Then, once in a while, I use Eclipse's formatting feature. I choose Source⇨Format on Eclipse's menu bar. Eclipse rearranges the active editor's code according to my preferred style rules.

And what, you ask, are my preferred style rules? Are they the same as your preferred style rules? Well, it doesn't matter. If you don't like mine, you can use your own. And if you don't have rules of your own, you can use Java's official recommended rules.

Eclipse's Format menu actions

Listing 8-1 shows you what I have before Eclipse formats my code.

Listing 8-1: **Ugly Code**

```
package com.
allmycode.io;
                  /**
* @author bburd

*/public      class EndOfFileChecker
{public static boolean
          isEndOfFile (String fileName){FileState
          fileState=DummiesIO.open( fileName) ;
          while(fileState.tokenBuffer==null){DummiesIO
          . fillTokenBuffer(fileState); } return
          fileState.isAtEOF ;}}
```

Listing 8-1 is awful. With Listing 8-1, I can't see the code's structure at a glance. I can't easily see that the class contains a method, and that the method contains a single `while` statement.

That's enough for Listing 8-1! Listing 8-2 shows what I have after Eclipse formats my code.

Listing 8-2: **Lovely Code**

```
package com.allmycode.io;

/**
 * @author bburd
 *
 */
public class EndOfFileChecker {
    public static boolean isEndOfFile(String fileName) {
        FileState fileState = DummiesIO.open(fileName);
        while (fileState.tokenBuffer == null) {
            DummiesIO.fillTokenBuffer(fileState);
        }
        return fileState.isAtEOF;
    }
}
```

The formatted version in Listing 8-2 is much better. I can see all the code's structure in Listing 8-2. There's no doubt about it. Well-formatted code is less expensive. People spend less time and money maintaining easy-to-read code.

Eclipse offers two ways to format your Java source code: Format and Format Element.

The Format action

When you choose Source⇨Format, Eclipse formats an entire file or a whole bunch of files at once. It depends upon the focus.

And where is your focus? Is the focus squarely on the editor? If so, then choosing Source⇨Format affects code in whatever file you're currently editing.

And what about the old Package Explorer? Is the focus on a branch of the Package Explorer? If so, then Source⇨Format affects all Java files in that branch. (For example, if you select a package's branch, then Source⇨Format affects all files in the package.)

In fact, by using the Package Explorer you can quickly format a whole bunch of files. The files don't even have to live in the same project. Just do whatever you normally do to select more than one branch of the tree. In Windows and in many flavors of Linux, use Ctrl+click to add a branch to your selection. Use Shift+click to extend your selection from one branch to another (including all branches in between). After selecting a bunch of branches, choose Source⇨Format.

Whenever I ask Eclipse to format my code I always finish up by choosing File⇨Save. Sometimes the Save action is grayed out, but I don't care. I try clicking the Save option anyway. When it comes to saving or not saving my source code, I'd rather err on the side of "SAVE-tee." (Groan!) I remember so many times when I thought I had no need to save the code. I thought Eclipse's Format action didn't change my code at all. But I was wrong. The Format action deleted blank spaces at the end of a line, or made some other changes that were difficult to see. So the code on my hard drive wasn't up to date, and Eclipse interrupted with all kinds of Save Resources dialogs. So take my advice, and always Save after you Format.

The Format Element action

When you choose Source⇨Format Element, Eclipse formats whatever piece of code contains your cursor.

For instance, if I put my cursor somewhere inside the `while` loop in Listing 8-1, I get partially formatted code. (See Listing 8-3.)

Listing 8-3: Half Ugly (or Half Lovely) Code

```
package com.
allmycode.io;
                /**
 * @author bburd

*/public       class EndOfFileChecker
  {
    public static boolean isEndOfFile(String fileName) {
        FileState fileState = DummiesIO.open(fileName);
        while (fileState.tokenBuffer == null) {
            DummiesIO.fillTokenBuffer(fileState);
        }
        return fileState.isAtEOF;
    }}
```

Eclipse formats the enclosing element (the isEndOfFile method) but not the entire Java source file.

The Format Element action is handy when most of the code is exactly the way I want it. For instance, I have a program that works fine, but that needs a few additional statements. I add the statements, and then call Source⇨ Format Element on those statements. I don't want Eclipse to mess with the entire source file, so I choose Format Element instead of plain old Format.

If you try to get Eclipse to format code that contains syntax errors, the formatting probably won't work.

Java elements

To get the formatting shown in Listing 8-3, I place my cursor inside the while statement. So why doesn't Eclipse format only this while statement? Why does Eclipse format the entire isEndOfFile method?

The answer is, Eclipse has a list of things that it calls *Java elements*, and statements aren't in that list. Instead, the list includes things like classes, import declarations, fields, and methods. When I place the cursor inside the while

loop and choose Source⇨Format Element, Eclipse looks for the smallest enclosing element. In Listing 8-1, that element happens to be the isEndOfFile method.

To find out more about what Eclipse calls (and doesn't call) a Java element, read the Eclipse API Javadoc's IJavaElement page. You can find the Eclipse API Javadocs at www.jdocs. com/eclipse/3.0/api/index.html.

Eclipse's Format actions change the look of your code, but they don't check the code's content for subtle stylistic errors. They don't look for unnecessary if statements, duplicate string literals, empty catch blocks, and other such things. To apply such rigorous style tests, use a third-party plug-in. The plug-in that I recommend is called PMD. For more information (which doesn't include the origin of the three-letter PMD name) see Chapter 17.

Configuring Eclipse's formatting options

For many years I put open curly braces on separate lines of code. I wrote code like this:

```
if (amount < 100.00)
{
```

Then one day I read the official *Code Conventions for the Java Programming Language* document. (I found the document by visiting java.sun.com/docs/codeconv.) This document told me not to put open curly braces on separate lines. According to the document, I should write code like this:

```
if (amount < 100.00) {
```

Okay. Now I know. But what if my style preferences differ slightly from the official rules? (Worse yet, what if my boss's style preferences differ slightly from the official rules?) What's an Eclipse user to do?

The answer is simple. You can customize the way Eclipse formats your code. Just follow these steps:

1. **Visit the Java⊏ゝCode Style⊏ゝCode Formatter page of the Window⊏ゝ Preferences dialog.**

   A page like the one in Figure 8-1 appears on your screen.

   For details about visiting the Preferences dialog, see Chapter 6.

2. **Click New.**

   The New Code Formatter Profile Wizard appears. (See Figure 8-2.)

   With Eclipse, you don't change the formatting settings willy-nilly. Instead, you combine settings to create a *profile*. Because each profile has a name, you can easily switch back and forth among profiles.

   By default, Eclipse uses the Java Conventions formatting profile. (The profile is based on the *Code Conventions for the Java Programming Language* document. I mention the document at the beginning of this section.) In this example, your new profile maintains most of the Java Conventions rules. Like the old Java Conventions profile, your new profile indents lines by exactly four spaces, puts one blank line between method declarations, and so on.

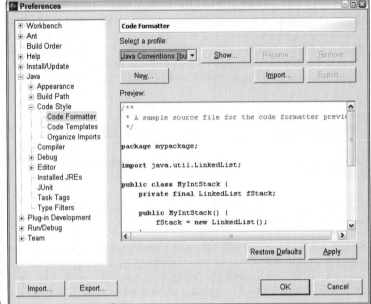

Figure 8-1:
The Code
Formatter
page of
Eclipse's
Preferences
dialog.

But your new profile makes some adjustments for open curly braces. Unlike the old Java Conventions profile, your new profile puts certain curly braces on lines of their own.

Back to the New Code Formatter Profile Wizard . . .

3. In the Profile Name field, type a name.

In Figure 8-2, I typed **My New Formatting Profile**. The Initialize Settings with the Following Profile field tells Eclipse that my new profile is to be almost like the existing Java Conventions profile.

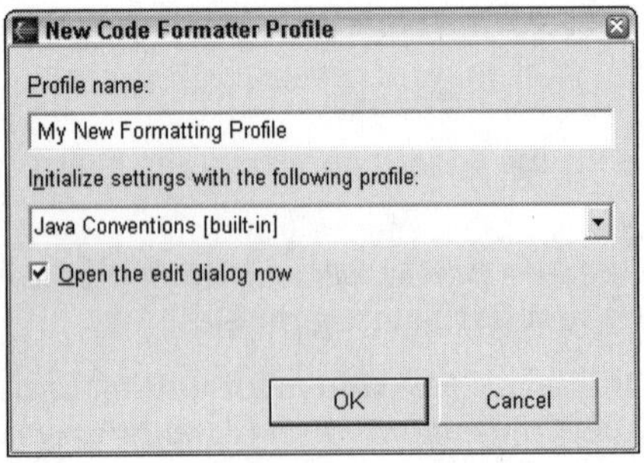

Figure 8-2:
The New
Code
Formatter
Profile
Wizard.

4. Click OK.

. . . at which point Eclipse opens an enormous and glorious Edit Profile dialog.

5. Select a tab in the Edit Profile dialog.

In this example, I selected the Braces tab. (See Figure 8-3.)

6. Make changes on the left. See the effects of your changes in the Preview pane on the right.

In the Constructor Declaration box in Figure 8-3, I selected the Next Line option. The instant I make this selection, the curly brace after `Example()` jumps down to the beginning of the next line in the Preview pane.

The same kind of thing happens with my `'switch' statement` selection. I selected Next Line Indented. Immediately, in the Preview pane, the curly brace after `switch (p)` jumps downward and four spaces to the right. (Of course, you can control the number of indentation spaces. That's part of the Edit Profile dialog's Indentation tab.)

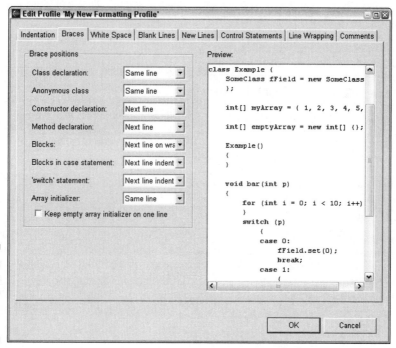

Figure 8-3:
The Braces
tab of the
Edit Profile
dialog.

7. **In the Edit Profile dialog, click OK.**

8. **In Eclipse's all-encompassing Preferences dialog, click OK.**

Back in the workbench, you can choose Source⇨Format. Eclipse pretties up your program according to your new code formatter profile.

For more information about Eclipse's placement of curly braces, see the section on smart typing in Chapter 6.

I give up. What effect does that formatting option have?

In the Edit Profile dialog, some selections have no effect on the Preview pane's puny code example. For instance, in the Blocks box of Figure 8-3 I selected the Next Line on Wrap option. (In the figure, it looks like Next Line on Wra, or something like that.) Anyway, when I change from Same Line to Next Line on Wrap, I see no difference in the Preview pane's code. I figure this selection has something to do with line wrapping, but I don't know the details. I find nothing about this option in Eclipse's documentation, and a Web search for the phrase Next Line on Wrap comes up completely empty.

So to figure out what Next Line on Wrap means, I performed some experiments. I created a new profile that's almost exactly like the Java Conventions profile. The only difference is, my new profile doesn't use the Same Line option. Instead, my new profile uses Next Line on Wrap.

I jumped back and forth from Java Conventions to my new profile, making slight changes to my code as I go. At first, the two profiles produce the same formatting results. But after a while, I stumble on a difference in the two profiles' behaviors.

The Edit Profile's Line Wrapping tab has a Maximum line width field. By default, this field's value is 80. If a line of code is 80 characters long or longer, then the formatter breaks the line in a convenient place. (This line breaking is fairly smart. Eclipse doesn't break at any old blank space. Instead, Eclipse looks for a logical place to break the line of code.)

My Next Line on Wrap profile tries hard to keep a curly brace on the same line of code. But the two goals — having a maximum line width and keeping a curly brace on the same line — can conflict with one another. If a line becomes very long, and the best place for the break is just before the curly brace, which rule wins? I tested each profile's rules on a line like

```
while
    (booleanVariableThatMakesThe
    Line81CharactersLong) {
```

The Java Conventions profile, with its Same Line rule, leaves the curly brace in the 81st position. The profile refuses to wrap the curly brace to the next line, even if it means violating the maximum line width rule. But my Next Line on Wrap profile drags the curly brace to a new line, giving the maximum line width rule precedence over keeping the brace on the same line.

Fixing indentation

Not long ago, I was preparing code for an hour-long presentation. For my special audience I needed certain oddball style conventions. I didn't have time to configure Eclipse's formatting preferences. (To be honest, I had neither time nor interest, but that's another story.) Halfway through the preparation, I realized that I'd messed up the code's indentation. (Somewhere in the middle of a big source file, I had forgotten to press the spacebar. From that point downward, everything was slightly misaligned.)

For this situation (and for similar situations), I choose Source⇨Correct Indentation. The Correct Indentation option doesn't mess with things like line wrapping, blanks between operators, or braces staying with their header lines. Instead this option moves entire lines sideways.

As a case study, consider the code in Listing 8-4. If you select the entire main method, and then choose Source⇨Correct Indentation, Eclipse moves the `public static void main` line. You end up with the nicely indented code in Listing 8-5.

Listing 8-4:   Poorly Indented Code

```
public class SecondClass {

        public static void main (String[] args)
    {
        //Well formatted code?
    }
}
```

Listing 8-5:   Nicely Indented Code

```
public class SecondClass {

    public static void main (String[] args)
    {
        //Well formatted code?
    }
}
```

Eclipse may not be completely happy with Listing 8-5. (The placement of parentheses and braces violates the default style conventions.) But Eclipse is willing to live with the code in Listing 8-5. After all, you chose Correct Indentation. You didn't ask for a complete reformatting.

When you select code, and apply Source⇨Correct Indentation, Eclipse uses any unselected code as a baseline. Look again at Listing 8-4, and imagine that you select only three lines. You select the comment and the curly braces before and after the comment. (Your selection doesn't include the main method header.) What happens when you choose Source⇨Correct Indentation? Eclipse uses the method header as a guide, and indents the three selected lines accordingly. (See Listing 8-6.)

Listing 8-6:   Strangely Indented Code

```
public class SecondClass {

        public static void main (String[] args)
        {
            //Well formatted code?
        }
  }
```

After seeing the kind of code that's in Listing 8-6, you may realize that you goofed. You want the method header to move toward the braces, and not the other way around. But that's okay. You still have a good baseline. The first line in Listing 8-6 is properly aligned, so select everything except that first line, and then choose Source⇨Correct Indentation. In response, Eclipse moves the main method leftward, giving you the code in Listing 8-5.

Shifting lines of code

In the previous section, Eclipse fixes indentation automatically while you do other code formatting manually. In this section, even more of the burden is on you. (That's okay. Think of it as a form of empowerment.)

Put your cursor on a line of code, or select a chunk of code in the editor. Then, when you choose Source⇨Shift Right, Eclipse moves lines rightward by a predetermined amount. But wait! What's a "predetermined amount?"

The answer comes from a few different Preferences pages. To make things confusing, the options on these pages seem to overlap one another. These options include the Insert Spaces for Tab check box and the Tab Size field. To find these options, follow a few simple steps:

1. **In the Window⇨Preferences dialog, visit the Java⇨Editor page.**

2. **On the Editor page, select the Appearance tab.**

    The Displayed Tab Width field lives on this Appearance tab page. (See Figure 8-4.)

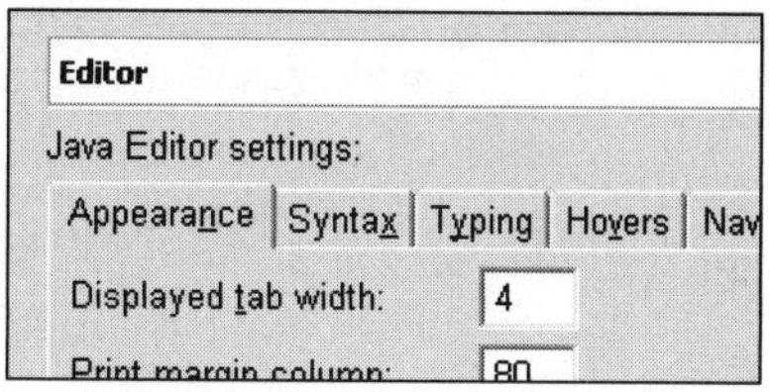

Figure 8-4:
The
Displayed
Tab Width
field.

3. **Without leaving the Editor page, select the Typing tab.**

   The Insert Spaces for Tab check box is on this Typing tab page. (See Figure 8-5.)

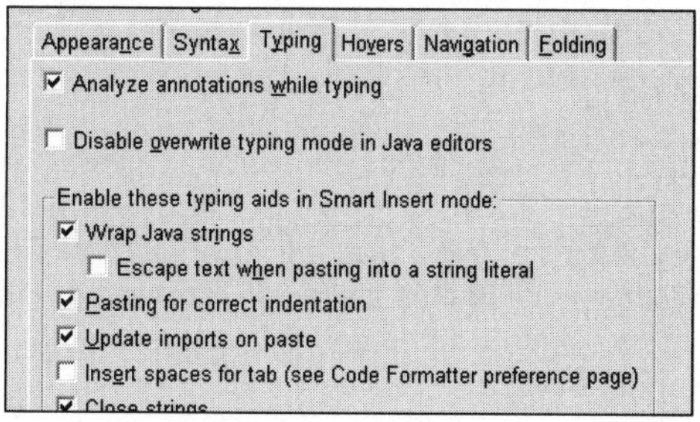

Figure 8-5:
The Insert
Spaces for
Tab check
box.

4. **Leave the Editor page and move to the Java⇨Code Style⇨Code Formatter page.**

5. **On the Code Formatter page, click Show or Edit (whichever button appears).**

6. **On the resulting Show Profile or Edit Profile dialog, select the Indentation tab.**

   The Tab Size field and the Use Tab Character check box live on this Indentation tab page. (See Figure 8-6.)

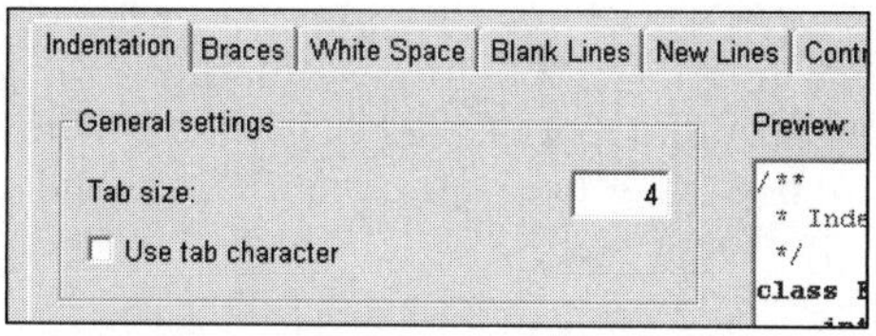

Figure 8-6:
The Tab Size
field and the
Use Tab
Character
check box.

Here's how these options affect the behavior of Source➪Shift Right:

```
if Insert Sspaces for Ttab is unchecked
    Eclipse inserts a tab.
    //Take whatever number is in the Displayed Ttab Wwidth
    //field. The tab looks like that number of spaces.
else
    Eclipse inserts the number of spaces in
    the Tab Ssize field.
```

Notice that the Use Tab Character check box in Figure 8-6 has no effect on shifting. The Use Tab Character check box affects only the Source➪Format and Source➪Format Element actions.

With all the noise in this section about the Shift Right action, you're probably feeling nonchalant about Shift Left. When you choose Source➪Shift Left, Eclipse eliminates tabs or spaces from the beginnings of your selected lines.

One strange thing can happen with the Shift Left action. Suppose you select ten lines of code, and one of these lines starts with only three blank spaces. (This three space gap is smaller than the value 4 in the Tab Size field. See Step 6 in this section's instructions.) In this situation, choosing Source➪Shift Left has no effect. None of the selected lines get shifted. Oh, well!

A line of code can contain both tabs and blank spaces. If you don't know which you have, things can become really confusing when you choose Shift Right or Shift Left. Unfortunately, the editor in Eclipse Version 3.0 provides no way to display tabs or spaces as visible characters.

Sorting Members

I don't have much to say about the Source➪Sort Members action. When you choose this menu option, Eclipse rearranges the things inside your Java class's source code. (By "things" I mean fields, initializers, constructors, methods, and inner classes.) Sorting things in an agreed upon order makes code much easier to maintain.

You can change which things Eclipse puts before which other things. Just visit the Java➪Appearance➪Sort Members Order page of the Window➪ Preferences dialog. Select an item in either of the page's lists, and press the corresponding Up or Down button.

All other things being equal, Eclipse sorts things in alphabetical order. For example, with the `boolean isClosed` and `double accountBalance` fields, Eclipse moves the `accountBalance` declaration above the `isClosed` declaration. (Eclipse doesn't sort on type names such as `boolean` and `double`. Instead, Eclipse sorts on member names, such as `isClosed` and `accountBalance`.)

 The Sort Members action doesn't work on local variables inside methods. If your local variables aren't in the right order, get ready for some good, old-fashioned cutting and pasting.

Dealing with Imports

Someday soon, someone will extend Eclipse with colorful graphics. Before you use an import handling action, you'll see Barbara Eden coming out of a bottle.

"Jeannie, do anything that needs to be done with import declarations in my code."

"Yes, Master."

That's how Eclipse's Import actions work. You can ignore everything having to do with imports until the very last minute. Then choose Source⇨Organize Imports or Source⇨Add Import, and Eclipse performs its magic.

The Organize Imports action

Eclipse provides at least two ways to play with your code's import declarations (declarations like `import java.util.Iterator` that you put near the top your code). This section deals with the first way — choosing Source⇨ Organize Imports. Many things happen when you apply this Organize Imports action:

✔ **Eclipse removes any import declarations that you don't use.**

If your code starts with

```
import javax.swing.JButton;
```

but you never use a JButton, then Eclipse deletes the `JButton` import declaration. Eclipse deletes the declaration even if you use JButton, but all of your references to JButton are fully qualified (as in `button = new javax.swing.JButton("Help")`).

✔ **Eclipse adds any missing import declarations.**

If your code includes

```
button = new JButton("Help");
```

but you have no import declaration for JButton, Eclipse adds

```
import javax.swing.JButton;
```

near the top of your code. I've even seen Eclipse uncomment a declaration that I'd commented out earlier.

What if your code refers to a mysterious Element type? The Java API has four different Element types, each in its own little package. Because Eclipse can't decide which Element type you want, Eclipse asks. (See Figure 8-7.)

In Figure 8-7, you can start typing the name of your favorite package, or you can double-click one of the names in the list.

✔ **Eclipse sorts your code's import declarations.**

By default, `java` packages come first, then the `javax` packages, then the `org` packages, and finally the `com` packages. Within each category, Eclipse sorts declarations alphabetically. (That way, the declarations are easy to find.)

Of course you can change the sorting order. Visit the Java⇨Code Style⇨ Organize Imports page of the Window⇨Preferences dialog. Move names up in the list, move names down in the list, add names, or remove names. It's all up to you.

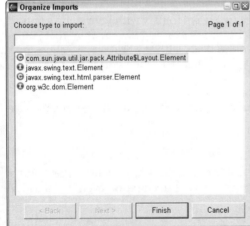

Figure 8-7: The Organize Imports Wizard.

✔ **Eclipse tries to eliminate import-on-demand declarations.**

An import-on-demand declaration uses an asterisk instead of a bunch of class names. Instead of writing many single-type import declarations

```
import javax.swing.ImageIcon;
import javax.swing.JButton;
import javax.swing.JCheckBox;
import javax.swing.JFrame;
import javax.swing.Popup;
import javax.swing.Spring;
```

you can achieve the same effect with just one import-on-demand declaration:

```
import javax.swing.*;
```

Some programmers use import-on-demand too much, and that offends Java's style gods. If your code starts with `import javax.swing.*` but you use only two Swing classes, Eclipse trades in your import-on-demand declaration for some single-type import declarations.

Of course, if you have too many of these single-type import declarations, your code topples from its own weight. That's why you can configure the number of single-type declarations that Eclipse tolerates. To configure this number, visit the Java⇨Code Style⇨Organize Imports page of the Window⇨Preferences dialog. Then change the value in the page's Number of Imports Needed for .* field.

Personally, I think the default number 99 is too many. But who am I to say? I'm just an author.

The Add Import action

The Source⇨Add Import action is a kind of mini Organize Imports command. But Add Import does things a bit differently:

✔ **Add Import acts on only one name at a time.**

Place your cursor on a type name, and then choose Source⇨Add Import. If only one package contains a class or interface with that name, Eclipse immediately adds an import declaration to your code. If more than one package contains a class or interface with that name, Eclipse offers you a choice of packages, as in Figure 8-7.

Before you use Add Import this way, select as little source code as you can. If you select the entire line

```
JButton button;
```

then Add Import does nothing. If you select the word `button`, on that same line, then Add Import still does nothing. But if you select only `JButton` (or just click your mouse anywhere inside the word `JButton`), then Add Import can create a new `javax.swing.JButton` import declaration.

✔ **Whereas Organize Imports removes unnecessary import declarations, Add Import can turn them into necessary import declarations.**

Start with both of the lines

```
import javax.swing.JButton;
```

and

```
panel.add(new javax.swing.JButton("Help"));
```

in your code, and make sure that you don't use the name JButton anywhere else.

- If you choose Source⇨Organize Imports, then Eclipse removes the import declaration.

- If you select the `JButton` in `new javax.swing.JButton`, and then choose Source⇨Add Import, Eclipse simplifies the constructor call. You end up with this statement:

```
panel.add(new JButton("Help"));
```

Add Import simplifies only one name at a time. So if your code contains the line

```
javax.swing.JButton button = new javax.swing.JButton();
```

then one application of Add Import can simplify either the first or the second `javax.swing.JButton`, but not both.

Don't apply Add Import when your cursor is on an import declaration. When I try it, Add Import turns `import javax.swing.JButton` into an invalid `import JButton` declaration.

Chapter 9

More Eclipse "Sourcery"

*T*he word "boilerplate" comes from nineteenth century typography. The process for distributing syndicated newspaper articles involved pouring boiling lead into a prepared mold. (Sounds like fun, doesn't it?) The result was a plate that stamped out hundreds of copies of the original newspaper article.

These days, you can write boilerplate Java code. In fact, if you practice enough, you can create constructors, getters, and setters in your sleep. But why interrupt your sleep? Have Eclipse do the work instead.

Creating Constructors and Methods

Constructors and methods are the workhorses of any computer program. First, the constructors create objects. Then the methods take over and do useful things with objects.

Eclipse's Source menu includes several actions for adding constructors and methods. These actions are fairly smart, so you don't have to do much work on your own.

Override and implement methods

Figure 9-1 shows you what happens when you choose Source➪Override/ Implement Methods. The dialog offers to create some skeletal method code.

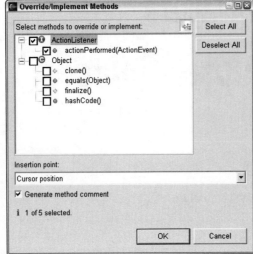

Figure 9-1:
The
Override/
Implement
Methods
dialog.

In Figure 9-1, notice how Eclipse automatically puts a check mark next to a method like `actionPerformed`. (When I created Figure 9-1, I was working on a class that implements `ActionListener`. Without an `actionPerformed` method, my code wouldn't compile.) Eclipse doesn't put check marks next to the other method names (names like `clone`, `equals`, and so on). My code can compile even if I don't implement these methods.

If I click OK in Figure 9-1, I get code of the kind shown in Figure 9-2.

Figure 9-2:
Eclipse
creates a
method.

```
    /* (non-Javadoc)
     * @see java.awt.event.ActionListener#actionPerformed(java.awt.event.ActionEvent)
     */
    public void actionPerformed(ActionEvent e) {
        // TODO Auto-generated method stub

    }
```

Better getters and setters

You can find getters and setters in almost every object-oriented program. A getter method gets an object's value:

```
public typename getValue() {
    return value;
}
```

A setter method sets an object's value:

```
public void setValue(typename value) {
    this.value = value;
}
```

Like the paintings in cheap hotel rooms, most getters and setters are very much alike. Here and there you find an unusual getter or an atypical setter. But in general, these getter and setter methods are mechanical copies of one another. So why write getters and setters by hand? Have Eclipse write these methods for you.

If you choose Source⇨Generate Getters and Setters, you see a dialog like the one in Figure 9-3. The dialog offers to create methods for each of the fields in your source file. The resulting methods look like the ones in Figure 9-4.

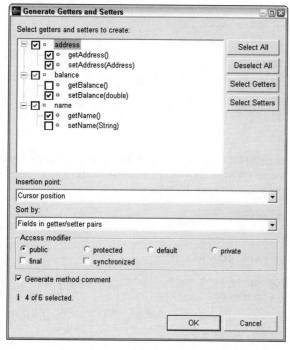

Figure 9-3:
The Generate Getters and Setters dialog.

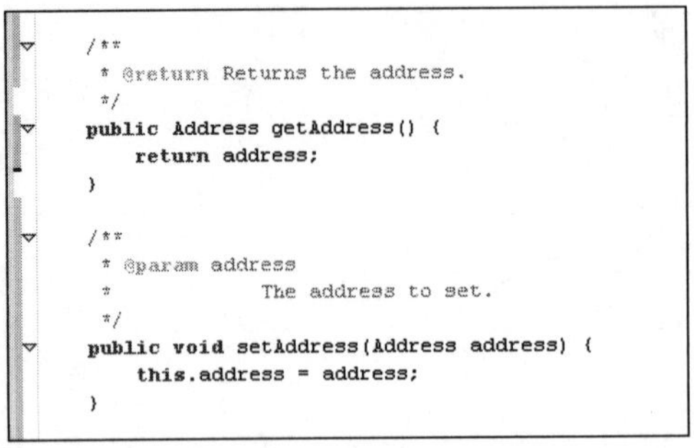

```
/**
 * @return Returns the address.
 */
public Address getAddress() {
    return address;
}

/**
 * @param address
 *          The address to set.
 */
public void setAddress(Address address) {
    this.address = address;
}
```

Figure 9-4: Eclipse creates getter and setter methods.

Don't wait. Delegate!

A *delegate* does work on behalf of some other piece of code. Here's a tiny example. You start with an innocent looking Address class:

```
public class Address {
    private int number;
    private String street;
    private String city;
    private String state;
    private int zip;

    public void print() {
        // Create an address label
    }

    // Blah, blah, blah...
}
```

The Address class prints its own mailing labels. Then some new piece of code comes along and creates an Address instance. So you delegate the work of printing to one of the new code's methods:

```
public class HandleAccount {
    public String name;
    private double balance;
    private Address address;

    public void print() {
        address.print();
    }

    // Blah, blah, blah...

}
```

The HandleAccount class's print method is a delegate method. Delegate methods can save you from some potentially awkward programming situations. To make Eclipse write a delegate method, select the class that will contain the delegate method. (In the example above, select HandleAccount in either the editor or the Package Explorer.) Then choose Source➪Generate Delegate Methods.

In response, Eclipse gives you a dialog like the one in Figure 9-5. After clicking OK, you get a method like the one shown in Figure 9-6. With this new method, the address object delegates its print functionality to the object that contains the address field.

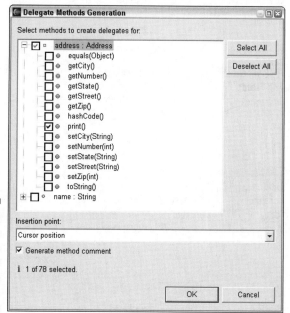

Figure 9-5:
The Delegate Methods Generation dialog.

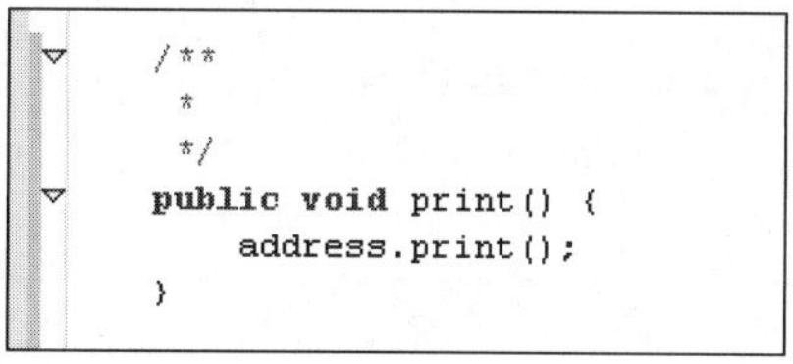

Figure 9-6:
Eclipse creates a delegate.

```
/**
 *
 */
public void print() {
    address.print();
}
```

Creating constructors

Eclipse's Source menu gives you two ways to create constructors.

✔ When you choose Source⇨Generate Constructor Using Fields, Eclipse gives values to the subclass's fields.

✔ When you choose Source⇨Add Constructor from Superclass, Eclipse gives values to the parent class's fields.

Figure 9-7 illustrates the point. The Generate Constructor Using Fields action uses assignment statements; the Add Constructor action passes parameters. Both actions call the parent class's constructor. So, in some situations, both actions give you the same result.

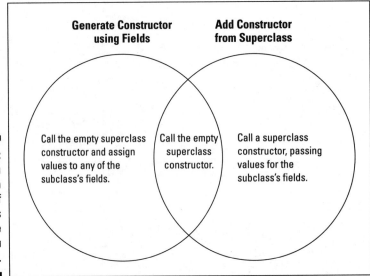

Figure 9-7:
Things you
can do with
two of
Eclipse's
Source
menu
actions.

Generate Constructor using Fields

Add Constructor from Superclass

Call the empty superclass constructor and assign values to any of the subclass's fields.

Call the empty superclass constructor.

Call a superclass constructor, passing values for the subclass's fields.

For a concrete example, look over the code in Listing 9-1.

Listing 9-1: A Class and a Subclass

```
class Employee {
    private String name;

    private String jobTitle;

    public Employee() {
        super();
    }
```

```
    public Employee(String name, String jobTitle) {
        super();
        this.name = name;
        this.jobTitle = jobTitle;
    }

    ... Etc. (No additional constructors)
}

class PartTimeEmployee extends Employee {
    private double hourlyRate;

    ... Etc. (No constructors)
}
```

If I choose Source➪Generate Constructor Using Fields with the
PartTimeEmployee class in the editor, I see the dialog in Figure 9-8. This
dialog creates one constructor. To create two constructors, I have to choose
Generate Constructor Using Fields twice.

Figure 9-8:
The
Generate
Constructor
Using Fields
dialog.

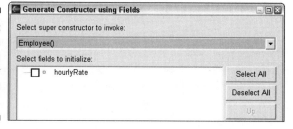

I use this dialog in Figure 9-8 twice — once with hourlyRate unchecked, and
a second time with hourlyRate checked. When the dust settles, I have the
code shown in Figure 9-9.

Figure 9-9:
Eclipse
generates
construc-
tors using
fields.

```
/**
 *
 */
public PartTimeEmployee() {
    super();
}

/**
 * @param hourlyRate
 */
public PartTimeEmployee(double hourlyRate) {
    super();
    this.hourlyRate = hourlyRate;
}
```

Some people have strange notions of what it means to have "fun." Just for
fun, I wiped the slate clean. I deleted the code that I created using Generate

Constructor, and I returned to the pristine code in Listing 9-1. Then I do it all again. But this time around, I choose Source⇨Add Constructor from Superclass. As a result, I see the dialog in Figure 9-10.

Figure 9-10:
The Add
Constructor
from
Superclass
dialog.

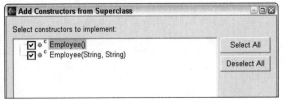

If I put check marks in both of Figure 9-10's boxes, I get the constructors shown in Figure 9-11. One constructor is the same as a constructor created by the Generate Constructor Using Fields action. The other constructor is unique to the Add Constructor from Superclass action.

Figure 9-11:
Eclipse
generates
construc-
tors from
the
superclass.

```
/**
 *
 */
public PartTimeEmployee() {
    super();
    // TODO Auto-generated constructor stub
}

/**
 * @param name
 * @param jobTitle
 */
public PartTimeEmployee(String name, String jobTitle) {
    super(name, jobTitle);
    // TODO Auto-generated constructor stub
}
```

Creating try/catch Blocks

A try/catch block is like a safety net. If anything goes wrong inside the block, your program can recover gracefully.

Choosing Source⇨Surround with try/catch Block is like applying the `try` template. But the Surround with try/catch Block action is much smarter than the `try` template.

To find out more about the `try` template, see Chapter 7.

To see how smart the Surround with try/catch Block action is, march over to the editor and select the following lines of code:

```
FileInputStream stream = new FileInputStream("myData");
Thread.sleep(2000);
```

Then choose Source⇨Surround with try/catch Block. When you do all this, you get the following result:

```
import java.io.FileNotFoundException;
...

try {
    FileInputStream stream = new FileInputStream("myData");
    Thread.sleep(2000);
} catch (FileNotFoundException e) {
    // TODO Auto-generated catch block
    e.printStackTrace();
} catch (InterruptedException e) {
    // TODO Auto-generated catch block
    e.printStackTrace();
}
```

Eclipse even adds the import declaration for the `FileNotFoundException`.

If you apply the `try` template to the same code, you get the following wishy-washy result:

```
try {
    FileInputStream stream = new FileInputStream("myData");
    Thread.sleep(2000);

} catch (Exception e) {
    // TODO: handle exception
}
```

It gets even better. If you apply Surround with try/catch Block to code that contains a `super` call, Eclipse answers back with a message: `Cannot surround a super constructor call`. (How about that! Eclipse knows that you're not allowed to put a `super` call inside a try/catch block!)

What if you apply the Surround with try/catch Block action to the following code?

```
fib = previous + prePrevious;
prePrevious = previous;
previous = fib;
System.out.println(fib);
```

The code doesn't throw any checked exceptions, so Eclipse asks you if really need a `try/catch` block. (See Figure 9-12.)

Figure 9-12:
Would you
care to
catch a
Runtime-
Exception?

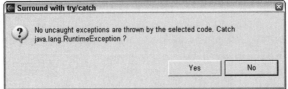

If you ignore Eclipse's caution and click Yes, Eclipse gives you the following sensible code:

```
try {
    fib = previous + prePrevious;
    prePrevious = previous;
    previous = fib;
    System.out.println(fib);
} catch (RuntimeException e) {
    // TODO Auto-generated catch block
    e.printStackTrace();
}
```

Instead of using `RuntimeException`, the `try` template would have used a plain, old `Exception`. That would be adequate, but for this particular piece of code, `RuntimeException` is a better fit.

"118n"

My high school French courses come in handy at times. After college, I went bumming around Europe, walking the city streets, hitch-hiking, and taking odd jobs here and there. (I was young and energetic. The usual tourist sites didn't interest me.)

One evening, while I roamed the streets of Paris, some English- speaking tourists stopped me to ask for directions. Nervously, they pointed to a map. "*Eiffel Tower?*" they said. "*Oooo essst la Eiffel Tower?*" they repeated, using French that they'd learned from a guidebook that day.

Not wanting to break the illusion, I answered them in French. "*Allez vers la droite,*" I said, as I pointed down the street. I probably got it wrong myself, but it didn't matter. I was thrilled as they walked away saying "*Murcee, murcee.*"

As the third millennium moves onward, you need to fine-tune your applications so that people all over the world can use them. More and more, people who don't speak your native language want to use your code, and they're not always interested in translating text themselves. That's why Java comes with internationalization features.

And don't forget . . . If you want to be cool, abbreviate "internationalization" with the name "i18n." The name "i18n" stands for "i" plus eighteen more letters, followed by "n." All the popular geeks use this terminology.

Preparing your code for internationalization

Eclipse's *string externalizing* tools can help you internationalize your code. (They're called "externalizing" tools because they move strings outside of your source code.) Here's an example to show you how the tools work:

1. **Create a new project.**

   In this example, I called it my **HelloProject**.

2. **Create a new class.**

   The class name **Hello** works for me.

3. **In the** Hello **class's main method, add the usual** System.out.println("Hello") **statement.**

   See Figure 9-13.

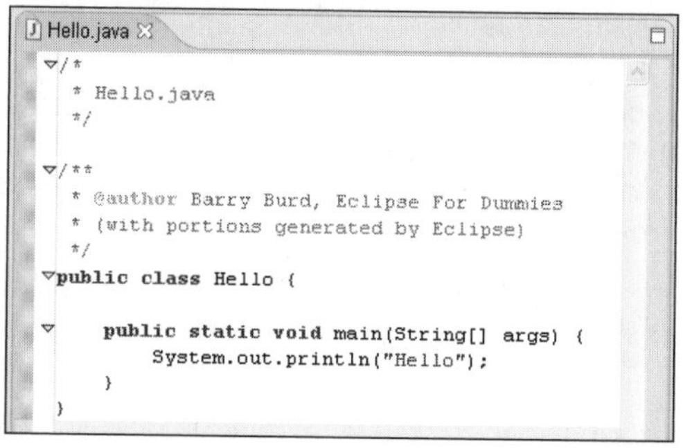

Figure 9-13: Monolingual code.

```
J Hello.java ⊠
▽/*
 * Hello.java
 */

▽/**
 * @author Barry Burd, Eclipse For Dummies
 * (with portions generated by Eclipse)
 */
▽public class Hello {

▽    public static void main(String[] args) {
        System.out.println("Hello");
    }
}
```

4. **Run the program.**

   The program prints Hello. Big deal!

5. **In the Package Explorer, select the project's branch.**

   In this example, select the HelloProject branch.

6. **Choose Source⇨Find Strings to Externalize.**

   The Find Strings to Externalize dialog appears with a list of source files containing strings. (See Figure 9-14.)

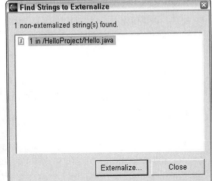

Figure 9-14:
The Find
Strings to
Externalize
dialog.

Eclipse's Source menu has two actions for externalizing strings. The Find Strings to Externalize option works after you select an entire project, package, or folder in the Package Explorer. The alternative Externalize Strings action works after you select a Java source file in the Package Explorer (or after you click your mouse on a file in the editor). In general, Externalize Strings is good for small projects and Find Strings to Externalize is better for large projects. Either way, you get the same results.

7. In the dialog (refer to Figure 9-14), select a source file whose strings you want to eventually translate into other languages. Then click Externalize.

The next thing you see is a page of Eclipse's Externalize Strings Wizard. (See Figure 9-15.) In the big Strings to Externalize list, some rows may be checked, and others may contain an X or an arrow. In this example, the one and only Hello row is checked.

For now, leave the check mark in the Hello row. For more info about the check marks in rows, see the next section's "Marking strings for externalization" sidebar.

By clicking Configure (in the Externalize Strings Wizard of Figure 9-15) you can change all kinds of little things about the way externalization works. I call these things "little" because, even though they may be very important in some applications, they don't make a big difference in the way externalization works.

8. Click Next.

A page like the one in Figure 9-16 appears. On that page, don't let the words "Found problems" make you nervous. Eclipse is just telling you that it's about to add a file to your project.

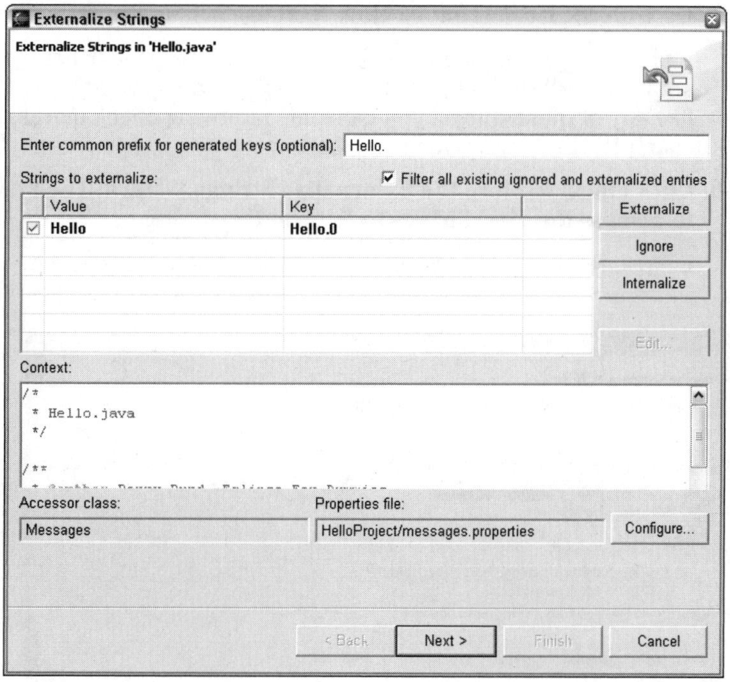

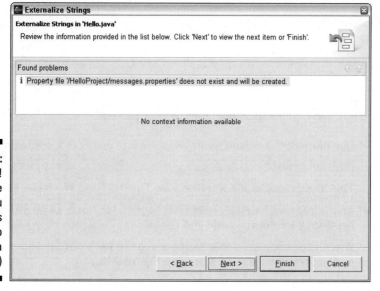

Figure 9-15: Selecting strings for externalization.

Figure 9-16: Oh, no! (Eclipse warns you that it's about to create a file.)

9. **Go with the flow. (That is, click Next again.)**

   A page like the one in Figure 9-17 appears. This page is handy because it shows you all the things Eclipse is about to do to your code. If you don't like any of these things, you can start removing check marks. But in this example, leave everything checked.

10. **Click Finish to close the Externalize Strings Wizard. Then click Close to dismiss the Find Strings to Externalize dialog.**

    Eclipse returns you to your regularly scheduled workbench.

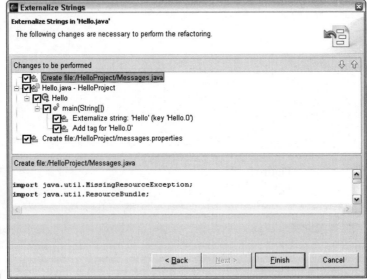

Figure 9-17: Eclipse tells you how your project is about to change.

You now have some additional files in your project.

- One file with the default name `messages.properties`, **contains a line like**

  ```
  Hello.0=Hello
  ```

  This line describes a key/value pair. The `Hello.0` key has a `Hello` value.

- Another file with default name `Messages.java` acts as an intermediary between your source code and the `messages.properties` file.

  When your code calls this `Messages.java` file's `getString` method, the method returns a key's value. (See Figure 9-18.)

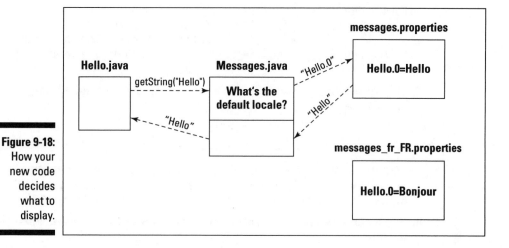

Figure 9-18:
How your
new code
decides
what to
display.

Adding other languages to your code

When you finish following the previous set of steps, Eclipse makes some
changes in your Java source file. To see what I mean, compare Figure 9-13
("before") with Figure 9-19 ("after"). In place of an ordinary string (like
"Hello") Eclipse puts a key (like "Hello.0").

Figure 9-19:
Potentially
multilingual
code.

```
public class Hello {

    public static void main(String[] args) {
        System.out.println(Messages.getString("Hello.0")); //$NON-NLS-1$
    }
}
```

The key represents the translation of the original string into any number of
languages. To find out how this works, follow the next several steps.

1. **Create an alternate version of the** messages.properties **file.**

   In this example, I create a file named messages_fr_FR.properties.
   The first two letters fr stand for the French language. The next two
   letters FR stand for the country France. No matter what language or
   country you use, you must include the underscore characters. That's
   the way Java recognizes these internationalization files.

For the official list of two-letter language and country codes, visit `www.iso.ch/iso/en/prods-services/iso3166ma/02iso-3166-code-lists/list-en1.html`. (Wouldn't you know it? That Web address includes `en`, which stands for "English." You can find other versions of the page at `www.iso.ch`.)

2. **In your new properties file, add a line that assigns a value to the original key.**

In my `messages_fr_FR.properties` file, I add the line

```
Hello.0=Bonjour
```

With this addition, the original `Hello.0` key becomes associated with two different words — *Hello* in the `messages.properties` file and *Bonjour* in the new `messages_fr_FR.properties` file. (Refer to Figure 9-18.)

3. **Buy a plane ticket to a country where you can test your new properties file.**

Alternatively, you can change your program's default locale. In this example, I add a call to Java's `Locale.setDefault` method. (See Figure 9-20.) When I run the modified code, the program displays the word *Bonjour*.

Java's API has constants for some of your favorite locales. In Figure 9-20, instead of calling the `Locale` class's constructor, you can write `Locale.setDefault(Locale.FRANCE)`.

Figure 9-20:
When in
Paris, do as
the
Parisian's
do.

```
public class Hello {

    public static void main(String[] args) {
        Locale.setDefault(new Locale("fr", "FR"));
        System.out.println(Messages.getString("Hello.0")); //$NON-NLS-1$
    }
}
```

Marking strings for externalization

The dialog in Figure 9-15 has three interesting buttons — Externalize, Ignore, and Internalize. To show you what each of the buttons does, I create the code in the following figure. The code contains three strings, and each string tells me what button to push.

```
public class HelloAgain {

    public static void main(String[] args) {
        System.out.println("Externalize me.");
        System.out.println("Go ahead. Ignore me.");
        System.out.println("Please. Won't you Internalize me?");
    }
}
```

When I reach the appropriate page in Eclipse's Externalize Strings Wizard, I take care to heed each string's advice. For instance, in this figure, I select the `Ignore me` string's row, and then I click Ignore. Sure enough, the Ignore button is grayed out. This graying out indicates that I've already clicked the Ignore button for the `Ignore me` string. (The little X in the `Ignore me` row's check box is further confirmation that I chose to ignore this string.)

Value	Key		
☑ **Externalize me.**	**HelloAgain.0**		Externalize
☒ **Go ahead. Ignore me.**			Ignore
⟳ Please. Won't you Internalize me?			Internalize

Strings to externalize: ☑ Filter all existing ignored and externalized entries

But what does it mean to "ignore" or to "internalize" a string? After finishing up with the Externalize Strings Wizard, I get the code shown in the following figure. Eclipse substitutes a key for the original `Externalize me` string, but makes no substitutions for the `Ignore me` or `Internalize me` strings. So that's Part 1 of the answer to the "ignore and internalize" question.

```
public class HelloAgain {

    public static void main(String[] args) {
        System.out.println(Messages.getString("HelloAgain.0")); //$NON-NLS-1$
        System.out.println("Go ahead. Ignore me."); //$NON-NLS-1$
        System.out.println("Please. Won't you Internalize me?");
    }
}
```

Part 2 is a little more complicated. In the figure, notice how Eclipse adds `//$NON-NLS-1$` comments. A `NON-NLS` comment reminds Eclipse not to offer to externalize a particular string again. So, the next time I invoke Eclipse string externalizing on this code, I see the stuff in this figure. Eclipse knows better than to waste my time on strings like `"HelloAgain.0"` or `"Go ahead. Ignore me"` (strings marked with `NON-NLS` comments).

(continued)

(continued)

Strings to externalize:		☑ Filter all existing ignored and externalized entries	
Value	Key		Externalize
☑ Please. Won't you Internalize ...	HelloAgain.1		Ignore
			Internalize

So that's the difference. When you tell Eclipse to ignore a string, you mean "ignore this string in all future externalizations." Eclipse reminds itself by adding a NON-NLS comment for this string. (A number inside the comment identifies each such string. For instance, if a line of code has two ignorable strings, the line may contain two comments — //$NON-NLS-1$ and //$NON-NLS-2$.)

But when you tell Eclipse to internalize a string, you mean "leave the string as internal during this round of externalization." Eclipse doesn't add a NON-NLS comment, so the string is a candidate for future rounds of externalization.

Now take one more look at the third figure. Notice the NON-NLS comment for the "HelloAgain.0" string. If you think about it, this makes sense. The HelloAgain.0 key already stands for *Hello*, *Bonjour*, or whatever else you put into your properties files. Only a maniac or a theoretical computer scientist would consider externalizing a string that's already been externalized.

Chapter 10

Refactoring: A Burd's Eye View

*T*he *Free On-line Dictionary of Computing* defines *refactoring* as "Improving a computer program by reorganising its internal structure without altering its external behaviour."*

According to Paul Furbacher (of the Amateur Computer Group of New Jersey), the current trend in integrated development environments is to better one another with useful refactoring features.

Author Barry Burd says "the goal of refactoring is to move seamlessly from correct code to more correct code."**

Without refactoring, you improve code by messing with it. You start to edit your working code. While you edit, you break the code temporarily. Sure, when the editing is done, your code works again. But this "working, then not working, then working again" cycle can lead to errors.

With refactoring, you skip the "not working" part of the cycle. You do all the editing in one big atomic step. During this step, the code doesn't have time to be incorrect.

---

* From The Free On-line Dictionary of Computing, www.foldoc.org/, Editor Denis Howe

** In fact, in Eclipse For Dummies, Burd says that "Burd says that 'the goal of refactoring is to move seamlessly from correct code to more correct code.'" He goes on to say that "Burd says that 'Burd says that 'the goal of refactoring is to move seamlessly from correct code to more correct code.'"

Refactoring didn't originate with Eclipse, or even with Java. Refactoring started around 1990, when programmers were looking systematically for ways to improve their code. Many of Eclipse's refactoring actions are commonly known tools that stem from computer science research. For an in-depth look at the world of refactoring, visit www.refactoring.com.

Eclipse's Refactoring Tools

Figure 10-1 shows Eclipse's grand Refactor menu. Each menu option represents a particular refactoring *action*. For instance, if you select the bottommost option, Eclipse performs its Encapsulate Field action. The top two actions are a little bit different. These Undo and Redo things are "actions that affect other actions."

Refactor	Navigate	Search	Project	Run	Window	Help
Undo - Rename Java p...o:'MyBigApplication'						Alt+Shift+Z
Redo - Move Members						Alt+Shift+Y
Rename...						Alt+Shift+R
Move...						Alt+Shift+V
Change Method Signature...						Alt+Shift+C
Convert Anonymous Class to Nested...						
Move Member Type to New File...						
Push Down...						
Pull Up...						
Extract Interface...						
Generalize Type...						
Use Supertype Where Possible...						
Inline...						Alt+Shift+I
Extract Method...						Alt+Shift+M
Extract Local Variable...						Alt+Shift+L
Extract Constant...						
Introduce Parameter...						
Introduce Factory...						
Convert Local Variable to Field...						Alt+Shift+F
Encapsulate Field...						

Figure 10-1: The Refactor menu.

Each action does different things to different pieces of code. For instance, the Rename action changes the names of variables, methods, and other elements. The Move action relocates methods, classes, and other things from one file to another or even from one package to another.

Occasionally, I need to distinguish between a refactoring action and a refactoring *operation*. An operation is one round of performing an action. For example, you choose Refactor⇨Rename to change the variable name rose to the variable name violet. That's one operation. Later, you choose Refactor⇨Rename again to turn the method name display into the method name show. That's a second operation. But both the first and second operations are instances of the same Rename refactoring action.

Each refactoring action has its own special quirks and tricks. But behind all the quirks lie many common features. This chapter emphasizes those common features. (The next chapter emphasizes quirks.)

The Three Ps

At first glance, an Eclipse refactoring operation seems to be a big production — something you'd see in a Busby Berkeley musical. After starting an operation, you deal with one dialog, then another, and then another. By the time the operation finishes, you may have forgotten what you were trying to accomplish when you started the operation.

Fortunately, the refactoring dialogs come in only three different flavors:

✔ In one or more *parameter pages,* you select options that control the refactoring operation's behavior.

✔ In a *preview page,* you selectively approve the changes that the operation can make in your code.

Sometimes, you can skip the preview page.

✔ In a *problem page,* Eclipse tells you a "doom and gloom" story about the operation's possible aftereffects.

Thank goodness! You seldom see a problem page.

This chapter covers all three kinds of pages. When you're used to dealing with these pages, Eclipse's refactoring operations no longer feel like big productions.

In the next several sections, I introduce each of the three Ps — parameter, preview, and problem pages.

Eclipse's Help files differentiate between the parameter pages that I describe in this section, and a simpler *input page* that you see with certain refactoring actions. I don't distinguish between parameter pages and input pages. I have two reasons for calling them all "parameter pages." First, the distinction isn't important to the novice Eclipse user. And second, the word "input" doesn't begin with the letter "p."

Parameter pages

You ask Eclipse to pull declarations out of a class and into a parent class. Eclipse begins the operation by asking you questions. Exactly which declarations do you want to pull? Exactly where do you want the declarations to go? The dialogs for all these questions are parameter pages (a.k.a. input pages). To see how the pages work, try the following experiment:

1. **Create a new project containing the code from Listing 10-1.**

   Remember, you don't have to retype the code in Listing 10-1. You can download the code from this book's Web site.

2. **In the editor, place the cursor anywhere inside** `MyClass`**. (Alternatively, select** `MyClass` **in the Package Explorer or in the Outline view.) Then choose Refactor⇨Pull Up.**

   Eclipse responds by showing you a parameter page (the Pull Up page in Figure 10-2).

   Each refactoring action has its own kind of parameter pages. The page in Figure 10-2 represents only one kind of parameter page — a parameter page for the Pull Up action.

   In the next few instructions, you feed information to parameter pages.

3. **Inside the Specify Actions for Members list, check the** `i` **and** `display` **boxes. Leave the** `j` **box unchecked. (Again, see Figure 10-2.)**

   Depending on where you put the cursor in Step 2, some of these boxes may already contain check marks.

4. **In the Select Destination Class drop-down list, select** `MySuperclass`**.**

   You can pull members up to a parent, a grandparent, or any ancestor class.

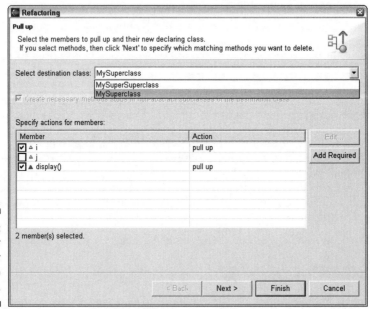

Figure 10-2:
A parameter
page for
Pull Up
refactoring.

5. Click Next.

This click brings you to another parameter page. (See Figure 10-3.)

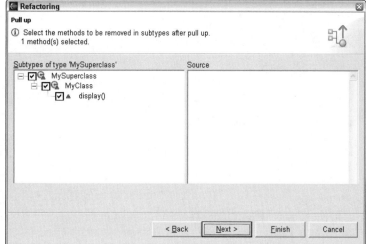

Eclipse realizes that your request to pull up the `display` method may mean two different things. You may want to *copy* the method from `MyClass`, or you may want to *move* the method from `MyClass`. In Figure 10-3, Eclipse offers choices.

- **If you leave check marks in the** `MySuperclass`, `MyClass`, **and** `display` **boxes, then Eclipse moves the** `display` **method.**

  That is, Eclipse removes the `display` method from `MyClass`.

- **If you uncheck the** `MySuperclass`, `MyClass`, **and** `display` **boxes, then Eclipse copies the** `display` **method.**

  In other words, Eclipse doesn't remove the `display` method from `MyClass`.

The check boxes in Figure 10-3 can be confusing. At first glance, you may think that you can selectively check the `MySuperclass`, `MyClass`, and `display` boxes. Would a check mark in only one of the boxes have any meaning? No, it wouldn't. In Figure 10-3, the little hierarchy of check boxes simply shows what's a subclass or member of what else. If you uncheck any of these three boxes, Eclipse removes check marks from the other two. Taken together, these three check boxes settle only one issue — whether Eclipse removes the `display` method from `MyClass`.

In this experiment, leave the boxes in Figure 10-3 checked.

6. Click Finish.

In other words, ignore the Next button at the bottom of Figure 10-3.

7. **Notice how your code has changed.**

Eclipse has pulled the declarations of i and display from MyClass up to the parent MySuperclass. (Compare Listings 10-1 and 10-2.)

Listing 10-1:   Before Pull Up Refactoring

```
class MySuperSuperclass {
}

class MySuperclass extends MySuperSuperclass {
}

class MyClass extends MySuperclass {
    int i, j;

    void display() {
    }
}

class MyOtherClass extends MySuperclass {
}
```

Listing 10-2:   After Pull Up Refactoring

```
class MySuperSuperclass {
}

class MySuperclass extends MySuperSuperclass {

    int i;

    void display() {
    }
}

class MyClass extends MySuperclass {
    int j;
}

class MyOtherClass extends MySuperclass {
}
```

Look back at Figure 10-2, and notice the unassuming Add Required button. Clicking Add Required tells Eclipse to put check marks in certain members' rows. For example, start with these two declarations:

```
double amount;
double tax = 0.06*amount;
```

Choose Refactor⇨Pull Up. Then, in the preview page, put a check mark in only the tax variable's row.

The value of `tax` depends on the value of `amount`, so moving the `tax` declaration without moving the `amount` declaration makes no sense. (In fact, moving tax never makes *cents*. Ha ha!) So if you click Add Required, Eclipse adds a check mark to the `amount` check box.

But wait! Have you saved yourself any work by clicking the Add Required button? Click a button instead of checking a check box? What's so great about that? Well, for some programs, the parameter page contains dozens of check boxes, and figuring out what's required and what isn't required can be a messy affair. With such programs, the Add Required button is very useful.

The preview page

First you initiate an operation by choosing an action from the Refactor menu. Then you fill in some information on one or more parameter pages. With the information that you give on the parameter pages, Eclipse can create a preview page. The preview page shows you exactly how Eclipse plans to modify your code. You can selectively veto any of the proposed modifications. Here's an example:

1. **Start with the code in Listing 10-2.**

   This section's instructions don't work unless each of the classes is in its own separate Java source file. You need files named `MySuperclass.java`, `MyClass.java`, and so on.

2. **In the editor, place the cursor anywhere inside** `MySuperclass`. **(Alternatively, select** `MySuperclass` **in the Package Explorer or the Outline view.) Then choose Refactor⇨Push Down.**

   Eclipse responds by showing you a parameter page (the Push Down page in Figure 10-4).

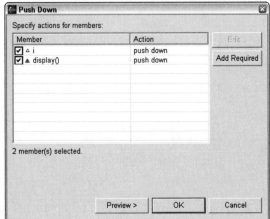

Figure 10-4: A parameter page for Push Down refactoring.

3. **Make sure that the boxes in the** i **and** display **rows contain check marks.**

Again, refer to Figure 10-4.

4. **Click Preview.**

A preview page appears. The top part of the preview page lists the things that can happen if you go through with the refactoring operation. The bottom part shows code before and after the proposed refactoring. In Figure 10-5, notice how MySuperclass goes from containing two declarations to being empty. And, in Figure 10-6, see how MyOtherClass goes from being empty to containing i and display declarations.

But what if you don't want MyOtherClass to contain the i and display declarations? What if you want to go from the code in Listing 10-2 back to the code in Listing 10-1? In the next step, you veto all MyOtherClass changes.

5. **Uncheck any of the** MyOtherClass **branch's check boxes.**

Your goal is to return to the original code in Listing 10-1 — the code in which only MyClass contains i and display declarations. You achieve the goal by removing some check marks in the preview page.

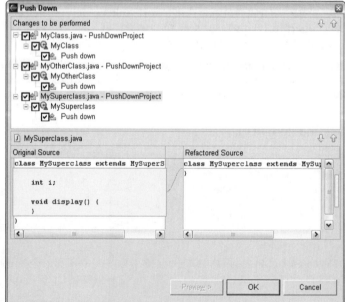

Figure 10-5: Selecting MySuper class on the preview page.

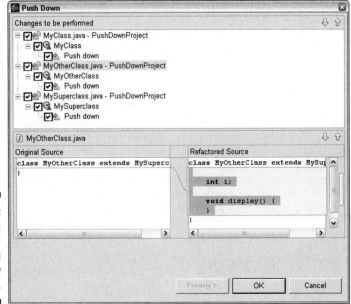

Figure 10-6:
Selecting
MyOther
Class on
the preview
page.

The code in the Refactored Source pane doesn't necessarily keep up with things you do to the preview page's check boxes. For instance, in Figure 10-6, the Refactored Source pane can contain declarations even after you uncheck the MyOtherClass branches. Regardless of what you may see in the Refactored Source pane, the boxes you check in the top half of the preview page have the final authority. These boxes determine what Eclipse does (or doesn't do) with your code.

You can't edit the code in either the Original Source or the Refactored Source panes of Figure 10-6. You can copy the code (for the purpose of pasting it some other place) but you can't delete or otherwise modify the code in these panes. To change the way refactoring works, you must use the check boxes in the top half of the preview page.

6. Click OK.

The preview page disappears.

7. Notice how your code has changed.

Because of the things you do on the preview page, Eclipse restores the original Java source code of Listing 10-1 — the code in which only MyClass contains i and display declarations.

This section's instructions do the opposite of what the "Parameter pages" section's instructions do. The "Parameter page" instructions go from Listing 10-1 to Listing 10-2, and this section's instructions go from Listing 10-2 back to Listing 10-1. Hey, wait! That sounds like Undo!

In fact, applying Refactor⇨Undo can roll back a refactoring operation's effects. But remember this: If you change anything after you refactor, then you can no longer apply the Refactor⇨Undo or Refactor⇨Redo actions. When I say "change anything" I mean "change the code with anything other than another refactoring action."

For example, imagine that you follow the instructions in this chapter's "Parameter pages" section. These instructions take you from Listing 10-1 to Listing 10-2. After following the instructions, you click your mouse inside the editor and add a blank space somewhere in the code.

That blank space puts the kibosh on any future Undo operation. After adding the blank space, you can no longer use Refactor⇨Undo to go back to the code in Listing 10-1. No, undoing your addition of the blank space doesn't help. The Refactor⇨Undo action simply refuses to perform.

The problem page

A refactoring operation can involve three kinds of pages: parameter pages, a preview page, and a problem page. This section describes a problem page.

Remember, you don't have to retype the code in Listings 10-3 and 10-4. You can download the code from this book's Web site.

1. **Create a project containing the code in Listings 10-3 and 10-4.**

2. **Select the** `computeTax` **method in Listing 10-3, and then choose Refactor⇨Move.**

   Eclipse opens the Move Static Members parameter page. (See Figure 10-7.)

Figure 10-7: Preparing to move a static method.

> **Move Static Members**
>
> Destination type for 'computeTax(double)':
>
> `CashRegister` ▼   Browse...
>
> Preview >   OK   Cancel

3. **Type** CashRegister **in the Destination Type field.**

   When you type **CashRegister** you tell Eclipse that you want to move the `computeTax` method to the code in Listing 10-4.

4. **Click OK.**

   Oh, oh! Eclipse shows you the problem page of Figure 10-8. According to this problem page, moving `computeTax` to the `CashRegister` class may not be a good idea. After all, the `computeTax` method refers to a `taxRate` field. The code inside the `CashRegister` class can't access that private `taxRate` field. And Eclipse isn't willing to drag the `taxRate` declaration to the `CashRegister` class for you.

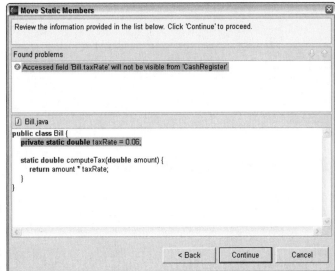

Figure 10-8:
A problem
page.

5. Live dangerously. In spite of everything that you see in the problem page, click Continue.

When you click Continue, Eclipse bows reluctantly to your wishes. But the new refactored code has errors, as you can see in Figure 10-9.

Of course, for a short time, you may be able to tolerate a few errors. If you cut and paste instead of refactoring, you probably have some errors to clean up anyway. Good refactoring means going from correct code to correct code (without having any incorrect code in between). But sometimes you can't afford to do good refactoring. That's when the Continue button on the problem page comes in handy.

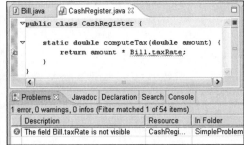

Figure 10-9:
The sad
result of
ignoring the
problem
page's
advice.

Listing 10-3:   The File Bill.java

```
public class Bill {
    private static double taxRate = 0.06;

    static double computeTax(double amount) {
        return amount * taxRate;
    }
}
```

Listing 10-4:   An Empty Cash Register

```
public class CashRegister {
}
```

More Gossip about Refactoring

All of Eclipse's refactoring actions share a few interesting (and sometimes bothersome) traits. This section lists a few of those traits.

Selecting something

Here's a quote from an Eclipse Help page: "In a Java view or in the Java editor, select the method that you want to move." For my money, this instruction is a bit vague. What does it mean to "select a method?" If you're selecting text in the editor, do you select the method's header, the method's name, the method body, or a method call?

Mind you, I'm not complaining about the Help page instruction. I'm just making an observation. Whoever wrote the instruction volunteered his or her time to create Eclipse documentation. So to whoever wrote this instruction I say "Thanks. Now allow me to clarify."

✔ **For a Java element, "select" can mean "click a tree branch in a view."**

Eclipse has this notion of *Java elements.* A Java element is something that can appear as a branch in a view's tree. A method is one of Eclipse's Java elements. So if I say "select a method," you can find that method's branch in the Package Explorer or Outline view, and click the branch.

For more info on Java elements, see Chapter 8.

✔ **For a Java element or for something that isn't a Java element, "select" can mean clicking once inside the editor.**

For instance, you click between the a and the i in main, and then choose Refactor➪Move. Then Eclipse offers to move the main method to a different class.

The same thing happens if you select the `main` branch of the Package Explorer's tree, and then choose Refactor⇨Move. Eclipse offers to move the `main` method.

You can select a branch or click a word. In this example, it makes no difference.

✔ **For a Java element or for something that isn't a Java element, "select" can also mean highlighting text.**

In the editor, you double-click the word `main`. In response, Eclipse highlights that word in the editor. Next, you choose Refactor⇨Move. Then Eclipse offers to move the `main` method.

Alternatively, you sweep your mouse from the `p` in `public static void main` to the close curly brace that ends the `main` method's body. Again, Eclipse offers to move the `main` method.

When you sweep your mouse across the `main` method's body, don't include any characters before the `p` in `public`. No, don't even include the blank space before the word `public`. If you include that blank space, Eclipse thinks you're trying to move the entire class, not just the `main` method.

Here's another example: A single statement isn't a Java element, so you can't find a statement in the Package Explorer or the Outline view. But sweep your mouse across a statement and then choose Refactor⇨ Extract Method. In response, Eclipse offers to create a new method containing that statement.

✔ **In many cases, selecting any reference to an item is like selecting the entire item.**

Look again at Listing 10-1, and imagine that both `MyClass` and `MyOther Class` have `int i` declarations. If you apply Pull Up refactoring to either `MyClass` or `MyOtherClass`, Eclipse offers to pull `i` out of *both* `MyClass` *and* `MyOtherClass`.

✔ **In many cases, selecting text is the same as selecting neighboring text.**

For example, you select the word `allmycode` in the line

```
import com.allmycode.gui.MyFrame;
```

and then choose Refactor⇨Rename. Then Eclipse offers to rename `com.allmycode`. But select the word `allmycode` in the line

```
new com.allmycode.gui.MyFrame();
```

and then choose Refactor⇨Rename. Then Eclipse offers to rename `MyFrame`.

So be careful what you select, for Eclipse may rename it.

When I describe refactoring, I get tired of writing long-winded instructions — instructions like "Click your mouse, highlight a word in the editor, or select a branch in a view's tree." What's worse, you can easily get tired of reading long-winded instructions. So instead of repeating these alternatives over and over again, I write simple instructions — instructions like "select a method" or "select a declaration." If you want to read about alternative selection techniques, or if you run into trouble selecting anything, just refer back to this section for all the gory details.

Why is that menu item gray?

A particular refactoring action works on some kinds of Java elements, and doesn't work on other kinds. To see this, select a .java file in the Package Explorer tree, and then choose Refactor from Eclipse's main menu bar. When you do this, most actions in the Refactor menu are grayed out. The only actions that you can apply are the few that aren't grayed out.

In many instances, actions that aren't grayed out are still not usable. For example, try selecting a method's name in the method's header. (Select the word main in public static void main.) Then choose Refactor➪Generalize Type. Eclipse responds by telling you that your text selection isn't suitable for the Generalize Type action. (See Figure 10-10.)

Figure 10-10:
Sorry, you can't generalize something that's not a type.

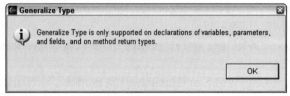

After making a selection, you can get *some* information on the permissible refactoring actions by pressing Alt+Shift+T. This keyboard shortcut creates a context menu containing (more or less) the refactoring actions that apply to your selection. (See Figure 10-11.)

Figure 10-11:
Pressing Alt+Shift+T.

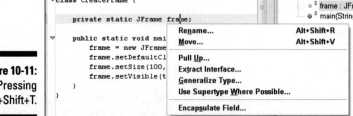

The trouble is, some actions that aren't applicable can creep into the Alt+ Shift+T context menu. Look again at Figure 10-11, and notice the context menu's Pull Up option. You can't use this Pull Up option because the class in Figure 10-11 has no `extends` clause. If you want to pull something upward, you have no place to go. So much for one of the actions in the Alt+Shift+T menu!

The class in Figure 10-11 extends `java.lang.Object`. But for the purpose of Pull Up refactoring, extending `java.lang.Object` doesn't count. Eclipse doesn't normally store the `java.lang.Object` source code, so Eclipse isn't willing to pull a declaration up to the `java.lang.Object` level.

Calling Eclipse's bluff

Some actions that don't look like refactoring are refactoring actions in disguise. Other Eclipse actions look like refactoring, but aren't really refactoring. Here are some examples:

✔ **Select a branch in the Package Explorer. Then choose File➪Rename.**

Even though File➪Rename isn't part of Eclipse's Refactor menu, File➪ Rename is a refactoring action. Choosing File➪Rename is the same as choosing Refactor➪Rename. When you choose File➪Rename, you see the usual parameter, preview, and problem pages. Also, any action you take as a result of choosing File➪Rename gets placed on Eclipse's big Undo stack. (By choosing Refactor➪Undo, you can reverse the effects of choosing File➪Rename.)

This File➪Rename trick can be confusing. After going to the editor and selecting a name inside the source code, you can't use File➪Rename. Eclipse grays out that option unless your most recent click is on a Package Explorer branch.

✔ **Select a non-static field declaration, like the `int i = 10;` declaration. Then choose Refactor➪Move.**

The Move refactoring action can't move non-static fields. So Eclipse offers to do a *textual move*. With this textual move, Eclipse drags the `int i` declaration from one class to another. But Eclipse doesn't do its usual refactoring chores. In the process of textually moving `int i`, Eclipse doesn't bother to scan your code for references to the variable `i`.

If things go wrong as a result of a textual move, if some references to `i` are left dangling, if moving `int i` breaks your code, then that's just too bad. With a textual move, any undesirable after effects are your fault, not Eclipse's fault. You asked for a textual move, so you got one.

Textual changes remind me of alphabet soup. I have thousands of letters floating around in a greasy, nebulous broth. And if by accident I manage to spell a word correctly, it's a miracle.

✔ **Open the Resource perspective. Right-click a branch in the Navigator view's tree. Then, in the resulting context menu, select Rename.**

In response, Eclipse does what many operating systems do when you start renaming something on a branch of a tree. Eclipse creates a tiny, one-line editor for the label on that branch.

So type a new name inside that little editor, and then press Enter. Eclipse does a *textual rename*. That is, Eclipse changes the name of a file or a folder, but doesn't update any references to the name. Like the textual move, the textual rename isn't a refactoring action. If you want refactored renaming, you can't start in the Navigator view.

If you stop and think about it, the Navigator view and textual renaming go hand-in-hand. After all, the Navigator view is part of the Resource perspective, and the Resource perspective isn't much like the Java perspective. Whereas the Java perspective deals with Java elements (classes, methods, fields, and those kinds of things) the Resource perspective deals with big lumps on your hard drive — lumps such as files, folders, and projects. The Resource perspective (along with its friend the Navigator view) isn't supposed to be smart about package names and other Java-specific things. So when you rename something in the Navigator view, Eclipse doesn't bother to consider the overall Java picture. In other words, Eclipse does textual renaming, not refactored renaming.

Chapter 11

Refactor This!

· ·

· ·

*I*magine yourself working on a large Java application. The application involves several people or even several teams. Some people are in nearby cubicles, on opposite sides of those gloomy partitions. Other people working on the application are halfway around the world. You write code that counts wombats in Australia. A colleague writes code that analyzes your wombat count. Then you write code that uses your colleague's analysis.

What a tangled web you weave! When you change `wmbtCnt` to `wombatCount`, your colleague's analysis code falls apart at the seams. Your code (which uses the analysis code) also stops running. Your computer hangs, and that causes the server in the back office to crash, and that causes your Java-enabled coffee pot to brew decaf instead of regular. As a result, you fall asleep and miss a deadline.

Yes, things can be very complicated. But no, things aren't unmanageable. When you write small programs or big applications, Eclipse's refactoring tools keep track of all the cross-references. If you change things in one part of an application, Eclipse automatically changes things in another part. With all the ripple effects under control, you can manage the tangled web of references, cross-references, and cross-cross-references in your code. You can concentrate on the application's overall logic (or you can have more time to goof off and surf the other kind of web).

What Am I Doing Here in Chapter 11?

Chapter 10 emphasizes some features that all refactoring actions have in common. For example, all refactoring operations start with your selection of something in an editor or a view. And almost all refactoring actions involve the three Ps: a parameter page, a preview page, and in the worst cases, a problem page.

This chapter takes a slightly different approach. In this chapter, I list Eclipse's refactoring actions, and describe each action in some detail. I gloss over the things refactoring actions have in common. That way, you don't have to read about things like the "parameter, preview, problem page" cycle over and over again.

Remember, you don't have to retype the code in this chapter's listings. You can download the code from this book's Web site.

Renaming Things

To rename a Java element, select the element and then choose Refactor⇨ Rename. Now, the resulting parameter page differs depending on the kind of element that you select, but in more than a few cases the parameter page is going to have the check boxes shown in Figure 11-1.

Figure 11-1:
A parameter
page for
renaming.

To see what these check boxes do, look at Listing 11-1.

Listing 11-1:   Rename of the Rose

```
/*
 * MyFrame.java
 *
 * Thanks to rose friedman for her help in creating this code
 */

import java.awt.Color;
import java.awt.Image;
import java.awt.Toolkit;

import javax.swing.JFrame;

public class MyFrame extends JFrame {

    MyImagePanel panel = null;

    final Color rose = new Color(255, 0, 100);

    public MyFrame() {
        Image rose =
          Toolkit.getDefaultToolkit().getImage("rose.jpg");
        panel = new MyImagePanel(rose);
    }

    public void changeBackground() {
        setBackground(rose);
    }
}
```

Suppose you select the word rose in the final Color rose = new Color(255, 0, 100) declaration. Then you choose Refactor⇨Rename, wait for the parameter page in Figure 11-1 to appear and then enter **violet** in the page's New Name field. Here's what happens when you check or uncheck the boxes in Figure 11-1:

   ✔ If you leave the Update References box checked and then accept everything in the preview, Eclipse changes the following two lines:

```
final Color violet = new Color(255, 0, 100);

setBackground(violet);
```

   Eclipse doesn't change any occurrences of the word rose inside the MyFrame constructor. (Eclipse understands that you can have different variables, both named rose.)

   ✔ If you uncheck the Update References box and then accept everything in the preview, Eclipse doesn't change the name in the call to setBackground:

```
final Color violet = new Color(255, 0, 100);

setBackground(rose);
```

When you don't check the Update References box, Eclipse modifies only the occurrence that you select.

✔ If you check the Update Textual Matches in Comments and Strings box and accept everything in the preview, Eclipse makes the following changes:

```
Thanks to violet friedman for her help in creating ...

final Color violet = new Color(255, 0, 100);

Toolkit.getDefaultToolkit().getImage("violet.jpg");
```

Even with this Update Textual Matches in Comments and Strings box checked, Eclipse doesn't change variables inside the `MyFrame` method. Eclipse doesn't change `Image rose` to `Image violet`, and doesn't change `new MyImagePanel(rose)` to `new MyImagePanel(violet)`.

While hunting for text in comments and strings, Eclipse ignores everything except whole words. In this example, Eclipse doesn't consider changing `System.out.print("rosey")` to `System.out.print("violety")`.

✔ If you leave the Update Textual Matches in Comments and Strings box unchecked and accept everything in the preview, Eclipse leaves `rose friedman` and her buddy `"rose.jpg"` alone. In this case, Eclipse doesn't change `rose` words inside comments or strings.

Eclipse's Rename refactoring is very smart. For example, when you rename an interface's abstract method, Eclipse hunts down all implementations of that method and applies renaming to those implementations.

Moving Things

When I was new to object-oriented programming, I obsessed over questions about where things should go. For instance, when you pay an employee, you write a check. You use a `PayrollCheck` object. Should a `PayrollCheck` object contain its own `write()` method, or should a `DoPayroll` object contain a `write(PayrollCheck check)` method?

These days I don't worry about those issues so much, but I still change my mind as I develop a project's code. I discover things that didn't occur to me during the design phase, so I move Java elements from one part of my application to another. Fortunately, Eclipse helps.

Hiring a mover

Consider the code in Listings 11-2 and 11-3. The `PayrollCheck` class defines what it means to be a check (something that an employee can take to the bank). And the `DoPayroll` class writes checks.

Listing 11-2:   What Is a PayrollCheck?

```
package com.allmycode.payroll;

public class PayrollCheck {
    public String name;

    public double amount;

    public PayrollCheck(String name, double amount) {
        super();
        this.name = name;
        this.amount = amount;
    }
}
```

Listing 11-3:   Who Writes a PayrollCheck?

```
package com.allmycode.accounting;

import com.allmycode.payroll.PayrollCheck;

public class DoPayroll {

    public static void main(String[] args) {
        new DoPayroll().write
            (new PayrollCheck("Barry", 100.00));
    }

    public void write(PayrollCheck check) {
        drawCompanyLogo();
        System.out.print("Pay ");
        System.out.print(check.amount);
        System.out.print(" to ");
        System.out.println(check.name);
    }

    public void drawCompanyLogo() {
        System.out.println("**Our Logo**");
    }
}
```

The code in Listings 11-2 and 11-3 raises some stylistic questions. Why should the DoPayroll class take responsibility for writing a check? Why not have the PayrollCheck class write its own darn check?

After thinking about these issues for three whole seconds, you decide to move the write method to the PayrollCheck class. To do this, select the write method, and then choose Refactor⇨Move. Eclipse gives you the parameter page in Figure 11-2. (The parameter page can be confusing, so I give it my undivided attention in this chapter's "Dissecting a parameter page" section.)

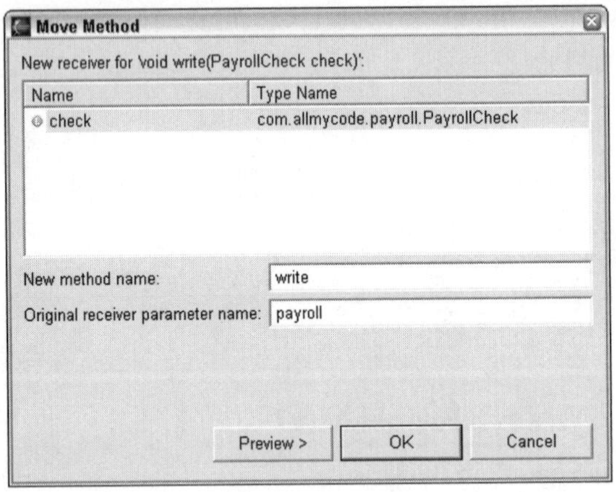

Figure 11-2:
Moving a non-static method.

When you click Preview, you see all the things that happen with just one application of the Move action. (See Figure 11-3.)

If you leave all the preview page's boxes checked, you end up with the code in Listings 11-4 and 11-5.

Figure 11-3:
Many things change when you move a non-static method.

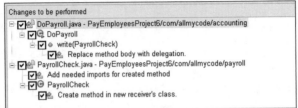

Listing 11-4:   A Check that Writes Itself

```
package com.allmycode.payroll;

import com.allmycode.accounting.DoPayroll;

public class PayrollCheck {
    public String name;

    public double amount;

    public PayrollCheck(String name, double amount) {
        super();
        this.name = name;
        this.amount = amount;
    }

    public void write(DoPayroll payroll) {
        payroll.drawCompanyLogo();
        System.out.print("Pay ");
        System.out.print(amount);
        System.out.print(" to ");
        System.out.println(name);
    }
}
```

Listing 11-5:   Streamlined Work for the Payroll Department

```
package com.allmycode.accounting;

import com.allmycode.payroll.PayrollCheck;

public class DoPayroll {

    public static void main(String[] args) {
        new DoPayroll().write
            (new PayrollCheck("Barry", 100.00));
    }

    public void write(PayrollCheck check) {
        check.write(this);
    }

    public void drawCompanyLogo() {
        System.out.println("**Our Logo**");
    }
}
```

Dissecting a parameter page

If you look back at the parameter page in Figure 11-2, you see things like "New receiver" (right there at the top) and "Original receiver" (right around the middle). Personally, I find this receiver terminology confusing. So in the next several bullets, I untangle some of the confusion. As you read the bullets, you can follow along in Figure 11-4.

- ✔ A *receiver* **is a class that contains, at one time or another, whatever method you're trying to move.**

  In this example, you're trying to move the `write` method so you have *two* receivers — the `DoPayroll` class and the `PayrollCheck` class.

- ✔ **The** *original receiver* **is the class that contains the method before refactoring.**

  In this example, the original receiver is the `DoPayroll` class.

- ✔ **The** *new receiver* **is the class that contains the method after refactoring.**

  In this example, the new receiver is the `PayrollCheck` class. To be contrary, I like to call `PayrollCheck` the *destination* class. (The `write` method is moving, and the `PayrollCheck` class is the method's destination.)

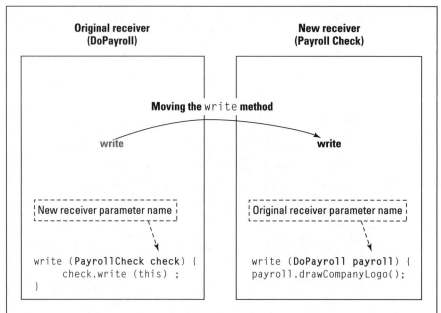

Figure 11-4:
Receivers
everywhere.

With that in mind, you can read about the roles that the fields in Figure 11-2 play:

- ✔ **The New Receiver list offers a choice of destinations for the method that you plan to move.**

  This example has only one possible choice — move the `write` method to the `PayrollCheck` class.

- ✔ **The New Receiver list also tells you how other classes refer to the destination class.**

  In Figure 11-2, the Name part of the New Receiver list contains the word `check`. Sure enough, after refactoring, the newly formed `write` method in Listing 11-5 has a `PayrollCheck check` parameter. In other words, Listing 11-5 refers to a `PayrollCheck` instance with a `check` parameter.

- ✔ **The New Method Name field tells you the name of the method after being moved to the destination.**

  If you change the name `write` to the name `bubbleblinger` in Figure 11-2, then Eclipse creates a `bubbleblinger` method in the `PayrollCheck` class's code.

- ✔ **The Original Receiver Parameter Name field tells you how other classes refer to the original receiver class (to the class containing the method before refactoring).**

  In Figure 11-2, the Original Receiver Parameter Name field contains the word `payroll`. Sure enough, after refactoring, the reworked `write` method in Listing 11-4 has a `DoPayroll payroll` parameter. In other words, Listing 11-4 refers to a `DoPayroll` instance with a `payroll` parameter.

An immovable object meets irresistible source

The year is 1979. The place is Milwaukee, Wisconsin. I'm moving from a one-room apartment to a larger place three streets away. Like any other one-room apartment, my apartment contains an upright piano.

The piano has its own tiny furniture wheels and my friends are collected to help me roll the thing through busy Milwaukee streets. But it's a rickety old piano. Any twisting force will tear the piano apart. (If half the piano is resting on the sidewalk and the other half is dangling over the edge onto the street, the piano can bend until it's in two pieces. That's how old this piano is.)

So what do I do? I call the *Milwaukee Journal* and tell the editor to send over a photographer. Certainly five people rolling a wobbly piano down Prospect Avenue makes a good human-interest story. Besides, if the piano collapses, the newspaper gets an even better story.

So what's the point? The point is, some things are meant to be moved. Other things aren't.

The Refactor⇨Move action can move only certain kinds of Java elements. Unfortunately, the list of movable elements isn't easy to remember until you get practice moving things. For example, the rules governing the movement of static methods are quite different from the rules for non-static methods.

But the idea underlying all the rules makes sense. The Move action wants to turn your valid code into other valid code. So if you ask Eclipse to move something that can't easily be kept valid, Eclipse balks. At that point, you fall back on things like good old cutting and pasting.

Here's a list of things you can move with Eclipse's refactoring action:

- ✔ Methods
- ✔ Static fields
- ✔ Classes and interfaces
- ✔ Java source files and folders
- ✔ Packages and projects

Notice some things that aren't in the list. The Move refactoring action doesn't work on non-static fields or on variables defined inside methods. The action moves some non-static methods but refuses to move others. (Of course, Eclipse's willingness to move a non-static method isn't arbitrary. It depends on the method's context in the Java program.)

The Eclipse Help page titled "Refactor actions" has a more carefully worded list of things that you can and cannot move.

Using views to move things

You can move Java elements by dragging and dropping things within views. To see this in motion, try the following:

1. **Start with the code in Listings 11-2 and 11-3.**

   This code lives in two different packages — com.allmycode.payroll and com.allmycode.accounting.

2. **In the Package Explorer, select the** `PayrollCheck` **branch.**

3. **Drag the** `PayrollCheck` **branch to the** `com.allmycode.accounting` **package's branch.**

   In response, Eclipse opens a parameter page with all the bells and whistles of any other refactoring action. If you accept everything in the preview page, Eclipse modifies the project's package declarations and input declarations. When I look at the new code, I'm really impressed!

When you move a class, file, or folder, you can't reverse the move's effects with Refactor➪Undo. Eclipse simply refuses to apply the Undo action. Of course, you can still reverse the effects of moving a class. To do so, just do a second move. Return to the Package Explorer, and drag the class back from its new package to its old package.

For many kinds of elements, dragging and dropping makes Eclipse do a textual move, not a refactored move. For example, suppose you start afresh with the code in Listings 11-2 and 11-3. In the Package Explorer, drag the `write` method from the `DoPayroll` branch to the `PayrollCheck` branch. Then Eclipse does something stupid. Eclipse cuts text from the `DoPayroll.java` file, and pastes that text into the `PayrollCheck.java` file. The result is a bunch of error-ridden code.

For more information on textual moves, see Chapter 10.

Changing a Method's Signature

The Change Method Signature refactoring action isn't complicated. It does a few things very well, but it doesn't try to do everything you may want it to do. To see what I mean, try this:

1. **Create a project containing the code in Listings 11-6 and 11-7.**

2. **Select the** `display` **method in Listing 11-6 or 11-7. Then choose Refactor➪Change Method Signature.**

   Eclipse shows you the parameter page in Figure 11-5.

3. **Click Add in the parameter page.**

   Eclipse adds a new row in the Parameters list in the Change Method Signature parameter page. The new rows entries are `Object`, `newParam`, and `null`.

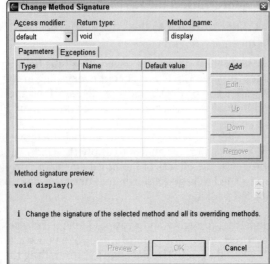

Figure 11-5:
A Change
Method
Signature
parameter
page.

4. **Select the word** *Object* **in the Type column. Replace** *Object* **with the word** String. **(See Figure 11-6.)**

Figure 11-6:
Creating a
new
parameter.

Parameters	Exceptions		
Type	Name	Default value	Add
String	whatToDisplay	"Goodbye"	Edit

5. **Repeat Step 4 twice. The first time, replace** *newParam* **with** whatToDisplay. **The second time, replace** *null* **with** "Goodbye".

6. **Click OK to dismiss the parameter page.**

Eclipse gives you the code in Listings 11-8 and 11-9.

Listing 11-6: Oh No! Another Hello Program!

```java
public class Class1 {

    public static void main(String[] args) {
        display();
    }

    static void display() {
        System.out.println("Hello");
    }
}
```

Listing 11-7:   Invoking the Hello Program

```
public class Class2 {

    public Class2() {
        super();
        Class1.display();
    }
}
```

Listing 11-8:   A Refactored Version of Listing 11-6

```
public class Class1 {

    public static void main(String[] args) {
        display("Goodbye");
    }

    static void display(String whatToDisplay) {
        System.out.println("Hello");
    }
}
```

Listing 11-9:   The Refactoring of Listing 11-7

```
public class Class2 {

    public Class2() {
        super();
        Class1.display("Goodbye");
    }
}
```

Eclipse changes the display method's signature, and fills any display method call with whatever *default value* you specify in Figure 11-6. Of course, Eclipse doesn't change everything. Eclipse has no way of knowing that you intend to replace "Hello" with whatToDisplay in the System.out.println call.

Try the same experiment again, this time asking Eclipse to change the display method's return type. (See Figure 11-7.)

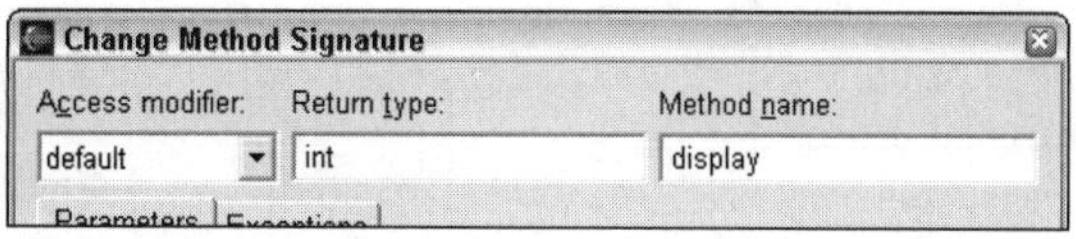

Figure 11-7:
Changing a
method's
return type
to int.

When you click OK, Eclipse shows you the problem page of Figure 11-8. The bad news is, Eclipse doesn't plan to add a return statement at the bottom of the display method. And Eclipse doesn't change the call

```
display();
```

to a call like

```
int returnValue = display();
```

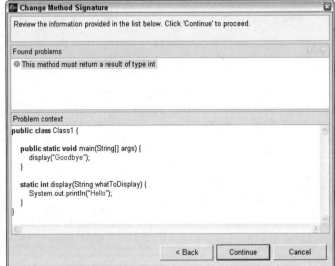

Figure 11-8:
Excuse me.
Eclipse says
you have a
problem.

Kicking Inner Classes Out

This section introduces two refactoring actions that do (more or less) the same thing. One action starts a trend, and the other action continues the trend. In this case the trend is to pull class definitions from being inside things to being outside of things.

Listing 11-10 contains an anonymous inner class named . . . Well, the class doesn't have a name. That's why they call it "anonymous." Anyway, to my mind, an anonymous inner class is more "inner" than a named inner class. So the first step in pulling out the class is to change it from being anonymous to being an ordinary named inner class.

Listing 11-10:   As "Inner" as Inner Classes Get

```
package com.allmycode.gui;

import java.awt.event.WindowAdapter;
import java.awt.event.WindowEvent;

import javax.swing.JFrame;

class CreateFrame {

    static JFrame frame;

    public static void main(String args[]) {
        frame = new JFrame();
        frame.addWindowListener(new WindowAdapter() {
            public void windowClosing(WindowEvent e) {
                frame.dispose();
                System.exit(0);
            }
        });
        frame.setSize(100, 100);
        frame.setVisible(true);
    }
}
```

Don't be fooled by Eclipse's folding mechanism. By default, whenever you open the code in Listing 11-9, the editor folds any inner classes. In the marker bar, you see a rightward pointing arrow. And in place of the folded code, you see a little rectangle. (The rectangle has two dots inside it. See Figure 11-9.) If you don't expect the folding, you may not realize that the code has an inner class. To unfold the class, click the little arrow in the editor's marker bar. To make sure that this automatic folding doesn't happen again, visit the Folding tab of the Java⇨Editor page in the Window⇨Preferences dialog. On that page you can disable auto folding for certain kinds of things, or disable auto folding altogether.

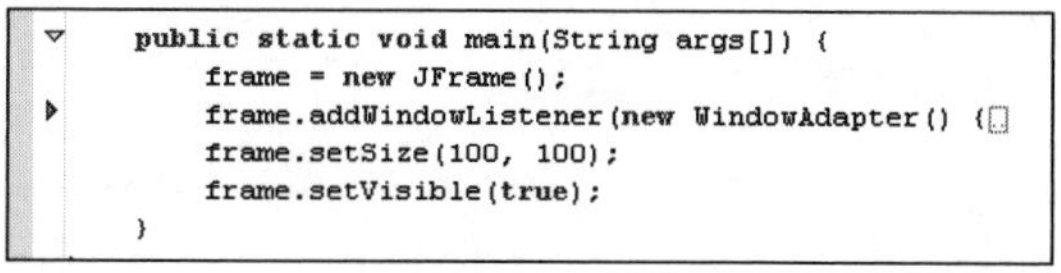

Figure 11-9:
A folded
inner class.

```
▽      public static void main(String args[]) {
           frame = new JFrame();
▸          frame.addWindowListener(new WindowAdapter() {▢
           frame.setSize(100, 100);
           frame.setVisible(true);
       }
```

For details on folding, see Chapter 6.

To give the anonymous class in Listing 11-10 a name, select that anonymous class, and then choose Refactor⇨Convert Anonymous Class to Nested. In response, Eclipse gives you the mercifully simple parameter page of Figure 11-10.

Figure 11-10: A parameter page for the Convert Anonymous Class to Nested action.

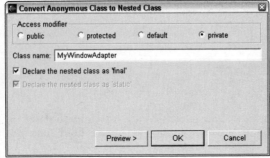

Clicking OK in Figure 11-10 gives you the code of Listing 11-11.

Listing 11-11:   Your Inner Class Is No Longer Anonymous

```java
package com.allmycode.gui;

import java.awt.event.WindowAdapter;
import java.awt.event.WindowEvent;

import javax.swing.JFrame;

class CreateFrame {

    private static final class MyWindowAdapter
            extends WindowAdapter {

        public void windowClosing(WindowEvent e) {
            frame.dispose();
            System.exit(0);

        }
    }

    static JFrame frame;

    public static void main(String args[]) {
        frame = new JFrame();
        frame.addWindowListener(new MyWindowAdapter());
        frame.setSize(100, 100);
        frame.setVisible(true);
    }
}
```

If the `MyWindowAdapter` class doesn't feel too uncomfortable being exposed as it is in Listing 11-11, you can take things a step further. You can send the class out into the world on its own. To do this, select the `MyWindowAdapter` class in Listing 11-11, and then choose Refactor⇨Move Member Type to New File.

After choosing this Move Member Type to New File action, you're in for a real shock. What? No parameter page? All you get is a preview page!

So click OK in the preview page. In response Eclipse hands you the code in Listings 11-12 and 11-13.

Listing 11-12:   Exposing a Class to the Great Outdoors

```
package com.allmycode.gui;

import java.awt.event.WindowAdapter;
import java.awt.event.WindowEvent;


final class MyWindowAdapter extends WindowAdapter {
    public void windowClosing(WindowEvent e) {
        CreateFrame.frame.dispose();
        System.exit(0);
    }
}
```

Listing 11-13:   Calling the Newly Created Class

```
package com.allmycode.gui;

import java.awt.event.WindowAdapter;
import java.awt.event.WindowEvent;

import javax.swing.JFrame;

class CreateFrame {

    static JFrame frame;

    public static void main(String args[]) {
        frame = new JFrame();
        frame.addWindowListener(new MyWindowAdapter());
        frame.setSize(100, 100);
        frame.setVisible(true);
    }
}
```

In order for Move Member Type to New File to work, certain names have to be accessible outside of their classes. Just to be ornery, go back to Listing 11-11, and add the word **private** to the `static JFrame frame;` declaration. Then select `MyWindowAdapter`, and perform a Move Member Type to New File operation. When the dust settles, you have bad code. After all, the `MyWindowAdapter` class in Listing 11-12 refers to the `CreateFrame.frame` field. If the `frame` field is private, this reference doesn't work.

Pulling Up; Pushing Down

When I was a young lad, I strengthened my arm muscles doing pull ups and push ups. But when I reached middle age, I gave up on my arm muscles. Instead of pull ups and push ups, I did Pull Ups and Push Downs. Eclipse can't make me look better on the beach, but it can help me move things from one Java class to another.

For examples of Pull Up and Push Down refactoring, see Chapter 10.

Extracting an Interface

Here's a common scenario. You have a class that you use over and over again. Many other classes use the functionality that this class provides. Your `JFrame` subclasses use this class; your `Account` subclasses use this class; all kinds of things use this class in new and unexpected situations. So useful is this class that you want other classes to share its wealth. Somehow, you feel that this class should be living in a higher plane (whatever that means).

So you decide to create an interface. Each of those other classes can implement your new interface. Best of all, your `MyJFrame` class can continue to extend `javax.swing.JFrame` while it implements the new interface.

So start with a useful class, like the one in Listing 11-14.

Listing 11-14:   Love Nest

```
package com.allmycode.feelings;

public class Love {

    public void happiness() {
        System.out.println("Love me; love my code.");
    }
```

```
    public void misery() {
        System.out.print("When all else fails,");
        System.out.println(" become manipulative.");
        startAllOverAgain(new Love());
    }

    void startAllOverAgain(Love love) {
        love.happiness();
    }
}
```

To see how useful the Love class is, look at all the references to Love in Listing 11-15.

Listing 11-15:   Calling the Code of Listing 11-14

```
import com.allmycode.feelings.Love;

public class MakeLoveNotWar {

    public static void main(String[] args) {
        Love love = new Love();
        love.happiness();
        love.misery();
    }
}
```

Select the Love class, and then choose Refactor⇨Extract Interface. Eclipse answers with the parameter page in Figure 11-11. Among other things, the parameter page offers to declare two methods in the new interface. The page also offers to change some outside references to the Love class.

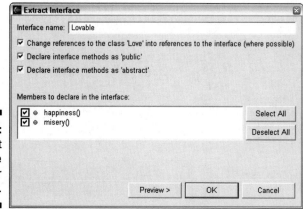

Figure 11-11:
An Extract Interface parameter page.

In deciding which methods to propose for the new interface, Eclipse looks for methods that are public. If a method isn't already public, then the method doesn't appear in the Members to Declare in the Interface list. That's why, in Figure 11-11, the happiness and misery methods appear in the list, but the startAllOverAgain method doesn't.

In Figure 11-11, I assign the name Lovable to my new interface. I confess, when I constructed this example, I was looking for parallels to established Java API interface names — names like Runnable, Cloneable, and Serializable. I got caught up in the whole Love/Lovable business and the result was the goofy code in Listing 11-14.

Anyway, click OK to the stuff in Figure 11-11, and you get the code in Listings 11-16 through 11-18.

Listing 11-16:   My, You Have a Lovable Interface!

```
package com.allmycode.feelings;

public interface Lovable {
    public abstract void happiness();

    public abstract void misery();
}
```

Listing 11-17:   Me? I Have a Lovable Implementation.

```
package com.allmycode.feelings;

public class Love implements Lovable {

    public void happiness() {
        System.out.println("Love me; love my code.");
    }

    public void misery() {
        System.out.print("When all else fails,");
        System.out.println(" become manipulative.");
        startAllOverAgain(new Love());
    }

    void startAllOverAgain(Lovable love) {
        love.happiness();
    }
}
```

Listing 11-18:   I Love Both Listings 11-16 and 11-17.

```
import com.allmycode.feelings.Lovable;
import com.allmycode.feelings.Love;

public class MakeLoveNotWar {

    public static void main(String[] args) {
        Lovable love = new Love();
        love.happiness();
        love.misery();
    }
}
```

Eclipse creates the Lovable interface and makes the Love class implement the Lovable interface. In addition, Eclipse changes Love to Lovable wherever possible in the code. Because interfaces don't have constructors, and new Lovable() wouldn't make sense, Eclipse leaves things like new Love() alone.

Eclipse dodges bullets

The Extract Interface refactoring action is pretty smart. (This action would get good grades in a computer programming course.) For example, in Figure 11-11 I check both the happiness and misery boxes. That's great, but what happens if I check only the happiness box as in Figure 11-12? Then Eclipse creates a Lovable interface containing only one method. (See Listing 11-19.)

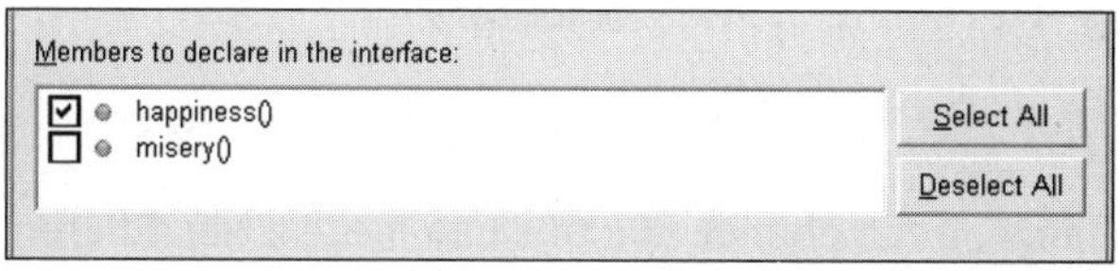

Figure 11-12:
Excluding a
member
from the
interface.

```
Members to declare in the interface:
☑ ● happiness()                          Select All
☐ ● misery()
                                         Deselect All
```

Listing 11-19:   An Interface with Only One Member

```
public interface Lovable {
    public abstract void happiness();
}
```

With the feeble interface in Listing 11-19, the following code (from Listing 11-18) isn't legal:

```
Lovable love = new Love();
love.happiness();
love.misery();
```

So Eclipse avoids this pitfall. With only one method in Listing 11-19, the Extract Interface refactoring action doesn't change `Love` to `Lovable` inside the `MakeLoveNotWar` class.

Even with the skimpy interface of Listing 11-19, the following code from Listing 11-17 is legal:

```
void startAllOverAgain(Lovable love) {
    love.happiness();
}
```

So with the choices in Figure 11-12, Eclipse changes `Love` to `Lovable` in the `startAllOverAgain` method's parameter list.

Promoting types

Suppose your code contains the following declaration

```
MyFrame frame = new MyFrame();
```

and that `MyFrame` is a subclass of Java's `JFrame` class. Knowing about all the code that uses `JFrame`, you decide to make the declaration a bit more versatile. You change `MyFrame` to `JFrame` as follows:

```
JFrame frame = new MyFrame();
```

It's not a big change, but a change like this can make a big difference in the amount of casting you have to do later.

Eclipse provides two refactoring actions to help with such things. The weaker of the two actions is Generalize Type, and the stronger is Use Supertype Where Possible.

To see how this stuff works, look over the code in Listings 11-20 through 11-23.

Listing 11-20:   A Parent Class

```
public class MySuperclass {
    int i;
}
```

Listing 11-21:   A Class

```
public class MyClass extends MySuperclass {
}
```

Listing 11-22:   Another Parent Class

```
public class OtherSuperclass {
}
```

Listing 11-23:   Help! I'm Running Out of Ideas for Code Listing Titles!

```
public class OtherClass extends OtherSuperclass {

    void doSomething() {
        MyClass mine1 = new MyClass();
        MyClass mine2 = new MyClass();
        OtherClass other1 = new OtherClass();
        OtherClass other2 = new OtherClass();
        mine1.i = 55;
    }
}
```

Now try these experiments:

- **Select `mine1` in Listing 11-23. Then choose Refactor⇨Generalize Type.**

  After the usual round of parameter pages and preview pages, Eclipse gives you the following modified code:

  ```
  MySuperclass mine1 = new MyClass();
  MyClass mine2 = new MyClass();
  ```

  Eclipse changes the `mine1` variable's type, but doesn't change any other types. Heck, Eclipse doesn't even call the `MySuperclass` constructor.

- **Select `other1` in Listing 11-23. Then choose Refactor⇨Generalize Type.**

  Eclipse does the same kind of thing that it does in the previous bullet. You end up with

  ```
  OtherSuperclass other1 = new OtherClass();
  OtherClass other2 = new OtherClass();
  ```

- **Starting with the code in Listing 11-23, select `OtherClass`. Then choose Refactor⇨Use Supertype Where Possible.**

  After parameter paging and previewing, Eclipse gives you the following modified code:

  ```
  MyClass mine1 = new MyClass();
  MyClass mine2 = new MyClass();
  OtherSuperclass other1 = new OtherClass();
  OtherSuperclass other2 = new OtherClass();
  ```

Eclipse changes one or more occurrences of `OtherClass` to `OtherSuperclass`. In this case, Eclipse doesn't fiddle with references to `MyClass`.

In my version of Eclipse, the Use Supertype Where Possible action suffers from a behavioral fluke. If I don't opt to see the preview page, Eclipse sends me into what seems to be an unending parameter page loop. After the first parameter page, I see the words "no possible updates found." And Eclipse performs the refactoring action, even if I click Cancel. If I pay even the most cursory visit to the preview page, none of this strange behavior happens.

✔ **Move the `int i` declaration from `MySuperclass` to `MyClass`. (That is, move the declaration from Listing 11-20 to Listing 11-21.) Then redo the experiment in the first of these four bullets.**

Surprise! Eclipse nags you with a page like the one in Figure 11-13. Because your code contains the line

```
mine1.i = 55;
```

Eclipse refuses to change the declaration of `mine1`. Changing the declaration to `MySuperclass mine1` would create invalid code.

Figure 11-13:
Sorry!
In this
example,
you can't
generalize
a type.

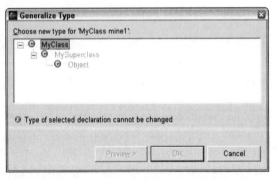

This section's refactoring actions complement the Pull Up and Push Down actions. After all, with Pull Up, Push Down, and this section's actions, Eclipse bounces things back and forth between classes and their superclasses. Often, when I invoke Generalize Type or Use Supertype Where Possible, I find myself using Pull Up or Push Down soon afterward.

Moving Code In and Out of Methods

What? You're tired of retyping code? The old cut-and-paste routine makes you queasy? Then take heart. Eclipse's Inline and Extract Method actions come to the rescue.

Start with the code in Listing 11-24. Notice the ugly repetition of all the `System.out.println` calls.

Listing 11-24:   Repetitious Code

```
public class Account {
    String name;

    double balance;

    void doDeposit(double amount) {
        balance += amount;
        System.out.println("Name:                " + name);
        System.out.println("Transaction amount: " + amount);
        System.out.println("Ending balance:      " + balance);
    }

    void doWithdrawl(double amount) {
        balance -= amount;
        System.out.println("Name:                " + name);
        System.out.println("Transaction amount: " + amount);
        System.out.println("Ending balance:      " + balance);
    }
}
```

You can repair the ugliness in Listing 11-24. In either the `doDeposit` or the `doWithdrawl` method, select the three `System.out.println` lines with your mouse. Then choose Refactor⇨Extract Method. In response, Eclipse shows you the parameter page depicted in Figure 11-14.

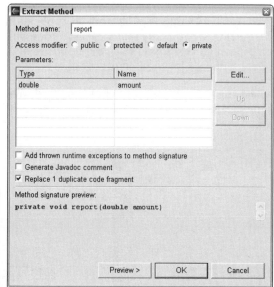

Figure 11-14:
An Extract
Method
parameter
page.

In Figure 11-14, notice the little Replace 1 Duplicate Code Fragment check box. Eclipse sees two identical copies of all the `System.out.println` code — one copy in `doDeposit`, and another copy in `doWithdrawl`. Because Eclipse aims to please, it offers to replace both copies with a call to your new method.

If you skip the preview page (or accept everything in the preview), you get the code in Listing 11-25.

Listing 11-25:   An Improved Version of the Code in Listing 11-24

```java
public class Account {
    String name;

    double balance;

    void doDeposit(double amount) {
        balance += amount;
        report(amount);
    }

    void doWithdrawl(double amount) {
        balance -= amount;
        report(amount);
    }

    private void report(double amount) {
        System.out.println("Name:                   " + name);
        System.out.println("Transaction amount: " + amount);
        System.out.println("Ending balance:       " + balance);
    }
}
```

Sometimes you need to trim every ounce of fat from an application. You want the application to run quickly, without any unnecessary processing time for things like method calls. In such cases, you want the opposite of the Extract Method action. You want Eclipse's Inline refactoring action.

So in Listing 11-25, select the `Account` class's `report` method. When you choose Refactor⇨Inline, Eclipse answers back with the parameter page shown in Figure 11-15.

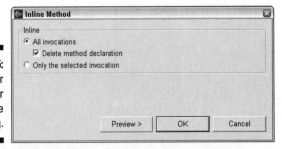

Figure 11-15:
A parameter
page for
Inline
refactoring.

If you check boxes as I do on the parameter page, the Inline refactoring action takes you right back where you started. You go from the code in Listing 11-25 back to the code in Listing 11-24. There's no place like home!

You can select the Account class's report method in many ways. If you select either method call in Listing 11-25, then Eclipse gives you an Only the Selected Invocation option (as in Figure 11-15). But if you select the report method's declaration, Eclipse grays out the Only the Selected Invocation option.

Eclipse practices conflict resolution

When you perform Inline refactoring, you merge one method's code with some other method's code. Occasionally, merging code can lead to conflicts. Take, for instance, the following snippet:

```java
void display() {
    int count = 100;
    count = increment(count);
    System.out.println(count);
}

int increment(int value) {
    for (int count = 0; count < 20; count++) {
        value *= 1.15;
    }
    return value;
}
```

If you try to move increment inline, and you're not careful, you may end up with the following incorrect code:

```java
void display() {
    int count = 100;
    int value = count;
    for (int count = 0; count < 20; count++) {
        value *= 1.15;
    }
    count = value;
    System.out.println(count);
}
```

The code is incorrect because Java doesn't let you declare a duplicate variable name inside a for loop.

But once again, Eclipse comes to the rescue. When moving `increment` inline, Eclipse automatically renames one of the `count` variables. Here's what you get:

```
void display() {
    int count = 100;
    int value = count;
    for (int count1 = 0; count1 < 20; count1++) {
        value *= 1.15;
    }
    count = value;
    System.out.println(count);
}
```

Eclipse becomes stubborn (for good reasons)

Some code doesn't want to be moved inline. Either the code is too complicated for Eclipse to move, or the code doesn't make sense when it moves inline. Take, for instance, the code in Listing 11-26.

Listing 11-26:   I Dare You to Apply Inline Refactoring to getAverage!

```
void display() {
    System.out.println(getAverage(10.0, 20.0, 30.0));
}

double getAverage(double i, double j, double k) {
    double avg = (i + j + k) / 3.0;
    return avg;
}
```

If you try to apply the Inline refactoring action to the `getAverage` method in Listing 11-26, you get nowhere at all. In fact, you get the problem page of Figure 11-16. This page tells you that the stuff in Listing 11-26 is too complicated for Eclipse's Inline refactoring action.

The question is, what's "too complicated" for Eclipse to move inline? No single thing about Listing 11-26 makes the code too complicated. Instead, it's a combination of two things:

✔ Inside the `display` method, the `getAverage` call is inside a `System.out.println` call.

   You don't just assign the call's return value to a variable.

✔ The `getAverage` method's body contains more than one statement.

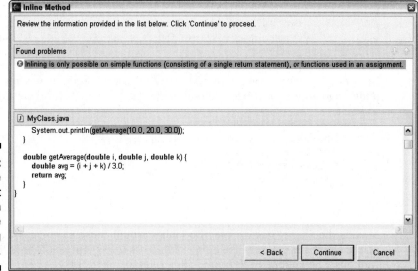

Figure 11-16:
Eclipse
can't
perform
this Inline
refactoring
operation.

Eclipse can overcome either of these stumbling blocks, but not both of them at once. Here's what happens if you remove one stumbling block at a time:

✔ Separate the `getAverage` and `System.out.println` calls in Listing 11-26:

```
void display() {
    double average = getAverage(10.0, 20.0, 30.0);
    System.out.println(average);
}

double getAverage(double i, double j, double k) {
    double avg = (i + j + k) / 3.0;
    return avg;
}
```

Then the Inline refactoring action gives you this reasonable code:

```
void display() {
    double avg = (10.0 + 20.0 + 30.0) / 3.0;
    double average = avg;
    System.out.println(average);
}
```

✔ Turn the `display` method into a one-liner:

```
void display() {
    System.out.println(getAverage(10.0, 20.0, 30.0));
}

double getAverage(double i, double j, double k) {
    return (i + j + k) / 3.0;
}
```

Then Eclipse gives you even more reasonable code:

```
void display() {
    System.out.println(((10.0 + 20.0 + 30.0) / 3.0));
}
```

In rare cases, when you try to do Inline refactoring, Eclipse may respond with a message about a *recursive call.* This means that the method contains a call to itself.

```
void chaseYourTail(int i) {
    if (i > 0) {
        chaseYourTail(i - 1);
    }
    System.out.println(i);
}
```

Moving the chaseYourTail method inline would cause an endless, nonsensical sequence of statements, like a pair of mirrors facing one another in a carnival funhouse. So Eclipse can't apply Inline refactoring to the chaseYourTail method.

If you know what recursion is, and you're trying to use it, remember that you can't move a recursive method inline. If you don't know what recursion is, and you get a "recursive call" message, please examine your code carefully. Your code probably contains some unintentional bit of self-reference.

Creating New Variables

Often, when I fish for information on the Internet, I find things that are close to what I want but not exactly what I want. For example, my daughter is taking high school chemistry. She needs to convert from Fahrenheit to Celsius. So of course, I reach for my laptop computer. After a quick search, I find the code in Listing 11-27.

Listing 11-27:   A Program Written in Sunny California

```
public class Converter {

    double fahrenheitToCelsius() {
        return (70.0 - 32.0) * 5.0 / 9.0;
    }
}
```

In Listing 11-27, 70.0 stands for the Fahrenheit temperature. But that's silly. What good is a conversion program if I can apply it to only one temperature? For plain old room temperature this code works very well. But if I want to convert values other than 70 from Fahrenheit to Celsius, this code stinks!

Maybe I should turn 70.0 into a parameter. With Eclipse, it's easy. I select 70.0 in the editor and choose Refactor⇨Introduce Parameter. Then after a few more clicks and keystrokes, I get the following improved code:

```
public class Converter {

    double fahrenheitToCelsius(double fahrenheit) {
        return (fahrenheit - 32.0) * 5.0 / 9.0;
    }
}
```

When I get started I can't stop. The freezing point of water is 32 degrees. That number hasn't changed since I was a boy. In fact, it hasn't changed since the Big Bang. So I turn that number into a constant. I select 32.0 in the editor, and then choose Refactor⇨Extract Constant. After a quick encounter with some refactoring dialogs, I get the following code:

```
public class Converter {

    private static final double FREEZING_POINT = 32.0;
    double fahrenheitToCelsius(double fahrenheit) {
        return (fahrenheit - FREEZING_POINT) * 5.0 / 9.0;
    }
}
```

Later I'll want to break down the formula inside the fahrenheitToCelsius method. So for now, I decide to assign the formula's value to a variable. Once again, the task is easy. I select the entire (fahrenheit - FREEZING_POINT) * 5.0 / 9.0 expression, and then choose Refactor⇨Extract Local Variable. Then, after another a little more clicking and typing, I get the following beautiful code:

```
public class Converter {

    private static final double FREEZING_POINT = 32.0;
    double fahrenheitToCelsius(double fahrenheit) {
        double celsius =
            (fahrenheit - FREEZING_POINT) * 5.0 / 9.0;
        return celsius;
    }
}
```

But I thought I selected an expression!

Eclipse is picky about the things you can select for this section's refactoring actions. For example, in Listing 11-27, select 5.0 / 9.0. Then try to start any of the three refactoring actions. Eclipse refuses to refactor. You see a dialog warning An expression must be selected to activate this refactoring. Hey! What's going on?

Eclipse knows that in the big conversion formula of Listing 11-27, you multiply by 5.0 before you divide by 9.0. It's as if the formula has hidden parentheses:

```
((fahrenheit - FREEZING_POINT) * 5.0) / 9.0
```

So when you select 5.0 / 9.0, Eclipse behaves as if you're selecting 5.0) / 9.0 — a string of characters that doesn't quite form a valid expression. That's why Eclipse gives you the expression must be selected error message.

Giving higher status to your variables

Here's a common situation. You declare a variable inside a method. Later, you realize that other methods need to refer to that variable. You can pass the variable from one method to another like a hot potato in a children's game. Better yet, you can turn that variable into a class-wide field.

To see an example, start with the following *incorrect* code.

```java
import java.awt.event.ActionEvent;
import java.awt.event.ActionListener;

import javax.swing.JButton;
import javax.swing.JFrame;

public class MyFrame extends JFrame
    implements ActionListener {

    public MyFrame() {
        JButton button = new JButton("Click me");
        button.addActionListener(this);
        getContentPane().add(button);
    }

    public void actionPerformed(ActionEvent arg0) {
        button.setLabel("Thanks");
    }
}
```

This code is incorrect because the actionPerformed method doesn't know what button means. To fix the code, you decide to drag the button declaration outside of the MyFrame constructor. And with Eclipse, you can drag the declaration without doing any typing.

Select the word button in the JButton button declaration. Then choose Refactor⇨Convert Local Variable to Field. After wrestling with a parameter page, your code is fixed. (See Listing 11-28.)

Listing 11-28:   A Local Variable Becomes a Field

```
import java.awt.event.ActionEvent;
import java.awt.event.ActionListener;

import javax.swing.JButton;
import javax.swing.JFrame;

public class MyFrame extends JFrame
    implements ActionListener {

    private JButton button;

    public MyFrame() {
        button = new JButton("Click me");
        button.addActionListener(this);
        getContentPane().add(button);
    }

    public void actionPerformed(ActionEvent arg0) {
        button.setLabel("Thanks");
    }
}
```

Now that you have a button field, you can take the next logical step. You can surround your field with getter and setter methods. But life's filled with interesting choices. Here are three different ways to create getter and setter methods:

✔ **Place the cursor inside the MyFrame class of Listing 11-28. Type the word** getB, **and then press Ctrl+Space.**

   Eclipse's code assist offers to create a getButton getter method. If you go back and type **setB**, Eclipse can create a setButton setter method. With this technique, you create one new getter or setter method at a time.

   For details on code assist, see Chapter 7.

✔ **Put the cursor anywhere inside the MyFrame class of Listing 11-28. Then choose Source⇨Generate Getters and Setters.**

Eclipse offers to create getters and setters for any of the MyFrame class's fields. If you want, you can pick a getter and not a setter, or a setter and not a getter. When you're done, Eclipse creates all the getters and setters in one fell swoop.

For details on this Generate Getters and Setters action, see Chapter 9.

✔ **Select any occurrence of the word** button **in Listing 11-28 (or select the** button **branch in a view's tree). Then choose Refactor⇨ Encapsulate Field.**

Eclipse prompts you with the parameter page of Figure 11-17. With this technique, you create both a getter and a setter for exactly one field. (You can't create a getter without a setter, or a setter without a getter.)

The interesting thing in Figure 11-17 is the Use Setter and Getter radio button. If the button remains checked, Eclipse adds setter and getter calls throughout the MyFrame class's code. (See Listing 11-29.)

The alternative in Figure 11-17 is to check the Keep Field Reference radio button. With this other button checked, Eclipse creates getter and setter methods, but doesn't sprinkle getButton and setButton calls throughout the MyFrame class's code.

Figure 11-17: An Encapsulate Field parameter page.

Listing 11-29:   Using Your Own Getters and Setters

```
import javax.swing.JButton;
import javax.swing.JFrame;

public class MyFrame extends JFrame
    implements ActionListener {

    private JButton button;

    public MyFrame() {
        setButton(new JButton("Click me"));
        getButton().addActionListener(this);
```

```
        getContentPane().add(getButton());
    }

    public void actionPerformed(ActionEvent arg0) {
        getButton().setLabel("Thanks");
    }

    private void setButton(JButton button) {
        this.button = button;
    }

    private JButton getButton() {
        return button;
    }
}
```

The Facts about Factories

Once upon a time, a factory was a place where machines assembled parts. These days, a factory is a method that returns a new object. A factory is like a constructor, except that factories are more versatile than constructors.

Consider the following lovely code:

```
package com.allmycode.accounts;

public class Account {
    String name;

    double balance;

    public Account(String name, double balance) {
        super();
        this.name = name;
        this.balance = balance;
    }
}
```

To create a factory method, select this code's Account constructor, and then choose Refactor⇨Introduce Factory. After clicking OK on a modest-looking parameter page, you get the following cool code:

```
package com.allmycode.accounts;

public class Account {
    String name;

    double balance;
```

```
    public static Account createAccount
            (String name, double balance) {
        return new Account(name, balance);
    }

    private Account(String name, double balance) {
super();
        this.name = name;
        this.balance = balance;
    }
}
```

Eclipse makes a new factory method. (In this example, createAccount is the new method.) Eclipse can also mask the existing constructor by making the constructor's access private.

Sure, this example's new createAccount factory method doesn't do anything fancy. But after creating a factory method, you can add fancy code inside the factory method's body.

Each application of the Introduce Factory action creates one factory method from one constructor. If your class has several constructors, and you want to make a factory method from each of these constructors, you have to invoke the Introduce Factory action several times.

Chapter 12

Looking for Things in All the Right Places

I love living in the computer age. Yes, I'm an Internet addict and a shareware junkie. But more than that, I like not having to look for things. For example, I'm writing this chapter in early October. In the next two weeks I have to submit my yearly income tax form. (My two filing extensions are coming to an end.) The trouble is, I don't know where my W-2 forms are. I don't know what pile of papers currently contains my 1099 forms. I don't even want to look for my accountant's unlisted phone number.

But with a computer, finding something is easy. In the worst case, you type a few words and then press Search. In the best case, the computer knows what you need, and finds things without waiting for you to ask.

Finding versus Searching

Eclipse's "look for things" facilities fall into two categories, and the best way to distinguish the two is to call one category *finding* and the other category *searching.* I admit it — I often confuse the two words. But when I'm being careful, I make the following distinction:

✔ **I initiate a finding action from Eclipse's Edit menu.**

    See Figure 12-1.

✔ **I initiate a searching action from Eclipse's Search menu.**

    See Figure 12-2.

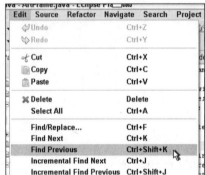

Figure 12-1:
Eclipse's
finding
actions.

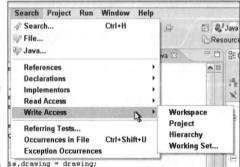

Figure 12-2:
Eclipse's
searching
actions.

The finding actions are like the kinds of things you do with a word processor. You type a word, click a Find button, and Eclipse moves to the next occurrence of that word in the editor. In general, I use a find action to locate something quickly in just one file.

The search actions are a little bit more elaborate — and I elaborate on that later in this chapter's "Searching" section. I use a searching action for an all-out hunt through many files at once.

Finding Text

Figure 12-3 shows Eclipse's Find/Replace dialog. To conjure up this dialog, choose Edit⇨Find/Replace. The dialog helps you find things in one file at a time. To find things that are distributed among several different files, close the Find/Replace dialog and skip to this chapter's "Searching" section.

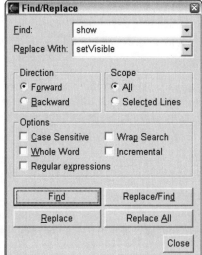

Using the Find/Replace dialog

The Find/Replace dialog's fields aren't shocking or unusual. So I give you a choice. You can read about each field, or you can skip the reading and experiment on your own.

Ah, hah! You've chosen to read on! Here are a few words about each of the Find/Replace dialog's fields:

- **Find:** Type the text that you want to find in the Find field. In Figure 12-3, I'm looking for the word **show**.

- **Replace With:** If you intend to replace the Find field's text, put the replacement text in the Replace With field. Otherwise, leave the Replace With field blank. In Figure 12-3, I prepare to replace **show** with **setVisible**.

The next two bullets refer to something called the *insertion point.* You probably know what the insertion point is, even if I don't explain it. But if you don't know, here's the scoop: When you click somewhere in the editor pane, the place where you click becomes the insertion point. Later, if you type something or press your keyboard's arrow keys, you move the insertion point. Most systems display a vertical line (or something like that) to mark the insertion point in the editor.

Returning to Figure 12-3 . . .

- ✔ **Forward:** Finds text from the insertion point downward.
- ✔ **Backward:** Finds text from the insertion point upward.
- ✔ **All:** Finds text anywhere in a file.
- ✔ **Selected Lines:** Limits your results to a specific collection of lines. This Selected Lines option has quirks that make it difficult to use. For more information see the section titled "Using the Selected Lines option."
- ✔ **Case Sensitive:** Distinguishes between things like `myObject` and `MYoBJECT`.
- ✔ **Wrap Search:** Makes Eclipse jump from the bottom of the file to the top.

  When you check the Forward radio button:

  - With Wrap Search, Eclipse reaches the bottom of a file, and then jumps to the top to look for more occurrences of the text in the Find field.
  - Without Wrap Search, Eclipse doesn't jump to the top of the file. When Eclipse hits the bottom of the file, Eclipse reports String Not Found.

  Of course, if you check the Backward radio button, everything happens (or doesn't happen) in reverse. Eclipse jumps to the bottom of the file, or gets stalled at the top of the file, depending on the status of that Wrap Search check box.

- ✔ **Whole Word:** Looks for whole words. Avoid finding **println** when you're looking for plain old **print**.
- ✔ **Incremental:** Looks for text while you type. I'm very proud of Figure 12-4, so please take a good, long look at it. This figure shows the progression of selections as you type the partial word **ArrayLi** with a check mark in the Incremental box.

  Before you start typing, Eclipse selects nothing. (Refer to the frame in the upper leftmost corner of Figure 12-4.) When you type the letter **A**, Eclipse selects the A in `Applet` (as in the upper rightmost frame). Then, after you type **Ar**, Eclipse jumps to highlight the Ar in `Area` (as in the left frame on the second row). And so on.

✔ **Regular Expressions:** Finds something that matches a pattern.

For example, the pattern `^\t..[a-e]*$` matches an entire line that starts with a tab, then contains any two characters, followed by any number of letters (as long as each of those letters are in the range a through e). To see a list of available pattern symbols (and to find out what each pattern symbols means), do the following:

1. **Choose Edit⇨Find/Replace to open the Find/Replace dialog.**

2. **Put a check mark in the Regular Expressions check box.**

3. **Click anywhere in the Find field.**

4. **Press Ctrl+Space.**

For a tutorial on the use of regular expressions in Java, visit `java.sun.com/docs/books/tutorial/extra/regex`.

The patterns in the Find/Replace dialog are like the patterns in the Java Element Filters dialog. For more information on the Java Element Filters dialog, see Chapter 3.

If you check the Regular Expressions box, then you can't use the Whole Word or Incremental options. Eclipse grays out these two options.

The big buttons at the bottom of the Find/Replace dialog do all the heavy lifting.

- ✔ **Find:** Locates the next occurrence of whatever text is in the Find field.

- ✔ **Replace:** Changes one occurrence of the Find field's text to the Replace With field's text. When you click Replace, Eclipse's editor highlighting stays on the newly replaced text. Eclipse doesn't move on to the next occurrence of the Find field's text.

  Eclipse can do a Replace operation even if you put nothing in the Replace With field. When you click the Replace button, Eclipse replaces the selected text with nothing. (In other words, Eclipse deletes the selected text.)

- ✔ **Replace/Find:** Does two useful things as once — changes an occurrence of the Find field's text, and then moves on to highlight the next occurrence of the Find field's text. To change that next occurrence, click Replace/Find again. Keep clicking Replace/Find until you reach the end of the file.

  This Replace/Find button is handy if you want to preview (and then accept or reject) each substitution.

- ✔ **Replace All:** Changes every occurrence of the Find text to the Replace With text. Use only if you don't need to preview each text substitution and you're feeling very confident.

Using the Selected Lines option

Maybe I'm just dense. I spent an hour figuring out what to do (and what not to do) to use the Find/Replace dialog's Selected Lines option effectively. To help me remember what I learned, I created a brief experiment. Here's how it works:

1. **Create a project with a class containing the code in Listing 12-1.**

   Your goal is to change the middle two `println` calls into `print` calls. That way, the words `Please log in with your username and password` appear along one line on the user's screen.

2. **Select any occurrence of the word `println`. Then choose Edit⇨Find/Replace.**

   Selecting `println` isn't necessary. It's just convenient. When you open the Find/Replace dialog, Eclipse populates the dialog's Find field with any text that happens to be selected. So selecting `println` saves you the effort of manually typing `println` in the Find field. (Hey! That's worth something.)

Don't start by selecting the lines in which you want to replace text. If you select a bunch of lines and then choose Edit⇨Find/Replace, then Eclipse populates the Find field with all the text in those lines. Most of the time, you have to delete all that text in the Find field.

3. **In the Replace With field, type the word** print.

4. **In the editor, drag your mouse from the** Please log in **line to the** your username **line.**

   You can select any parts of those two lines. (You don't have to select the two lines in their entirety.)

5. **Back in the Find/Replace dialog, check the Selected Lines radio button.**

   If you checked the Selected Lines radio button before Step 4, you must check the button again. For some reason, the stuff you do in Step 4 turns the Selected Lines button off and turns the alternative All radio button on.

6. **Click Replace All.**

   In response, Eclipse changes the middle two println calls (in Listing 12-1) into print calls.

Listing 12-1: Some Search Worthy Code

```
public class Greeting {

    public static void main(String[] args) {
        System.out.println
            ("You have reached the AllMyCode server.");
        System.out.println("Please log in with ");
        System.out.println("your username and ");
        System.out.println("password: ");
    }
}
```

Searching

Eclipse's Find/Replace dialog works interactively. You click Find and Eclipse locates text in the editor. Click Find again, and Eclipse locates the next occurrence.

In stark contrast to this interactive behavior, Eclipse search actions work in batch mode. These search actions report their results in a separate *Search view.* Figure 12-5 has a snapshot of the Search view. The view lists all relevant occurrences of the name `Drawing` anywhere in the current workspace. To jump to a particular occurrence in the editor, you double-click a branch of the Search view's tree.

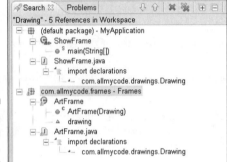

Figure 12-5: The Search view.

Here's another difference between search actions and the Find/Replace dialog. Search actions can cross file boundaries (or even project boundaries). To see what I mean, look back at Figure 12-2. When you search for Java elements, you can search within the current project, workspace, class hierarchy, or within a particular working set.

Eclipse has more than one search facility. It has File Search, Java Search, and a few other kinds of search. The next several pages describe Eclipse's most commonly used search facilities.

File Search

To do a File Search, you start by selecting something. The thing you select can be text in an editor, or a branch of a view's tree. After making your selection, choose Search⇨File. In response, Eclipse shows you the dialog in Figure 12-6.

Pattern matching

File Search supports two kinds of pattern matching mechanisms.

> ✔ If you check the Regular Expression box in Figure 12-6, File Search behaves almost exactly like the Find/Replace dialog. (For details, see the section on "Using the Find/Replace dialog.")

✔ Without checking the Regular Expression box, you can still use patterns. The non-regular-expression pattern language is much less powerful, and uses different symbols to match text, but the non-regular-expression language is useful nevertheless.

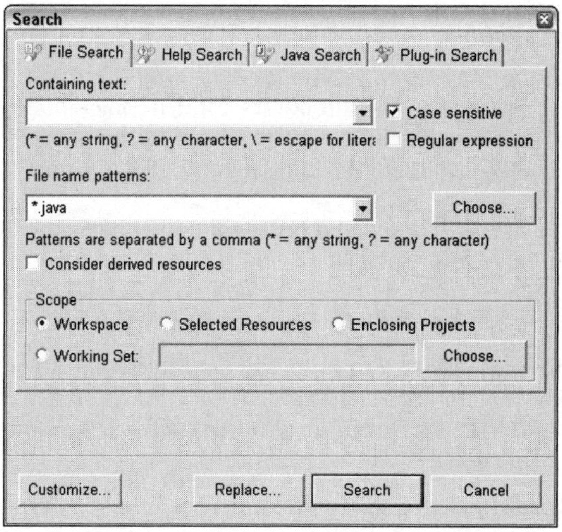

Figure 12-6:
The File
Search tab
of Eclipse's
Search
dialog.

Table 12-1 presents a few examples to illustrate the differences between searching with and without regular expressions.

Table 12-1	**Using Search Patterns**	
Searching For . . .	*With Regular Expressions*	*Without Regular Expressions*
Any single character	. a dot	? a question mark
Any string of characters	. * a dot followed by an asterisk	* an asterisk
A dot	\ . a backslash followed by a dot	. a dot
Tab character	\t	Copy and paste a tab character from an editor into the Containing Text field
The end of a line	$	As far as I know, there's no way to indicate a line end without using regular expressions

On some systems, the full label beneath the Containing Text field doesn't show up. So in case you can't read the entire label, the label says (* = any string, ? = any character, \ = escape for literals: * ? \). In plain English, typing **?** makes Eclipse search for any character, but typing **\?** makes Eclipse search for a question mark.

Selecting a search scope

Many items in Eclipse's File Search tab behave the way their counterparts in the Find/Replace dialog behave. But unlike the Find/Replace dialog, the File Search tab has a group of *Scope* radio buttons. This Scope group represents the File Search tab's ability to hunt through several files at once.

When you check one of the Scope radio buttons, you answer the "Which files?" question. You have four options:

- ✔ **Workspace:** Search in every file in the current workspace.

- ✔ **Selected Resources:** Before you open the Search dialog, select one or more resources. For instance, you can click a branch on the Package Explorer tree, and then Ctrl+click another branch on the same tree. When you do, you've selected two resources.

  With a check mark next to Selected Resources, Eclipse searches through the selected files, folders, packages, or projects. Eclipse searches through all the selected items (and through only the selected items).

  After opening the Search dialog, you can no longer select resources. If you want to change your selection of resources, you must close the Search dialog, select other resources, and then open the Search dialog again.

  Sometimes you find that the Selected Resources radio button is grayed out. If so, it's probably because your most recent selection is in an editor, and not in the Package Explorer or the Outline view. For the purpose of searching, Eclipse doesn't think of your selection in an editor as a resource.

- ✔ **Enclosing Projects:** I spent quite a while figuring this one out. Imagine that you select Class1A.java and Class2B.java as in Figure 12-7. Then you choose Search⇨File and you check Enclosing Projects. Finally, you type something in the Containing Text field, and click Search.

  As a result, Eclipse searches through all files in ProjectA and ProjectB. It searches all of ProjectA because ProjectA "encloses" Class1A.java. And it searches all of ProjectB because ProjectB "encloses" Class2B.java. Looking back at Figure 12-7, Eclipse searches Class1A.java, Class2A.java, Class1B.java, and Class2B.java.

If, instead of checking Enclosing Projects, you check Selected Resources, then Eclipse searches only the selected `Class1A.java` and `Class2B.java` files.

✔ **Working Set:** Search every file within a particular working set.

For details on working sets, see Chapter 3.

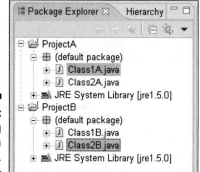

Figure 12-7:
Selecting
two Java
source files.

Java Search

The previous section covers Eclipse's File Search actions. These File Search actions don't know parameters from fields, or keywords from strings. In fact, the File Search actions know almost nothing. If you search for `s`, then File Search finds anything containing a letter `s` — things like `class`, `switch`, `case`, and `swing`.

In contrast, Eclipse's Java Search actions are *Java-aware*. These actions know that parameters aren't the same as fields, that method declarations aren't the same as method calls, and all that good stuff.

To see what I mean, imagine that you're editing the following `ArtFrame` class:

```
import javax.swing.JFrame;

public class ArtFrame extends JFrame {
    Drawing drawing;

    public ArtFrame(Drawing drawing) {
        this.drawing = drawing;
    }
}
```

On Eclipse's main menu bar, choose Search⇨Java. In response, Eclipse displays the Java Search tab of Eclipse's Search dialog. (See Figure 12-8.)

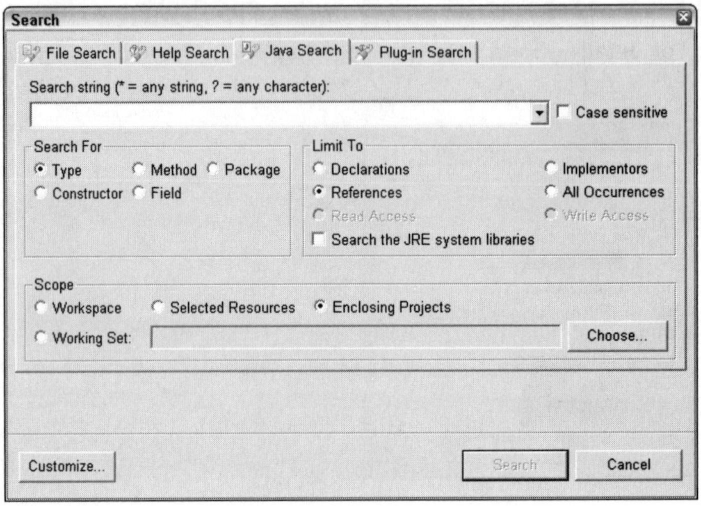

Now try the following:

1. **In the Search String field, type** drawing.

2. **In the Search For group of radio buttons, select Field.**

3. **In the Limit To group, select Write Access.**

4. **Click Search.**

Eclipse's response is shown in Figure 12-9. Eclipse locates the only place in the code in which a value is written to the drawing field. (Instead of saying "written to," most programmers say that a value is "assigned to" the drawing field. But let's not fuss about the wording.)

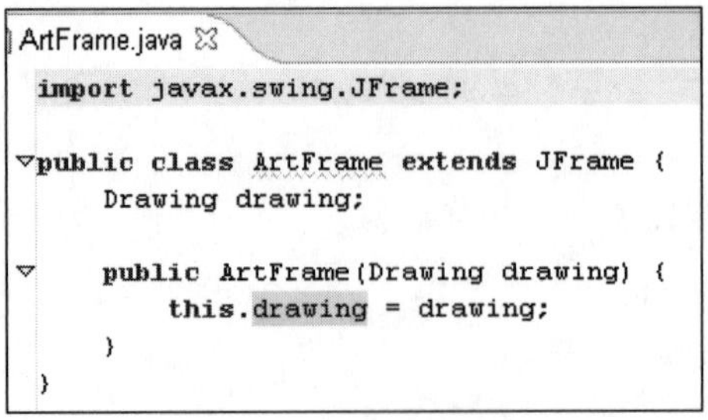

```java
import javax.swing.JFrame;

public class ArtFrame extends JFrame {
    Drawing drawing;

    public ArtFrame(Drawing drawing) {
        this.drawing = drawing;
    }
}
```

Here's another example. In Eclipse's editor, select the word `drawing`. Select the entire word in the `ArtFrame` constructor's parameter list. (Don't select only part of the word. If you do, this experiment doesn't work.) Then, on the main menu bar, choose Search⇨References⇨Project.

Choosing Search⇨References⇨Project triggers another Java Search action. Eclipse, with all its wisdom, responds as in Figure 12-10. Eclipse highlights the `drawing` parameter on the right side of the line.

```
this.drawing = drawing;
```

But Eclipse doesn't highlight the reference to the `drawing` field on the left side of the same line. How about that? It's not just a rumor. The Java Search facility is truly Java-aware.

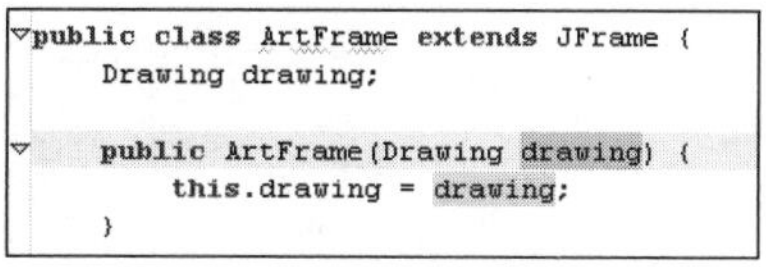

Figure 12-10:
Eclipse
searches
wisely.

```
public class ArtFrame extends JFrame {
    Drawing drawing;

    public ArtFrame(Drawing drawing) {
        this.drawing = drawing;
    }
```

Figure 12-8 shows the Java Search tab of Eclipse's Search dialog. With the Search For and Limit To groups, you narrow the search to specific kinds of Java elements. You can combine selections in the Search For and Limit To groups in many different ways. Instead of enumerating all the possibilities, I describe a few examples. In each example, I assume that Eclipse is set to search the code of Listings 12-2 through 12-4.

Listing 12-2:   A Class that Creates a MyFrame Instance

```
package com.allmycode.apps;

import com.allmycode.frames.MyFrame;

public class MyApp {

    public static void main(String[] args) {
        new MyFrame("I like Eclipse!");
    }
}
```

Listing 12-3: The MyFrame Class

```
package com.allmycode.frames;

import javax.swing.JFrame;

import com.allmycode.util.Chewable;

public class MyFrame extends JFrame implements Chewable {
    String title = "";

    public MyFrame(String title) {
        this.title = title;
        setTitle(title);
        setSize(200, 100);
        setVisible(true);
    }

    public void chew() {
    }
}
```

Listing 12-4: The Chewable Interface

```
package com.allmycode.util;

public interface Chewable {
    void chew();
}
```

✔ **Search for the MyFrame type and limit the search to declarations. (See Figure 12-11.)**

Eclipse finds the MyFrame class. (See Figure 12-12.)

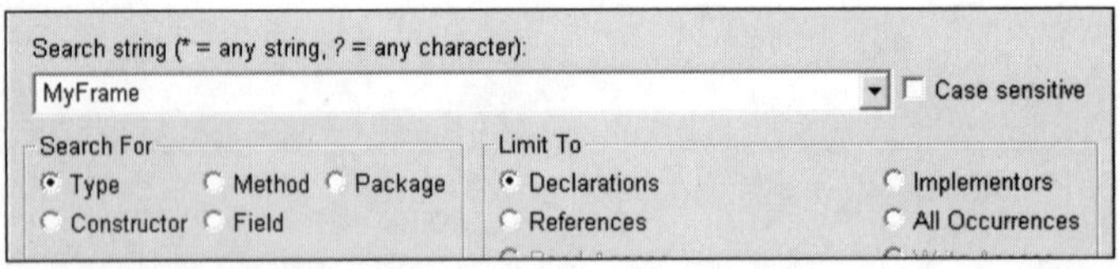

Figure 12-11:
Searching for the MyFrame type and limiting the search to declarations.

✔ **Search for the MyFrame type and limit the search to references. (See Figure 12-13.)**

Eclipse finds a MyFrame import declaration and a MyFrame constructor call. (See Figure 12-14.)

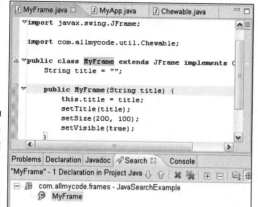

Figure 12-12:
The result
of the
search in
Figure 12-11.

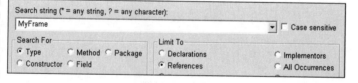

Figure 12-13:
Searching
for the
MyFrame
type and
limiting the
search to
references.

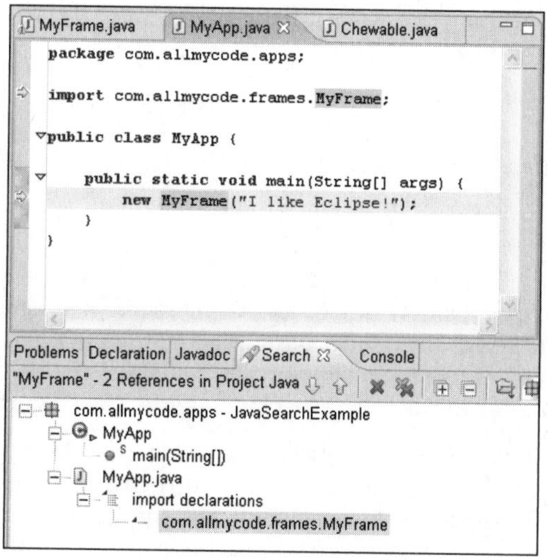

Figure 12-14:
The result of
the search in
Figure 12-13.

✔ **Search for the** MyFrame **type and don't limit the search. (That is, limit the search to all occurrences, as in Figure 12-15.)**

Eclipse finds the `MyFrame` class, a `MyFrame` import declaration, and a `MyFrame` constructor call. (See Figure 12-16.)

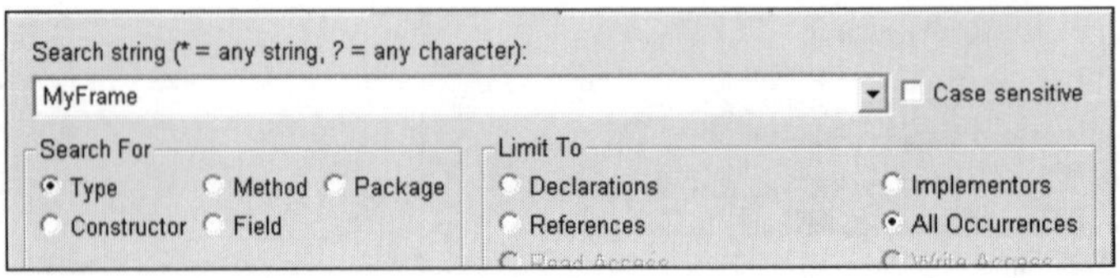

Figure 12-15:
Searching for the MyFrame type without limiting the search.

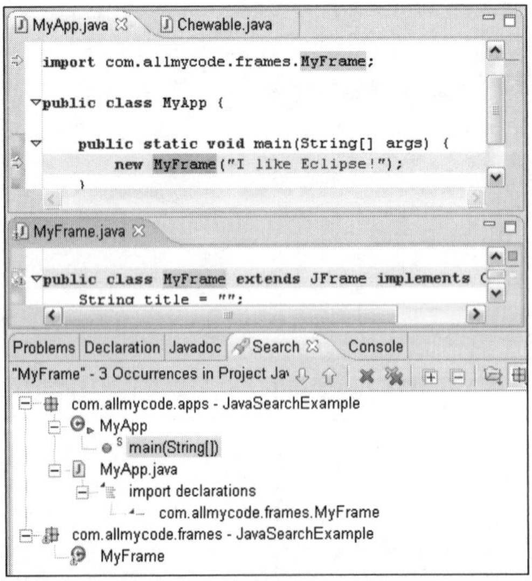

Search string (* = any string, ? = any character):

MyFrame ▾ □ Case sensitive

Search For
● Type   ○ Method ○ Package
○ Constructor ○ Field

Limit To
○ Declarations   ○ Implementors
○ References   ● All Occurrences
○ Read Access   ○ Write Access

```
J MyApp.java ☒   J Chewable.java

    import com.allmycode.frames.MyFrame;

    ▽public class MyApp {

    ▽    public static void main(String[] args) {
             new MyFrame("I like Eclipse!");
         }
```

```
J MyFrame.java ☒

    ▽public class MyFrame extends JFrame implements (
       String title = "";
```

Problems Declaration Javadoc ⚲ Search ☒ Console

"MyFrame" - 3 Occurrences in Project Ja

```
⊟ ⊞ com.allmycode.apps - JavaSearchExample
   ⊟ ⊖ MyApp
      └ ● ˢ main(String[])
   ⊟ J MyApp.java
      ⊟ import declarations
         └ ← com.allmycode.frames.MyFrame
⊟ ⊞ com.allmycode.frames - JavaSearchExample
   └ ⊕ MyFrame
```

Figure 12-16:
The result of the search in Figure 12-15.

You can quickly search a single file for all occurrences of a particular name. For example, select the `title` parameter in the code of Listing 12-3. Then choose Search➪Occurrences in File. Eclipse finds the three uses of the `title` parameter in the `MyFrame` class's code. (See Figure 12-17.)

The Search➪Occurrences in File action is Java aware. When you search for the `title` parameter, Eclipse doesn't find any occurrences of the `title` field. And like other Java Search actions, the Occurrences in File action searches only for a type, method, package, constructor, or field. (Refer to the Search For group in Figure 12-15.) If you select the word `public` and then choose Search➪Occurrences in File, then Eclipse does absolutely nothing.

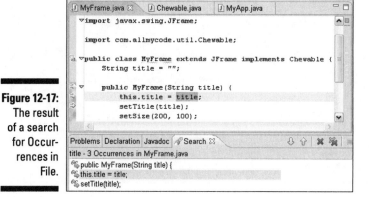

Figure 12-17: The result of a search for Occurrences in File.

✔ **Search for any** *Frame **type and limit the search to references. (See Figure 12-18.)**

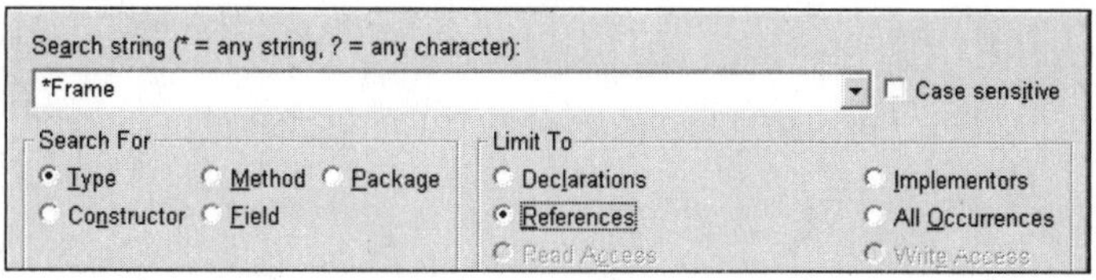

Figure 12-18: Searching for any `*Frame` type and limiting the search to references.

The asterisk is a wildcard. (The asterisk stands for any sequence of characters.) So Eclipse finds a `MyFrame` import declaration, a `MyFrame` constructor call, a `JFrame` import declaration, and an `extends JFrame` clause. (See Figure 12-19.)

✔ **Search for the** Chewable **type and limit the search to references. (See Figure 12-20.)**

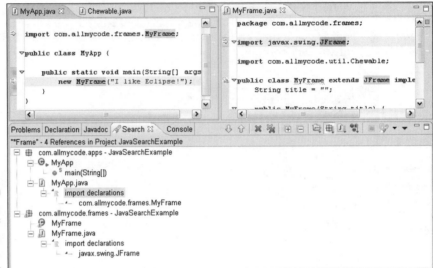

Figure 12-19:
The result of
the search in
Figure 12-18.

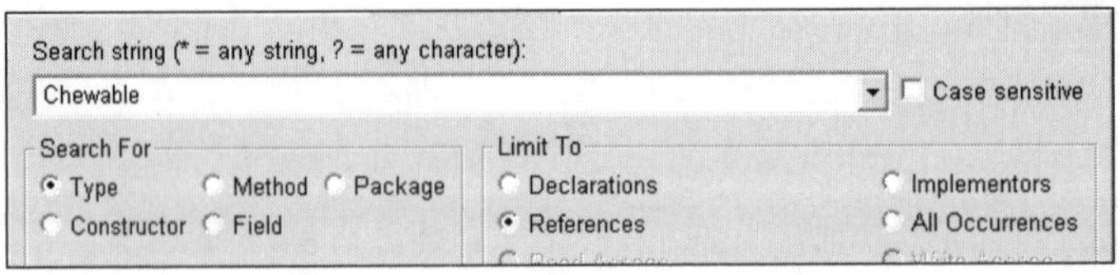

Figure 12-20:
Searching
for the
Chewable
type and
limiting the
search to
references.

Eclipse finds a Chewable import declaration and an implements
Chewable clause. In other words, searching for an interface yields the
same results as searching for a class. (See Figure 12-21.)

✔ **Search for the Chewable type and limit the search to implementors.
(See Figure 12-22.)**

Eclipse finds an implements Chewable clause. (See Figure 12-23.)

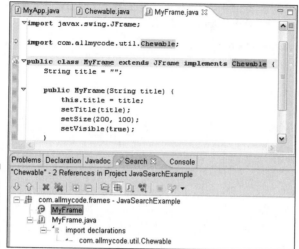

Figure 12-21:
The result of
the search in
Figure 12-20.

Figure 12-22:
Searching
for the
Chewable
type and
limiting
the search
to imple-
mentors.

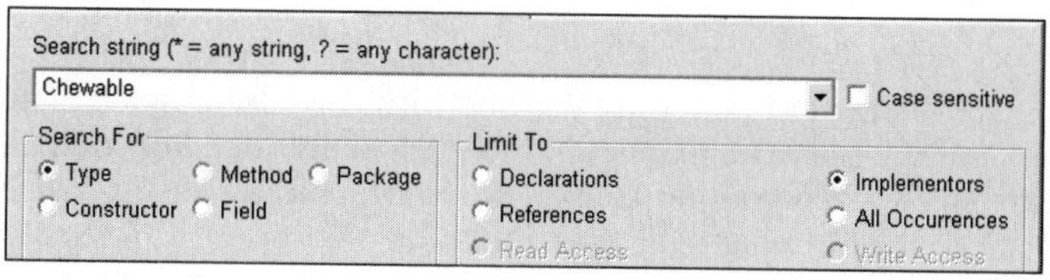

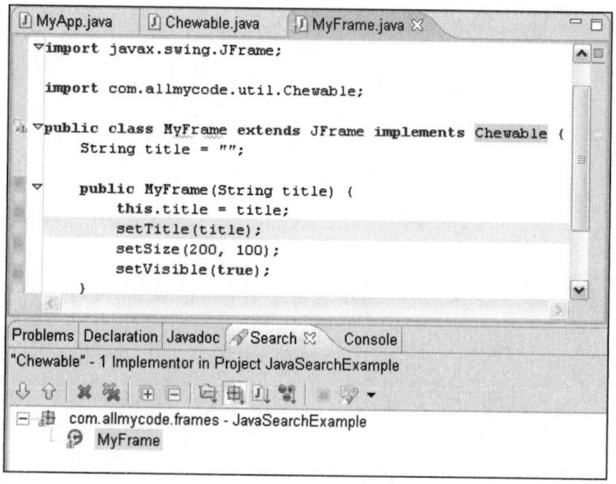

Figure 12-23:
The result of
the search in
Figure 12-22.

✔ **Search for the** com.allmycode.util.Chewable **type and limit the search to implementors. (See Figure 12-24.)**

Once again, Eclipse finds an `implements Chewable` clause. (Refer to Figure 12-23.)

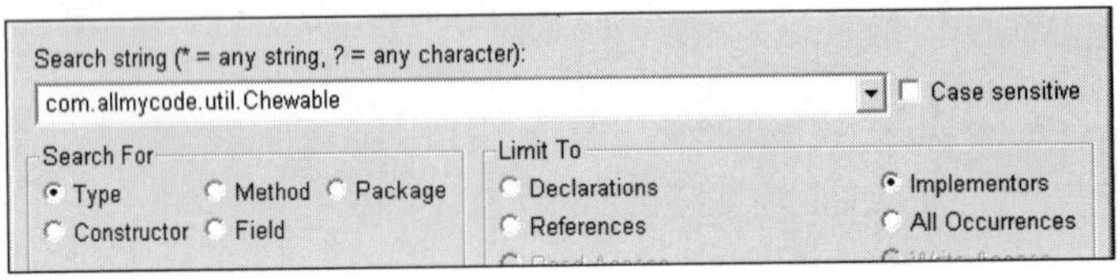

Figure 12-24:
Searching
for the
`com.`
`allmy`
`code.`
`util.`
`Chewable`
type and
limiting the
search to
imple-
mentors.

Search string (* = any string, ? = any character):		Case sensitive

```
com.allmycode.util.Chewable
```

Search For
- Type ○ Method ○ Package
- ○ Constructor ○ Field

Limit To
- ○ Declarations
- ○ References

- • Implementors
- ○ All Occurrences

Unlike the kind of matching you see with the File/Replace dialog or with a File Search, the Java Search knows about things like fully qualified package names. So when you perform a Java Search on the entire `com.allmycode.util.Chewable` name Eclipse finds the `implements Chewable` clause. Eclipse finds this `implements Chewable` clause even though the clause doesn't explicitly contain the words `com.allmycode.util`.

✔ **Search for any** com.allmycode.* **packages and limit the search to declarations. (See Figure 12-25.)**

Once again, the asterisk is a wildcard. Eclipse finds three packages — `com.allmycode.apps`, `com.allmycode.frames`, and `com.allmycode.util`. (See Figure 12-26.)

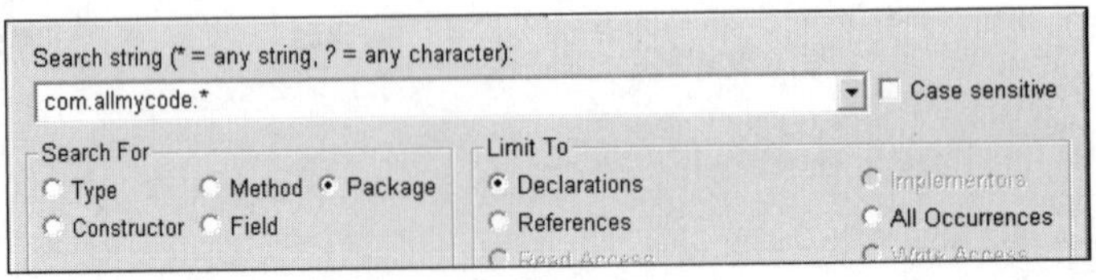

Figure 12-25:
Searching
for `com.`
`allmy`
`code.*`
packages
and limiting
the search
to declara-
tions.

Search string (* = any string, ? = any character):		Case sensitive

```
com.allmycode.*
```

Search For
- ○ Type ○ Method • Package
- ○ Constructor ○ Field

Limit To
- • Declarations
- ○ References

- ○ Implementors
- ○ All Occurrences

Figure 12-26:
The result of
the search in
Figure 12-25.

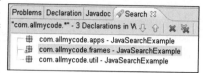

Eclipse doesn't associate the packages with Java source files. Even if the code that you're examining contains ten `package com.allmycode.util` files, the Search view's tree lists only one `com.allmycode.util` item.

✔ **Search for the** title **field and limit the search to write access. (See Figure 12-27.)**

Figure 12-27:
Searching
for the
`title` field
and limiting
the search
to write
access.

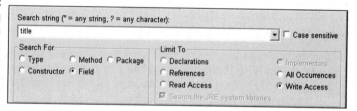

Eclipse finds places where a `title` field is given a value. (See Figure 12-28.) This includes places in the JRE system libraries. For example, the `java.awt.Frame` class contains a `title` field, and the `Frame` class's code contains three lines in which `title` is given a value.

When you limit the search to either write access or read access, Eclipse grays out its Search the JRE System Libraries check box so you can't deselect it. (Refer to Figure 12-27.) This means that Eclipse finds occurrences in the JRE system libraries whether you like it or not.

You can't see the code in any of the JRE system libraries unless you tell Eclipse where the libraries' source code lives. To find out how to do this, see the section about the Declaration view in Chapter 5.

✔ **Search for the** title **field and limit the search to read access. (See Figure 12-29.)**

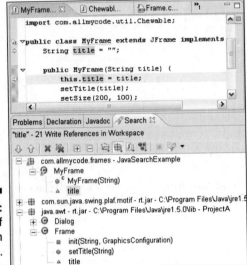

Figure 12-28:
The result of
the search in
Figure 12-27.

Eclipse finds places where the code uses a `title` field's value. In this example, the only such places are in the JRE system libraries. Nothing in Listing 12-3 uses the `title` field's value. (Some statements use the `title` parameter's value, but not the `title` field's value.)

Suppose Listing 12-3 contained a getter method.

```
public String getTitle() {
    return title;
}
```

Then searching for read access to a `title` field would find the getter method's `return` statement.

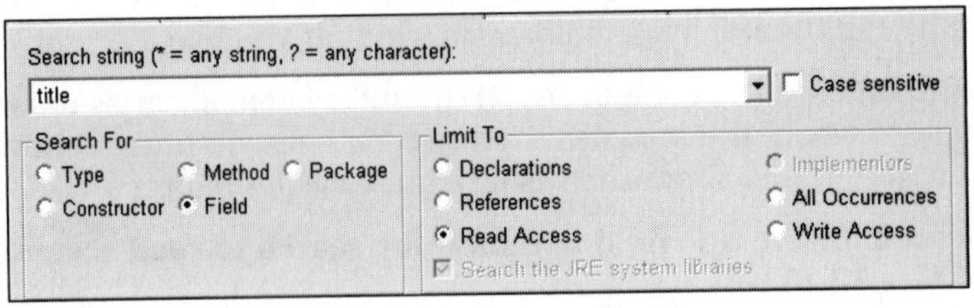

Figure 12-29:
Searching
for the
`title` field
and limiting
the search
to read
access.

✔ **Search for** Chewable **and limit the search to references in the** Chewable **hierarchy.**

What? You say you see nothing about a hierarchy on the Java Search page? To search for Chewable references in the Chewable hierarchy, select Chewable (in the editor or in a view). Then choose Search➪ References➪Hierarchy. (See Figure 12-30.)

Eclipse finds an implements Chewable clause. (See Figure 12-31.)

Figure 12-30:
Searching
for
Chewable
and limiting
the search
to refer-
ences in a
hierarchy.

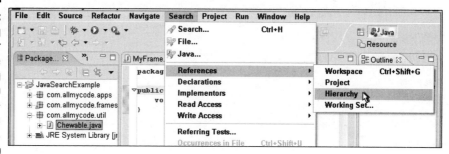

Figure 12-31:
The result of
the search in
Figure 12-30.

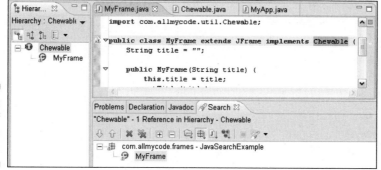

Using the Exception Occurrences action

At the end of Chapter 6, I describe a cool Mark Occurrences feature. If you select an exception, Eclipse highlights all the statements that can throw the exception.

You can do the same kind of thing with a Search action. Select an exception in the editor. Then choose Search➪Exception Occurrences. As with the Mark

Occurrences feature, Eclipse highlights all statements that can throw the exception. In addition, Eclipse lists all those statements in the Search view. (See Figure 12-32.)

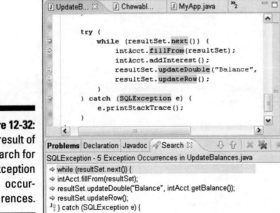

Figure 12-32:
The result of a search for exception occurrences.

Part III
Doing More with Eclipse

The 5th Wave — By Rich Tennant

In this part . . .

When I think about this part of *Eclipse For Dummies*, the word *tweak* comes to mind. Tweak your project, tweak the Java compiler, or tweak the way your program runs. Parts I and II give you the cake. This part gives you the icing.

Chapter 13

Working with Projects

Many years ago I visited a computer store to try out the latest version of FinalWord. (At the time, FinalWord was my favorite word processing program.) I was amazed when the salesperson opened a box containing nine 5¼-inch floppy disks. "That's a huge program," I said. And the salesperson replied, "That's the way software comes these days."

A huge program indeed! At least 100 copies of FinalWord would fit on one of today's CD-ROMs. And a program for home use can come packaged as a set of CD-ROMs. But that's not all. A program for commercial use can be enormous. Commercial programs can be divided into parts, with the parts running on several processors, and on several computers in several geographical locations.

I can't describe all the tools for managing this size and complexity. But I can describe a few simple tricks — ways that Eclipse helps you move from chaos to organization.

The Typical Java Program Directory Structure

Take a look at Figure 13-1. My hard drive's JavaPrograms directory contains a com directory, which in turn contains allmycode\gui and burdbrain\io directories. At the bottom level, my gui directory contains ShowAFrame.java, which (take my word for it) begins with the line

```
package com.allmycode.gui;
```

The directory structures in Figure 13-1 have nothing to do with Eclipse. These com*something**somethingelse* directory structures are standard fare. (Well, they're standard for people who do a lot of Java programming). In fact, when I created the directories in Figure 13-1, I hadn't even heard of Eclipse.

I talk a lot about the kinds of directory structures that you see in Figure 13-1. So I have handy names for these directories:

- ✔ **In Figure 13-1, I call** JavaPrograms **the** *source directory.*

  The source directory is the directory where the Java compiler and Java Virtual Machine begin looking for your Java source files.

- ✔ **In Figure 13-1, I call** com, allmycode, **and** gui **the** *package directories.*

  The package directories are all the directories whose names are part of a dotted package name. Because allmycode is part of the dotted com. allmycode.gui package name, the allmycode directory in Figure 13-1 is a package directory.

- ✔ **In Figure 13-1, I call** com **the** *top-level package directory.* **I call** gui **a** *bottom-level package directory.*

I use the words "directory" and "folder" to mean exactly the same thing. Sometimes, one word feels a bit more appropriate, so I use one word instead of the other. But these feelings of mine about appropriateness and inappropriateness don't mean much. Eclipse's Help pages tend to favor the word "folder." And I, in my capacity as a computer geek, tend to favor the word "directory." It doesn't matter. The two words are interchangeable.

Working with Source Folders

The more elaborate your application, the more your application needs to be well organized. If your project is a small one, you can keep everything in one folder. But an industrial-strength project spans dozens, or possibly even hundreds of folders. This section helps you manage a project with several folders.

Creating a separate source folder

In earlier chapters, your project's source folder is the project folder itself. This unified folder contains all kinds of code, including .java files and .class files.

For instance, with a project named MyProject, your eclipse workspace directory has a subdirectory named MyProject, which in turn has a com subdirectory, and a few subdirectories below the com directory. In Figure 13-2, the lowest level stuff directory contains both a .java file and a .class file.

Figure 13-2:
The project folder is the source folder.

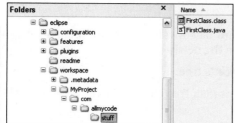

The structure in Figure 13-2 is good for very small projects, but bigger projects demand a higher level of organization. That's why all the big-time Java programmers create separate directories for a project, for the project's .java files, and for the project's .class files.

So in this chapter, you create richer directory structures. Here's how you start:

1. **On the Eclipse menu bar, choose File⇨New⇨Project.**

2. **In the New Project dialog, select Java Project and click Next.**

   You see the New Java Project Wizard.

3. **In the Project Name field, type a name for your new project.**

   In this example, I typed **BigProject**.

4. **In the Project Layout section of the wizard select the Create Separate Source and Output Folders radio button. (See Figure 13-3.)**

   Selecting the "separate folders" option makes this section's project different from the previous chapters' projects. In this project, all .java files go in a src directory, and all .class files go in a bin directory. That's what you get (by default) when you select the option. The bin folder (or any folder that stores all the .class files) is called an *output folder*.

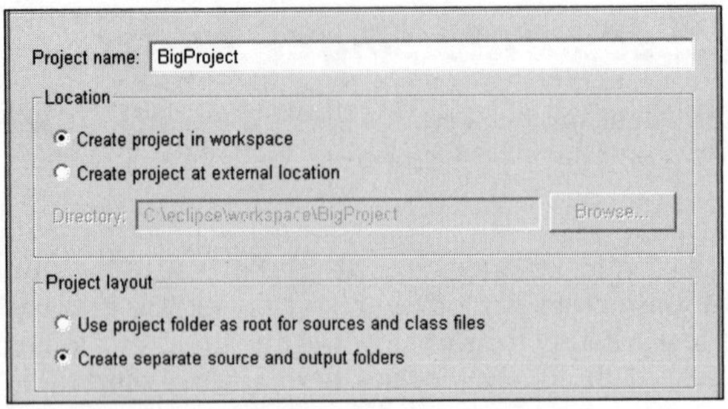

Figure 13-3:
Creating
separate
folders.

Project name: BigProject

Location
◉ Create project in workspace
○ Create project at external location

Directory: C:\eclipse\workspace\BigProject   Browse...

Project layout
○ Use project folder as root for sources and class files
◉ Create separate source and output folders

5. Click Finish.

The New Project Wizard disappears. In the workbench's Package Explorer view, you see the newly created `BigProject`.

6. Expand the new project's tree.

When expanded, the project tree contains a `src` folder. (See Figure 13-4.)

Figure 13-4:
A new
source
folder.

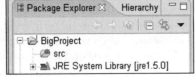

Package Explorer ⊠   Hierarchy

BigProject
  📁 src
  📚 JRE System Library [jre1.5.0]

7. Create a package and create a class inside the package.

In this example, name the package **com.allmycode.bigpackage**. And while you're at it, name the class **BigClass**.

In the New Java Package and New Java Class Wizards, Eclipse automatically fills in the Source Folder field. In Figure 13-5, the Source Folder field contains `BigProject/src`. In this example, all the files live inside the `BigProject` subdirectory of Eclipse's workspace directory. In particular, the `.java` files live in the `src` subdirectory of that `BigProject` directory.

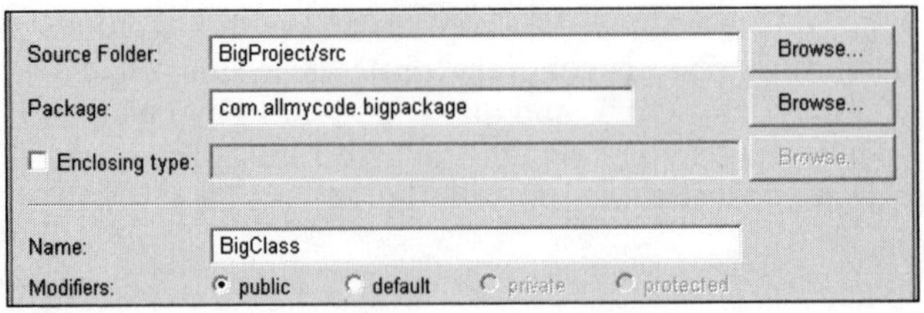

Figure 13-5:
Creating
a class in
the `Big`
`Project/`
`src`
directory.

Source Folder: BigProject/src   Browse...
Package: com.allmycode.bigpackage   Browse...
☐ Enclosing type: Browse...

Name: BigClass
Modifiers: ◉ public   ○ default   ○ private   ○ protected

Eventually, you click Finish to close the New Java Class Wizard. The wizard disappears, to reveal your old friend — the Eclipse workbench.

8. Expand branches in the Package Explorer's tree.

You see a new class inside the src folder. (See Figure 13-6.)

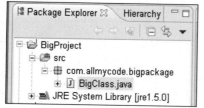

Figure 13-6: A class in the src directory.

As soon you as you create a .java file, Eclipse compiles the .java file and creates a corresponding .class file. If you ask for separate folders (Step 4), the new .class file goes into a bin folder. But in Figure 13-6, the Package Explorer's tree doesn't display the bin folder. If you want to see the bin folder, you have to open the Navigator view. (See Figure 13-7.)

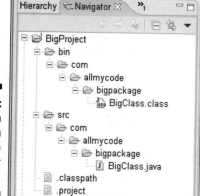

Figure 13-7: The bin directory in the Navigator view.

For tips on opening the Navigator view, see Chapter 4.

Your previous projects don't have bin directories. If you look at one of these projects in the Navigator view, you see a much simpler directory structure. (See Figure 13-8.)

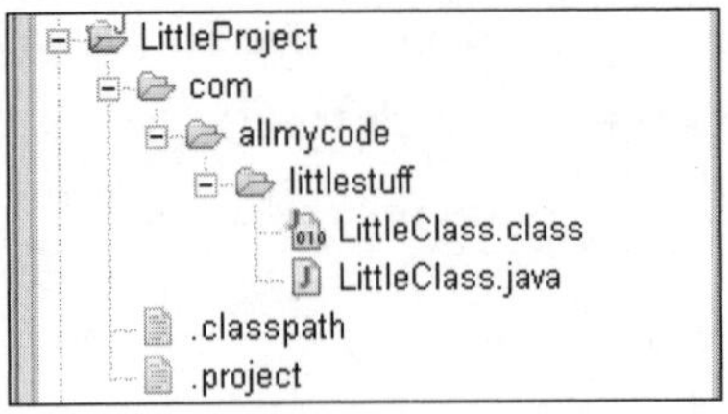

Figure 13-8:
A project
with no b i n
directory
(in the
Navigator
view).

```
⊟ 🗁 LittleProject
   ⊟ 🗁 com
      ⊟ 🗁 allmycode
         ⊟ 🗁 littlestuff
               🗎 LittleClass.class
               🗎 LittleClass.java
      🗎 .classpath
      🗎 .project
```

Oops! I forgot to create a separate source folder.

I have a very bad habit. I avoid creating new directories until circumstances force my hand. I think the habit comes from the olden days — the days of floppy disks. On a floppy that stores 360K, subdirectories are unnecessary.

So here's what happens: I start what I think is going to be a small programming task. When I create an Eclipse project, I don't do all the stuff in the "Creating a separate source folder" section. (That is, I don't create a separate source folder.) As the project grows and I see things becoming more complex, I start regretting my original decision not to create a separate source folder.

So what can I do? Can I create a separate source folder after I've been tinkering with a project for several hours? Of course I can. Here's how:

1. **Create a Java project. In the New Java Project Wizard, don't create separate source and output folders.**

   Leave the creation of separate folders until after the project is underway.

2. **Add a package and a class to your new project.**

   In this example, I named the package **com.allmycode.growing**. I named the class **GrowingClass**.

3. **In the Package Explorer, right-click the project that's begging to have a new source folder.**

   That is, right-click com.allmycode.growing.

4. **On the resulting context menu, choose New⇨Source Folder.**

   A New Source Folder dialog appears. (See Figure 13-9.)

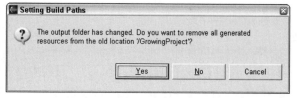

Figure 13-9:
The New
Source
Folder
dialog.

5. **In the Folder Name field of the New Source Folder dialog, type a name for your new source folder.**

   In Figure 13-9 I typed **src**. Notice the innocent looking message in Figure 13-9. In addition to creating the src directory, Eclipse plans to create a directory named bin (a separate directory for all your .class files).

6. **Click Finish.**

   A message box asks you if you want to remove things like .class files from the project folder. (See Figure 13-10.) Sure, you want to remove those .class files.

Figure 13-10:
Do you want
to remove
stuff?

7. **Click Yes.**

   The Package Explorer displays your new src folder. But the com directory isn't inside the new src folder.

   Look carefully at the message box in Figure 13-10, and notice what the message doesn't say. The message doesn't say anything about generating new .class files. Nor does the message say that Eclipse intends to move the existing .java files. When you click Yes, the only thing Eclipse does is delete .class files. All the other moving and generating has to wait until Step 8.

8. **In the Package Explorer, drag the com directory to the src directory.**

   Eclipse moves the source code to the src directory and creates a compiled .class file in the bin directory. To see the src directory's contents, look over the Package Explorer in Figure 13-11. To see both the src directory and the bin directory, look at the Navigator view in Figure 13-12.

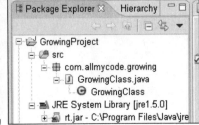

Figure 13-11:
A new source folder appears in the Package Explorer.

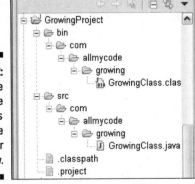

Figure 13-12:
The source files and the `.class` files in the Navigator view.

Working with even bigger projects

In the previous section I show you how to create a project with one source folder and with a separate output folder. That's fine for a big project. But for a truly humongous project, you may need more than one source folder. In this section, you create a project with two source folders and two output folders.

What follows may seem to be a very long sequence of steps. But trust me. If you create big projects often, you eventually perform these steps on autopilot.

1. **Repeat Steps 1 to 4 from the "Creating a separate source folder" section.**

   This time, name your project **HumongousProject**.

2. **Instead of clicking Finish, click Next.**

   The Java Settings page appears. (See Figure 13-13.)

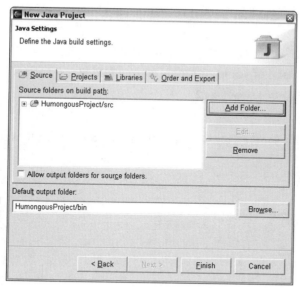

Figure 13-13:
The Java
Settings
page.

3. **On the Source tab of the Java Settings page, click the Add Folder button.**

   A Source Folder Selection dialog appears. (See Figure 13-14.)

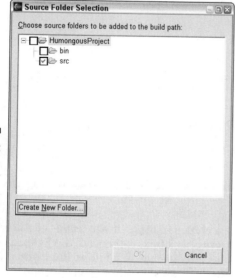

Figure 13-14:
The Source
Folder
Selection
dialog (with
only one
source
folder).

4. **On the Source Folder Selection dialog, click the Create New Folder button.**

   Guess what? A New Folder dialog appears.

5. **Type the name of your additional source folder.**

   In this example, I typed **src2**.

6. **Click OK.**

7. **Back on the Source Folder Selection dialog, make sure that** src2 **is checked.**

   See Figure 13-15.

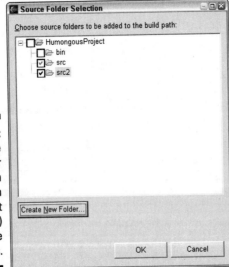

8. **On the Source Folder Selection dialog, click OK.**

   Now the Source tab of the Java Settings page displays two source folders — src and src2.

9. **Expand all branches of the Source Folders on Build Path tree.**

   See Figure 13-16.

   At this point, you have a choice to make. If you leave the Allow Output Folders for Source Folders check box unchecked, the Eclipse compiler dumps all its .class files into a single bin folder. But if you check the Allow Output Folders for Source Folders box, you have more control over the use of output folders.

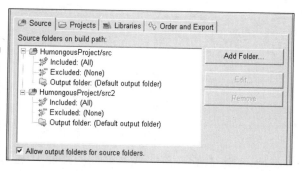

10. **Put a check mark in the Allow Output Folders for Source Folders box.**

   Notice how the tree grows some new branches. These new branches represent output folders for each of the project's source folders. (See Figure 13-17.)

Figure 13-17: A separate output folder for each source folder.

Renaming your new output folder

In the previous section, you create two output folders — one for each of two source folders. By default, each output folder is named bin. Of course, you can override a default name. Here's how you do it:

1. **Work through the instructions in the previous section.**

   At the end of Step 10 you have the situation illustrated in Figure 13-17.

2. **Select an output folder, and then click Edit.**

   I selected the output folder for src2. When I clicked Edit, the Source Folder Output Location dialog appears. (See Figure 13-18.)

3. **Select the Specific Output Folder radio button, and then click Browse.**

   The Folder Selection dialog appears.

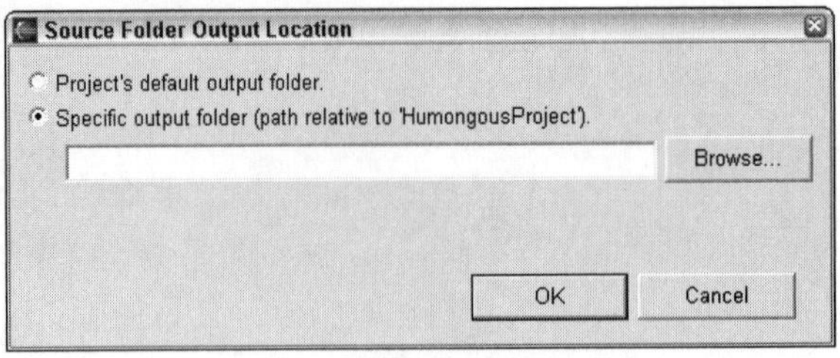

Figure 13-18:
The Source
Folder
Output
Location
dialog.

4. **Click Create New Folder. On the resulting New Folder dialog, type a name for the new output folder.**

   In this example, I typed **bin2**.

5. **Click OK to dismiss the New Folder dialog. Then, back on the Folder Selection dialog, select the new bin2 folder. (See Figure 13-19.)**

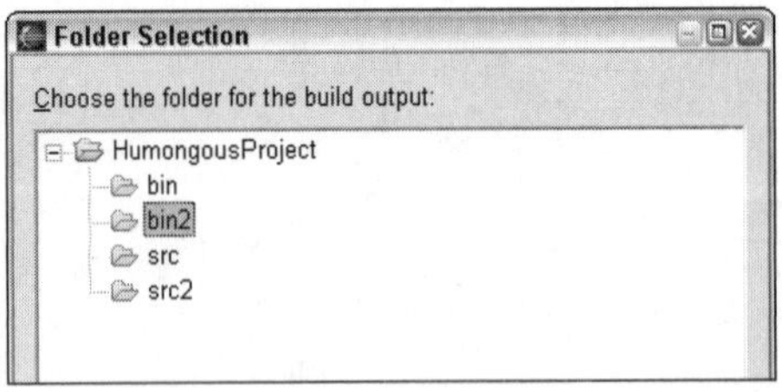

Figure 13-19:
Selecting a
new output
folder.

6. **Click OK to dismiss the Folder Selection dialog. Then click OK again to dismiss the Source Folder Output Location dialog.**

   After all that clicking, you see the Java Settings page. On the Java Settings page, the output folder for src2 is now bin2. (See Figure 13-20.)

7. **Click Finish to dismiss the Java Settings page.**

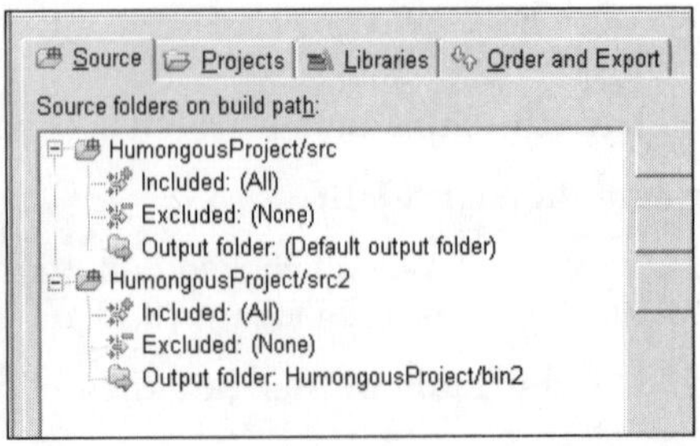

Figure 13-20:
At last! The
second
source
folder has
an output
folder
named
bin2!

After performing all these steps, you probably want to examine the fruits of your effort. To see the stuff that you've created, open Eclipse's Navigator view.

Better yet, add classes to the `src` and `src2` folders. Have the code from one source folder call code in the other source folder. Eclipse manages this call without blinking an eye.

Working with colossal applications

With programs becoming bigger and better, it's hard to imagine a single Eclipse project holding an entire industrial-strength application. That's why Eclipse lets you link several projects together.

Start with the code in Listings 13-1 and 13-2.

Listing 13-1: A Class in the ReferencedProject

```
/*
 * ReferencedProject
 * ReferencedClass.java
 */
package com.allmycode.referenced;

public class ReferencedClass {
    public int value = 42;
}
```

Listing 13-2: A Class in the ReferringProject

```
/*
 * ReferringProject
 * ReferringClass.java
 */
package com.allmycode.referring;

import com.allmycode.referenced.ReferencedClass;

public class ReferringClass {

    public ReferringClass() {
        new ReferencedClass().value = 22;
    }
}
```

According to Figure 13-21, the code in Listings 13-1 and 13-2 lives in two separate Eclipse projects — `ReferencedProject` and `ReferringProject`. But the code in Listing 13-2 refers to the `value` field in Listing 13-1. If you don't tell Eclipse that one project's code can refer to the other project's field, then Eclipse displays red error markers. By default, all projects are independent of one another, even if they live in the same workspace.

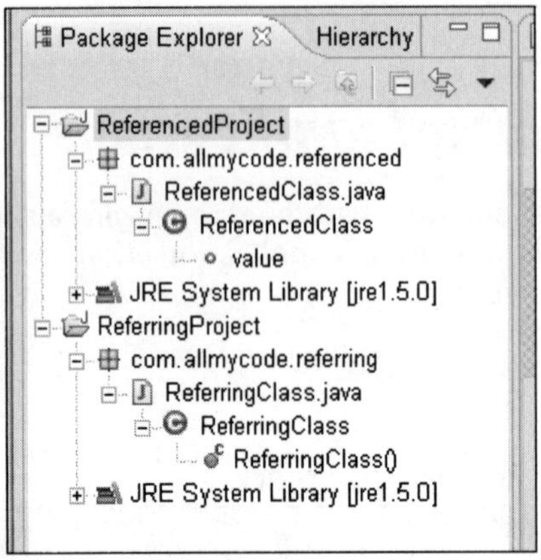

Figure 13-21:
A program
that
straddles
several
Eclipse
projects.

To connect one project to another, do the following:

1. **In the Package Explorer, right-click the project that refers to the other project's code.**

   In this example, right-click `ReferringProject`.

2. **In the resulting context menu, choose Properties.**

   A big dialog appears on-screen. This dialog describes all the properties of `ReferringProject`.

3. **On the left side of the dialog, select Java Build Path.**

   The *build path* is what many people call the CLASSPATH — the collection of folders in which Eclipse looks for classes.

4. **On the right side of the dialog, select the Projects tab. (See Figure 13-22.)**

   You can add an entire project's folders to another project's build path.

5. **Put a check mark next to the project whose code is referenced.**

   In Figure 13-22, I put a check mark in the `ReferencedProject` box.

6. **Click OK.**

   Any red error markers in the referring project's code disappear. If they don't disappear immediately, they disappear the next time you save the code.

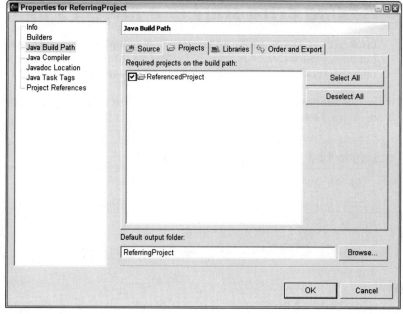

Figure 13-22:
Adding one
project to
another
project's
build path.

Eclipse gets upset if you create circular build paths. If ProjectA's build path includes ProjectB, and ProjectB's build path includes ProjectA, then Eclipse displays messages like the ones in Figure 13-23. When you try to run your code, Eclipse displays a box like the one in Figure 13-24. In spite of the word "Errors" in Figure 13-24, you can run code that contains a circular build path. If you click OK in the Errors in Project dialog, Eclipse executes your program.

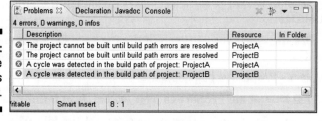

Figure 13-23:
The
Problems
view.

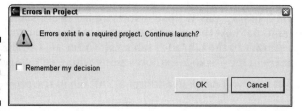

Figure 13-24:
Errors in
your code.

Adding extra stuff to a project's build path

Look back at Figure 13-22, and notice how complex a project's build path can become. Figure 13-22 has Source, Projects, Libraries, and Order and Export tabs. Each tab manipulates the build path in one way or another.

In this section, I focus on the Libraries tab. And to stretch the build path's muscles, I introduce a JUnit test. The test code is in Listing 13-3.

Listing 13-3:   A Really Simple JUnit Test

```
import junit.framework.TestCase;

public class Arithmetic extends TestCase {

    public void testGetName() {
        assertEquals(2 + 2, 5);
    }
}
```

If you're a Java programmer and you've never used JUnit, then you're missing out on all the fun. JUnit is a "must have" tool for testing Java programs.

The test case in Listing 13-3 is pretty simple. The code fails if 2 + 2 doesn't equal 5. (And where I come from, 2 + 2 doesn't equal 5.)

This section describes the setup in Eclipse for running the code in Listing 13-3. As you follow the steps, you find out how to mess with the project's build path.

1. **Create a new project.**

   On the Select a Wizard page, select Java Project. For the project name, use **JUnitDemo**.

2. **Right-click the** `JUnitDemo` **branch of the Package Explorer and choose Properties.**

   The project's Properties page appears.

3. **On the left side of the Properties page, select Java Build Path.**

4. **On the right side of the Properties page, select the Libraries tab. (See Figure 13-25.)**

   As part of the Libraries tab, Eclipse displays a list of JARs and class folders on the build path. At this point, you're probably not surprised to find JRE System Library in the Libraries tab's list. (After all, the JRE System Library appears in the Package Explorer along with every single project.)

   To run a JUnit test, you need an additional JAR file in the project's build path.

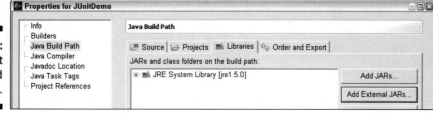

Figure 13-25:
The default
Java build
path.

5. **Click the Add External JARs button.**

   A JAR Selection dialog appears. This dialog looks just like an ordinary Open dialog that you see when you open any new document.

6. **In the JAR Selection dialog, navigate to the** eclipse plugins **directory.**

   That is, look in the directory in which you installed Eclipse. Directly under that installation directory, look for a subdirectory named plugins.

7. **Within the** plugins **directory, navigate to a directory whose name begins with** org.junit.

   In Eclipse 3.1, the directory's name is org.junit_3.8.1. But by the time you read this book, the name may be org.junit_99.9.98, or something like that.

8. **Inside the** org.junit **directory, look for a** junit.jar **file and double-click it.**

   As if by magic, Eclipse returns you to the project's Properties page. Now the list of JARs and class folders has an additional entry. Naturally, the entry's label is junit.jar. (See Figure 13-26.)

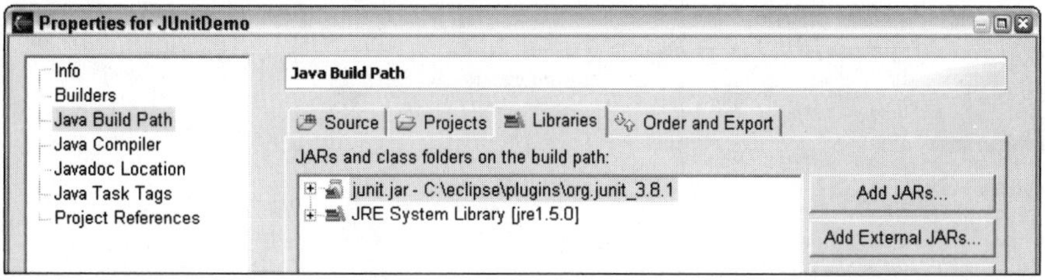

Figure 13-26:
An
enhanced
Java build
path.

9. **Click OK to dismiss the project's Properties page.**

   Eclipse returns you to the workbench. In the Package Explorer, you see the additional junit.jar entry. (See Figure 13-27.)

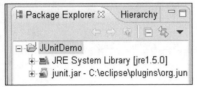

Figure 13-27:
A project
with two
libraries.

Now all you need to do is add the code in Listing 13-3. You can add it just like any other class, but my obsessive/compulsive streak tells me to call it a JUnit test case.

10. **Right-click your project's branch in the Package Explorer. In the resulting context menu, choose New⇨JUnit Test Case.**

Eclipse's New JUnit Test Case Wizard appears.

11. **Type a name for your new test case.**

In the wizard's Name field, type **Arithmetic**.

12. **Click OK to dismiss the New JUnit Test Case Wizard and return to the workbench.**

13. **In the editor, type the code from Listing 13-3 (or download the code from this book's Web site).**

14. **On Eclipse's main menu, choose Run⇨Run⇨JUnit Test.**

After much sound and fury, you see the JUnit view in Figure 13-28. The number of errors is 0, but the number of failures is 1. If you look down at the Failure Trace, you can see what failed. The trace says expected: <4> but was: <5>. How much more explicit can a failure message be?

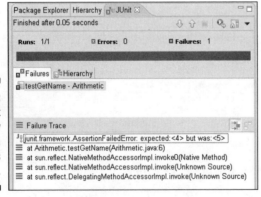

Figure 13-28:
The JUnit
view
displays a
program's
failures.

Importing Code

In most of this book's examples, you create brand-new programs using Eclipse. That's fine for new code, but maybe you weren't born using Eclipse. Maybe you have Java code that you created before you started using Eclipse. What do you do with all that older Java code? The answer is, you *import* the code. You bring existing code into a newly created Eclipse project.

You have two import techniques to choose from. You can drag and drop, or you can use the Import Wizard.

Using drag and drop

As an importing technique, dragging and dropping works only with certain operating systems. (With Eclipse 3.0, the technique works only in Windows.) In addition, this technique is like a blunt instrument. The technique imports everything from a particular directory on your hard drive. If you want to import only a few files from a directory, this technique isn't your best bet.

Of course, if you use Windows, and you like the intuitive feel of dragging and dropping, then this technique is for you. Just follow these steps:

1. **Create a new Java project.**

   In this example, I named the project **MyImportedCode**.

2. **Double-click My Computer, and then navigate to a source directory that's outside of the Eclipse workspace.**

   In other words, navigate to the directory containing the stuff that you want to import. For example, take a look back at Figure 13-1. To import all the stuff in Figure 13-1, navigate to the JavaPrograms directory.

3. **Drag the top-level package directory to the new project's branch in Eclipse's Package Explorer.**

   In plain English, drag the stuff that you want to import to your new Eclipse project.

You must be careful to drag the proper directory. If you don't, then your Eclipse project ends up having the wrong directory structure. For example, in Figure 13-29 I drag the top-level com package directory from the My Computer window into the MyImportedCode project.

The result is in Figure 13-30. Within its own workspace, Eclipse creates a copy of the com directory (and of everything inside the com directory). As you may expect, Eclipse ignores the JavaPrograms directory.

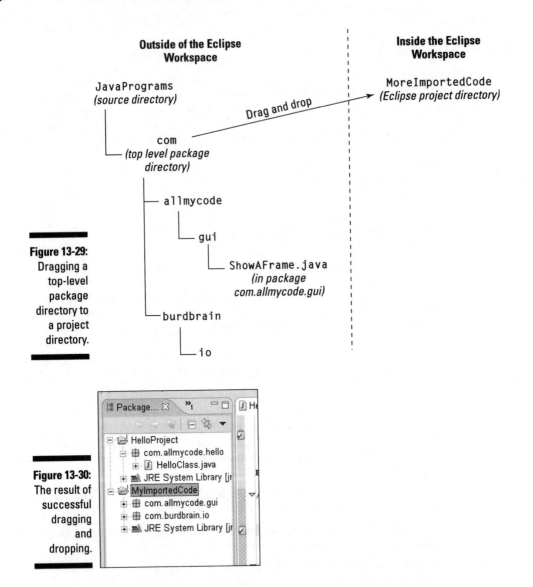

Figure 13-29:
Dragging a
top-level
package
directory to
a project
directory.

Figure 13-30:
The result of
successful
dragging
and
dropping.

I admit it. I find these directory names to be a bit confusing. If I don't do it for a while, I forget which directory to drag. I'm usually off by one level. (I select either the parent or the child of the appropriate directory.) Then my directory structure doesn't match my Java package structure, and I have to start over again. My brain doesn't process this particular concept very easily. Who knows? Maybe your brain does a better processing job.

Dragging and dropping selected directories

In the previous section, I show you how to drag all the code from the com.*anything.anythingelse* packages into the Eclipse workspace. That's fine if you're not too picky. But what if you want to drop only some of the code from a particular directory into the Eclipse workspace?

For instance, from all the stuff in Figure 13-1 I may want com\allmycode\gui, but not com\burdbrain\io. So which directory do I drag? If I drag the com directory, then the burdbrain\io directory comes along with it. And if I drag allmycode, then the new Eclipse directory structure doesn't match the package name. (The new Eclipse directory is allmycode\gui, but the package name in the code is still com.allmycode.gui.)

So here's what I do. I manually create a com directory in the Eclipse project. I call com an *un-dragged directory* because I don't drag com from My Computer to the Eclipse project.

After creating this un-dragged directory inside the Eclipse project, I can drag allmycode into the Eclipse project. To do all this on your own, follow these steps:

1. **Create a new Java project.**

   If you want to follow along with my clicks and keystrokes in this set of steps, name your project **MoreImportedCode**.

2. **In the Package Explorer, right-click your new project's branch.**

   To follow along with me word for word, right-click the MoreImportedCode branch.

3. **On the resulting context menu, choose New⇨Folder.**

   Be sure to choose New⇨Folder, and not New⇨Source Folder. The Source Folder option is for creating a source directory. And in this example, com is a package directory, not a source directory. (See the discussion of source directories and package directories in my section titled "The Typical Java Program Directory Structure.")

   A New Folder dialog appears.

4. **In the Folder Name field of the New Folder dialog, type the un-dragged directory's name.**

   In this example, I typed **com**.

5. **Click Finish.**

   The New Folder dialog disappears. In the Eclipse workbench, your project tree contains a new `com` entry.

6. **On your Windows desktop, open My Computer.**

7. **Drag the stuff that you want to import, and drop it in Eclipse's Package Explorer. Drop it into the un-dragged directory.**

   In Figure 13-31, I drag `allmycode` from My Computer into the `MoreImportedCode` project's `com` directory (in the Package Explorer).

8. **Check your work by looking for error markers in the Package Explorer.**

   Figure 13-32 shows the results of two attempts to import files. One attempt is successful; the other isn't.

   - In the successful attempt, I dropped `allmycode` in the `com` directory of the `MoreImportedCode` project. The resulting `com.allmycode.gui` directory contains the `ShowAFrame.java` file.

   - In the unsuccessful attempt, someone else (who shall remain nameless) makes a mistake. This person manually creates a `com` directory, but doesn't drop `allmycode` into the `com` directory. Instead, this poor programmer drops `allmycode` directly into the `PoorlyImportedCode` branch of the Package Explorer's tree.

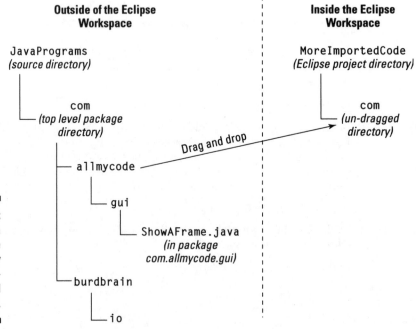

Figure 13-31:
Dragging a package directory into the un-dragged directory.

So unfortunately, the newly copied `allmycode` directory isn't a subdirectory of the `com` directory. Eclipse immediately attempts to compile the code. But the directory structure doesn't match the `com.allmycode.gui` package name inside the `ShowAFrame.java` file. To indicate the error, Eclipse displays tiny red error markers.

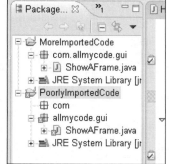

Figure 13-32: Successful and unsuccessful importing.

Using the Import Wizard

If you don't use Microsoft Windows, or if you want to carefully pick and choose what you import, you can't use drag-and-drop. Instead, you have to use the Import Wizard.

1. **Create a new Java project.**

   In this example, name your project **ImportWizardTest**.

2. **In the Package Explorer, right-click your newly created project. Then, on the resulting context menu, choose Import.**

   An Import Wizard appears.

3. **In the Import Wizard, select File System. Then click Next. (See Figure 13-33.)**

   The File System page appears.

4. **In the From Directory field, enter the name of a Java source directory.**

   In this example, I'm importing some of the stuff in Figure 13-1. In that figure, the source directory's name is `JavaPrograms`. So in Figure 13-34, I typed **JavaPrograms** in the From Directory field.

   This source directory (a.k.a. the From Directory) is the immediate parent of the top-level package directory. For instance, in Figure 13-34, the `JavaPrograms` source directory is the immediate parent of `com` (the top-level package directory).

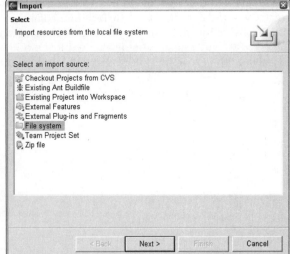

Figure 13-33:
The first
page of the
Import
Wizard.

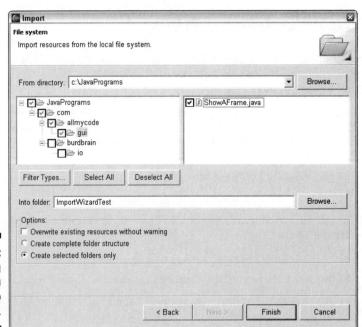

Figure 13-34:
Selecting
the files you
want to
import.

TIP

To fill in the From Directory field, you can either browse or type characters. If you type characters, then Eclipse may exhibit some slightly peculiar behavior. The two white panes directly beneath the From Directory field stay empty until you do something else (whatever "doing something else" means). After typing a name in the From Directory field, I clicked my mouse inside one of the big white panes. As soon as I click, Eclipse starts to populate these panes with check box structures.

5. **Expand the left check box tree, looking for a directory containing the code that you want to import. When you find such a directory, select it with your mouse.**

   In this example, I selected the gui directory.

6. **In the list on the right, put a check mark next to any file that you want to import.**

   In Figure 13-34, I put a check mark next to the ShowAFrame.java file. In response, Eclipse automatically puts check marks next to some of the directories in the left check box tree.

7. **In the Options group, select the Create Selected Folders Only radio button.**

   With Create Selected Folders Only checked, you import the com, allmy code, and gui directories. With the alternative Create Complete Folder Structure box checked, you import the JavaPrograms directory as well. (That's bad, because JavaPrograms isn't part of the package name.)

8. **Click Finish.**

   The Import Wizard disappears. In the Eclipse workbench, your project tree contains new entries. In Figure 13-35, these new entries are in the com.allmycode.gui package.

Figure 13-35:
The newly imported com.all mycode. gui package.

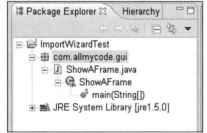

Getting rid of unwanted directories

In this chapter, you create one directory after another. Occasionally, you make a mistake and create a directory that you don't really want. Who knows? Maybe you create a whole set of directories within directories that you don't really want.

If you create a bad directory, you can delete the directory and try again. To delete a directory, right-click the directory's branch in the Package Explorer and choose Delete.

At some point, when you try to delete a directory, you may see an annoying out of sync with file system message. Chances are, you're trying to get rid of something that's already been deleted. Just click the message's OK button. Then in the Eclipse workbench, choose File⇨Refresh. When you do, the non-existent directory disappears from the Package Explorer.

Adding Javadoc Pages to Your Project

When you create a new Java class, Eclipse puts Javadoc comments in the newly generated code. That's good because some programmers forget to add Javadoc comments of their own. (Of course, you never forget to add Javadoc comments, and I never forget either. But some programmers forget, so Eclipse creates the comments automatically.)

Of course, Javadoc comments aren't very useful until you sift the comments out of your code. As a result of the sifting, you get a bunch of nice looking Web pages. These Web pages (which also happen to be called *Javadoc pages*) are indispensable for anyone who uses the names defined in your code.

Eclipse associates each collection of Javadoc pages with a particular project. To sift out a project's Javadoc comments and create Javadoc Web pages, follow these steps:

1. **Create a Java project, and add a class with Javadoc comments to your project.**

2. **On the Eclipse menu bar, choose Project⇨Generate Javadoc.**

   The Generate Javadoc Wizard appears. If this is your first time using Eclipse to generate a Javadoc, the Javadoc Command field is empty. (See Figure 13-36.)

3. **If the Javadoc Command field is empty, click the Configure button.**

   In the Generate Javadoc Wizard, what you normally call the Browse button is labeled Configure. Navigate to a file on your computer named javadoc or javadoc.exe. This javadoc file (an executable) sifts comments out of your code for insertion into Web pages.

The javadoc executable is part of the JDK (Java Development Kit). You don't need the JDK to do most of the things you do in this book, so you may not have the JDK on your computer. To get the JDK, visit java.sun.com. After you install the JDK, look for a bin directory inside another jdk5.0 directory (or something like that). The bin directory contains lots of other java*something* filenames — names like javac, javah, javaw, and (yes!) javadoc. The directory also contains some non-java names — names like appletviewer and jarsigner.

Figure 13-36:
Your first visit to the Generate Javadoc Wizard.

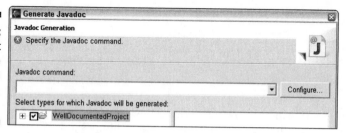

After you successfully browse for the javadoc executable, the top of the Generate Javadoc Wizard looks something like the page in Figure 13-37.

Figure 13-37:
The Generate Javadoc Wizard, after filling in the Javadoc Command field.

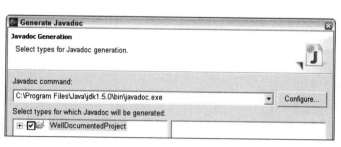

4. Click Finish to bypass the wizard's other pages.

The Generate Javadoc Wizard gives you lots and lots of options. As for me, I often accept the defaults.

Clicking Finish gives you a dialog in which you're asked to confirm the location of the new documents.

5. Click Yes to accept the default Javadoc document location (unless you don't like the default location, in which case click No).

The Eclipse workbench reappears. Then after lots of hard drive spinning and chirping, a new Console view shows up in the workbench. This Console view contains a blow-by-blow description of the Javadoc generating process. (See Figure 13-38.)

Figure 13-38:
Eclipse
keeps you
posted as it
generates
Javadoc
pages.

Eclipse doesn't generate Javadoc pages quickly, so be patient. You may think that your computer isn't doing anything. But if you wait a few minutes, you'll see some action in the Console view.

When the dust settles, you have some brand-new Javadoc pages. If you want to be sure that the pages exist, look at the Package Explorer (as it's pictured in Figure 13-39.)

Figure 13-39:
The
Package
Explorer
displays
the names
of your
project's
Javadoc
pages.

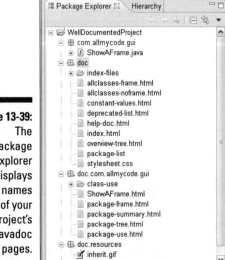

In Figure 13-39, all the filenames are very nice. But you may want to view your new Javadoc pages. Here's how you do it:

1. **Select your project's branch in the Package Explorer.**

   Alternatively, select a class inside your project in either the Package Explorer or the editor.

2. **On Eclipse's main menu, choose Navigate➪Open External Javadoc.**

   A bright, new Javadoc page appears in your computer's Web browser.

 You can get more from your Javadoc pages if you tell Eclipse where the Java System Library's pages live. To do this, right-click an rt.jar branch of the Package Explorer's tree, and choose Properties. On the resulting Properties page, select Javadoc Location. Then in the Javadoc Location Path field, type the name of a directory that contains the package-list and index.html files.

Chapter 14

Running Code

*B*ack in 2002, I wrote *Java & XML For Dummies*. As part of my research, I joined a local Special Interest Group on XML. The meetings were interesting. People argued for hours over the most esoteric issues. Should a certain piece of information be expressed as an element attribute or should that information be the element's content? The term "religious wars" came to mind, but I never uttered that term aloud in any of the group's discussions.

Every field of study has its religious wars. In the world of Java programming, people argue over all kinds of things. For instance, you want a program to get a small piece of information at runtime. Where do you put this piece of information? Do you make it a program argument or a virtual machine argument? And what if you don't know the difference between these two kinds of arguments? (And what if you don't care?)

This chapter covers program arguments, virtual machine arguments, and a few other tricks. The chapter tells you how to use each of these things in Eclipse.

Creating a Run Configuration

A *run configuration* is a set of guidelines that Eclipse uses for running a particular Java program. A particular run configuration stores the name of a main class, the values stored in the main method's args parameter, the JRE version to be used, the CLASSPATH, and many other facts about a program's anticipated run.

Whenever you run a program, Eclipse uses one run configuration or another. In the previous chapters, Eclipse uses a default run configuration. But in this chapter, you create customized run configurations. Here's how you do it:

1. **Select a class that contains a main method.**

   You can select any class you want. Select this class by clicking a branch in the Package Explorer or the Outline view. Alternatively, you can click the class's editor tab.

2. **On Eclipse's menu bar, choose Run⇨Run.**

   The big Run dialog appears. (See Figure 14-1.)

   Starting with Eclipse version 3.1, the Run menu has two Run items that look almost identical. One of the Run items has an ellipsis (three dots) and the other Run item doesn't. In this example, the Run item you want is the one with the ellipsis. If, after choosing Run⇨Run, you don't get the dialog shown in Figure 14-1, then you've chosen the wrong Run item.

3. **In the Configurations pane (on the left side of the Run dialog), double-click the** `Java Application` **branch.**

   Double-clicking `Java Application` creates a brand new item. The item's name comes from whatever class you selected in Step 1.

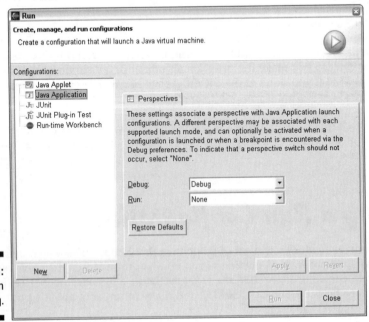

Figure 14-1: The Run dialog.

When I selected a class in Step 1, the class's name was `DeleteEvidence`. So in Figure 14-2, the Configurations pane has a new item named `DeleteEvidence`. This `DeleteEvidence` item represents a brand-new run configuration.

Figure 14-2:
A new item in the Configurations pane.

Eclipse's run configurations come in five different flavors. In Eclipse version 3.0, these "flavors" are named Java Applet, Java Application, JUnit, JUnit Plug-in Test, and Run-time Workbench. (Again, see Figure 14-2.) By the time version 3.1 rolled in, someone had replaced Run-time Workbench with Eclipse Application.

Anyway, each flavor of run configuration stores certain kinds of information. For example, a Java Applet configuration stores applet tag parameters — things like `Width` and `Height`. (See Figure 14-3.) A Java Application configuration doesn't store any applet tag parameters because a stand-alone application doesn't use an applet tag.

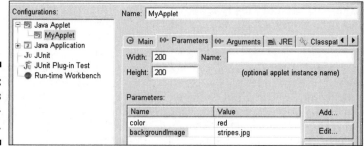

Figure 14-3:
An applet's run configuration.

Using Program Arguments

Listing 14-1 contains a very useful program. The program deletes a file of your choosing. To choose a file, you send the file's name to the `args` parameter.

Listing 14-1:   How to Delete a File

```
package com.allmycode.monkeybusiness;

import java.io.File;

public class DeleteEvidence {

    public static void main(String[] args) {

        if (args.length > 0) {
            File evidence = new File(args[0]);
            if (evidence.exists()) {
                evidence.delete();
                System.out.print("Evidence? ");
                System.out.println("What evidence?");
            }
        }
    }
}
```

In the old days of plain, white-on-black command windows, you invoked this `DeleteEvidence` program by typing the following line of text:

```
java DeleteEvidence books
```

That was the original idea behind this `String[] args` business. You typed a program's name, and then typed extra words on the command line. Whatever extra words you typed became part of the `args` array. Each extra word (like the word `books`) was called a *program argument*.

Even now, in the third millennium, you can run a Java program by typing a command like `java DeleteEvidence books`. When you run Listing 14-1 this way, your computer hands the word `"books"` to `args[0]`. So if your hard drive has a `books` file, the program of Listing 14-1 deletes the file. (Of course, the `books` file has to live in a certain directory on your hard drive. Otherwise, the program of Listing 14-1 can't find the `books` file. For more details, read on.)

Running with program arguments

Eclipse isn't just a plain, white-on-black command window. So with Eclipse, you don't type a command like `java DeleteEvidence books`. Instead, you click buttons and fill in fields when you want to send `"books"` to the `args` parameter. Here's how you do it:

1. **Create a new Java project.**

   In this example, call your project **CoverUpProject**.

2. **Create a new Java class containing the code of Listing 14-1.**

3. **Create a file of any kind in the project directory.**

   Select the `CoverUpProject` branch in the Package Explorer and choose File⇨New⇨File. In the New File dialog's File Name field, type a name for your file (a name like **books**). Then click Finish.

   If all goes well, the new `books` file appears in the Package Explorer. It appears at a level immediately beneath the `CoverUpProject` branch itself. (See Figure 14-4.) The `books` file also appears in an editor. If you want, you can add text to the `books` file by typing stuff in the editor. Or if you're lazy, you can skip the typing. In this example, it doesn't matter one way or the other.

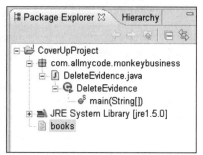

Figure 14-4: The books file is part of the Package Explorer's tree.

Next you run the `DeleteEvidence` code, and you give `args[0]` the value `"books"`.

4. **Create a run configuration for the `DeleteEvidence` class.**

   At first, the run configuration contains a bunch of defaults. So in the next several steps you change some defaults.

   If you don't know how to create a run configuration, see the section "Creating a Run Configuration."

5. **On the right half of the Run dialog, select the Arguments tab.**

   A page containing some empty fields appears.

   If you can't find the Run dialog's Arguments tab, don't panic. You may have glossed over Step 3 in this chapter's "Creating a Run Configuration" section. On the left side of the Run dialog, look for an `DeleteEvidence` item. If you find such an item, select it. If you can't find such an item, double-click the `Java Application` branch.

6. **Type values in the Arguments tab's fields.**

   In this example, type **books** in the Program Arguments field. (See Figure 14-5.) That way, when Eclipse runs the code, `args[0]` will refer to the String value `"books"`.

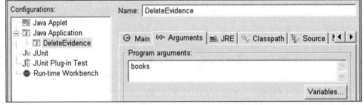

Figure 14-5:
Typing a value in the Program Arguments field.

   Anything you type in the Program Arguments field becomes part of the `args` array when Eclipse runs the code. For example, if you type **cooked books** in the Program Arguments field, then `args[0]` is `"cooked"` and `args[1]` is `"books"`. Any blank spaces between `cooked` and `books` separate `args[0]` from `args[1]`.

   To circumvent the business about blank spaces, enclose words in quotation marks. For instance, if you type **"freeze dried" books** (with one pair of quotation marks), then `args[0]` is `"freeze dried"` and `args[1]` is `"books"`.

7. **Near the lower-right corner of the Run dialog, click Apply.**

   Though it's not necessary in this example, clicking Apply is a good habit for you to have.

8. **Near the lower-right corner of the Run dialog, click Run.**

   Eclipse runs the code of Listing 14-1. Because `args[0]` stands for `"books"`, the program's run deletes the `books` file.

9. **Look at the Package Explorer's tree.**

   Hey, what gives? You can still see the `books` branch. The Package Explorer doesn't update its listing unless you specifically call for a refresh.

10. **Select the project's branch of the Package Explorer tree. Then, on the menu bar, choose File⇨Refresh.**

    In this example, select the `CoverUpProject` branch. When you choose File⇨Refresh, the books branch disappears.

Is there such a thing as a rerun configuration?

A run configuration stays attached to a project. And what in the world does it mean for a configuration to be "attached?"

Imagine that you perform all the instructions in the "Running with program arguments" section. Then you redo Step 3, creating the `books` file anew. To delete the `books` file a second time, you don't have to repeat all the run configuration steps. Instead, march over to the menu bar and choose Run⇨Run⇨ Java Application. Eclipse automatically reuses the run configuration that you created in the "Running with program arguments" section.

Of course, you can always change a project's run configuration. Just return to the Run dialog and make whatever changes you want to make. (To return to the Run dialog, follow the "Creating a Run Configuration" section's steps.)

Starting with Eclipse version 3.1, the Run menu has two Run items that look almost identical. One of the Run items has an ellipsis (three dots) and the other Run item doesn't. In this example, the Run item you want is the one without the ellipsis. If, after choosing Run⇨Run, you get the dialog shown in Figure 14-1, then you've chosen the wrong Run item.

Finding the elusive Refresh action

Where's the File menu's Refresh item when I need it? More often than not, that Refresh item is grayed out. What nerve! Who do these volunteer Eclipse developers think they are?

But wait! Maybe it's my fault. Ah, yes! The thing I just selected is outside of the Package Explorer. (I clicked my mouse on a word in the editor.) Then there's nothing to refresh. So naturally, the Refresh item is grayed out.

Occasionally, when I select a branch in the Package Explorer's tree, the Refresh item is grayed out. For instance, if I select JRE System Library, then Eclipse refuses to do a refresh. I guess that's reasonable. The JRE System Library doesn't change often enough to need a refresh.

Piling on those run configurations

You can create several different run configurations for the same project. Return to Step 3 of this chapter's "Creating a Run Configuration" section, and double-click the `Java Application` branch several times. Each time you double-click, Eclipse creates an additional run configuration. And each run configuration can have different argument values.

So what if you create ten run configurations for the code in Listing 14-1? When you choose Run⇨Run⇨Java Application, which run configuration does Eclipse use?

If the code you're trying to run is associated with more than one run configuration, Eclipse displays a Launch Configuration Selection dialog. The dialog lists all applicable run configurations. You just select a configuration, and then "run with it."

Using Properties

The "Running with program arguments" section shows you how to use the main method's parameter list. So to balance things out, this section's example uses something else — a *property*. A property is like a program argument, except that it's different. (How's that for a clear explanation?)

In ancient times, program arguments were things you typed on the command line at runtime. In contrast, properties were pieces of information that you stored in a little file. These days, with things like Eclipse run configurations, the distinction between program arguments and properties is quickly fading.

Just like the example in the "Running with program arguments" section, this section's example deletes a file. In the "Running with program arguments" section, the program gets the file's name through the main method's parameter list. But in this section's example, the program gets the file's name using a property.

A property is something with two parts — a *name* and a *value*. Speaking for myself, I have a property with name `sex` and value `male`. I have another property with name `citizenOf` and value `United States`. Another person's `citizenOf` property may have value `Australia`.

When you start running a Java program, you can feed properties to the Java Virtual Machine (JVM). In this section's example, I give the JVM a property whose name is `file_name`, and whose value is `books`. In turn, the JVM hands that property to my Java program. Here's how it works:

1. **Create a new Java project.**

   In this example, call your project **CoverUpProject2**.

2. **Create a new Java class containing the code of Listing 14-2.**

3. **Create a file of any kind in the project directory.**

   Name this file `books`. For details, see the "Running with program arguments" section.

4. **Type** -Dfile_name=books **in the VM Arguments field. (See Figure 14-6.)**

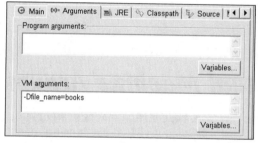

Figure 14-6:
Creating a
runtime
property.

The abbreviation "VM" stands for "Virtual Machine." No, it doesn't stand for any old Virtual Machine. It stands for the Java Virtual Machine. So in this example, the abbreviations "VM" and "JVM" stand for the same thing. I can live with that.

In this step, you type `-Dfile_name=books` in the VM Arguments field. This `-Dfile_name=books` stuff creates a property with name `"file_name"` and with value `"books"`. So far, so good.

5. **Follow Steps 7 through 10 in the "Running with program arguments" section.**

   When you use this example's run configuration, you hand that `"file_name"/"books"` property to the Java Virtual Machine. Then, when you run the code in Listing 14-2, the code retrieves the property's value with a call to `System.getProperty`. At last, the cycle is complete. The code in Listing 14-2 gets the needed `file_name=books` information.

   Whether it's a program argument or a VM argument, the word `books` represents a file. The code in Listing 14-2 deletes that `books` file.

Listing 14-2:   How to Use a Property

```
package com.allmycode.monkeybusiness;

import java.io.File;

public class DeleteEvidence {

    public static void main(String[] args) {
        File evidence =
            new File(System.getProperty("file_name"));
        if (evidence.exists()) {
            evidence.delete();
            System.out.print("Evidence? ");
            System.out.println("What evidence?");
        }
    }
}
```

Using Other Virtual Machine Arguments

In the "Using Properties" section, I use virtual machine arguments to feed a property to a program. That's great, but virtual machine arguments are good for all kinds of things, not just for creating properties. Here's an example.

I have a program that's supposed to generate a number from 1 to 6. The program is in Listing 14-3. This program better not give me a number like 0 or 7. If it does, I'll accuse the program of cheating (in the style of an old western barroom brawl).

Listing 14-3:   Did I Use the nextInt Method Correctly?

```
import java.util.Random;

public class RollEm {

    public static void main(String[] args) {
        int dieRoll = new Random().nextInt(6);
            //Between 0 and 5 or between 1 and 6 ??
        System.out.println(dieRoll);
        assert 1 <= dieRoll && dieRoll <= 6;
    }
}
```

Because I'm not absolutely sure that the program creates numbers from 1 to 6, I add an assert statement. The assert statement is a feature of Java 1.4, and by default this feature is not normally available.

So if you run the RollEm program from the command line, you have to type some extra stuff.

```
java -enableassertions RollEm
```

The extra -enableassertions business activates one of the virtual machine's many options. In other words, -enableassertions is an argument that you pass to the virtual machine. To do the same thing without a command line, you can tweak Eclipse's run configuration. The next set of instructions gives you all the details.

1. **Create a new Java project.**

2. **Add the** RollEm **class of Listing 14-3 to your project.**

3. **Notice how Eclipse seems to despise the** assert **statement.**

   Eclipse puts an ugly red blob in the editor's marker bar. The blob's hover tip tells you that you shouldn't use assert as an identifier. (See Figure 14-7.)

Figure 14-7:
An error
indicates
that the
word
assert is
problematic.

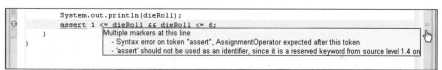

Before you can use an assert statement, you have to clear two hurdles. The first hurdle is the compiler; the second is the Java Virtual Machine.

By default, Eclipse's compiler treats assert statements like pariahs. To fix this problem, you have to dig in to the big Preferences window.

4. **Visit the Java⇨Compiler page of the Window⇨Preferences dialog. Within that page, select the Compliance and Classfiles tab.**

   See Figure 14-8. In the figure, the Use Default Compliance Settings box contains a check mark. That check mark is the assert statement's enemy.

You can tweak the compiler's settings on a project-by-project basis. To do so, right-click a project's branch on the Package Explorer tree. On the resulting context menu, choose Properties. Then, on the project's Properties page, select Java Compiler.

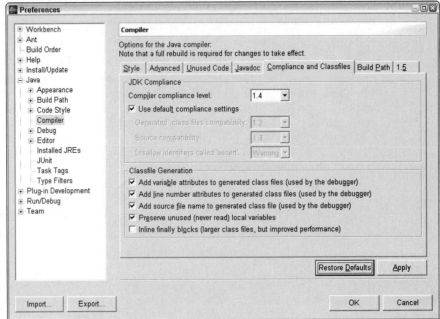

Figure 14-8:
Using the
default
compiler
compliance
settings.

Don't confuse a project's Properties page with any of the properties in this chapter's "Using Properties" section. A project's Properties page describes features of an Eclipse project. In contrast, the properties in the VM Arguments field feed short strings of information to a running program. These two kinds of properties have very little in common.

5. **Remove the check mark from the Use Default Compliance Settings box. Then change the Generated .class Files Compatibility and Source Compatibility lists to values 1.4 or higher.**

See Figure 14-9. When you insist on compatibility with Java 1.4, you tell Eclipse to accept things like `assert` statements — things that creep into Java with version 1.4.

Figure 14-9:
Setting the
compiler for
Java 1.4.

6. **Click Apply.**

   Eclipse responds with a dialog about rebuilding the source code.

7. **Click Yes to rebuild the source code.**

   After a brief rebuild, you see the Preferences dialog.

8. **Click OK to dismiss the Preferences dialog.**

   The editor's marker bar no longer displays a nasty red blob. Eclipse happily compiles the `assert` statement in Listing 14-3.

   But wait! Remember the two hurdles in writing code with `assert` statements. The first hurdle is the compiler, and the second is the Java Virtual Machine. You still have to tell the Java Virtual Machine about that `assert` statement.

9. **Select the `RollEm` class, and follow the steps in the "Creating a Run Configuration" section.**

10. **On the right half of the Run dialog, select the Arguments tab.**

    Congratulations! You've arrived at a page like the one in Figure 14-10. In the Configurations pane, the highlighted item is named `RollEm`.

Figure 14-10:
Adding the
`-enable`
`asser`
`tions`
argument.

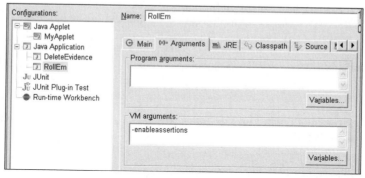

11. **In the VM Arguments field, type** -enableassertions.

    Again, see Figure 14-10.

12. **Click Apply.**

13. **Click Run.**

    The `RollEm` program's output is random. So chances are good that your first run puts a number between 1 and 5 in Eclipse's Console view. But run the program again (by choosing Run⇨Run⇨Java Application). Keep running the program until you see a zero in the Console view.

When the value of dieRoll is 0, the Java Virtual Machine throws an AssertionError. (See Figure 14-11.) This happens because, in Step 11, you tell the virtual machine to enable exceptions. If you don't add this virtual machine argument, then the virtual machine simply ignores the assert statement. You get an output of 0, with no AssertionError message.

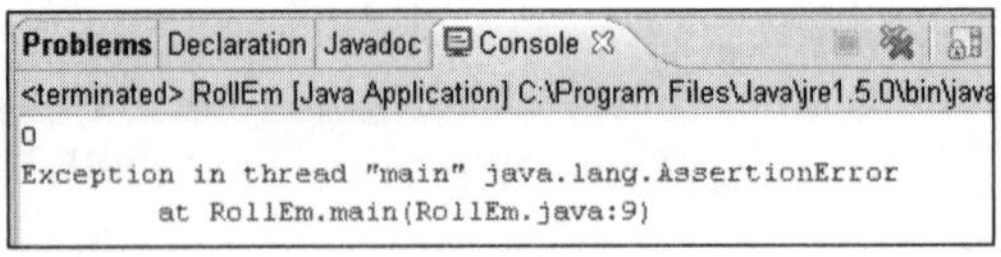

Figure 14-11:
Adding the
-enable
asser
tions
argument.

Problems	Declaration	Javadoc	🖳 Console 🔀		▣ ✹ ▯

```
<terminated> RollEm [Java Application] C:\Program Files\Java\jre1.5.0\bin\java
0
Exception in thread "main" java.lang.AssertionError
        at RollEm.main(RollEm.java:9)
```

Using Environment Variables

In their purest form, environment variables are pieces of information that an operating system stores. Running processes use these variables to coordinate activities, and to communicate with the rest of the system.

For example, on my Windows XP computer, I can open a command window. When I type

```
set user
```

in the command window, I get back the following list of environment variables and values:

```
USERDOMAIN=GROUCHO
USERNAME=bburd
USERPROFILE=C:\Documents and Settings\bburd
```

My Windows XP system has a USERDOMAIN environment variable. And the value of my USERDOMAIN variable is GROUCHO.

In their less-than-pure form, environment variables are just name/value pairs. (They're a lot like the properties in the "Using Properties" section.) For instance, in the same command window, I can type

```
lunch=cheeseburger
```

and then every program on my computer knows what I had for my noontime meal. With tools like Eclipse, I can change environment variables from one run to another. So one Java program can think I had a cheeseburger for lunch, and another can think I had pizza. (Please Note: No program thinks that I had salad for lunch.)

The material in this section is controversial. The section's example works on some versions of Microsoft Windows, but not on Linux or other operating systems. To make matters worse, Java experts discourage the use of environment variables (the principle point of this section's example). So enjoy this section if you want, and by all means, skip this section if you're not interested.

The code in Listing 14-4 uses some Windows XP environment variables and some variables that I can create on my own. In Listing 14-4, calls to System. genenv grab the values of these environment variables.

Listing 14-4: Displaying the Values of Some Environment Variables

```
package com.allmycode.env;

public class ShowEnvironment {

    public static void main(String[] args) {
        System.out.println(System.getenv("USERNAME"));
        System.out.println(System.getenv("COMPUTERNAME"));
        System.out.println(System.getenv("PATH"));
        System.out.println(System.getenv("CLASSPATH"));
        System.out.println(System.getenv("TEMP"));
        System.out.println(System.getenv("SETUPS"));
    }
}
```

The output from a run of Listing 14-4 is shown in Figure 14-12.

Figure 14-12:
A run of the
code in
Listing 14-4.

Problems	Declaration	Javadoc	Console ⊠

```
<terminated> ShowEnvironment [Java Application] C:\Program Files\Java\jre1.5.0\bin\javaw.exe (Oct 5, 2004 12:2
bburd
GROUCHO
C:\Program Files\WinOne;C:\WINDOWS\system32;C:\WINDOWS;C:\WINDOWS\System32\Wbem;C
.
C:\DOCUME~1\bburd\LOCALS~1\Temp
null
```

Well whadaya' know! My system has no SETUPS variable! So, in Figure 14-12, System.getenv("SETUPS") is null.

That's okay. Eclipse gives you the ability to create new environment variables on a run-by-run basis. You can even change the values of existing environment variables. Here's how:

1. **Create a project containing the code in Listing 14-4.**

2. **Follow the steps in the "Creating a Run Configuration" section.**

3. **On the right half of the Run dialog, select the Environment tab.**

   At first, you may not be able to see the Environment tab. To find this tab, click the little scroll arrow to the right of all the other tabs.

   In the next several steps, you create a brand new environment variable. This variable applies only to runs that use the current run configuration.

4. **Click New.**

   The New Environment Variable dialog appears.

5. **Type a name and a value for your new variable.**

   In Figure 14-13, I created a variable with name **SETUPS** and value **c:\Setups**.

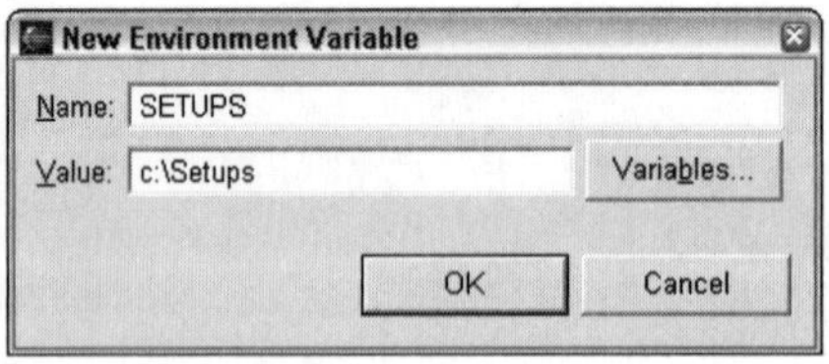

Figure 14-13: Creating a new environment variable.

6. **Click OK to dismiss the New Environment Variable dialog.**

   Your new SETUPS variable appears in the Environment Variables to Set list. (See Figure 14-14.)

   Next, you modify the value of an existing environment variable.

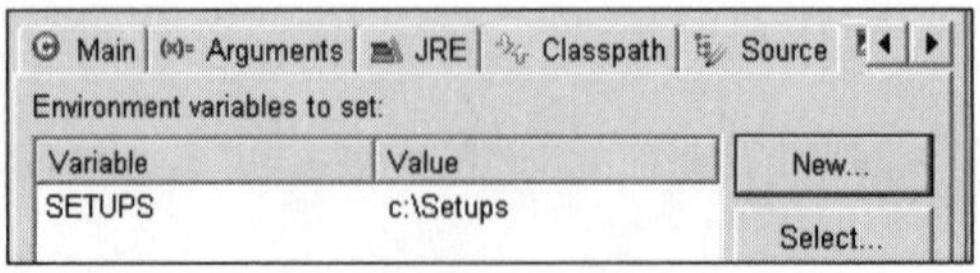

Figure 14-14: The Run dialog displays your new environment variable.

7. Click Select.

The Select Environment Variables dialog appears. (See Figure 14-15.)

8. Put a check mark next to TEMP.

9. Click OK.

Back in the Run dialog, the Environment Variables to Set list now contains a TEMP row. The TEMP row's value is your system's default temporary folder. (See Figure 14-16.)

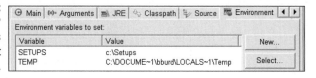

10. Select the TEMP row, and then click the Edit button.

An Edit Environment Variable dialog appears. The dialog looks very much like the dialog in Figure 14-13.

11. **Change the Value field in the Edit Environment Variable dialog.**

    On my computer, I have a c:\Junk folder. So I type **c:\Junk** in the Value field.

12. **Click OK to dismiss the Edit Environment Variable dialog.**

13. **Back in the Run dialog, notice the change in the Environment Variables to Set list.**

    On my computer, the value of TEMP is now c:\Junk.

14. **Click Apply, and then click Run.**

    The output of Listing 14-4 includes a value for SETUPS, and includes a brand new TEMP value. (See Figure 14-17.) In this experiment, you simply display variables' values on-screen. But in real life, the values of environment variables can be very useful.

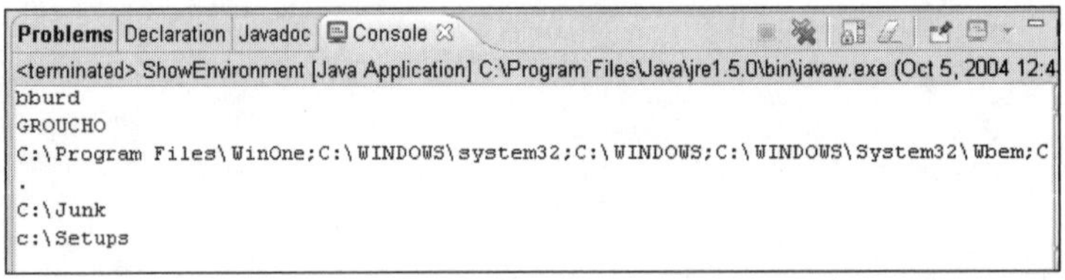

Figure 14-17:
Updated
values
of the
environment
variables.

Problems	Declaration	Javadoc	🖳 Console ⌗				❋	🖩 ⫞	⌐ ⊟ ⸱ ⊐

```
<terminated> ShowEnvironment [Java Application] C:\Program Files\Java\jre1.5.0\bin\javaw.exe (Oct 5, 2004 12:4
bburd
GROUCHO
C:\Program Files\WinOne;C:\WINDOWS\system32;C:\WINDOWS;C:\WINDOWS\System32\Wbem;C
.
C:\Junk
c:\Setups
```

Chapter 15

Getting Help

● ●

● ●

1 know. It's hard to believe. You have a question that *Eclipse For Dummies* doesn't answer. If that happens, what do you do? Where do you go for help? How do you keep from going crazy?

One thing you can do is read Eclipse's Help documents. The documents answer all kind of questions — questions that I can't begin to answer in this 350-page book. These documents are fairly comprehensive, mostly up to date, and above all, authoritative.

But Eclipse has its own built-in Help system, and navigating the Help system can be somewhat confusing. So to help you find help when you need help, I provide this chapter's help about Help. (I hope it helps.)

Searching for Help

To search within Eclipse's Help pages, you have two options. Fortunately, both options lead to the same results.

> ✔ Choosing Search⇨Search opens either File Search or Java Search. Either way, select the Help Search tab at the top of the Search dialog. When you do, Eclipse reveals the Help Search page shown in Figure 15-1.

> ✔ Choosing Help⇨Help Contents opens a window like the one in Figure 15-2. This window is called the *Help view*.

With either option, you can enter a search string, use Boolean searching, and narrow the results to a particular help working set. The next few pages have all the details.

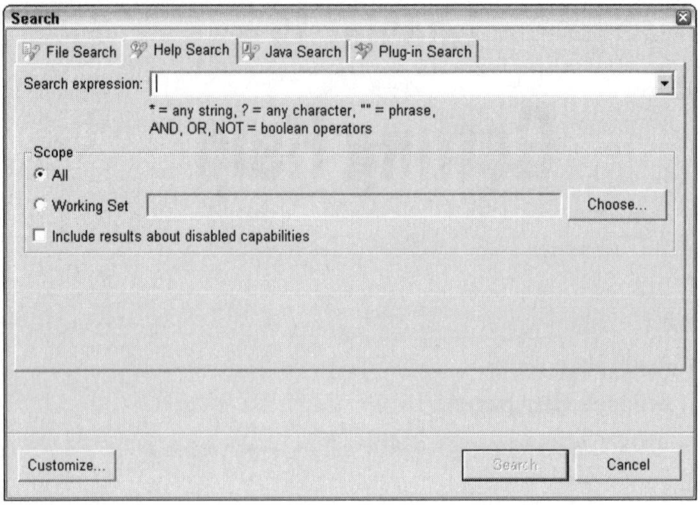

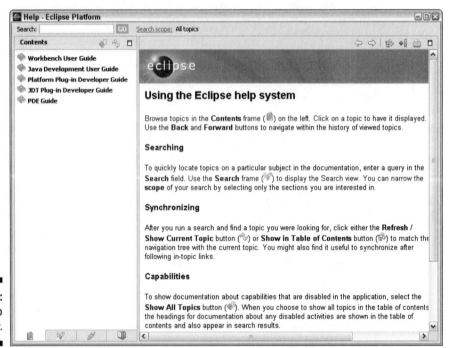

Figure 15-1:
The Help
Search
page.

Figure 15-2:
The Help
view.

Things you can use in a search expression

The Search Expression and Search fields in Figures 15-1 and 15-2 obey the rules that you use with many search engines on the Web.

✔ **You can combine terms using OR, AND, NOT.**

For instance, the expression **refactor OR parameter** searches for all Help pages containing either **refactor** or **parameter** (or both **refactor** and **parameter**).

Eclipse pastes an unseen **AND** between any two words that you type in the search field. So the expression **refactor parameter** along with **refactor AND parameter** yield the same results. In either case, each page in the results list contains both **refactor** and **parameter**.

You can use the word **NOT** to block results. For instance, if you type **refactor NOT parameter** in the search field, you get a list of pages that contain **refactor** but don't contain **parameter**.

A **NOT** phrase with nothing before the word **NOT** does absolutely nothing. For example, if you type **NOT parameter** (and nothing else) in a search field, you get a disappointing `Nothing found` message. When you use the word **NOT**, you have to type words both before and after the **NOT** (as in **refactor NOT parameter**).

✔ **You can use quotation marks to create search phrases.**

Searching for **"refactoring actions"** (with quotation marks) finds pages containing the phrase **refactoring actions**.

But searching for **refactoring actions** (without quotation marks) finds pages containing both the words **refactoring** and **actions**. (That is, in order to be found, a page must contain both words **refactoring** and **actions**, but not necessarily together.)

✔ **You can use a question mark to represent any character, or use an asterisk to represent any sequence of characters.**

Searching for **Abstract*Editor** looks for things like **AbstractTextEditor** and **AbstractDecoratedTextEditor** (names that happen to be part of Eclipse's own API).

✔ **You don't have to worry about capitalizing words (or about not capitalizing words).**

Eclipse's search strings are not case-sensitive.

✔ **You get similar results searching for** edit, editor, editing, edited, **or for other word variants.**

Eclipse's Help search uses something called *stemming*. With stemming, Eclipse takes a word like **editing** and looks for occurrences of the stem word **edit**. If you really, really need to search for **editing** and not for **edit**, **editor**, or **edited**, type the word **"editing"** in quotation marks inside the search field.

Using a help working set

Chapter 3 introduces the three kinds of Eclipse working sets — Java, resource, and help. A *help working set* is a collection of Help pages that you want included in a Help search. Creating a help working set narrows the search's results. That way, the list of pages in the Search view doesn't include dozens of pages that you know ahead of time are irrelevant.

With the following steps, you create an important help working set — a working set for people who *use* Eclipse, and who *don't modify or enhance* Eclipse's behavior.

1. **Choose Search⇨Search.**

   Eclipse's Search dialog appears.

2. **Select the Search dialog's Help tab.**

   A page like the one in Figure 15-1 appears.

3. **Select the Working Set radio button, and then click Choose.**

   The Select Working Set dialog appears. If you've already created Java working sets, they appear in this Select Working Set dialog.

   For information on Java working sets, see Chapter 3.

4. **Click New.**

   The New Working Set Wizard appears. If you've created a Java working set (Chapter 3), you're familiar with this page of the wizard.

5. **Under Working Set Type, select Help. Then click Next.**

   The Help Working Set page appears. (See Figure 15-3.) The page lists sections and subsections of Eclipse's Help documentation.

6. **Type a name for your new help working set.**

   In Figure 15-3, I typed **Eclipse User Working Set**.

7. **Select the sections and/or subsections that you want included in the Help Search results.**

   In Figure 15-3, I selected the Workbench User Guide and the Java Development User Guide. *Remember:* I only selected sections that are relevant for people who use Eclipse; these sections don't concern people who modify or enhance Eclipse's behavior (sections specifically for Eclipse plug-in developers).

8. **Click Finish.**

   The Select Working Set dialog reappears. Your new Eclipse User Working Set is in the dialog's list of working sets. (See Figure 15-4.)

Figure 15-3:
The Help
Working Set
page.

Figure 15-4:
A newly
created help
working set
appears in
your list.

9. **In the Select a Working Set list, select your new working set. Then click OK.**

Now the Help Search page reflects your choice of the Eclipse User Working Set. (See Figure 15-5.)

Figure 15-5:
You have
chosen
a help
working
set.

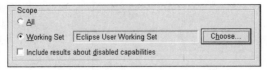

In the previous list of instructions, you start with the Help Search page and create a help working set. You can do the same thing if you start with the Help view (refer to Figure 15-2). Clicking the Search Scope link gives you a dialog similar to the Select Working Set dialog (refer to Figure 15-4). From there, you can select an existing help working set, or create a brand new help working set.

Some useful Search view tricks

You want to know something about Eclipse's refactoring actions. So you choose Search➪Search, select the Help Search tab, and then type **refactoring actions** in the Search Expression field.

Finally, you click Search. After a brief waiting period, you see the Search view in Figure 15-6. This view lists all the Help pages that match your **refactoring actions** search expression.

When you double-click an item in the Search view, Eclipse opens the Help view (refer to Figure 15-2). The right side of the Help view contains a big browser pane, and that browser pane visits the page that you double-clicked. From that point on, you can continue to visit pages in the Help view, or you can return to the Search view for more tinkering.

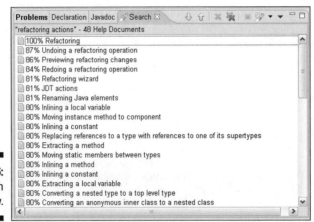

Figure 15-6:
The Search
view.

Returning to the Search view, you look over the view's list of Help pages. You remember seeing some of these pages in previous help searches. You know that certain pages don't contain the information that you want. So you eliminate some pages from the list. To do so, Ctrl+click the items that you want to eliminate. Then click the X button in the Search view's toolbar. (See Figure 15-7.)

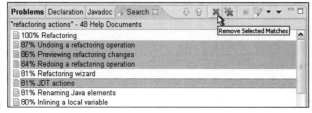

Figure 15-7: Selecting items in the Search view for removal.

Clicking the X button cleans up the current list. But it doesn't blacklist any pages. The pages that you remove can appear in future search lists.

Eventually you decide that one of your previous searches yielded better results. To retrieve an earlier search's results, click a button on the Search view's toolbar. (See Figure 15-8 for the exact location of that particular button.)

Sometimes I have trouble locating the toolbar button that lists previous searches. If you have trouble finding this button, let your mouse hover over the buttons on the Search view's toolbar. The button you're looking for has a hover tip that reads `Show Previous Searches`.

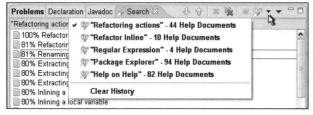

Figure 15-8: Returning to a previous search.

Using the Help View

The heart of Eclipse's Help system is the Help view (refer to Figure 15-2). The Help view has four tabs on the left side, a browser pane taking up two-thirds of the view's window, and some other miscellaneous stuff. Unlike other Eclipse views, the Help view is a loner. You can't drop the Help view into another view's area. The Help view lives in a window of its own.

A ten-cent tour of Eclipse's Help view

Figure 15-2 shows the Help view as it first appears on your screen. The lower left-hand corner of the view has four tabs — Contents, Search Results, Links, and Bookmarks.

The word *tab* has two meanings, and I use both meanings in this section. In fact, I probably use both meanings in a single sentence. First, a tab is a little button that looks like the edge of a piece of paper. (The lower left-hand corner of Figure 15-2 contains four of these tabs.) And second, a tab is a page that you see after you click one of the little buttons. (The left side of Figure 15-2 displays a tall tab labeled *Contents*.) I'd like to use two different words for the little tab and the tall tab. But if I did, I'd clash with the terminology in Eclipse's documentation pages.

The Contents tab

The Contents tab displays a table of contents for Eclipse's Help pages. Figure 15-2 shows the table's five main headings. Figure 15-9 shows what you get when you start expanding the headings.

Figure 15-9:
Expanding
the Help
table of
contents.

The Search Results tab

If you enter something in the Search field and click the GO button, a list of pages appears in the Search Results tab, which is similar to the Search view (refer to Figure 15-6).

The Links tab

The Links tab is like the Search Results tab. The big difference is, the Links tab shows the results of *context-sensitive help* requests.

Here's how it works: At any point in your Eclipse experience, you can press F1. In response, Eclipse shows you a list of help topics that apply to your current activity. (See Figure 15-10.) Although I can't imagine why, Eclipse's documentation calls this list an *infopop*.

If you're a Linux user, press Ctrl+F1 to access context-sensitive help. If you're a Mac user, press the Help key.

Eclipse can't read your mind. Sometimes, the topics in the infopop don't apply to your current activity. For example, in Figure 15-10, my cursor is planted on the word System inside the editor. So Eclipse offers help on various aspects of the editor. But if you're looking for help on the selected word System (or if you're not thinking about Java and you're looking for advice to the lovelorn), then pressing F1 does you no good at all. (For info on the System class, just hover your mouse over the word System in the editor. For advice to the lovelorn, read Dear Abby.)

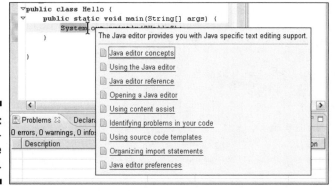

Figure 15-10: Context-sensitive help.

When you select a topic from the infopop, Eclipse opens the big Help view. The big browser pane of the Help view shows whichever documentation page you selected. And the left side of the Help view displays the Links tab. (See Figure 15-11.) This Links tab contains the same list of topics as the infopop. That's good because the infopop is no longer visible. You can browse the original list of topics without having to hunt for the infopop.

Figure 15-11:
The Links
tab and the
Help view's
browser.

The Bookmarks tab

This tab had me fooled for a long time. Figure 15-12 shows the Bookmark
Document button. This button lives in the upper-left corner of the Help view.
If you click this button, nothing much seems to happen. Lights don't flash
and rockets don't fire. Heck, you don't even see an "Eclipse bookmarked the
page" message box.

Figure 15-12:
The
Bookmark
Document
button.

But when you click the Bookmark Document button, Eclipse adds the current
page to your favorites list. To view the list in its entirety, select the appropriate
tab in the Help view's lower-left corner. (The tab you want has a picture of a
bookmark on it. That makes sense.) When you click this little tab, Eclipse displays the big Bookmarks tab.

Figure 15-13:
Barry's
bookmarks.

Figure 15-13 shows a portion of my Bookmarks tab. To revisit a page that you bookmarked, click the page's title in the Bookmarks tab.

To remove a page from the Bookmark tab, right-click the page's entry in the tab and choose Delete.

Some useful Help view tricks

I'm interested in Eclipse's renaming facilities. So I choose Help⇨Help Contents to open the browser (refer to Figure 15-2). I typed **renaming** in the Search field, and then clicked the GO button.

After clicking GO, I see a message about indexing. The message reminds me that the indexing process may take a few minutes, and that the process runs only once after I install Eclipse. So I wait patiently. Eventually, I see a list of search results. It's a list like the one in Figure 15-6, except that this new list appears in the Help view's Search Results tab. Each item in the list represents an Eclipse Help page. If I click an item in the list, the Help view's browser visits the corresponding page.

Eclipse uses a little built-in Web server to manage all the browser's Help pages. Sometimes this server is a bit sluggish. You click an item in the list of search results, and then nothing happens for several seconds. My advice is, be patient. You may not see the Help page right away, but rest assured that the page eventually appears.

Sometimes, I type a word or phrase in the Search field, click GO, and then I see a strange message — a message like the one in Figure 15-14.

Figure 15-14:
A misleading
message in
the Search
Results tab.

The message in Figure 15-14 is very misleading. The message tells me to do something that I've already done. The message makes me think I didn't type anything in the Search field. Instead of saying `type a query in the Search field`, this message should say `please wait while Eclipse works on fulfilling your search request`. Anyway, after a few seconds, Eclipse replaces this message with a list of Help pages.

Finding words and phrases in the Help view's browser

Here's another scenario. I search for the word **renaming**. Among its results, Eclipse lists a Renaming Java Elements page. (Eclipse gives the page a 68% rating, whatever that means.) When I click that item in the list, I see the Renaming Java Elements page shown in Figure 15-15.

Figure 15-15: Eclipse highlights words in the search expression.

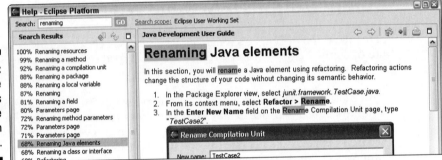

Notice how Eclipse highlights the word I typed in the Search field. (In fact, with stemming, Eclipse highlights any word that's like the word **renaming**.) I didn't type the word "preferences" in the Search field, so Eclipse doesn't highlight occurrences of the word "preferences."

As an afterthought, I decide to hunt for the word **preferences** on the Renaming Java Elements page. How can I hunt for a word on a page? To find the word "preferences" on the Renaming Java Elements page, do the following:

1. **Click anywhere in the browser pane.**

   That is, click in the right side of the Help view window, which puts the focus on the browser pane.

2. **Press Ctrl+F.**

   A Find dialog appears. (See Figure 15-16.)

3. **Type the word** preferences **in the Find What field.**

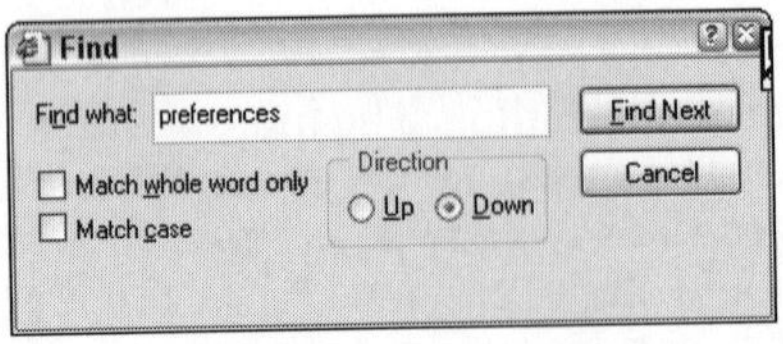

Figure 15-16: The Find dialog.

4. **Click Find Next.**

   Eclipse locates the first occurrence of the word **preferences** on the current Help page. (See Figure 15-17.)

Figure 15-17:
Using the
Find dialog
pays off.

Finding a page's place in the table of contents

Look again at the Renaming Java Elements page (refer to Figure 15-15), and notice the wording at the top of the Help page. "In this section, you will rename . . ." This section? What section? All you did was click something in the Search Results tab.

The Renaming Java Elements page is part of a tutorial. When writing "In this section," the tutorial's author assumes that you're working your way sequentially from one tutorial page to another. But you're not doing that. You're just parachuting into the middle of the tutorial, wondering where you are and how you got there.

If only you knew which page comes before this page in the tutorial! Reading the previous page could help you make sense of this Renaming Java Elements page.

Looking back at the Search Results tab doesn't help at all. The Search Results tab says nothing about pages coming after other pages. To find the previous page in the tutorial, you need a table of contents . . .

Well, you're in luck. You can tell Eclipse to display a table of contents. In the upper-right corner of the Help view, you can find a button with the `Show in Table of Contents` hover tip. (See Figure 15-18.) My eyesight isn't very good, but I think the picture on the button has a little tree and a couple of rounded arrows.

Figure 15-18:
The Show in
Table of
Contents
button.

Anyway, when you click this Show in Table of Contents button, Eclipse activates the Contents tab and highlights the current Help page in the table of contents. (See Figure 15-19.) You can click entries above and below the highlighted entry to see the current Help page's context.

Figure 15-19:
Eclipse
locates a
page in the
Help
system's
table of
contents.

Need More Help?

I have nothing but admiration for people who write Help documents. It's tedious work, and it seldom garners praise. A good Help document goes into just the right amount of detail — not too little, and not too much. Of course, some people need more detail than others, so what's good for one reader can be bad for another.

As for me, I like to read details, more details, and even more details. That's why I need more information than I find in Eclipse's Help pages. So after lots of poking around, I've found the following useful resources:

- ✔ **The newsgroups at** `www.eclipse.org`

  Search for answers written by Eclipse experts. If you don't find the answer you need, then post a new question. In most cases, some knowledgeable person responds within 24 hours.

  Access to these newsgroups requires a one-time registration. But don't worry. No one sells the registration list or bothers you with annoying e-mail. It's just a group of professionals sharing useful ideas.

- ✔ **Articles and newsletters from** `www.eclipsenews.com`

  Find up-to-date information on new developments. Subscribe to the newsletter or read articles online.

✔ **Eclipse API Javadocs at** `www.jdocs.com/eclipse/3.0/api/`
`index.html`

If you want the barebones facts, this resource is for you. These API
Javadocs describe the inner workings of Eclipse. Even if you never contribute to the Eclipse open source project, you'll probably find these
docs useful.

At `jdocs.com` you find multifaceted documentation. Visitors annotate
the Javadocs with their own comments and insights. No longer must you
read between the lines. Thanks to this innovative Web site, you can easily
get the inside scoop on All Things Java.

✔ **A repository of Eclipse plug-ins at** `eclipse-plugins.2y.net/eclipse/`
`index.jsp`

In Chapter 1, I describe Eclipse's ingenious plug-in architecture. If Eclipse
doesn't support drag-and-drop form design, no problem! You can add
plug-ins that take care of all that.

At this superb Web site you can search for plug-ins, browse plug-ins by
category, find the newest plug-ins, and even download the most popular
plug-ins. It's a big toy store for Eclipse users.

Chapter 16

Squashing Bugs

*W*hen you write a computer program, many kinds of things can go wrong. Here are some possibilities:

✔ **Eclipse can't build your code.** You've violated Java's grammar rules. Eclipse puts an error marker (an X and maybe a light bulb) next to one or more lines of code.

Errors of this kind are called *compile-time errors*. A typical compile-time error involves only a line or two of code. Usually, you don't have to look hard to find the error. If you right-click the error marker, Eclipse may be able to apply a quick fix. (For details on error markers and the Quick Fix feature, see Chapter 2.)

✔ **Your program compiles. But when you run the program, it doesn't do what you expect it to do.** Chances are, the program has a *logic error*. The program's instructions tell the computer to do the wrong thing.

Logic errors can be nasty beasts. They can involve long, complicated chains of lines, spanning one or more Java source files. In the simplest case, you can stare at your code and figure out what's wrong. But in thorny situations, you need an automated debugger. (For details, see Chapter 16. Hey, wait! This is Chapter 16! See this chapter!)

✔ **Your program compiles and runs correctly. But your boss or your client makes last-minute changes in the program's requirements.** You've fallen victim to a *no win situation error.*

Next time, try to set up better communication with your boss or your client from the very start of the project. (For details, read *Software Project Management Kit For Dummies,* by Greg Mandanis.)

This chapter helps you through the second kind of error by introducing you to Eclipse's automated debugging tools.

A Simple Debugging Session

Consider the code in Listing 16-1. This code is supposed to exchange two values in an array named stuff. (Starting with values 15, 4, 9, 3, 0, the stuff array should end up with values 4, 15, 9, 3, 0.)

Listing 16-1:   Buggy Code

```
public class Swapper {

    int stuff[] = { 15, 4, 9, 3, 0 };

    public static void main(String[] args) {
        new Swapper();
    }

    public Swapper() {
        swap(0, 1);

        for (int i = 0; i < stuff.length; i++) {
            System.out.print(stuff[i]);
            System.out.print(" ");
        }
    }

    /*
     * THIS METHOD DOESN'T WORK.
     */
    public void swap(int i, int j) {
        stuff[i] = stuff[j];
        stuff[j] = stuff[i];
    }
}
```

If you run this code, you get the following unpleasant output:

```
4 4 9 3 0
```

Instead of swapping the values 15 and 4, this code replaces 15 with 4.

You may already know what's wrong with the swap method in Listing 16-1. But that doesn't matter. What matters is the way you can examine a run of the Swapper class. You use Eclipse's debugging facilities. Here's how you do it:

1. **Create a new project containing the code of Listing 16-1.**

2. **On Eclipse's main menu bar, choose Window⇨Open Perspective⇨ Debug.**

   The Debug perspective opens. (In some situations, you have to choose Window⇨Open Perspective⇨Other. Then, in the resulting Select Perspective dialog, double-click Debug.)

3. **Select the editor area's Swapper.java tab.**

4. **Find the point in the editor's marker bar that's immediately to the left of the swap(0, 1) call.**

5. **Double-click that point in the editor's marker bar.**

   Eclipse marks the point with a tiny blue ball. You've created a *breakpoint* at a particular line of code.

   Eclipse can suspend a program's execution at each breakpoint. And while execution is suspended, you can do some useful detective work. For instance, you can examine and change the values of the program's variables. For more info, follow the next several steps.

6. **On Eclipse's main menu bar, choose Run⇨Debug⇨Java Application.**

   Eclipse begins running the Swapper class's code. Instead of continuing to the very last statement, Eclipse pauses at the swap(0, 1) call.

   Eclipse has suspended execution of the program at the breakpoint that you created in Step 5. Your computer hasn't yet executed the swap(0, 1) call. Instead, the computer waits for your next command.

   Just above the editor area, Eclipse's Debug view displays information about the Swapper class's run. In particular, the Debug view displays any threads of execution that are currently running, and any method calls that are currently in progress. (In this context, each method call is known as a *stack frame*.)

   Not sure anymore how a Debug view might differ from Debug perspective? Refresh your memory by reading Chapter 3.

7. On the Debug view's toolbar, click the Step Into button, as shown in Figure 16-1.

The Step Into button tells Eclipse to execute the swap(0, 1) call, and to suspend execution at the first statement inside the swap method. (In a way, the Step Into button creates an ad hoc breakpoint inside the swap method.)

Figure 16-1:
The Debug view's toolbar.

8. In the upper-right area of the workbench, select the Variables tab.

Eclipse's Variables view comes to the fore.

9. Expand all branches of the Variables view tree.

The tree in Figure 16-2 displays the values of the program's variables. That's useful information.

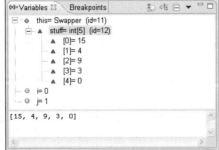

Figure 16-2:
The Variables view (before executing stuff [i] = stuff[j]).

10. Click the Step Into button again.

The computer executes stuff[i] = stuff[j].

The Variables view tree shows the result of this statement's execution. (You can't see colors in Figure 16-3, but on your computer screen, [0]= 4 is red. The red color tells you that the stuff[i] = stuff[j] statement assigned a value to stuff[0].)

In the Variables view, both stuff[0] and stuff[1] have a value of 4, and the number 15 has disappeared. That's bad. Now you can't put the number 15 anywhere. If you're trying to swap the values 4 and 15, you're out of luck.

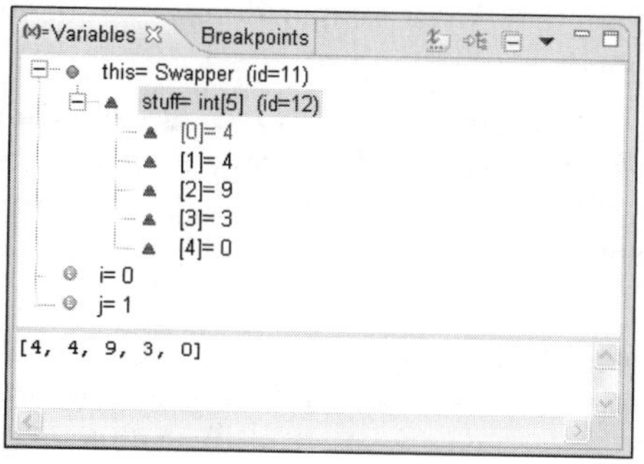

Figure 16-3:
The
Variables
view (after
executing
stuff[i]
=
stuff[j]).

So the trouble starts when you execute stuff[i] = stuff[j]. Instead of stuff[i] = stuff[j], you need a statement that stores 15 for safekeeping. Here's a better version of the swap method:

```
public void swap(int i, int j) {
    int safekeeper = stuff[i];
    stuff[i] = stuff[j];
    stuff[j] = safekeeper;
}
```

The Debug View's Buttons

The Debug view's toolbar has some very useful buttons. This section describes a few of them.

✔ **The leftmost button (a vertical yellow strip and a green wedge) is the *Resume* button.** Click this button for a more-or-less normal run of the rest of the program. (With the Resume button, Eclipse doesn't suspend the program's run at every new statement; Eclipse suspends the run only at the breakpoints.)

✔ **The red square is the *Terminate* button.** If you click this button, your program stops running. To start another run (starting at the beginning of the main method), choose Run➪Debug➪Java Application again.

- ✔ **The leftmost yellow arrow is the *Step Into* button.** See the section titled "A Simple Debugging Session," earlier in this chapter, for more on the Step Into button.

- ✔ **Moving from left to right, the second yellow arrow is the *Step Over* button.** See Figure 16-4. When you click the Step Over button, Eclipse executes the current statement. What Eclipse does next depends on the current statement's form.

  - **Suppose the current statement isn't a method call. Then Eclipse suspends execution at the start of the very next statement.** If the current statement is stuff[i] = stuff[j], then Eclipse suspends execution at the start of the stuff[j] = stuff[i] statement. (See Listing 16-1.)

  - **Suppose the current statement is a method call. Then Eclipse suspends execution after executing the entire method call.** If the current statement is swap(0, 1), then Eclipse zips through the statements inside the swap method. Eclipse suspends execution at the start of the for statement. (See Listing 16-1.)

  Compare the Step Over button with the old Step Into button. If the current statement is swap(0, 1) and you click Step Into, then Eclipse suspends execution inside the swap method.

Figure 16-4:
The Step
Over button.

Experimenting with Your Code

While a program's run is suspended, you can fiddle with the program's values. For instance, in the Variables view of Figure 16-3, right-click the [0]= 4 branch. In the resulting context menu, choose Change Value. Eclipse displays a Set Value dialog. Type a new number (such as **15**) in the Set Value dialog, and then click OK. After doing all that, you can click the Step Into button again. You can see what would happen if stuff[0] had a value of 15.

Here's another trick you can try:

1. **Follow Steps 1 to 9 in the section titled "A Simple Debugging Session."**

2. **Type stuff[0] + stuff[1] in the lower half of the Variables view.**

The lower half of the Variables view is called the *Detail pane*. (See Figure 16-5.)

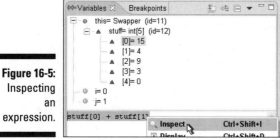

Figure 16-5:
Inspecting
an
expression.

3. **Select the** `stuff[0] + stuff[1]` **text in the Detail pane.**

4. **Right click the** `stuff[0] + stuff[1]` **text. Then, in the resulting context menu, choose Inspect.**

   A big hover tip appears. On the face of the tip you see `"stuff[0]+ stuff[1]"= 19`. That's pretty cool. The information on the tip inspires you to write a brand new version of the `swap` method (a version that doesn't involve an additional `safekeeper` variable). To find out exactly what you write when you're inspired, visit this book's Web site.

Part IV
The Part of Tens

The 5th Wave   By Rich Tennant

In this part . . .

If you can say only ten things about your family, what ten things do you say? What about your living quarters? And what about your life? What are the ten most important ideas about your story from birth to the present moment?

That's the game I play in this part's chapters. If I can say only ten things about some aspect of Eclipse, what ten things do I say? Read on and find out.

Chapter 17

Ten Frequently Asked Questions (And Their Answers)

In This Chapter

▶ Solving some common problems

▶ Working with Eclipse's less intuitive features

Some features of Eclipse are simple and intuitive. Others aren't. That's true of any piece of software. (In fact, it's true of anything — not just software.)

But what happens if you stumble upon too many unintuitive features? If you don't watch out, you can become frustrated. Then you miss out on Eclipse's many benefits.

That's why I wrote this chapter. The chapter helps you use some of Eclipse's less unintuitive features.

I Can't See My New Project

I just created a new project. Why can't I see my project in the Package Explorer's tree? — Albert from Albuquerque

Dear Albert, When you create a Java working set, you choose the projects that belong to the working set. Any projects that aren't in the working set don't show up in the Package Explorer. So when you select a working set, some of the projects disappear from the Package Explorer. That's okay (because it's what you expect to happen when you select a working set).

But when you create a brand new project, you're probably not thinking about that working set. You expect the new project to appear in the Package Explorer, but it doesn't. New projects aren't added to the active working set. So after you create a new project, the project seems to be invisible.

To see the new project visible in the Package Explorer, edit the working set. (Add the new project to the existing working set.)

A New File Doesn't Appear

I used Windows Notepad to create a new file. I put the file in a project folder, but the file doesn't show up in the Package Explorer's tree. Why not? — Curious in Canarsie

Dear Curious, The Package Explorer doesn't watch for changes in your computer's file system. If you sneak away from Eclipse and create a new file, then Eclipse isn't aware of the change. So the new file doesn't appear in the Package Explorer's tree.

You can force Eclipse to update the Package Explorer's contents. Select the project whose directory contains the new file. Then choose File⇨Refresh. In response, Eclipse examines the contents of the project's directory and updates the display in the Package Explorer's tree.

Failure to Format

After choosing Source⇨Format, my code's indentation looks really strange. Why? — Tex from Louisiana

Dear Tex, Eclipse can't format code that it doesn't understand. If your code has a missing semicolon, unmatched parentheses, or some other abnormality, then Eclipse's formatting mechanism can choke. Sure, you may think your code makes perfectly good sense. But a missing semicolon can confuse a compiler.

When your code has compile-time errors, Eclipse's formatter does its best to interpret what you've written. But the errors keep the formatter from seeing the code's real structure. So you end up with some very strange formatting. The solution is, go back and fix those compile-time errors.

Renaming Is Broken

I'm trying to rename something. I can't use File➪Rename because the Rename option is grayed out. Why? — Rhoda from Rhode Island

Dear Rhoda, The Rename action works only when you select something in the Package Explorer. What's more, your most recent selection must be a selection in the Package Explorer.

Imagine that you can select something in the Package Explorer and then click somewhere in the editor. Sorry, the Rename action is grayed out. Your most recent selection is in the editor rather than the Package Explorer, so renaming isn't available.

If you must select a name in the editor, then right-click the name. In the resulting context menu, select Show in Package Explorer. In response, Eclipse selects the corresponding branch in the Package Explorer. With the branch selected, you're free to choose File➪Rename.

Searching Is So Complicated

I choose Search➪Java to find something in a Java source file. Instead of an easy-to-use search dialog, I get a complicated window with a thousand options. When I finally click Search, I get a long list of stuff (and no guidance telling me what to do with this list). Whatever happened to user-friendly interfaces? — Phil from Philadelphia

Dear Phil, Eclipse has several searching and finding dialogs. The most intuitive of these dialogs is the Find/Replace dialog. You can get to that dialog by choosing Edit➪Find/Replace. The dialogs that you get when you choose Search➪Java or (Search➪*Whatever Else*) are much more complicated.

So for now, stick with Edit➪Find/Replace. When you become more comfortable using Eclipse, and you become bored with the Find/Replace dialog, then move on to the Search➪Java action.

Large Isn't the Same as Maximized

No matter what I do, my Eclipse window seems to be maximized. Am I doing something wrong? — Max from Minnesota

Dear Max, On many people's screens, Eclipse starts in a peculiar state. Eclipse's workbench window takes up the entire screen, but the window isn't maximized. Instead, the workbench window is just stretched to fit the entire screen.

To make the window smaller, do two things. First, look at the picture on the window's Maximize button. Make sure that the picture indicates an un-maximized window. Then, move your mouse cursor to the very edge of the window (on the very edge of your screen). Watch carefully to see the mouse cursor turn into an arrow of some kind. When the mouse cursor becomes an arrow, hold down the mouse button and drag the edge of Eclipse's window to another place on your screen.

Illegal Imports

I have code that compiles and runs correctly. But when I import the code into my Eclipse workspace, I see dozens of red error markers. What gives? — Indignant in Indiana

Dear Indignant, This symptom may have many different causes. But the first thing to check is the way you imported the code. Did you import from the correct directory to the correct directory? For instance, if you dragged a com directory into your Eclipse workspace, did you drag this directory into a Java source folder? If you dragged a subdirectory of a com directory, did you drag this directory into a com directory in your workspace?

This stuff can be pretty complicated. For more details, see Chapter 13.

Finding a Bookmark

I find a Help page that I really like. When I click the Bookmark button, nothing happens. Is the button broken? — Clueless in Kalamazoo

Dear Clueless, The button isn't broken. To see your bookmarks, you have to visit the Bookmarks tab. To find this tab, look at the lower left-hand corner of the Help view. Notice the four tabs, all containing tiny, hard-to-decipher icons.

The icon on one of these tabs resembles an open book. There's even a book-mark dangling on the open page. Hover your mouse over this icon, and you can see Bookmarks in the hover tip. Finally, if you click this icon's tab, Eclipse displays a list of bookmarked pages.

The Case of the Missing Javadocs

I select something in the editor and then choose Navigate⇨Open External Javadoc. Instead of seeing the Javadoc pages, I see a message telling me that a documentation location has not been configured. What's up with this? — Larry from Tarrytown

Dear Larry, You're probably requesting one of the JRE System Library's Javadoc pages. Eclipse doesn't automatically know where the JRE System Library's Javadoc files live.

To fix this, expand a JRE System Library branch in the Package Explorer's tree. Then right-click an `rt.jar` branch. In the resulting context menu, select Properties. A Properties dialog appears. On the left side of the Properties dialog, select Javadoc Location. Then on the right side of the dialog, fill in the Javadoc Location Path field.

On my computer, the Javadoc Location Path field contains `file:/C:/ Program Files/Java/jdk1.5.0/docs/api/`. Your field may point to a different location. One way or another, the location that you choose must contain files named `package-list` and `index.html`. If the location contains these two files, then you're probably all set.

Get Right to the Source

I select something in the editor and then choose Navigate⇨Open Declaration. Instead of seeing source code, I see a "Source not found" message. What does a guy have to do to see some source code? — Harry from Tarrytown

Dear Harry, Are you related to Larry by any chance? Your problem is very similar to Larry's. Eclipse can't display the JRE System Library's source code unless you tell Eclipse where the source code is.

Expand a JRE System Library branch in the Package Explorer's tree. Then right-click an `rt.jar` branch. In the resulting context menu, select Properties. A Properties dialog appears. On the left side of the Properties dialog, select Java Source Location. Then on the right side of the dialog, fill in the Location Path field.

On my computer, the Location Path field contains `C:/Program Files/Java/ jdk1.5.0/src`. Your field may point to a different location. One way or another, the location that you choose must contain directories named `com`, `java`, and `javax`.

And please give Larry my regards.

Chapter 18

Ten Great Plug-Ins for Eclipse

In This Chapter

▶ Finding plug-ins

▶ Adding cool tools to Eclipse

*I*n a way, the word "plug-in" is misleading. When you hear "plug-in" you think of an add-on — an extra piece of software that doesn't come with the regular product.

But with Eclipse, almost everything is a plug-in. The user interface is a plug-in, the compiler is a plug-in, the whole kit and caboodle is a plug-in. The rock bottom, bare bones Eclipse product is just an empty frame — a place to put plug-ins.

This chapter isn't about the run-of-the-mill plug-ins — the ones you get when you download Eclipse itself. Instead, this chapter deals with the extras, the additions, the things you download separately.

Each plug-in has its own Web site, but you can find pointers to most plug-ins at `eclipse-plugins.2y.net`. This Web site is an official repository for the world's Eclipse gadgetry.

Most plug-ins are easy to install and run. Here's what you do:

1. **Download the compressed file containing the plug-in.**

2. **Uncompress the file.**

3. **Copy the file's contents to your Eclipse directory's** `plugins` **subdirectory.**

   The stuff you're copying has a name like `com.allmycode.myplugin_ 1.2.0`. In some cases, you find several of these `com.allmycode.blah-blah_1.1.1` folders inside the uncompressed download. You can find many similarly named things in the `plugins` directory. (So you know you're copying these folders to a place where they're welcome.)

   In some instances, you find `plugins` and `features` folders inside the uncompressed download. If you do, then installing the plug-in is a two-step process. First, copy everything from the downloaded `plugins` folder into your Eclipse directory's `plugins` subdirectory. Then, copy everything from the downloaded `features` folder into your Eclipse directory's `features` subdirectory.

4. **Restart Eclipse.**

   If Eclipse is already running, you can do a quick restart by choosing File⇨Switch Workspace. When the Workspace Launcher appears, leave the name of the workspace as it is, and then click OK.

   Eclipse stops running, and then starts running again.

5. **Poke around for signs of the new plug-in's existence.**

   Many plug-ins provide new views. So choose Window⇨Show View⇨ Other and look for new items in the Show View dialog. You may also find new options in the Preferences dialog, in the Help view's table of contents, and in other places within the Eclipse environment.

   Of course, when poking around doesn't get you anywhere, check the plug-in developer's Web site for useful documentation.

Checkstyle

```
sourceforge.net/projects/eclipse-cs
```

Eclipse's Format action fixes your code's stylistic anomalies. But sometimes you need an extra layer of style protection. Checkstyle is the number one style checking tool for Java. You can use Checkstyle on its own, or use it as an Eclipse plug-in.

Cheetah

```
dev.eclipse.org/viewcvs/index.cgi/%7Echeckout%7E/jdt-core-
        home/r3.0/main.html#updates
```

I don't know when you're reading *Eclipse For Dummies,* but as I write this chapter, my calendar is open to the October 2004 page. For the time being, Eclipse doesn't support the new Java language features in JDK 5.0. If you want to experiment with things like generics, enum types, and autoboxing, you have to install some extra support.

The extra support comes as a plug-in named *Cheetah*. This plug-in is still in its early development stages, but if you're anxious to get started with Java 5.0, then download Cheetah and give it a try.

If Cheetah isn't ready to meet your needs, you can still run JDK 5.0 in Eclipse. Create an Ant project that bypasses Eclipse's compiler, and run the Ant project in Eclipse's Ant view. For details, visit this book's Web site.

Eclipse Instant Messenger (Eimp)

`eimp.sourceforge.net`

Use Eclipse's workbench to exchange messages with your buddies. Move seamlessly from your Eclipse code to Eimp's Multi-Session Board view.

Gild (Groupware enabled Integrated Learning and Development)

`gild.cs.uvic.ca`

As an educator, I use Eclipse to teach Java programming courses. Along with Eclipse's standard features, I use features designed specifically for students and teachers. I get these features with the Gild plug-in.

Jigloo

`www.cloudgarden.com/jigloo`

Some integrated development environments support drag-and-drop design tools. To create a graphical user interface, you drag text fields and buttons from a tools palette onto an empty form. Eclipse doesn't come with tools of this kind. But the Jigloo plug-in adds drag-and-drop tools to Eclipse. Try it. It's fun.

Lomboz

`forge.objectweb.org/projects/lomboz`

Are you a J2EE developer? Do you like creating EJBs from scratch? Do you enjoy all the routine coding that J2EE requires?

Or are you tired of organizing J2EE applications on your own? Do you want some tools to take the drudgery out of EJB code creation? If you do, then download and install the Lomboz plug-in.

Open Shell

`coderush.org/projects/OpenShellPlugin`

This cute plug-in does one thing and does it well. Open Shell adds a new item to some of the Package Explorer's context menus. Clicking this Open Shell item starts a Command Prompt or a Shell window. The window's working directory is whatever directory houses the selected Eclipse project. For a command line veteran like me, Open Shell is a dream come true.

PMD

`pmd.sourceforge.net`

The PMD plug-in goes beyond style checking. This plug-in analyzes code for things like unused variables, empty statements, the use of classes when interfaces are available, excessive statement nesting, methods that contain too much code, statements that are more complicated than they need to be, and much more.

VE (Visual Editor)

`www.eclipse.org/vep`

The Visual Editor is Eclipse's official entry in the drag-and-drop design department. Like Jigloo, VE provides visual design capabilities for graphical interfaces. Jigloo has been around longer than VE, and Jigloo is easier to install, but Jigloo costs slightly more than VE. (Jigloo is free for non-commercial use, but a professional license costs $75. In contrast, VE is just plain free.)

My advice is, try both Jigloo and VE. Find out which plug-in you like better.

XMLBuddy

`www.xmlbuddy.com`

When I first started using Eclipse, I was amazed to learn that Eclipse doesn't have its own XML code editor. At the time, I was doing some heavy-duty deployment descriptor development, so I needed some good XML tools. No problem! I downloaded XMLBuddy, and I've been using it ever since.

Index

●*Q*●

●*R*●

EL REFUGIO

Colección Lumía

UNIVERSIDAD AUTÓNOMA METROPOLITANA

RECTOR GENERAL
Eduardo Abel Peñaloza Castro
SECRETARIO GENERAL
José Antonio de los Reyes Heredia

UNIDAD AZCAPOTZALCO
SECRETARIA DE UNIDAD
Norma Rondero López
COORDINADOR GENERAL DE DESARROLLO ACADÉMICO
Eduardo de la Garza Vizcaya
COORDINADORA DE EXTENSIÓN UNIVERSITARIA
Bárbara Velarde Gutiérrez
JEFE DE LA SECCIÓN DE PRODUCCIÓN
Y DISTRIBUCIÓN EDITORIALES
Juan Arroyo Galván Duque

Primera edición.

El refugio
Colección Lumía
Serie Narrativa
D.R. © David Poireth, 2018.
D.R. © Diseño de portada: Ricardo Velmor, 2018.
D.R. © Textofilia S.C., 2018.

D.R. © 2018, Textofilia Ediciones
Limas No. 8, Int. 301,
Col. Tlacoquemecatl del Valle,
Del. Benito Juárez, Ciudad de México.
C.P. 03200
Tel. (52 55) 55 75 89 64
editorial@textofilia.mx
www.textofilia.mx

Universidad Autónoma Metropolitana Azcapotzalco
Avenida San Pablo 180, Ciudad de México, 02200

ISBN: 978-607-8409-51-8, Textofilia Ediciones
ISBN: 978-607-28-1269-7, Universidad Autónoma Metropolitana

Esta obra literaria se realizó con apoyo del Fondo Nacional para la Cultura y las Artes
a través del Programa Jóvenes Creadores 2016-2017.

Impreso y hecho en México.
Printed & made in Mexico.

[EL REFUGIO]

DAVID POIRETH

A Diana, por su silencio amable

[EXÉGESIS]

Al escribir esta historia, una pregunta sólo me rondaba: ¿cuántas páginas resistirá el lector las descripciones de lo inhumano y mi aburrimiento?

De ahí el olvido y la gracia de la estupidez.

[EL REFUGIO]

Sin embargo, tengo esperanza, lo juro, de poder un día contar una historia, una más con hombres, con especies de hombres, como en otros tiempos en que no dudaba de nada, casi.

Textos para nada, Samuel Beckett

Sólo hay vida si hay olvido.

La escritura del desastre, Maurice Blanchot

Vivir es de necios.

1 *(Refugio)*: y escribir sobre ella sería, pienso, como si fuera a escribir sobre una mula. Cosa o árbol muerto, gris, que respira. Aunque más pudiera ser aquella mula que espera resignada, con los corvejones tiesos y el pescuezo pellizcado, la gentileza del rifle que vendría a reventarle el seso en pedazos; obsoleta, con los ojos ciegos ya antes de desplomarse en la llanura y hundirse en la boca de las sabandijas de rapiña. No obstante, de una mujer se trata si bien casi de una cosa con tripas y aún con hambre: una vieja tetrapléjica. O un tronco podrido con venas y sangre que le fluye. Su cuerpo es una cáscara, y es su sangre lo único que acontece. La atraviesa un río... y ella intacta, quieta. ¿Qué la mantiene con vida?, ¿ya para qué?

Entonces, es la mula anciana que rumia y estorba. Tosca, que ya no anda, que es agresiva. Un experimento de la naturaleza, un engendro de matrimonios monstruosos, y mi esposa.

La miro arruinada y tan de lleno que es como si ignorase su humanidad, su habilidad de vergüenza, su memoria..., ¿pero es que acaso puede sentirse a un tiempo amor y asco? Sin embargo, la quiero. Es un fantasma, un objeto que obsta, que desordena, que atasca la vida de su movimiento ordinario, falso e ideal. Y la quiero. Ahora, como antes y siempre, la miro, y ella no puede hacer por ocultarse; está atada al camastro, que es más una mesa de comedor antiguo, con sus piernas duras y débiles y sus brazos tirados. Está, quiero decir, encadenada a su cuerpo. Y es más bien como que se manifiesta: Mi Mujer, la vieja tetrapléjica. Así, al verla de diario en su yacija, tan callada y concreta, me da una sensación de certeza insoportable; la angustia de saber que es cierto que todo existe y que, al día de mañana, será todo igual.

2 (*Refugio*): no habría que sentirle lástima o, en todo caso, no una mayor a la que habría que sentir por todos nosotros. Por mí. La simpatía habría que dejarla fuera: no hay. Yo no sufro lo que ella sufre ni me cabe imaginarlo ni me da la gana hacerlo y, sin embargo, tenerla aquí siempre y saber que existe... Ojalá no la sintiera. Como alojada en mí. Tiesa y moribunda. Quizá me pesa que sea cierto; caer en cuenta que es real, mi vieja, y que hay formas de vida inimaginables. Y es en este sentido que estorba, como un estancamiento de agua sucia, como el perro sarnoso, muerto, que repugna y duele y se esquiva y que luego, en algún momento, se fundirá al suelo y al aire y a todo. Pero el perro muerto es al hombre muerto, a mi vieja tetrapléjica, lo mismo. Y todos respiramos el resto de perro que ahora se pudre. Por ello es preferible no saber; el saber estorba, angustia, pesa...los otros, todos, pesan. Y sentir. Y seguramente sólo para desembarazarme de ella tengo la necesidad de hacerle el cuento, y a mí; para no verla como lo que es: una vieja aburrida e inmóvil que se desgasta, se echa a perder. Y sea también para no ver lo que soy: un intento fallido, porque nuestras vidas se van en aquellas obras que se escriben sin escribirse, los sueños..., y el resto, la nada, es lo que somos: lo que no hicimos. Somos lo que no hicimos de nosotros. Un resto, *una especie de hombres.*

Y nos queda la eternidad.

Me detengo de escribir cada tres segundos. Son tierras estériles y no es de extrañar que los piojos se arrimen a cual sea la mollera que se cruce. Llegaron antes de que nos instalara aquí, y tal parece que están resignados a quedarse y mi calva y cuerpo los cobijan. Tanta soledad y aún así resulta imposible que nos dejen solos.

3 *(Afuera)*: su madre septuagenaria la cuida, la alimenta. Le talla bajo la lonja y le escurre los granos. Le humecta las estrías y las úlceras. La friega luego de zurrarse y, todavía así, ni una sola palabra se cruzan. Si acaso algunas pocas. Y no son tan diferentes: un par de trastajos. En su recámara, Mi Mujer está echada en el camastro haciendo de desperdicio, mientras la atiende sentada a su lado su madre con una bandeja donde un vaso de agua, un pedazo de chivo y un cigarro hacen de merienda. Ella se aguanta las fermentaciones de mi vieja, su hija, y es que hace unos segundos, al tiempo que tragaba la segunda rebanada de chivo, Mi Mujer ensució. No puede notarlo, entonces gruñe de inmediato para que le sirvan en la boca un chorro de agua y luego el cigarro. Es así sucesivamente. Y ya que no cae en cuenta, o cayendo por las narices, pero haciéndose la idiota, mi suegra decide esperar a que termine la merienda y luego alzarla, remolcarla, para lavarle primero a ella antes de enjugar los platos sucios. Así es más fácil y menos el repudio. Y es que no es tan sencillo como atender los pañales de las criaturas, porque no hay comparación entre las nalguitas sonrosadas y gordas de los bebés y las nalgas destruidas, ruinosas, de una vieja de cincuenta y paralítica.

Su madre también rumia, se masca la lengua o las palabras, los gritos de desesperación, y se los engulle como jugo de bilis, aunque se enferme. Todavía más. Están tan cerca sus caras que, seguramente, se alcanzan a escuchar sus respectivas masticaciones de lengua y parece que hasta se comunican. Se aburren y así pasan las horas, como si para mi vieja, su madre no supiera sino sólo ponerle en la boca la carne y el cigarrillo, y quizás algo más sepa, pero a nadie le importa. Son este tipo de personajes protagonistas de algún tipo de vida y olvido. Es decir, protagonistas de una Historia ajena, otra, y, de nuevo, que a nadie le interesa. Ignoradas más, tal vez, por aburridas que por duras. Son una morbosidad: "¿te imaginas?". Y no. Sin embargo, aunque tuviera intenciones de más, de inventar alguna cosa…, y podría decirse que son estos personajes los que nos enseñan cómo es que se vive. Hoy. Y pudiera, incluso, mortificar darse cuenta; si dentro, si de pronto, se despertara algún resto de falsa tierna humanidad. O lo que fuera aquello.

En fin, que ahora deja los trastes a un lado y comienza su labor con Mi Mujer. No hace bien las cosas: la remolca, dije, hasta que la deja bocabajo, le desnuda las nalgas y comienza a fregotearla. Yo estoy ahí y miro todo desde mi sillón en el rincón, donde por las noches acompaño a Mi Mujer y a su madre a la merienda. Su piel irritada se estira, y se le miran mejor las llagas y pústulas encendidas mientras le pasa por encima una esponja y un trapo, pero muy pronto retrocede de nuevo el cuero, acurrucándose una arruga en otra como una parva de escombros.

Y yo no he terminado de comer.

4 *(Refugio)*: recuerdo que pensé ese día, como hice en muchas otras ocasiones, que esa señora, achaparrada y fea, sería capaz de matar a mi esposa. De hacer el favor por puro rencor o hasta por hastío y puro hartazgo: aburrimiento. No obstante, de inmediato rectifiqué por la imposibilidad de aquello, y me dije que sería más probable que fuera ella, su madre, la que se muriera primero. Si no de anciana, sí de tedio, de cansancio o de decepción. Porque cargábamos, todavía, con un remedo de pudor moral y andábamos sin la desnudez cruel de ahora. Sin embargo, pensé siempre que su madre también fue una terca al seguir viviendo y, quizás, al ayudarla a vivir.

¿Tendría que relatarlo todo en pasado y no en el tiempo abultado y confuso de hoy?, pero es que me parece que aquello, el pasado, no existe y que todo es ya puro presente: la memoria y el futuro; toda una carga. Todo está aquí y todo el tiempo, y el Refugio está abarrotado y es inhóspito. Todo se recoge en nosotros, en el cuerpo de Mi Mujer que yace sobre la mesa despatarrada donde alguna vez comimos, donde la enfermedad la aplasta; la gravedad que la tumba, aunque no termine de morirse porque su espíritu, inmóvil también, atado a la carne, débil, atorado entre los órganos y huesos, no se decide a abandonarla. Y es él, más bien en ambos, pesado y perezoso; el espíritu, *un esfuerzo inútil y una estúpida simplicidad.* Si bien ahora tengo la sensación, una vez dicho eso, de que el presente es lo que no

existe. Nosotros. Y que el vacío que la naturaleza aborrece, niega, aniquila, es lo real. Y todo ya fue y todo lo que está por venir
ya viene en ruinas. Sin embargo, sea el caso que fuere, comprendo de inmediato lo irremediable que es el que estemos aquí, que
existamos aquí, en el Refugio, los dos, aunque todo pudiera ser,
de tan real, una ilusión.

Qué desastre.

5 (Afuera): casi arrastrándome de tan cabizbajo, con la cabeza enterrada entre los hombros, entro al edificio gris del H. Ayuntamiento del pueblo donde trabajo en las bodegas. Y es que hoy comienza una nueva etapa en mi carrera: he sido degradado de una oficina, de un uniforme de burócrata, a bodeguero. Aunque valdría más decir que es casi una promoción de mi cargo, pues lo que hacía antes era todavía más inútil que lo que haré a partir de ahora. Hago el intento por dejar fuera, por unas horas, a mi vieja inmóvil y a su madre. La vida pasiva, la lentitud de todo. Y mientras la voy dejando tras de mí como un camino espeso de baba, pasan a mis costados todos corriendo y todos en uniformes de burócratas o del ejército en posesión, salvo yo, dije, que traigo otra clase de prisas y de trapos. Entonces, me detengo. Dentro de estos muros, tan aseados y blanquecinos, me hurga una sensación vomitiva, y quizá liberadora: la mentira. Pero, me vuelvo, miro los pisos rechinantes y sigo en línea recta hasta donde el jergón se llena de la suciedad de los caminos por los que ando, y así todos nosotros sin importar los trajes o los vestidos. Luego, mi mirada se alza hasta donde la puerta de cristal hace de lo de afuera un espejismo. Veo el pueblo destruido, olvidado. Los muros embarrados de tierra que ya no se borra, y todo del color del excremento enfermo y pálido de los hombres que los ocupan. Ganaderos vendedores de las tripas descoloridas y los filetes pellejudos de sus bestias, granjeros de pampas baldías que casi regalan sus cosechas, funcionarios de gobierno, militares en guardia, gente quemada y yo, que ni animales desnutridos ni campos secos ni uniformes de manchas o de corbatas ya tengo. Y ahí está el revoltijo en mi vientre. La vida pasiva y la vida inútil. Yo y Mi Mujer. Yo y Mi Mujer y su parálisis. Y la propia, y la de todos. Cuando abro la puerta de las bodegas, al fin, y miro el desmán de baratijas al que he de acoplarme quizá por el resto de mis días, y con una tarea fija, especial: las 8,000 latas; cuatro por cada persona del municipio. Porque es probable que todo acabe pronto, o esa es la amenaza, que es más bien una promesa que nos han anunciado: el asedio inminente, las matanzas. Y hay que sobrevivir, dicen. Luchar por sobrevivir. Entonces, fisgoneo rápidamente en lo que se amontona, el polvo, las cajas roídas. Alguna rata que me cruza por la mente, anticipándose a la que habría que encontrar luego. Y comienzo a ocuparme en la primera lata, la segunda, la tercera.

Y así la vida sin aspavientos. Sin embargo, hay en las Oficinas una mujer de tacón alto y fuertes corvas; un pasatiempo, una luz. Casi ni se alcanza a percibir que anda con la pierna izquierda más corta. Y me gusta la renga, mi paticoja, a quien apenas me dispongo a evocar cuando llega al almacén y me interrumpe. De 8,000 latas no llevo ni 80, y llega y me interrumpe y me encara con una mano en la cintura y me pregunta si sé en dónde quedó enterrada la caja del archivo personal del pasado Intendente. No, le digo. Sea, quizá, que me identifico con ella a causa de mi solo testículo; pero, de verdad me resulta bonita, apetecible. Estoy tirado al suelo de frente a ella con mis espaldas empolvadas e irritadas mis narices. La bodega que alberga lo viejo. Le miro las rodillas, las articulaciones malogradas, los músculos disparejos de los jarretes, las nalgas descompuestas, y me subo a la falda verde corta hasta la blusa arremangada de donde ya soltó algunos botones del escote porque la tierra arde. Puedo buscar, repongo. Ella frunce la boca que apenas se hincha, cruza los brazos que le alzan los senos y no dice nada. Por su silencio logro, al fin, dejar de verla fragmentada o, más bien, despedazada, y la concibo entera. Ah, mi patizamba. Y, como harta de que le ande husmeado la pelvis imaginándome sus bragas con sus caderas chuecas, resopla y se da vuelta azotando los pasos, indignados, y la puerta. Tendría que volver, pienso. Y el problema es que el Intendente falleció allá en su despacho y en plena holgazanería. Desgane. Ya estaba viejo, aunque eso no sea excusa suficiente en este mundo ni para holgazanear ni para morir. De cualquier modo, el barragán estaba también algo loco y dormía, de tanto en tanto, en su oficina. No era difícil, por ello, encontrarlo jetudo y seboso, en calzones, camisa blanca y calcetas azules solamente. No tenía a nadie y, cuando murió, todo lo que encontraron suyo lo pusieron en esa inútil, tal vez importantísima caja, donde se mezclan una sarta de locuras con papeles de primer orden. Apenas la pusieron acá se perdió entre la multitud de escombros, tragada la indiferencia. Y ahora, al fin, alguien, ella quizá, tiene que revisarla. Revivirlo. Y quizá quiera hacerlo yo también.

Sin embargo, seguiré antes hasta llegar, aunque sea, a las 20 latas, porque estoy con todo aquí tan amontonado que tardaré un buen rato en encontrarla. Son tantas cosas, y nadie sabe lo que aquí hay. Ésta, como todas las bodegas, alberga puros olvidos, esconde las vergüenzas. Y se aglomera la basura.

Y yo. Y el abandono.

6 *(Refugio):* están aquí ahora las latas, Mi Mujer y aquel archivo del Intendente que me pidió mi paticoja entonces. Y pienso que nunca ha sido justa la comparación que hice y hago entre mi esposa y la patizamba; aquí no gana el que más tenga sino el que, por decirlo de algún modo, tenga menos carencias. Le miro las piernas muertas a Mi Mujer, el músculo consumido. La miro a ella entera, pero despedazada de veras. Por dentro y como si todo su cuerpo no fuera sino sólo un pedazo de materia olvidado, cercenado de lo que antes fue. Toda ella, es decir, un órgano palpitante abortado, una pieza de carne magra. Y, sin querer hacerlo, vuelvo a compararla con la coja. Y me inunda algo similar a la tristeza.

7 (Refugio): babea y la limpio. Le sueno las narices y me mira pelándose los ojos, ¿qué más? Furiosa y aguijándose dentro con un odio para que su cuerpo despierte y se mueva. Me mira, digo, como amenazan los ojos negros del caballo de boca herida, o mula, una vez que el freno le ha destrozado los carrillos. La mirada animal hueca, enloquecida y cansada, aunque pronto vuelva a la pasividad y a la obediencia. La mirada confundida que no comprende. Y así me mira Mi Mujer, como cualquier otra bestia hambrienta que no se decide, o no sabe cómo hacerle para devorarse a su dueño, maltratarlo. Gesticula demasiado y gime, jadea, y luego de torcerse dislocándose la cara, se truena el maxilar y me mira de nuevo. Abre y cierra la boca masticando aire y gimoteando. Muge. Luego me enseña los dientes hasta las encías negras, ya en silencio. La mula. Y es un asco; esconde sus labios desgastados hasta donde brotan las raíces de los dientes y me sigue mirando. Me nacen ganas de abofetearla, entonces, por mula terca, tozuda, porque no quiere comer de mis latas. Intento alimentarla y le digo: Aquí no, mujer. Aquí no hay otra cosa, ni madre ni chivo, y la única birria eres tú. Come. Pero, no me hace caso. Sólo tenemos estas latas, le digo, y hasta que alguien venga por nosotros o a matarnos, eso tendrás que comer. Y, como en protesta, se zurra. Es decir, como si pudiera al menos protestar y tener control de sus esfínteres. Entonces desiste, y los ojos, de tormenta, ya sólo se nublan, se ensombrecen. Voltea

23

al techo melancólica, porque seguramente el haber mencionado que han de asesinarnos le hizo pensar en su madre muerta. Casi con envidia de saber, quiero decir, que su madre es la muerta y no ella. Casi creyendo, me digo, que Mi Mujer aún piensa.

No es de adrede, sin embargo, ni de resentido que la vea como un animal; pero es que se hace la bruta y no me habla. Ya no pita ni pizca de palabra, y tal vez extrañe a su madre o... No sé. Pero ya querrá comer; siempre es igual, y cuando me escucha raspar el fondo de la lata berrincha, como las crías, la bebota. Si pudiera moverse, haría de sí un zarandeo, sobre la tabla donde yace, como en capricho. Aunque, después de tantos años así, ¿qué fuerzas podrían quedarle para ser humana? Pienso en eso, entonces, en que está cansada y triste, verdaderamente que sufre, y se me ablanda el pecho y le doy de comer, de beber y su cigarro. Quizá sea demasiada ya mi sinceridad, pero, de cualquier modo, en esos momentos me siento como un niño con su mascota y la acaricio. Le rasco en la cabeza como hacen conmigo los piojos, aunque no me sienta. Después ya sosegada y más como un cachorro, me mira preguntándome, quizá, qué es lo que estoy esperando, hasta que se duerme. Entonces pienso que las matanzas que se libran ahora allá afuera también nos van lentamente matando a nosotros.

Y ya todo así, cabe preguntarse qué es lo humano, pero se me agotan las fuerzas. Y me alzo de mi silla limpiándome la mugre detrás de las orejas con los hombros.

8 *(Afuera)*: viniéndome palabras como si fueran de otro, imaginaciones, me veo deslizando mis manos bajo las axilas de la coja para pellizcar, desde su espalda, sus senos. Desviar mi cuerpo un poco a la izquierda, a su altura inclinada y dispareja. Rasparme las manos con sus axilas rasuradas antes de envolver la suavidad y la blandura de sus tetas. Y así, repitiéndome una vez y otra con la obsesión y la impotencia de quien no puede imaginar lo que tendría que ocurrir después, termino mi jornada: con las latas apiladas, las cajas arrumbadas en todas las esquinas y mis manos exprimiendo los pechos de la coja. Como para sacarle el corazón, los pulmones y cortarle el aliento. Me alzo, entonces y al fin, del suelo y miro una mancha grasosa de sudor y mía extendiéndose en el muro blanco de la bodega. Una mancha que niega, cínicamente, mis pensamientos y las tetas que aprieto. Mis manos empuñan sólo el aire hasta ceñirse en sí mismas, y ensimismadas ya son el símbolo de la insatisfacción, de la lucha inútil por el cambio, por ser lo que no somos. Es decir, otra vez, la convicción aquella de que somos lo que apenas pudimos llegar a ser y no lo que quisimos. Ese páramo donde mi fe se agota, porque cada quien tendrá sus razones o pretextos para ser lo que es, pero a sabiendas, siempre, de que el motivo es simple y llanamente la impotencia. Y yo ya dejé de creer que la mía, mi ineptitud, tiene límites. Entonces me rebasa y me anula. Y encajándome las uñas salgo de las bodegas buscando en mí ese

par estrujado, rasguñado, de tetas desnudas que, por un segundo, me aliviaron de lo que soy. Pero ya no están. Sólo respiro el aire terroso de fuera mientras me cruza por delante un hombre que arrastra, ayudándole a andar, a un burro con los genitales picados, y bajo un cielo sin violencias.

La maldita calma, pienso, engañosa.

Otro hombre, desde la izquierda, se acerca, acaricia al borrico. Se asoma por entre sus patas, agachándose, y le mira los testículos hinchados. Hace un gesto de resignación y apoyo, camaradería, oprimiéndole los carrillos, el hocico, al asno como diciéndole que él lo entiende y que su dolor también le duele, como si fuera un niño. Entonces, bajo el pretexto del burro enfermo, se da forma a la conversación entre los hombres que andan y se acompañan en mi cara. Atardece y camino tras de ellos, y no son para mí sino sólo dos sombras, porque es como si nos separara todo un mundo. Y de esa manera, tomando distancia del compadrazgo genitálico de esos tres, voy de vuelta a casa. Al hogar que es más una celda. A Mi Mujer que es más una prisión. Aunque también fuera el amor. Y pienso en la coja y en nuestra plática de hoy: unas cuantas palabras escupidas al azar. Y en una suerte de futuro. En las posibilidades cortas de acercarme a ella y a quien fuera. Porque hablo tan poco y con nadie, si acaso conmigo mismo a quien no le salen más que palabras lastimosas. Me hablo como hacen mis manos que se hieren: clavándome las uñas. O bien a mi suegra sólo para enterarme de lo que va a haber luego para comer, aunque sea más bien que yo quiera que me diga, si lo sabe, cuánto nos queda. ¿Cuándo se muere ella? ¿Cuándo yo? ¿Cuándo todos? Sin embargo, no digo nada. Nos sentamos uno frente al otro en la mesa de la cocina por las mañanas, yo bebo café y ninguno interrumpe el silencio. Ese otro silencio que se hace cuando mi esposa duerme; menos denso o angustiante que aquel que escandaliza cuando está despierta. Que es un silencio pantanoso, tenso. Y todo corre como siempre: le doy sorbidos largos al café apenas tibio, mientras mi suegra se hurga con las uñas los dos únicos dientes, de los siete que le sobran, que están pegados uno al otro. Nos miramos. De hace tiempo que nos miramos, todos, sin mirarnos. Ella masca, entonces, el pedazo de ayer o anteayer recién liberado de los dientes y degusta, chascando la lengua, para atinar de qué resto se trata. Planta sus ojos en mis narices, o en mis ojos, o en cualquier parte de mi cara que ya no es sino sólo una cara. Porque ya no somos sino sólo partes, carne adherida a un cuerpo: somos cabeza, ojos, nariz, boca y eso, en conjunto, ya no significa nada más que nariz, ojos, boca y cabeza. Todo es su superficie. Oquedades sin fondo, y ya no hay profundidad que nos sostenga. Y allí, en el vacío, me imagino, con sus ojos que me perforan como yo miro a Mi Mujer, hueca, que me aconseja: el suicidio. Y lo considero cuando ella, ahora, se hurga cada orificio del rostro, sin embargo, sabiendo que hasta para negarse a vivir se requiere de un tanto de voluntad. Y, es más, digo yo, que somos la negación a secas. Negándose. Eso que soy sin ser. Es decir, *eso que no hago que me deshace*. Y una nostalgia de lo que nunca fue. Además, pienso en el riesgo que el suicidio implica: toda una apuesta, porque se puede correr con la suerte de que la muerte no sea un descanso, sino una imitación, apenas un poco más o menos tormentosa, de la vida. Y qué aburrimiento sería aquello. La eternidad. Y el retorno. El mareo.

Y allá voy ahora. Andando por mis atajos de costumbre, todos tan iguales, pensando en esa extraña sensación que me dejó mi paticoja al hablarme, al irrumpir en mí. Voy con el centro del pueblo ya dejado atrás, el sol ya casi caído, y de frente a los campos, a las granjas y al desencanto de mi hogar, cuando veo a orillas del camino de tierra a un crío que ha adoptado como mascota a una rata de campo. Enorme y ceniza. De tan grande que sobrepasa los puños y más del medio brazo, flaco, que la sujeta. La trae arrinconada a las costillas y la mima, serio, con la cara rígida y llena de lodo seco y de pústulas porque la suciedad, el sol que quema sin calentar y el frío que corta... su cara como las bolas gordas, los testículos del asno. Y es la mueca de ese niño la mueca de todos, el espíritu de todos... Mi Mujer... Pero él, de tan vivido, no le teme a ningún roedor ni a las piedras ni al viento que ya no corre ni a la inutilidad ni a la desnutrición.

Sin embargo, a ella, a la rata, la veo gorda. De todo el mundo, la más rolliza y sana porque es astuta, pienso, y no sólo se deja malcriar, sino que, me viene a la cabeza, se alimenta de a poco de la carne del niño. Sí, me digo, aprovecha las heriditas en la piel, las llagas y las ampollas, y hunde por allí la lengua y masca. Lo va llenando del doble de agujeros y, gracias a la enfermedad suya, como de leproso bíblico, no alcanza a percatarse su madre ni nadie de que se lo andan comiendo. Y tal vez él lo sepa, y sea ese su modo de dejarse morir: a pedazos. Porque el niño nació ya cansado y tampoco le teme a la muerte y, además, los mordiscos le deben de venir como besos. Habrá, entonces, llegado a un acuerdo, como de matrimonio contranatura, con la rata que lo excava, digo, pienso soñando y... bueno, qué se yo, ahora me imagino que será la rata la primera en morirse, y que será la carne pútrida del niño la que le envenene las vísceras. Luego, la felicidad será extrema, porque si el niño, caprichoso y terco, no había dejado a nadie meterle mano a su rata, ahora, ya muerta, no habrá mejor decisión que comérsela.

Vaya ciclo tóxico. Y me digo que el hombre sobrevive por pura necedad, y que es como aquella mancha mía de grasa en el muro, en las bodegas, que no se borra. Pero me recuerda mi infancia. Aunque yo no tuve ninguna rata, no. Antes bien, y por ser un niño de casa, tuve un gato. Un gato temeroso de salir y aterrorizado tanto por las callejas como por el campo abierto: se paraba en la puerta o en la ventana, se agazapaba mirándolo todo y, a la menor ventisca, espantado, correteaba hacia adentro. Se olvidaba pronto del deseo curioso de ensuciarse del mundo de fuera, y se distraía con cual sea la basurita que rodara frente a él o astilla de mueble que se encontrara. Cómo quise a ese gato. Y todavía así olvidé, siempre, ponerle un nombre. Afuera, mi madre tenía gallinas y puercos y él, de vez en vez, se acercaba a mí que los miraba desde la ventana, y se sentaba también a mirarlos. Alzaba el cuello y estiraba, en asombro, la cara como queriendo chapotear en la pocilga con los puercos o hundir su trompa en la tierra como las gallinas brutas que, confundiendo las piedritas con los granos, se desgraciaban los picos. Tendríamos la misma cara, el gato y yo, y quizá la misma sensación de vacío sedante. La contemplación: ese grado de la conciencia donde el hombre se asemeja a las sabandijas y se aleja, dios por delante, de los primates y otros hombres.

Se aburría él primero, aunque pudiera ser que yo estuviese siempre aburrido, y se iba. Las sirvientas, y luego el gañán cuando comadreaba con ellas antes de violarlas, me veían sentado a la ventana por horas y pensaban que se trataba de alguna deficiencia y me juzgaban de retrasado: Un soplo atorado tiene en el cerebro, decían. Pero yo creo más que es una expresión de inteligencia mirar a los animales. Y bueno, afuera también había nubes deformadas y, de tanto en tanto, alcanzaba a ver en los campos secos de atrás al gañán y a las sirvientas revolcándose, a veces de a una y a veces de a dos por uno. Casi los sentía.

Por eso fue una sorpresa el día que se escapó el gato. Quién sabe, tal vez sólo salió para morirse, ¿para qué más? Andaba enfermo, como todo, y ya algo viejo. Tiraba el pelo y maullaba como ahuyentando fantasmas.

Tocaron a la puerta. Fue una sirvienta a atender. Yo estaba con mi madre quien ya andaba en aquel entonces, también, algo moribunda. Estábamos en su recámara y, como de costumbre, callados y aburridos. Tenía diez años, y afuera llovía. No me permitió salir a los charcos, ni siquiera para aliviar mi tristeza. Comenzaron a escucharse, entonces, pasos graves y húmedos tronando el suelo de madera del pasillo. Se adelantó la sirvienta y dijo, apenas entornando: Señora…, cuando el mozo de labranza, el gañán, la empujó abriendo de par en par la puerta. Estaba empapado, traía una jeta de placer como la que ponía cuando encajaba en el culo de las sirvientas, y también llevaba del pescuezo lo que sería casi el puro pellejo de mi gato extraviado. Yo creo que lo vaciaron las ratas y los insectos, dijo acercándose a la cama y a mi madre, y sujetándolo sobre su cara para que lo mirara bien.

Se desfiguró, mi madre, en una mueca de pánico y se vio en ella el esfuerzo, marcado en la sien, por curarse, por reparar, en ese instante, el resto de vida y fuerza que pudieran quedarle. Pero ya no había nada de eso. El tipo sacudía el cuerpo descompuesto y decía: ¿Lo ve?, ¿lo ve? Ya lo traje, cuando uno de los parásitos que aun albergaban la tripa abierta del cadáver voló cayendo sobre el rostro de mi madre. Gimoteaba y sollozaba muda, y nadie más que yo se percataba de lo que estaba ocurriendo. Y no hice nada. El bicho se arrastró, succiono la piel de su mejilla, se encaminó hacia su boca y justo allí, cuando ya estaba por dejarse caer en esa tumba que era mi madre, se lo arrebaté exprimiéndolo en mi puño cerrado. Fue como si yo le dijera: Tú no me dejas salir a jugar a los charcos y aun así soy capaz de ayudarte. Y aquello entendía yo por piedad cuando tenía diez años.

Habrá sido uno o dos días después que murió al fin, con el rostro todavía vuelto un espantajo. Quizá, ya no sé, ella pensó en ese instante, al ver a mi gato, lo terrible que es convertirse en un cadáver y llenarse de tanta larva. Falleció llena de temores; encerrada en sí misma, en su angustia, en su vano esfuerzo por recomenzar a vivir. Tal vez como lo hiciera también mi gato al salir por primera vez. Ya tan tarde.

Llego pensando en todo ello, y siento que he perdido, envuelto en memorias tristes y estúpidas, los últimos momentos míos antes de volver a Mi Mujer, su tetraplejía y su madre. Llego, pues, relatándome mi pasado y sintiendo, extrañamente, que sería bueno emparejarme a los hombres y al burro y seguirlos hasta donde sea que se vayan. Descubrir qué ponzoña trae en los testículos. Y después, de golpe, repaso también las palabras, la voz de mi patizamba, que me recuerda, quizá vagamente, la de Mi Mujer cuando nos amábamos y ella podía, y yo a ella, sentirme. Sin embargo, me interrumpo antes de hallarme alguna clase de sentimiento. Ya cansado. Abro la puerta y me invade el fuerte olor a comadreja asada, otra clase de rata. Entro a donde mi vieja ya come y el silencio se ve embrutecido por su respiración y por la mezcla de su saliva con la carne correosa que masca. Doy un paso hacia donde me arrincono en mi sillón y, ya sentado, le encuentro de pronto a Mi Mujer un parentesco duro, evidente, ya no sólo con las bestias, sino con mi madre agonizante y, más y luego, con el cadáver de mi madre.

Tanta inmovilidad. Tanto parásito.

Y me digo, en ese momento, que he sido un tonto, que, así como tanto me tardé en descubrir que el cadáver de mi madre no era más mi madre, pueda ser que ya mi esposa haya dejado de ser, desde hace tiempo, mi esposa, y yo no haya caído aún en cuenta.

9 *(Refugio)*: estará ya todo oscuro allá arriba, y se seguirán matando. Insomnes obreros de la sangre, como si cobraran por horas extra de trabajo. Mientras que aquí nada pasa. Agonizamos... Es tan larga la espera..., ¿habría hecho mejor en no esconderme? ¿Cuántos muertos estarán ya regados sobre nuestras cabezas ahora? Se derraman. Y les guardo envidia, tal vez. No. Es el cansancio. Porque muy pronto me he cansado ya de escribir, y no es sólo que no pueda hacer más que esto, ninguna cosa, sino que el acto es más un defecto. Escribir es un defecto mío, un bulto tumoroso. Otra forma de gastar el tiempo. De morir la vida breve, pasiva, que transcurre tan lenta y se alarga ahora. Y de tan aburrido que ha sido todo, y tan limitada mi imaginación, escaso mi lenguaje, me viene la condena de escribir sobre la mía, mi vida. Mi Mujer. Este cuento de amor... Y quizá fuéramos todos iguales: ella, yo, mi gato, mi madre, porque pudiera ser que viví un tiempo y luego, de pronto, ya no. Ya no. Y aquí no pasa nada. Y es allí cuando la vida ya no es breve, cuando ya no se tiene expectativa alguna en vivirla. Y dura tanto. Habría, por ello, que no tener conciencia; eso, ya dije, de saber que estamos vivos. Ese otro defecto que es al acto de escribir tan parecido. Encallar en lo insoportable. Porque es todo tan real, tan duro, aunque vacío. Eso es tener conciencia, el bulto: tener el mundo dentro. Y aunque vacío, el mundo al fin. El vacío al fin. Reventamos tanto de eso. De la existencia. Por eso es preferible la ignorancia, no saber

y no escribir. Sin sentir nada. Ya que escriben los que vivos, sin vivir, se están muriendo.

Mi Mujer se despierta ahora. Tiene los labios mórbidos y frunce su boca. Pienso, primero, que es porque me pide que la bese. Gime como cuando los bebés que, dejados en los brazos de un desconocido, comienzan a hacer la mueca de donde luego nace el llanto. Y ella así despierta. La escucho, a mi vieja que para más la boca y la aprieta arrugándola, y pienso en el terror de esos niños, tan doloroso, cuando ven a su madre alejándose de espaldas. Presiento, luego, que el terror es la única señal verdadera de amor. Me acerco a Mi Mujer: ¿podría inclinarme aun hoy a besarla? Mi cara está frente a la suya; yo analizo sus labios púrpuras, veo la punta de sus dientes acabados por el cigarro, el gas gástrico y la falta de higiene. Entre negruzcos, escuálidos, cariados y pestilentes. ¿Podría todavía hoy hundir mi boca en ese agujero?, ¿sentir esos labios como lijas, lamerlos y ensalivarnos los dos? Ella me mira la mirada; sus ojos brotan de sus cuencas como si los empujaran desde dentro para sacarlos. ¿Acaso la estoy asfixiando? Me pregunto y miro: no. Tendría que hacerlo, me digo, besarla, tal vez por curiosidad y por ver si algo se enciende. Si se consigue algo que nos entretenga. Ella se chupa y yo la imito. Pero, después, al llegarme el tufo agrio de su boca, me convenzo de que no quiere sino sólo un poco de agua.

Es una trampa. El Refugio y todo, es una trampa. Y Mi Mujer es la forma del vacío. Tal vez cada uno. Mortinatos. La vida que se vive negándose. Que avanza sólo negándose.

10 *(Afuera):* va llegando. Arrastrando las chinelas. Con las piernas aletargadas y tan miopes como los ojos que frunce, hasta rasgarlos, cada que lo saludan. Con las orillas del pantalón sucias de la tierra que levanta y el piso que trapea. Desencajado. Desfajada la camisa y enflaquecido tanto que el saco del traje le cuelga en el cuerpo desaparecido casi como si fuese apenas un gancho de ropa. La corbata anudada en cruz, como agujeta sin conejo. El Intendente no encuentra sus zapatos, dice, y explica así lo de las babuchas. No tiene esposa, dice luego, y explica también así el desarreglo, la hambruna y el cabello reñido, aunque por lo demás blanquísimo. Y sonríe, porque es lo más cercano a la inocencia. Sin embargo, a veces confunde las historias y cuenta que la extraviada es su esposa y que son los zapatos los que no tiene. Y sonríe otra vez, y siempre, enseñando sus dientes minúsculos; el interior de su boca descalabrada. Así lo recuerdo, y cuánta lástima a todos provocaba por senil, por bruto, porque era antes su esposa, mucho más joven, la que lo vestía, aderezaba, y porque fue ella la que, pasados tantos años, al fin lo abandonó llevándose a su hija. Entonces, después de la sonrisa pícara del viejo al saludar, el rostro se le aguada y derrite, entristecido, y así pasa el resto de la jornada hasta que llega la noche y se despide otra vez sonriente.

Es ahora como si lo estuviese viendo. Obligando a sus piernas a andar, más bien escurriéndose sus pies por el suelo, y pasándose de largo el jergón donde tendría que limpiarse. Sí, dejando tras de sí sus huellas llenas de mierdas, terrosas, en el suelo hipócritamente limpio, y sonriéndome a mí y a todos.

¿Qué podría encontrar en esa caja?, me pregunto. Algo, quizás un recuerdo, de lo que ya no existe.

11 *(Afuera):* ya en las bodegas sigue conmigo en la cabeza el niño de ayer que abrazaba a su rata. La llenará de más arrumacos y besos que los que yo le he dado en toda mi vida a Mi Mujer, quien muy rápidamente, aun en la maternidad, mezcló el amor con el odio. La vida con la muerte. Y sin darse cuenta, como yo, que estamos en un limbo que no hace sino negarlo todo. Que estamos, quiero decir, purgándonos, vomitándonos tanto hasta quedar sedientos, y sin saber, con seguridad, si estamos del lado de la vida o de la muerte.

Llevo 30 latas y me viene de pronto pensar en el hijo casi abortado de mi vieja, cuando me interrumpe mi patituerta resplandeciente, de tan angélica y pulcra, bajo las manchas de humedad del techo. Sigo sin buscar, todavía, caja alguna, y me pregunta: ¿Ya la has encontrado? Otra vez estoy a la altura de sus rodillas, sentado en el suelo y con la espalda pegada a mi suciedad grasosa marcada en el muro. Porque laboro ahí tirado y no hago más que arrastrarme. Entonces, todo es lo mismo: el suelo, la mancha, las latas, la caja extraviada; todo salvo que ahora ella está más cerca de mí, tanto que al mirar hacia arriba para encontrar la cara que habla, mis ojos se atrancan entre sus senos abultados y estrangulados por el sostén, como si fuera por mis manos. Y al ver aquello me pregunto de inmediato cuánto tendría que arrastrarme a la derecha, hacia ella, hacia la puerta, para alcanzar a mirarle la maraña negra de su entrepierna, sus calzones, antes de que me suelte una patada. Y luego, cuánto tendría que hacerlo para que, en algún punto, me dejara entrar en ella y, tal vez, ya metido en su piel, nos amáramos. ¿Cuánto tendría que introducirme? Pero sólo son ensoñaciones, y entonces le digo: No. Me reclama porque ni siquiera la he buscado, y me dice que no dejo ni un segundo mis latas y que la bodega es un desorden. Pienso reprocharle, pero me lo guardo y me lo digo entre dientes: ser el responsable de estas latas es la empresa, ineludible, de la que me han solicitado hacerme cargo. Y, por otra parte, todas estas cajas en desarreglo son o fueron responsabilidades suyas olvidadas. Bueno, hicieron el intento de olvidarlas, pienso, porque esta basura los perseguirá, y a mí, hasta que ardamos todos en un incendio. Es la realidad que nos persigue, que ya hicimos y que no se puede borrar. Que ya fracasó. Y pudiera ser, imagino ahora, que la guerra que han comenzado después fuera sólo ideada con el propósito, firme, de tacharlo todo. De quemarlo todo. De ahorrarse, con la destrucción, la penosa tarea de buscarle a todas las malformaciones construidas un orden. Me mira. Aún no respondo nada. Bufa y afloja hacia un lado las caderas. Cruza los brazos. Zapatea desesperada por mi silencio, como si remachara esos golpes en mi cabeza. Yo sujeto en una mano el plumín de olor narcótico, mientras en la otra está una lata con aquellos números frescos que sólo se hacen significativos por los desastres y por los tercos hombres: las fechas. Datos que se sufren y demuestran mi punto, porque *sufrir la realidad significa ser una realidad fracasada.* Siempre incompleta y siempre necia a hacerse de nuevos fracasos. Nos atiborramos. Me percato, entonces, que no he terminado de escribirle la fecha correspondiente a la lata que sostengo, y le apunto, en premonición, la cifra faltante: caducará, como todas, el día_, el mes_ y el año_. Luego, todas mis latas serán inútiles. La coja gruñe furiosa una vez que me he vuelto a la lata sin responderle. Regreso a mirarla, pero sigo en silencio, y así me mantengo hasta que afloja los brazos con desgane y resignación, dando media vuelta para irse. Mientras abre la puerta, le miro las nalgas, y me insulta.

Me gusta verla. Y decido, por ello, aplazar cuanto pueda la búsqueda para luego, ya habiendo encontrado la caja, esconderla y aplazar así, también, su ausencia.

Porque me hace falta una mujer, me digo. Mi esposa en casa ya es otra cosa. Muy diferente. Aunque la quiera. Tomo una lata y escribo la fecha. Luego otra y después otra.

En pánico, quizás, o anticipándose, o sabiendo, más bien, lo que se vendría por ser ellos quienes lo han planeado todo, enviaron estas latas. Las 8,000 latas. Me dieron, después, una fecha y cinco plumines. La misma fecha que se dibuja en las cajas donde llegaron. Y al rayarlas con esos números, a veces, me siento cercano a la Parca. Asimilado. Y me lleno de una especie de orgullo, porque pienso que, de equivocarme en una sola cifra, mi error pudiera ser monumental. Como cuando la muerte se equivoca. Es decir, como cuando queremos creer que se equivoca. De ser así, pienso, su error sería, tal vez, no el eliminar "prematuramente" a alguien, sino, mejor dicho, dejar vivo a aquel otro al que le correspondía morir. Una desgracia. Pudiera ser, entonces, que siento algo muy parecido al control en mis manos, al poder. La grandeza. Y el cuarto se agranda, los muros se desplazan, y yo pierdo la calva y la flaccidez de mis músculos, y gano más cuerpo y me siento relevante. Único e irrepetible. Sin embargo, pronto, muy pronto, pasa aquella tiránica euforia de saber que podría afectar a tantos y me vuelvo a mí mismo, a la mancha de sudor, a la bodega, a las latas llenas de números, porque, honestamente, ¿quién no se arriesgaría, en hambres, a comer una lata de conservas echada a perder? Ya llegamos antes, vueltos otra vez nómadas, a desollar a los animales domésticos, perros y gatos, o a los salvajes muertos por famélicos, en costillas, y ya magullados por los quebrantahuesos. Llegamos a competir con otras bestias para alcanzar, aunque sea, mascar algunos pellejos y engañarnos. Y me pregunto: ¿una vez pasada esa fecha, al notar que ya expiró el longevo alimento, nos sentiremos afortunados de saber que le hemos sobrevivido? Es decir, ¿será motivo de celebración el percatarnos que hemos durado más allá de esta fecha tan lejana?

¿De qué otros restos estará hecho, entonces, nuestro mundo? Y, bueno, ¿quién querría vivir ya tanto? De cualquier modo, desde el nacer nos vamos pudriendo de a poco. Quizás estando desde la primera tragada de oxígeno ya caducos... Nuestros órganos pasan tanto tiempo embutidos en nuestro cuerpo y llenándose de tantas malarias, ¿quién nos almorzaría? Y se percibe, ¿o no?, en nosotros, en nuestra piel, en las uñas y los ojos con derrames, cómo nos va consumiendo toda la porquería de dentro. Entonces, quiero decir, estamos desde el inicio ya enlutados.

Miro las latas, lo que anuncian, y me siento ansioso, y visualizo, sin quererlo, tal vez, los estragos. Y allí, a mitad de mi presagio casi extático, pienso en el hijo bastardo de Mi Mujer. En su nacimiento y su "prematura" muerte. "Antinatural". ¿No te habrás confundido entre él y yo?, recuerdo haber dicho lloriqueando algunos años después de fallecido, ¿estás segura de que no era yo el que debía morir?

12 *(Refugio):* y es en este punto de la historia donde habría que olvidar para recordar. *Y acordarse por olvido.*

13 *(Afuera)*: entonces: nació. Lo que es ya en sí imposible. O absurdo. Digámoslo: un grave problema. Y al primer imbécil que rondó por su casa con una propuesta y atinándole al costo la entregaron como esposa. Siendo ambas familias latifundistas, la boda se planeó en grande y así su futuro. Un futuro deslumbrante que suponía repetir la vida de sus padres. Como debía ser, digo, porque el venir a la vida no es ya, y quizá nunca lo haya sido, un accidente milagroso, sino una redundancia insoportable. Se vive por imitación. Se siente, se piensa, por imitación. Y así se fue habitando la nueva casa de muebles, sirvientes, ilusiones: lo necesario. Y de igual forma se hizo la fiesta. La celebración tuvo lugar, también, con todo lo indispensable: la capilla, el sacerdote, el pueblo lambiscón entero, el blanco, el aire limpio, las nubes gordas. Y allí la conocí yo. A Mi Mujer. En su boda. Porque una vez muerta mi madre lo perdí todo: las gallinas, los marranos; me adoptaron la orfandad y todos los oficios, siendo en este caso el de trapero de las mesas de la fiesta y sin saber, ni ella ni yo, que ese día se festejaría el inicio de nuestra mutua desdicha. Sin embargo, todo comenzó, porque aún era posible, remedando en mayor medida lo humano; sintiendo, si acaso, felicidad y tristeza, emoción. Dicho de otro modo, el sentimiento descarnado y la angustia generada por tener, todavía, voluntad de vivir, de darnos, incluso, forma y no adoptar las malformaciones de lo que se gestaba a nuestro alrededor. A ser lo que somos

hoy, una negación de la forma: la pasividad. Otra vez, el fracaso. De manera que la vi llegar al festejo, flaca, con el pecho hinchado, con la boca que hoy llamo hocico pintada apenas de rosa y sonriente. Los dientes duros. Tan hermosa. Y tanta belleza no podía sino significar sólo el pronóstico de los desmanes que se vendrían. Ese equilibrio: los brazos rollizos, los senos rellenos de grasa blanda y firmes, las piernas ágiles y largas, la naricita tímida y los ojos grandes. No podía durar demasiado. Y quizá por su fragilidad, a sabiendas de su progresiva devastación, la amé. La amé tanto. Con miedo de morir sin ella. Todavía, y me asombro, con miedo a la muerte. Y apenas al verla, y luego escucharla, olerla, sentí la urgencia profunda, más que de poseerla, de abrazarla. Ser poseído. No de desnudarla, quiero decir, no de hacer violenta su desnudez sino suavemente, sin penas, sin deformidades. Con ansia, más que con miedo, de entregarme, de hacerme suyo como hiciera mi gato al atreverse a vivir y al mezclarse con la naturaleza violenta. Por ello no pudo ser más grande mi desgracia cuando la tomó por el brazo aquel otro hombre, a quien me di, desde entonces, la tarea de aborrecer hasta donde cupiera en mi cuerpo estrecho el asco; exprimirme el odio para desearle todos los males, a tiempo de comenzar a amar y desvivirme por su esposa.

Avanzada la fiesta, la veo en el baile; casi en cacería, buscando interceptar todo lo que pueda suyo: su mirada, su olor, y guardármelo. Nunca antes había tenido motivación de nada, y nunca más habré de tenerla. Esas intensidades en mi cuerpo que me rebasan engañándome, proyectando falsamente algo más aparte de mi carne. Haciéndome sentir, pues, que hay algo en mí que se desprende del músculo, de los huesos... La veo saltar, gritar, correr, bailar, divertirse. Reír. Mientras su esposo le restriega la boca, le muerde los labios, se los lastima, y la lame indecoroso porque está inundado en alcoholes. Él se tropieza, carcajea, bebe más, es decir, se engendra a sí mismo, se escupe, cada vez más repugnante. El resto de los invitados, los padres, no son sino sólo sombras pusilánimes que se balancean como si un viento los empujase.

Y quizás así sea ella también, pero no me percato. Ella se cansa, pronto, de ver a su marido bailar con las regordetas mujeres del pueblo con los senos obesos y llenos de lunares peludos, con la cara colmada de várices y la mala fama. Son sus amigas, dice. Y no lo duda, pero se cansa de andar de relevo con las gordas el día de su boda, aunque a nadie parezca importarle. El cinismo. Porque todos saben cómo funcionan las cosas, incluso ella, no obstante, se guarde una esperanza ingenua de cambiarlo todo. Yo que la miro así, espero que se canse tanto que llegue a notar los otros rostros fatigados: el mío. Sin embargo, va y se sienta en la mesa, come pastel. Se esconde. Y hasta que mira en dirección al vacío, de pronto, me encuentra. También mirándola. Y me sonríe, más por amabilidad que por el azar de mi existencia y su hallazgo. No soy diferente a la otra roña. Luego busca otra nada donde posar los ojos y me digo en ese momento, cuando veo la comisura de su boca deprimirse, que tengo que rescatarla y que sería capaz de hacer por ella lo que fuera. Tan heroico. Tan patético. De pronto, tan vivo. Y ahora lo sé, tan estúpido.

Van pasando las horas, la gente se va yendo en tumbos, cargándose mutuamente, olvidados ya de la pareja y del día de mañana, del romanticismo y la falsa pureza del evento. Se detienen, arquean sus cuerpos, se desentrañan en vómitos y continúan andando. Ella platica, platica tanto, conversa, y lo disfruta. Tiene cosas que decir, me parece, cosas que escuchar... tal vez algo invente e imagine, incluso. Y no quiero desencantarme ni creer que todo lo que estoy viendo es una farsa y que ella es igual a cualquiera: un defectuoso espécimen que me gusta sólo porque aún no le he encontrado su deformidad. Aunque sepa que existe. Después, veo que, discreta, sentada a la mesa, se quita las zapatillas, se soba los dedos, alguna recién ampolla, se truena los huesos tiesos y agotados de los pies. Infla los carrillos en cansancio y mira a su marido desenredándose de los brazos de una y enredándose en otra, hundiendo su nariz ancha entre las tetas de sus amigas, olisqueando algún perfume. Vociferando obscenidades. Ella vuelve a escupir aire y se pregunta si lo ama, y si eso, de verdad, importa. Aunque, casi de inmediato, sonríe de nuevo porque se dice que tiene que amarlo, porque guarda la ilusión de que mañana se abrazarán en su nueva cama, brillará el sol y cantará algún pájaro mofletudo. Porque le han enseñado a ilusionarse, y porque ama, entonces, también, por imitación. Y siento hacia ella, por vez primera, algo cercano al desprecio, pero lo olvido pronto. Entonces, decidida, se alza, va hacia él que la mira y la abraza y se la come con la boca café de tabaco y agria. Ella, como el niño de la rata, se deja comer. Y finge alegría.

Entrada ya la madrugada, quedan unos pocos: ella, su marido con sus amigos y amigas, y yo arrinconado en la sombra. Hace frío y ya se acaba la música y sólo se escuchan esas voces necias que alargan la noche. En la carreta de bodas, el cochero duerme también embriagado. Ronca. Entonces, anticipándome, me acerco y, empujando el bulto, lo dejo tirado al suelo y me hago, de la nada, el auriga. Ella comienza a despedirse de todos, toma de la mano a su esposo y, a la oreja, le dice algo. Él se voltea y manotea fastidiado como diciéndole: Ya te alcanzo, mosca. Resignada, tan cansada que no puede pensar en otra cosa que no sea dormir ni sentir nada con respecto a la actitud de su marido, se dice, embrutecida: Es la fiesta. Y de nuevo, se motiva y consuela pensando que en unas horas él estará allí y desayunarán juntos y todo tomará marcha y rumbo. Se sube al carretón, tal vez algo avergonzada y sin percatarse de quién lleva las bridas. Conduzco lento, rabioso. También ya estoy envinado y el alcohol se mezcla con lo que destila mi celo y el odio al hombre que la maltrata. El camino la habrá arrullado, pienso. O chilla como nena confundida, asustada de su error y esperando a que yo me aproveche de su llanto. O, quizá, sopese la oscuridad y se diga que es la última chanza que tiene para irse. Inmerso en esas cavilaciones, escuchando a las bestias dormir, enfureciéndome de veras de no ser yo su esposo, me viene la idea de secuestrarla. Atino pensar que, del secuestro y del tiempo, de la liberación mutua, ella encontrará la forma de amarme y hacerse conmigo. Lejos. Entonces, cargado así de esos ánimos, aprieto las cuerdas considerándolo ahora con el cuerpo. Me sudan las manos. Un chasquido, me digo, y los caballos corren y ella y yo nos fugamos. Un azote. No me hace falta nada más que hacerlo y todo se arregla, pienso. Alzo los brazos para fustigar, cuando caigo en cuenta de que ya estamos llegando y ella me avisa la parada. Mis manos antes impávidas se derrumban, y, como si ella hubiese podido escucharme las intenciones, me invade el ridículo. Como si se riera de mí la realidad. Se me eriza el cuerpo, empequeñecido, alienado, sin saber ya siquiera cómo moverse. La dejo en su casa, esa que todos vimos tan rápidamente construirse y amueblarse. Se apea y, al hacerlo, voltea a verme tal vez queriendo desahogarse conmigo, rogándome, quiero decir, que le asegure que todo estará bien. Que es normal, y que lo normal no es malo. Sin embargo, al mirarme me recuerda o reconoce: el vacío. Y se inmuta. No hay nada que pueda decirme. Sonríe, quizá más que por amabilidad, por reflejo, y se marcha.

Pensé en ella toda la noche, sintiéndome sucio. Idiota. De nuevo, y ahora se entiende, tan vivo. Esa desagradable sensación.

14 *(Refugio):* como tumbada por el peso de sus tripas negras...
derrumbada e inmóvil... durmiendo azotada contra el suelo...

Me interrumpe su olor y el sonido de su nariz que rezonga; el chasquido de su boca cuando babosea el aire que respira antes de expulsarlo. Saco mi cabeza, entonces, de los trazos, de las hojas arrugadas, de la mesa de madera tan podrida como sus piernas, y me busco, recordando aquello, alguna sensación, aunque sea vaga, que me estremezca, que me palpite. Que me diga, ya no que me asegure porque no puedo creerlo, que todo fue real. Que ella, quiero decir, que esas migajas que miro, fueron en algún punto la mujer de mis amores. Pero ya no hay nada. Cada músculo y nervio en mí se mantiene indiferente ante ella y ante la evocación del pasado. Y me digo ahora: estoy escribiendo las mentiras de otro, si bien suponen ser mis memorias. Otras falsedades. Es decir, memorias de lo que nunca ha sido; memorias, para decirlo mejor, que germinan insulsas desde la nada, desde el vacío. El vacío tan lleno de nada.

Y son mis palabras casi ruidos que roen sólo el hueso del interior de mi cráneo sin significar ninguna cosa, y es ella sólo ya, como dije, una cosa rellena, hasta reventar, de vísceras negras que apestan el cuarto y que se escapan por su boca y cada orificio de su cuerpo. La vida. Despanzurrándose, pudriéndose. Tan fastidiosas, sus vísceras, como las mías. Y es de sorprenderse que sólo de esto esté compuesto el hombre, e increíble que los otros de antes, los admirados, hayan cargado con lo mismo y hayan creado, todavía así, cosas bellas. Destruidas ya, porque fuimos viendo el mundo degradarse, vaciarse de toda belleza. Y así el lenguaje, despojado de lo que fuera.

Apago la luz que ilumina mis escritos y me recuesto en el suelo, como remedándola, cerrando los ojos duramente para que no vuelvan a abrirse. Y después, al quedarme dormido, acude a mí de nueva cuenta la mula atada a un árbol, cansada, con los ojos ya ciegos como dos bolas de vidrio. Sacude la cabeza para espantarse las moscas. Sopla el viento como ya no hace y despeina los pastos que ya no existen. No hay nada más que esa mula como una piedra. Pero ya se acerca el hombre con la escopeta cargada. Se planta frente a ella, se limpia con el antebrazo las narices, empuña el arma, apunta al medio del cráneo sobre el hocico. Tiene los mismos ojos que la mula que se desploma. Tan negros. Y me despierto.

No tendría que ser tan simple el acto de matarla, me digo. Pero tampoco puede ser más complejo.

Recostados los dos, le tomo a Mi Mujer la mano que yace fría, estriada, sobre la tabla de madera. Me giro a verla mientras emborrono de mi memoria la mueca tiesa del cadáver de la mula y luego la de mi madre: su lengua asomándose por entre su quijada dura; sus ojos, muertos, sobre mí mirando nada. Mirándome. Nada. Y es todo tan nítido: me veo y a Mi Mujer, y confirmo que es porque todavía existe el hombre que dudo de la existencia de Dios.

15 *(Afuera)*: pasada una noche después de la boda, al ir a buscarla a su enorme y nueva casa para siquiera mirarla, me topé con la Rabona; como por afecto la llamaba. Una mujer de culo metido, escamoteado. Piel quemada. Y qué jodida suerte, me dije, porque por aquel entonces me había olvidado ya de ella, aburrido ya hasta el desquiciamiento de ella, y liberado. Un día, como cualquier otro y simplemente, dejé de frecuentarla perdiéndole el rumbo. Ya me tenía cansado. Y quiso la fatalidad que me reencontrara con ella justo allí, sirviendo a la mujer que yo rondaba, y a la que luego nombraría mi esposa. La encontré harapienta, en cuclillas y poniéndome a los ojos sus nalgas planas. Daba de tragar a los perros de su dueña. Y ya no había dónde esconderme cuando se percató de mí: me amenazó, me insultó; echó frente a mí al suelo escupitajos espumosos en repetidas ocasiones para dar énfasis al sentido de sus insultos. De sus palabras. Me hizo quedar en sus gritos como una sabandija cualquiera, si bien poco me importó. Entonces le dije que estaba allí por ella y que quería recomenzar lo nuestro, revivirlo. Y fuera tal vez por su urgencia de un hombre o por su llana simplicidad, pero me tomó al tiro. Sin dudarlo. Le subí las faldas en la parte trasera de la casa, empujándola de cara al muro. ¿Y no se va a molestar la jefa?, le dije. No, me respondió entrecortada su voz por los gemidos. Está arriba llorando. Recién casada y ya la abandonaron, dijo mientras echaba para atrás la cabeza presentándome su boca sucia para besarla.

Su esposo no ha vuelto, terminó de decir mordiéndose los labios que dejé intactos. Nos mantuvimos así, sin cruzarnos más palabras, nuestros cuerpos también mordiéndose, hasta desahogar mi porquería en sus entrañas.

Terminada la boda, la fiesta de su marido demoró otros tres días. Por lo que me alcanza saber de voz de la Rabona, y luego de Mi Mujer, las cosas siguieron más o menos de la siguiente manera: corre la tercera noche y ella permanece sin todavía haber dormido. Espera apelotonada en las cobijas, confundida con sus emociones; entre rencorosa y angustiada; triste. Quizás aún le sobre un poco de la preocupación que comenzó a sentir hace dos días, pero ya no será tanta. Se ha mantenido insomne y en ayunas, y está tan debilitada que con esfuerzo alcanza apenas a limpiarse la costra de las lágrimas viejas, y moquea, más bien, seca, como en una reacción del llanto que ya no escurre. Es decir, ya en la pura asfixia del dolor que le estruja con brutalidad el pecho. Su cara trasnochada, ojerosa, es algo grotesco, y se pierde la identidad de su rostro. Nadie sabe nada de su esposo, y el pueblo entero ya conspira contra ella embarrándose la boca de monsergas que ensucian su nombre. La carcome la vergüenza, las opiniones, las miradas de los otros que la devorarán apenas la vean.

Está con los ojos enrojecidos pasmados en la ventana. Una luz tímida de luna que se asoma le deja saber que sigue despierta y que sigue esperando. Que sigue, quiero decir, viviendo, y que todo es verdad: que sigue sola. Que hace tres días que no ve a su esposo. Que hace tres días que se vistió con el camisón que usaría en su noche de bodas, donde reconocería en manos de él las formas de su cuerpo al violentarse, y la sensación del amor y la plenitud. Que se quedó atada a las cobijas, esperando, sintiendo pena de sí misma y como si la ropa le ahorcase la carne prohibiéndole olvidar que respira. Que trae aún puesto el mismo camisón de encaje blanco que ya está sucio de lágrimas, babas y mucosidades. Que no alcanza a comprender ni a decidirse qué es lo que ocurre; qué le ha pasado, si ha sufrido algún accidente, ha tenido algún altercado o sigue con la cara apelmazada en las tetas bofas de sus amigas regordetas. Que está deshecha y que pasa de la rabia a los gimoteos llorosos, al asombro por su paciencia o su ingenuidad, cuando con la cara alargada, pálida, la tripa encogida y los órganos torcidos, alcanza a escuchar la zancada de un caballo que, ahora siente, le patea el corazón. Porque ya llega. Se escucha rechinar la puerta de la estancia que se queda abierta, el rumor del viento que se arremolina y unos pasos torpes, embriagados, que se acercan. Después de tres días enteros, cierra al fin por un segundo los ojos y respira profundamente, aunque el pecho le arda. Cavila una idea que se ha ido gestando mientras escucha el cuerpo pesado de su esposo estrellarse con los muros como un bote ebrio que se destroza contra el terraplén. Entonces, dudando, estira su mano convulsa a la cómoda donde se esconden unas tijeras grandes. El sonido de los pasos se acrecienta hasta ya casi llegar a la puerta, y como si se impusiera la presencia del hombre sobre todo lo pasado y sentido, la invade una sensación fugaz donde se confunden la esperanza, el ridículo, la prudencia, la resignación y la estupidez, que le hace devolver su brazo bajo las cobijas. Toda su atención intenta concentrarse en su oído, pero el palpitar en su pecho, tan duro y renuente, fastidioso, no la deja escuchar otra cosa más que su sangre que se amontona. Está de espaldas a la puerta que se abre lentamente. Se encoje arrinconando sus piernas contra su pecho, escondiendo su cuerpo, cuando una corriente de aire azota aquella otra puerta que se había quedado abierta. El escándalo tumba al borracho al suelo, donde se queda dormido bocabajo. Ella, luego de estremecerse por el susto, se alza acolchándose el pecho y mirándolo: respira, roncando, con la boca atiborrada de saliva. Una vez más: las tijeras, piensa. Sin embargo, le vuelve la espalda y se recuesta de nuevo. Ahora mira el muro a un lado de la ventana, masculla algo ininteligible y se decide: se baja de la cama, se acerca a la masa corpulenta y deforme que gruñe y apesta, y antes de dejarse sacudirlo a golpes, lo intenta despertar, lo ayuda a ponerse en pie, lo tira en la cama, lo desviste. Regresa a su sitio en el colchón, donde mira que la jeta descompuesta, hinchada y con la boca rebosante de baba invade parte de su almohada y la humedece. Se recuesta y se recoge, diminuta, para que sus cuerpos no alcancen a tocarse.

Al día siguiente, se le vio al fin parada fuera de su casa, en la mañana pálida. Respirando el frío, abrazándose los brazos que el camisón, manchado, deja desnudos. Y allí estaba yo, lo suficientemente cerca para mirarla: los labios abultados, el pelo atado, el cuerpo palpitante, los pezones tiesos. Pasé los dos días anteriores desde temprano, y luego al anochecer, bajo el pretexto de cogerme a la Rabona, para tener noticias. Y al fin la miraba. La mirábamos todos. Y no le importó que la observaran, porque ella necesitaba sentir el aire, que el frío la envolviera, la tragara, le picara los pulmones purificándola. Fueron sólo unos minutos y luego volvió a su encierro. Él durmió todo el día.

Pasan de las cinco de la tarde y su marido despierta: la boca caliente, los músculos sueltos, la tripa apretada de hambre y así la entrepierna. Se la palma, se rasca los testículos y se debate: qué aflojar primero. Baja, luego, al comedor, donde su esposa está sentada, en absoluto repuesta del cansancio ni del insomnio, pero con las espaldas firmes, la mirada imperturbable y una terca gota de tristeza mojándole la mejilla. La saluda, le besa la frente empañando de su aliento agrio sus ojos. Ella lo observa sin camiseta, con las pelusas del sobaco tiesas de tres días de sudor, la cara desencajada y sin afeitar. Y como si se dijera decepcionada: Eres algo más de lo que pareces, se suelta en llanto. ¿Qué?, es lo único que alcanza a decir él, y con eso, todavía más, la deshace. Pero ella se guarda cualquier palabra y en silencio se encierra en el cuarto. Las sirvientas lo miran y escuchan todo: ella corriendo, él yendo detrás persiguiendo los pasos de su esposa, pero lentamente. Y luego, algunos gritos. Algunos reclamos de ella, que se envalentona: la luna de miel, la espera, la angustia, la vergüenza. Y pareciese que él sólo alcanza captar el tema del sexo, porque, forcejeando, le abre de par en par las piernas, luxándole las caderas y sangrándola. Dejándole, quiero decir, la piel sucia, roja, del sello del amor.

16 *(Afuera)*: se masca la boca. La cara entera le tiembla tragada por esa boca nerviosa, desvencijada, que muerde al aire. Está
sentada a la mesa de la cocina: las manos, como lijas, entrelazadas; desquiciada la mirada, perdida en el abismo que hay entre
ella y yo, donde se hunden sus ojos. En la negrura. La anciana, mi
suegra, no es sino sólo ese gesto maltrecho, ese pellejo surcado
por las tristezas; es decir, apenas alcanza a ser esa cara que le
cuelga y se agita por la boca que roe la nada, que se bate obse-
siva. Esa cara imbécil, pasmada en el dolor. Los ojos allí traba-
dos. Incrédula aún, quizá, de la suerte jodida de su hija que le ha
arruinado todo. Se levanta cada madrugada para sentarse unos
segundos a la mesa solamente y en completa soledad, porque es
esa toda la vida que vive; ese tiempo a solas. Y dudo que *tiemble
todavía ante el temor de perderla*; ya más bien hastiada de vivir.
Sin embargo, sufriría seguramente de poder aún decirse que es
absurdo que sólo eso signifique estar vivo: un hombre enclenque
que se aplasta con las uñas los piojos, una hija rota condenada a la
inmovilidad, una cocina bañada de luz pálida, un pedazo atorado
de chivo entre los dientes y una quijada suelta, descontrolada,
que la desespera. ¿Cómo se redujo todo a esto?, podría preguntarse con el pecho destazado en memorias ya irreconocibles y
que sólo la lastiman. Y es más bien su cabeza un silencio atrona-
dor interrumpido sólo por el sonido que hace su boca desdentada
al machucarse, babosa, a sí misma: la monotonía. Un mes que
sigue al otro sin notarse diferencia. ¿Cocinará hoy las vísceras

que ayer le traje?, le pregunto. Me inspecciona con los ojos como percatándose de mi existencia, si bien lleva cerca de treinta minutos con la mirada clavada en mí. Dejo mi taza de café vacía en el fregadero, me vuelvo a ella que me sigue mirando, y me responde sólo asintiendo con la cabeza. Habrá que disfrutarlas, le digo acercándome a la puerta, porque pronto ya no va a haber, y salgo. Es la parte trasera de la casa, y en frente mío quedan amplios páramos que parecen infinitos e inabarcables. Y siento el encierro. Desde el otro lado de la ventana, vuelvo a ver a mi suegra ahora con la cara fija en el muro y con su vida entre los dientes. Doy un respiro profundo, porque sé que aquí afuera todo es lo mismo y el mundo no es más que esta enorme burbuja que nos aprisiona, donde sólo es perceptible la vida como el chasquido ensalivado de la boca de una vieja.

Ya están en las bodegas las cajas que corresponden al resto del racionamiento. Ahora está todo, todavía más, revuelto, y ya no cabe espacio ni siquiera para arrastrarme. No nos sobran muchos días antes de que comiencen las entregas de los bonos y se aglomeren todos a hacer fila aquí afuera, y eso es casi como decir que no nos quedan muchos días y punto; sin embargo, la gente de este edificio y la otra, porque todos lo saben, no parece sentir pánico. Sentir nada. Las guerras son parte del mecanismo monótono que hace avanzar nuestros días; son parte, para decirlo mejor, del trayecto que hay, obligadamente, que seguir hasta alcanzar nuestra muerte natural. Están los que vienen aquí a llenar papeles y ven su posible muerte como efectos colaterales de su trabajo, y los que andan allá afuera, cargándose los pies en esfuerzos casi imposibles, que lo ven todo, otra vez la muerte, como cualquier trámite tedioso al que hay que ajustarse. Y eso es la naturaleza de hoy. ¿No debería yo, mejor, no permitir que se les entregara ni una sola lata? ¿Dejarlos morir una vez que se agoten sus ganados, sus reservas, y de una vez por todas, con la muerte tan natural como pueda serlo: en el exterminio? ¿Salvar a la humanidad de ser más inhumana?

Apenas pasan esas reflexiones, que duran sólo el segundo que tardo en ocupar mi lugar, vuelvo a mis latas. Comienzo con una y me detengo. Miro que me quedan miles de latas aún por marcar, pero me niego a mover un solo dedo. ¿Para qué? Y así dejo correr las horas. Estoy aburrido, confinado en mi muro, contagiado por la imbecilidad de mi suegra, y sólo respiro. A trancas, quiero decir, respiro y ya cansado de tener que hacerlo. Estoy con las piernas estiradas y en trenza, los brazos tirados al piso y las palmas mirando al cielo, como si estuvieran clavadas al pavimento. Estoy, pues, como un Cristo, más que vencido, perezoso. Indiferente. Lleno ya de morbosidades en el cuerpo, con una barriga parasitada y no un abdomen remarcado, a pesar de las flaquezas y la pobreza, en músculos. La sublimidad de mi rostro santo, deformado por los estragos del tiempo, está, también, más que en éxtasis místico, idiotizado y moroso. No vale la pena ya nada, me digo casi religiosamente. Y soy yo el que te abandona ahora, musito, también abandonándome. ¡Consumado es!

Sin embargo, no bien termino de decir aquello cerrando los ojos, me parece sin estar seguro, sentir algo en mí; un bulto hueco y pesado, porque ya tiene varios días sin aparecerse por aquí mi paticoja. ¿Y qué es esta sensación en el pecho?, me pregunto, pues ya no sólo suena ingenuo y hasta vulgar decir que algo se siente en el corazón, sino, incluso, que algo se siente y a secas. ¿Cómo fue que ocurrió?, ¿cómo le quitamos al corazón la carne?, ¿cómo fue que el sentir se redujo a un espasmo apenas perceptible? Y sea como fuere, me parece extrañar a la patizamba, y aunque se me ocurre pensar que ella no es, tampoco, más que un bulto de carnosidades, de glándulas violentas, siento la necesidad de verla, exprimirla. Quizá deba decirle ya que he encontrado la caja; que ha sido por accidente mientras le hacía espacio al racionamiento; que aún no la he revisado, y que me gustaría, si fuera posible, revisarla entera con ella. Ayudarle. Y ahora pienso que, tal vez deba ponerme en pie y andar hasta su oficina, hablar con ella. Enseñarle de mí lo que incluso yo ya desconozco. Dejar de ser lo que soy, pienso, este fracaso. Intentarlo de nuevo. *Fracasar otra vez. Fracasar mejor.* Es decir, encontrar el modo para salir de este marasmo, con ella; cruzar los páramos estériles enteros hasta encontrar algo distinto y antes de que llegue nuestra última hora. ¿No es posible?, me pregunto en ánimos, ahora, de redentor. ¿O es, más bien, que soy de aquellos que ya nacieron tarde, ya cuando no era posible intentar nada? Me pongo, entonces, de pie, aunque sé que lo que me ocurre es sólo un instante exagerado y falso, como la sensación fantasma de comezón en un miembro amputado y que pronto volveré a lo real y a decir que no existe nada más que estos campos planos y mierdosos. Que no soy más ni menos de lo que soy y no puedo serlo. Que es mi esperanza necia la amputada, la que me molesta y pica, casi como un instinto originario; una suerte de erección inevitable e inútil. Miro a mi alrededor, aprovechando que ya estoy erguido y me fluye la sangre, para buscar en dónde poner mi primer paso cuando caigo en cuenta de lo que ya he anticipado: todo lo que he dicho es inviable dentro del orden de lo racional: el corazón, sentir y etcétera, mi paticoja y los páramos, y todo aquello, vivo, que he sentido es mentira y no me interesa a mí, como a ningún otro, ser salvado ni redimido. Evitar la guerra. Nada. Además, al ver impedido mi paso por las cajas y sopesar, también, la divina pereza que hay en mi cuerpo molido de sortearlas, pasarles por encima y lo que fuera necesario hacer para llegar hasta donde está la coja, me vuelvo al suelo. Irremediablemente sé que éste es mi lugar. ¿Y qué diferencia hizo o haría hoy un Cristo en el mundo? No. No me sería extraño encontrar entre tanta basura inservible una cruz tallada a mano. Aquí pertenecemos.

La mancha de grasa en el muro es cada vez más grande. Como si mi existencia se fuera dilatando y reafirmando cada día. Ya revisaré más al rato el archivo del Intendente, a ver si me alcanza con sus manías para algún alivio.

Mejor no pensar. No sentir.

17 *(Afuera)*: el amor, entonces. ¿Es posible, aún, encapricharse con algo? ¿Enamorarse como los más grandes idiotas? Estoy con la Rabona dándome la espalda, poniéndome sus nalgas en huesos sobre la pelvis, hiriéndome, mejor dicho, con sus huesos filosos la pelvis mientras rezo aquellas preguntas, confundido por la necia necesidad que tengo de la mujer que duerme ahora, o llora, allá arriba. La dejó destrozada, me dice con la cara aplastada contra la pared blanca. Y son sus palabras, para mí, gestos aislados y apenas alcanzo a captar algunas frases. Tal vez sospeche de mis intenciones y guarde para ella algún placer el decírmelo todo: cuánto sufre la mujer que…, o quizá sea más bien que halle gusto en decirme aquellos chismes grotescos mientras le rebano aún más su raja. No, me imagino explicarle, no es más que por esa llaga entre tus piernas, depravada, masoquista, que te llaman mujer. Y sádica. Pone sus manos en mis nalgas, también desnudas, y las exprime acercándome más a ella. Está por terminar. Ayer, continúa diciendo, la violó. Y me rasguña. Su voz sólo se interrumpe por el mismo sonido que hace mi suegra y que engendra a todo el mundo: un balbuceo, una colisión de cuerpos desnudos y carne húmeda. Y no ha bajado en todo el día, dice, ni él tampoco desde ayer ha vuelto. Una de las otras sirvientas, más decrépitas aún y casi sordas, ciegas, asoma la cara por la ventana para vernos. Se emboba. Y nos miramos directamente, insensibles ella y yo, a los ojos. Ni se inmuta ni se excita. Y es

en su rostro de pez, cristiano, donde busco las formas ideales para quitarle a un hombre la vida. Quitarme del paso al marido de Mi Mujer. Asesinarlo… Mi Mujer, Mi Mujer…, me repito sin quererlo en voz alta y en sintonía con el ruido aguado que hacen nuestros cuerpos. ¿Qué dices?, pregunta la Rabona ahora con los dos codos pegados al muro y la frente protegida por las manos. Y sigue: escuchamos unos gritos; pegamos la oreja a la puerta para enterarnos; sólo se alcanzaba a escuchar la cama rechinando…, me imaginé… que… eran… los huesos… de la señora… los que crujían. Su voz está quebrada en vagidos porque se acerca el orgasmo. Convulsionan también sus palabras. Y es que la vida es para ella tan indiferente cuando yo, o alguien más, la coge por la espalda. Es casi, la vida, un milagro, casi es divertida y se le suelta la lengua. Entonces, para apurarla, la tomo por la cintura, la ahogo, le jalo los cabellos. Y es una pena, pienso, que yo no sienta nada. Después, dice, sólo alcanzábamos a oír un llanto cuando él, empujando contra nosotras la puerta, nos lanzó contra el suelo. Y no sabemos a dónde se ha ido. Saca deformado por el escote uno de sus senos y lo oprime; su pezón alzado asoma por la rendija entre sus dedos. La vimos tirada en la cama, tan desnuda… Y no sé yo con seguridad, al escucharla, cuántas intensidades existen de la desnudez, pero la entiendo. Estaba de espaldas a nosotras, abrazándose las piernas, reducida y la sangre le corría del sexo al culo. La última palabra se extiende en el largo y último gemido que da para cerrar, al fin, la boca. Obligada al silencio ya cuando hablar no otorga ningún placer. Vuelta otra vez al rostro llano e impávido, similar al de la otra sirvienta, se arranca de mí, se sube los calzones, desarruga la falda. También yo he derramado cada gota; sin goce y más bien pagando el costo. Me limpio con la mano lo que rebosa embarrándolo en el muro: y aquí quedó una existencia nonata, me digo, haciendo más pesada la mía. Pero no pienses mal, continúa aún mientras se ata el cabello, apenas al verla corrimos para ayudarla, pero nos echó de inmediato. Tan grosera. No nos dejó ni tocarla…, y pobrecilla, dice, porque debe de seguir todavía sucia y con la sangre ya seca.

Envuelta en el olor de esa sangre; ese olor cavernoso impregnado a las sábanas, termino yo por decir imaginándome aspirar el hedor para guardármelo. Y bueno ya vete que tengo trabajo, me dice con un bofetón al aire y desdeñosa.

La vieja sirvienta ya se ha ido.

Sin embargo, la convencí de dejarme quedar un rato en la cocina a beber un trago de café. Estoy ahora sentado solo. Las moscas rondándome las orejas, excitadas, porque al frente mío está la cena de ayer y el desayuno de hoy que la mujer que llora, que ha sido violada y abandonada dos veces, no ha querido tocar. La imagino deshabitada de sí, tanto como estas paredes permanecen deshabitadas de ella aún; habrá cruzado una vez por aquí, si acaso dos. No se habrá percatado aún de las termitas que ya han comenzado a roer el mueble de la alacena ni de la tierra sin limpiar que de a poco se irá comiendo el color de la fachada. Estará a oscuras, todavía tirada desnuda sobre la cama deshecha y en el medio del colchón. Sin cobijas, sin frío, sin sentir ningún dolor ni nada físico, sino sólo algo desde dentro que se le resquebraja. Duerme con la cara húmeda, ya acartonada de tanto llanto. Tan fea, seguramente. Y muy bien la veo. Un tenue resplandor ilumina en el aire una pelusa larga por su entrepierna asomándose. Las manos juntas bajo la cara como duermen las criaturas. La luz del baño encendida pero entrecerrada la puerta; las cortinas abajo, de manera que la luz apenas se inmiscuya tímida, silenciosa, para no tocarla ni herirla. El aire pesado, encerrado y oloroso; agrio. Me imagino entrando en el cuarto sin hacer ruido. Quitarme las botas sucias, los pantalones, la camisa, mientras me acerco. Veo sus ropas rotas mezclarse con las mías. Y ya desnudo, la miro más atentamente: los huesos resaltados de la columna, los pies fríos, la piel suave arañada, el vello largo entre sus muslos sucio también de sanguaza seca. Y me recuesto tras de ella, en la orilla de la cama, abrazándola, protegiéndola. Volviendo a nacer. La envuelvo en mí. El abdomen contracturado, el ombligo profundo, los senos graves aplastándose y amoratados; la boca abierta, los labios dilatados, mordidos, los párpados húmedos y cerrados; los brazos tersos, las costillas que la enjaulan hinchándose de aire, la cintura, el nacimiento del vello en el pubis, el calor de sus muslos aplastando mi mano. Una mosca en mi oreja, intentando entrar en mí, me despierta. Y no lo pienso dos veces. Me pongo en pie y camino fuera de la cocina. Nada se escucha. Las dos viejas están en el jardín y la Rabona en el sótano lavando trapos. Paso rozando con mi mano todo lo que me encuentro: la mesa de madera larga del comedor, una de las sillas, la pared rugosa. Veo las escaleras y ahora acaricia mi mano el barandal mientras subo. Hay tres recámaras. Dos de ellas con la puerta bien abierta por donde entra el sol al pasillo iluminando la única puerta que se halla cerrada. Las sirvientas la habrán cerrado, pienso, y no tendrá puesto el cerrojo. Doy vuelta al picaporte despacio, con placer, incluso. Y allí está. Diferente a como la imaginé, y me gusta más la versión de lo real. Las cortinas abiertas dejan entrar toda la luz de fuera evidenciando su existencia; manifestándola ante mí. Violenta y violentada. La cobija, enroscada serpentina, en una de sus pantorrillas. Manchada, enrojecida, en algunos puntos. Está cercana a la orilla, bocabajo, desnuda. Una pierna estirada y la otra encogida hacia un lado como los dibujos a gis de los cadáveres. Un brazo arriba y otro abajo, también; el cuerpo como a la mitad de una fuga. Está recostada su cara sobre la mejilla izquierda, en dirección a la enorme ventana y conmigo detrás. Duerme. El hedor es aún más denso y el calor me asfixia unos instantes. Cierro tras de mí la puerta y me detengo a mirarla. Estoy sudando. Ante mí sus nalgas. Y ahí están los pelos sucios que imaginé, embarrados al colchón blanco. Sigo la línea de su espalda mientras intento acercarme en callado. Paso por el armario, un estante de baratijas, una alfombra en el suelo frente a la cama que rodeo. Mi cuerpo le hace sombra al suyo y veo su cara. Hinchada, torcida, triste. Su mano flaca cerrada en un puño. En el suelo, debajo de mí, como un fantasma, su camisón de bodas. *Bodas de sangre.* Siento el ridículo de todo ahí dentro, lo exagerado que es para algunos vivir. Si pudiera recogerte en mis brazos e irnos, me digo. Si fueras mi esposa no te dejaría tumbada ni sucia; te alimentaría y te cuidaría. Te protegería en cada paso para evitarte la muerte. Te mantendría feliz y sana. Felices los dos. Porque es todavía posible la felicidad, ¿cierto? Me asomo por la ventana; veo los campos verdes, los bueyes y mulas arreando, los caballos guardados, el sol en el horizonte antes del mediodía. Prometería amarte diario, en la salud y en la enfermedad. Nos veo de frente, con la mirada agonizante de Dios juzgándonos, nuestro amor, yo sujetando su mano, repitiendo las palabras que el sacerdote me hace decir, convenciéndome de mi sinceridad. Hasta que la muerte nos separe. Y aún por toda la eternidad, digo entre dientes mirándola de nuevo. Desparramada, olorosa. Camino hacia la salida, mi mano otra vez acaricia lo que queda de paso: la cama, los dedos de un pie, la pierna ahogada por la sábana. Abro la puerta. Escucho que da un suspiro largo y cansado.

18 *(Refugio):* pudiera ser que al escribir todo esto me olvide de ti. Me cure de ti. Me alivie, me desembarace. Humanizados otra vez, los dos. Refugiado en momentos más vivos. Y vigorizado de nuevo con alguna ilusión; aunque sea con aquella de ser capaz de quitarme la vida. Porque *uno siempre se mata demasiado tarde,* como decía aquella voz que tanto he rezado. Las voces, mejor dicho, soterradas en mis oídos, como moscas. Sin embargo, escribir no ha hecho más que mostrarte a mí más real e insoportable. Cada día más lejos de lo que fuimos. Estás tirada a mis pies, sobre la mesa larga que acaricié el primer día que te vi desnuda. Y te miro ahora: el camisón transpirado adherido a tu cuerpo demacrado que no oculta tu tanta desnudez, tu fealdad. Tus costillas, las veo, tus senos desaparecidos, los huesos de tu esternón, a través de la tela. Como un sudario. Después tus brazos y pies flacos deshuesados. Tu cara que me mira aquí sentado en mi silla con los ojos fijos en ti, diciendo: *ciertamente así no muere un ser humano.* Porque quién sabe ya qué cosa seas y qué soy yo, y qué todos. Arriba, fuera de este sótano donde nos hallamos sepultados, los hombres se matan. ¿Y de qué nos estoy protegiendo en esta tumba? Fascinados los hombres, necios, en preservar vidas insignificantes. Qué contradicción. Y a sabiendas de que el infierno no es violento. Ni interesante. Sino la pasividad; una calma y un tedio que aniquilan. ¿Y no era yo capaz de estar allá arriba? ¿Qué estamos esperando?, ¿verdad?, me preguntas. Súbeme, me dices.

Entrégame a los hombres. Deja de sacrificarte por mí. Porque el sacrificio es estar vivo; resistir viviendo lo que se vive. Y se ha malentendido siempre. ¿Pero qué harían contigo los hombres? Sedientos, sudorosos. ¿Reconocerían en ti a una mujer? ¿Viva? ¿Violable? ¿O te confundirían con el resto de los cadáveres desperdigados? Y, sin embargo, sí. Para mí pudiera ser una oportunidad el dejarte allá afuera. Liberarme de ti y salvarme, ya que es egoísta tu empecinamiento en vivir y no un sacrificio como el mío: ¿por qué no te has dado por vencida? Si a todos, la vida ya nos ha derrotado. ¿Qué pretendes? ¿Qué esperas? ¿O será, más bien, que hemos dejado de vivir desde hace tiempo y estamos ya, solos tú y yo, en el infierno? Abandonados por Dios y los dioses y sin invitación para subir a la altura de las montañas. ¿Qué aire respiras en este sótano? Enterrado bajo la casa ya destruida, seguramente. La casa de tu matrimonio enterrada, también, en un mundo deforme. El mundo deforme. ¿Cómo decir? Vivir es respirar sin ahogarse. Hoy. Mejor dicho, vivir es aprender a respirar sin ahogarse. Y nosotros enterrados en el sótano, envueltos en cajas. Y en las cajas, las latas. Mundo deforme, digo. Qué asfixia. Tu olor y el mío aquí estancados, a la altura de los sepulcros. Sobre, bajo y a los costados de los muertos. Aburridos todos. Enterrado, yo también, en estas letras. Y dentro de mí, otra tumba como tú, la misma miasma que nos corroe: la memoria, la verdad. Y otras memorias póstumas.

Pero ya gimes de nuevo hambrienta. Y sé que es el hambre sólo otro dolor, y alimentarnos un paliativo. ¿Cuántos días resistirías si me negara a darte de beber y comer?, ¿si me hiciera de la vista gorda y me olvidara de ti y te dejara tirada al suelo bocarriba gimiendo, como si fueras sólo ya una voz necia que viene del más allá? No podrías atormentarme más, fantasma, de lo que ya lo has hecho. Y resistir unos días tu voz gangosa, espeluznante, sería poco. Sólo unos días, Mujer, vieja mula. Mi amor. Y te mueres. ¿No harías tú lo mismo por mí? Ayudarme a morir, que no matarme, para acabar con mi sufrimiento. El nuestro. Es decir, el hambre.

Acabar así con el hambre. Mejor no pensar. No sentir, me repito, porque nos matamos mutuamente. Y, sin embargo, me pongo de pie, arrastro una nueva caja hasta mi silla. Tomo una lata, ya otra vez sentado. ¿Serías capaz de arrancarme con tu boca los dedos sucios con los que te he alimentado? Son tus porquerías y las mías mezcladas, Mujer. Mula terca. Y yo también me los lamo y lo trago todo. Nos comemos una lata entre los dos, rápidamente. Bebemos agua. Veo mis dedos y siento más asco de tus babas que brillan en mi piel, que de toda la otra mugre que ya la ha ennegrecido. Cojo la segunda lata; es ésta toda nuestra ración del día. Me miras expectante y siento que lo más humano sería, de tu parte, morirte. Pero eres ya un animal a secas; ya no piensas, ya no sientes. El seso frito. Y no sabes ya siquiera qué es la muerte. Me llevas ventaja, pienso. Tú y todos los otros, allá arriba, que tampoco piensan, que tampoco sienten. Y me viene la idea, en este momento, tan extraña, de que yo soy lo más humano que resta en el mundo. Y me maldigo. Me sigues mirando. No parpadeas. Intercalas tu mirada entre la lata y yo. Igual que una perra. Una mula. Destapo la lata, pero ya no hay alimento en ella; sólo hay una enorme cucaracha que ya lo ha devorado todo. Al verla, lanzo la lata al aire. Cae al suelo de pie, corre perdida. ¿Cuánto tiempo sobrevivió ahí encerrada?, me digo mientras la veo, ahora, deteniéndose frente a mí. ¿Ya viste, Mujer? Algo que pudiera ser más despreciable que tú. Corre hacia donde me encuentro y, ridiculizándome aún más, me retraigo subiendo las piernas a la silla. No quiero que me toques, le grito. Mi movimiento la espanta. Está a la altura de tu cara y sé que me mira. ¿Tú la ves? En su enormidad, se alcanzan a distinguir los detalles de su cuerpo acorazado, sus antenas. Es una piedra negra, aplanada. Y me sorprendo de sentirme amenazado. Da un paso más hacia mí. ¡Que no me toques!, vuelvo a gritar. Nos tragará a los dos, Mujer. Entra a la lata tirada al suelo donde vivió quién sabe cuántos años encerrada, y luego a la otra, a aquella que tú y yo acabamos de vaciar. Se traga los restos. No nos dejará en paz, pienso, mientras la veo caminar de un lado al otro. Se acerca a tu cuerpo, ¿puedes verla?

Se sube en ti, a la altura de tu vientre, te cruza. Y se pierde en el fondo del sótano, entre las otras cajas. ¿Cuántas más podrían haberse inmiscuido en las demás latas?, me pregunto alzando la cara de mis notas, temeroso. Siento comezón en todo el cuerpo. ¿Te habrás estremecido de alguna manera cuando te pasó por encima?

Bárbara estupidez. Qué absurdo es todo esto.

19 *(Afuera):* decidido ya de hacer mías las latas, he dejado de marcarlas; sólo vengo aquí esperando ver a mi paticoja, y para alejarme, además, por unas horas de Mi Mujer y de la madre imbécil de Mi Mujer. Sin embargo, ella ya no ha vuelto a aparecerse y el tiempo se derrama tan lento aquí como en casa. Paso las horas más bien arrumbado en las bodegas, con la gravedad de mi cuerpo en el suelo, la huella de grasa en mi espalda, los brazos vencidos. Todavía como un Cristo derrotado que aguarda. Piadoso, sin embargo. Y no creo que la coja vaya a volver jamás, y mucho menos tengo fe en mis piernas, en mí, en la decisión que pueda tomar de ir por ella y buscarla, porque ya me he arrepentido, antes, de haberme interesado por alguna cosa, por alguna mujer. Resulta, asimismo, más congruente desviar mis esfuerzos, como lo hago, hacia la vida entera de los hombres que tomo en mis manos. Desinteresadamente, también, he tomado la decisión, pasados apenas unos momentos, de no hacer nada. No hacer nada por ustedes, que es a la vez salvarlos y hacerlo todo. Ayudarlos, quiero decir, quitándoles mis latas; mejor dicho, salvando a la humanidad a expensas de los hombres. Y de manera póstuma. ¿No es así como funciona?, ¿no es así como lo prometen los dioses y religiones: después de la vida, la salvación? Lo he considerado así los últimos días y en vistas de la ausencia de la coja. Se habrá adelantado a nosotros, pienso; salvada ella anticipadamente por su cuerpo pornográfico. Soborno de Dios

y de los hombres. Y aún muerta, quizá, su padre la habrá visto sobre su lecho, reprimiendo sus pensamientos impuros, porque valía la pena, la coja, el pecado. Inclinado sobre ella, pensando en su esposa e hija difuntas, llora todavía por querer tocarla. O sea, tal vez, que la haya tocado y punto. Después de haber sentido dolor, miedo por lo desconocido, se habrá acercado a ella, el rostro ya una piedra, y habrá rozado con sus dedos, primero, luego apretujando avorazadoramente con las manos sus dulzuras marchitas. Así debió ser. Y ahora cuelga de la rama de un árbol, ahorcado por la vergüenza. Siento dibujarse en mi rostro una sonrisa socarrona: ¿vergüenza?, me digo. Cualquiera lo hubiera hecho. Sólo me restan unos días, pienso mirando alrededor mío. Realmente es una cantidad inútil de cajas, insuficientes; como si esperaran que la ración alcanzara sólo para sobrevivir un par de semanas. Prolongando el sufrimiento. Y viéndolo bien, sólo estoy acelerando el proceso. Enfermos terminales, les ofrezco la buena muerte, digna, digo con mis ojos en el techo sucio, es decir, en el cielo. Vuelto ahora Juez. Y me pregunto cómo podré hacerlo. ¿Cómo sacar de aquí todas estas cajas?

El camino es largo, me digo mirando desde la puerta trasera, de carga y descarga, de las bodegas. Oscurecido ya el día. Hay que atravesar entera la avenida del pueblo que luego da a la carretera que, después de algunos kilómetros de puro campo seco, llega a la casa. Pasar por los rancheríos pobres, las granjas. Es imposible. Cierro tras de mí la puerta y comienzo la vuelta lentamente, como para contar los pasos. El crujir de la tierra en mis pies me planta en la realidad, en la debilidad de mis músculos, en mi desidia. Mi voluntad machacada; el espíritu de mi voluntad desvalida. La única voluntad posible, quiero decir, de no tener fuerza de voluntad alguna. Camino con las manos en los bolsillos frente a los puesteros del pueblo que ya se retiran. Si antes no tuve coraje ni carácter, *estando sano, suponiendo que así haya sido, cómo podría hoy, molido y deshecho, hacer cualquier cosa,* me pregunto. ¿Cómo trasladar 8,000 latas en cajas de las bodegas a la casa de mi vieja?

Cruzar el pueblo enterrado en mierdas; arrastrar los pies en la tierra suelta; pasar frente a la fuente seca de agua seca marrón; oír el sordo tañido de las campanas de la iglesia marrón; mirar a los costados de la calle las edificaciones inacabadas o destruidas, con las fachadas resquebrajadas y tragadas por más color marrón. Luego seguir por la carretera, bordeando los campos de puro abono. El llano, los páramos. El simple hecho de cruzar estos paisajes, un día solo, incluso, agota: desanima el espíritu. Y, además, y peor, ¿cómo hacerlo en callado, con sigilo? Es imposible, me repito, y ¿para qué tomarme tantas molestias? Comienzo a interrogarme, cuando alcanzo a distinguir a lo que me parece ser un mozo de mulas. De los que ya no existen, quiero decir, porque uno es ya sólo esclavo de uno mismo y de sus solas posesiones. Y son sólo sombras en la oscuridad, las mismas: el hombre de la otra noche jalando su burro y aquel otro que encontraba en los testículos inflamados de la bestia, si no lástima, un motivo de estimación. Como si no se pudiera ya encontrar aprecio más que por las cosas que se están muriendo. Y así habrán dicho sobre este mundo, los hombres, ya tan tarde: Lo están matando. Tan melodramáticamente para que, ahora que ya está muerto, el cadáver sólo nos aborrezca. Ojalá tuviera un burro o una, otra, mula, me digo rascándome el cráneo picado por los piojos, los brazos, detenido en la carretera por la aparición de las sombras como un simio idiota que tarda en reaccionar frente a lo que ocurre a sus ojos.

Marcho cerca de los hombres; escolta de las sombras que se acompañan. Los cuerpos torcidos por la fatiga. Van callados y se confunden los ruidos a la rastra de sus pies con las patas del burro; los tres, más bien, andando resignados de tener que andar. Y es en la noche silenciada, envolvente, lo único que se alcanza a oír, los pies y pesuñas machucados en la tierra, salvo cuando el agregado lanza intermitentemente preguntas apáticas que rellenan el momento: ¿Y cómo va su mujer?... La voz del burrero es débil y apenas la percibo como un barullo ronco, como los gorjeos de una rana, y por ello imagino sus respuestas.

Es decir, a través de su cuerpo, como si las palabras imitasen a su postura o fuesen, solamente, una extensión de los huesos. Mira a su interlocutor girando la cabeza; su gesto es bisilábico: triste, podría decir. Le leo el cuerpo; el verbo en la carne... ¿y los hijos?, pregunta el otro casi gritando. Rueda de nueva cuenta el cuello en su eje y se repite; en su asentir las sílabas, ...Tristes, dice, y se escucha la voz atorada en su gorja; la voz espesa, también, y las palabras tan apelmazadas como sus piernas. Vuelve a mirar al frente, al suelo que pisa, hundiendo tanto la cabeza que parece tener el cuello cercenado... ¿y los demás animales?... Sin mirarlo, finalmente, y con la cara todavía pegada al suelo, afirma nada más con la cabeza: Tristes... ¿Todos?... Y responde palpando en el lomo al burro que trae a cuestas. Dos manotazos que estresan a la bestia, *tan atenuada y flaca, con tanto espinazo, que muestra bien al descubierto* los tiempos que se viven en la granja del hombre. Difíciles. Enfermos. Aunque pudiera ser esto un diálogo distinto: los dos hombres se cruzan todos los días en el camino. Se saludan sin escándalos, bien si lo hacen como si fuese la primera vez que se encuentran después de mucho tiempo. Entonces se entrevistan, se ponen al tanto. Urgiendo uno las preguntas sin interesarse en las respuestas y, más bien, a la espera de ser él el interrogado: desahogarse; enterarse así, en alta voz, de su propia vida. Porque ya no la sabe. Porque ya no la siente. Y yo malinterpreto los gestos tristes con su concepto. No, él no responde así, pienso: ¿Y cómo va su mujer?... Hace, como cada día, la mueca de su respuesta y dice: Muerta. ¿Y cómo los hijos? Y se repite, limitado como es ya el lenguaje que imita al mundo bisilábico, también: Muertos. ¿Y los demás animales?, termina por preguntar mirando al burro superviviente, aunque ya sepa la respuesta. Luego hacen el trayecto ya en silencio; el interrogador mordiéndose las penas y pensando: Yo también tengo muertos que contar...

Pero, ya lo intentará de nuevo mañana.

Mundo deforme.

Pasamos de largo la casa de mi vieja, porque prefiero ver a dónde van a dar las sombras. Apenas a unos metros, sin embargo, se detienen. Las sombras no nos quedan lejos, me digo. Empuñan sus manos de gruesas venas. El hombre del burro hace la misma reverencia realizada durante todo el trayecto, y yo confundo en el vocabulario de su cuerpo los adioses con las tristezas con las muertes. Camina hacia el establo, un remedo algo menos higiénico que su choza, hacia donde luego se dirige. El otro lo mira alejarse y después sigue andando hasta confundirse, tragado, por la noche. A ella le contará toda la vida inútil que tiene guardada antes de llegarle el día apartado para morirse.

¿No hacemos todos lo mismo?

Triste noche.

20 *(Refugio):* "no es lugar para una criatura. Así decía. No. Sí, así decía luego de mirar a la niña sentada en la tierra. Así todos los días. Mi esposa en lágrimas. La pobre niña. *Víctima de la espera.* ¿Qué podía esperar? ¡Sácanos de aquí!, me gritaba. ¡Pronto! Nos estábamos volviendo locos".

Después algunos rayones aleatorios en la libreta. Distraídos. Para matar el tiempo. Aunque pudiera ser que, en su cabeza quebrantada, aquellas líneas deformes significaran alguna cosa. Más abajo, encimadas en los garabatos desordenados, las cifras de contabilidad del Ayuntamiento. Es el archivo del Intendente, el cuaderno de contaduría: balances, rayones simplones, caminos de tinta, recuerdos. Las memorias huecas de un desquiciado.

"Está enferma, digo yo. Su carita plana, sus brazos y piernas débiles, sin raspones. Sus huesos descalcificados, y quizás igual su alma. No es normal. Llévala al médico.

¡Enfermo estás tú y este miserable lugar!"

Paso las páginas. Son párrafos sueltos, incongruentes. Sería mejor decir, despedazados. Como su juicio.

"Quise ser padre. Ganaría más dinero, tendría una casa del doble de tamaño. Dejábamos atrás los muelles, las barcas, los escaparates, las trigueñas bañistas, el mar; pero, era un ascenso. Sería, para este pequeño pueblo, el hombre más grande. Sólo me hacía falta un hijo".

Y, sin embargo, pareciese ser que la escritura surgía en sus momentos de lucidez, tan escasos. Luego, tal vez perdiendo el hilo, saliéndose de nuevo de sus cabales, se deformaban las letras, las frases, en rayas negras. La baba vuelta otra vez al filo de la boca.

"Recibiste la noticia con emoción. Al fin la aventura, dijiste. Y apenas te mencioné la idea de traer un niño, te desnudaste. A mitad de la sala, tu vestido resbalando por tu cuerpo. Te mordí, me pellizcaste. ¡Hicimos el amor con los corazones reventados!

Después, aquí: Nos estás ahogando, decías delante de la ventana, tus manos sujetando algún traste sucio, mirándola. Pasiva. Sentada afuera, sus piernitas cruzadas, su cara rígida frente al hosco paisaje como frente a un muro; en *un sombrío letargo de idiotismo* encerrada. *Profundamente idiota.* Lo que habría dado por una risita, una carrera alrededor de la casa. Nos estás matando, decías después, vuelta de espaldas en la cama. Apagabas la luz. Nuestros cuerpos tan alejados. Y a mí sólo te unía ya tu desprecio; cada vez más grande".

Alzo la cara del cuaderno del Intendente. Me sosiega, quizá, leerme en sus palabras, porque me sirven de punto de partida para pensar, expresar alguna cosa que no sabía decir y que luego anoto. Con la cara fuera de las notas veo a Mi Mujer, la vieja tetrapléjica tumbada a la altura del suelo, quien me mira mientras leo. El gesto seco, así como el resto de su cuerpo. Cada vez más cadáver.

"La niña enferma era una pena, pero me resultaba imposible dejar el puesto. Te lo expliqué muchas veces. Y lo intenté todo, lo prometo, con abnegación. Lo intentamos todo, abnegados los dos. Resignados, los dos, a sufrir".

¿Qué trecho hay entre los abnegados y los resignados?, me pregunto mirando, otra vez, a Mi Mujer quien también, todavía, me mira. Sin mirar. Como la niña idiota, inmóvil. Como su madre mirándola. Mirando el muro. En nuestras narices, oprimiéndolas. En nuestros ojos astillados. El muro. Adentro.

21 *(Refugio):* no bien cierro apenas la libreta del Intendente para continuar escribiendo lo que por él me nace decir, la veo correr por encima de mis notas, casi rozándome. Ensuciándolo todo. Embarrando su cuerpo en la tinta fresca que se corre y urgida por participar de la historia. La cucaracha. El insecto que todo lo toca y ensucia y nos invade. Al verla, me echo para atrás de un salto tumbando la silla y, quizá por el temblor de la mesa que empujo, detiene su carrera a la orilla del mueble. Estupefacta, como juzgándome, me mira. Sus antenas largas revolviéndose en el aire. Y siento la misma repulsión que surge en mí por *la carne de Mi Mujer que se deshace,* pero acompañada de una suerte de angustia porque ella puede andar por donde le plazca, lamer con sus patas nuestros cuerpos, dejar sus secreciones virulentas en mis libretas, en mis latas, o acercarse a nosotros mientras dormimos. Acecharnos, cacharnos desprevenidos para embarazar de sus crías nuestras orejas. Pero, no. *Se estará muy bien junto a tu sangre,* le digo rechinando los dientes, rabioso, mientras retrocedo vigilándola. No te muevas, le ordeno, no te muevas, andando hacia las latas que se encuentran del lado opuesto del cuarto. Temo que de dejar de mirarla desaparezca. Y voy un paso a la vez, como si por el menor desperfecto en la estabilidad de mi cuerpo, ella pudiera leer mis pensamientos y huir. Es una amenaza, una amenaza con el cerebro entre las vísceras enterrado.

Mis pies rozan y esquivan lo que hay en el suelo: la caja del Intendente, rebosante de papeles y de escrituras: su vida; las cobijas que me abrigan al dormir; latas vacías que podría utilizar para terminar con esto de una buena vez. Pero no, prefiero hacerlo de la mejor manera posible para no repetir el acto: tomar una lata llena, más pesada, y asegurarme, así, de dejar triturado su cuerpo entero y a las alimañas nonatas que lo habitan. ¡Que reviente de veras! Aunque de tan sólo pensar que luego tendré que limpiar los restos dejados en la mesa, la mancha, como la mía en las bodegas, la marca de un cadáver y escribir todos los días junto a lo que fue su cuerpo... Sin embargo, no. Sería peor aún escribir con ella rondándome. Te mueres. Ya está decidido, le digo, cuando me siento trastabillar por algo bajo mi pie. Para no hacer movimientos bruscos que la espanten, piso firme con mi pierna izquierda la cosa en mi camino. No importa que la destruya. Nada aquí es importante. Siento, con mis ojos puestos en el insecto, aplastándose lo que está bajo mis pies: una premonición de su suerte. Y al ver la altura a la que estoy del camino, caigo en cuenta de que se trata del tobillo flaco, deshuesado, de mi esposa. Termino por hundir mi pie en él y me sorprende su blandura. En reflejo, giro para mirarle el rostro duro, buscando alguna reacción. Nada. La cara mirando al techo, los ojos allí pasmados. Mujer, ¿no eres tú ya un insecto aplastado en la tierra? Tus huesos ya molidos, la carne podrida. ¿Entre qué alimañas habito?, me pregunto llegando al otro extremo. Cojo lentamente una lata de las cajas abiertas, cuando ya corre de nuevo. Me lanzo hacia el escritorio empuñando la lata en lo alto, pero ya no está. Es una emboscada, pienso. Nos pone trampas. La busco en el suelo, bajo la mesa: está en la pared colgada. Me acerco a gatas; es un movimiento riesgoso pero necesario. Estoy cerca y percibo su inquietud. Nos cazamos. Será como clavar la lata en la pared, pienso alzando el brazo y midiendo el golpe, cuando huye de nuevo. Sale de debajo de la mesa, me pasa por un lado, ¡casi me toca! De prisa pego un brinco hasta donde se encuentra, camino con pasos largos tras ella para pisotearla. La persecución de los gigantes. El destierro. Rodeamos a Mi Mujer, que me sigue con los ojos. Se inmiscuye entre las cajas del racionamiento. Las empujo. No está. Las muevo todas hacia donde está mi esposa. Nada. Miro arriba, la pared, el techo. Otra vez. Nada. ¡¿Dónde te metiste?!, le grito con la lata bien aferrada en mi mano. Pateo las cajas, la busco por todos lados. Suelto, entonces, la lata al suelo, abro las cajas, saco las demás. Nada. Me arrastro de rodillas con la frente a la altura del suelo, como penitente, como rezando, buscándola. Es imposible. ¡¿Dónde?!, pregunto mirando a Mi Mujer a los ojos, quien se carga la misma estúpida cara de mula intacta. Burlándose de mí, como el insecto. Recorro a gatas el sótano entero hasta volver al punto donde la perdí de vista. ¡Un agujero! Hay un minúsculo agujero en el muro. Me pongo en pie, jalo mi silla. Me siento a esperarla. Ya vendrá.

Pasados unos minutos, sin embargo, me canso de mirar con tal concentración un hoyo en la pared. Sólo un hoyo. Además, mi esposa empieza, ahora, a gemir: sedienta, seguro. Tomo la caja del Intendente, pesada, la recargo contra el muro bloqueando el agujero. Todos moriremos ahogados aquí. Incluso tú, le digo.
Y es esto todo lo que ocurre. Nada puede hacerse. Uno sigue siendo lo que es, pienso sentado a la cabeza de Mi Mujer. Siempre ha sido así. Cuando no eres tú, vieja mula, es otro bicho repugnante. Mundo deforme. Vida inútil. Y seguimos tragándonos las latas, bebiendo agua.

22 *(Afuera):* ...desde entonces había comenzado ya, Mi Mujer, a desbaratarse. Antes de los huesos, su humanidad: destazada, disminuida...

Ya no tengo las nalgas planas de la Rabona en mis manos. Estoy sentado a la mesa de la cocina. Se ha hecho costumbre, pasados los últimos días, el quedarme a beber una taza de café después de haber sobado y herido cada una de sus partes, sus genitales. Cada vez, por imposible que parezca, todo más monótono: la Rabona contra el muro o la Rabona en cuatro. Nunca mirándonos las caras. La mujer, arriba, consumiéndose, y el hombre, su marido, yendo cada mañana para volver cada noche a ensartarla, cargado su miembro de orines, alcoholes y de la porquería de sus testículos. Va y vuelve, se tumba en la cama, aplasta con su cuerpo a la mujer enflaquecida, tan en huesos que se asfixia el alma. Se trata de un itinerario de disciplina y rigor: día tras día. Noche tras noche. Como animales los cuatro, y, sin embargo, demasiado humanos y cogiéndonos por las espaldas, porque no es el hombre ya una conciencia compleja, sino apenas la repetición de actos distintos, repetición que es, a su vez, la negación de todos los actos y de la posibilidad real de actuar. Y no soy yo ninguna excepción. Ella ya come, bien como si estuviera en una prisión encerrada y sólo a mordiscos diminutos dejando la mayoría en el plato, pero come. Le llevan alimento en una bandeja, ella lo traga dejando los restos al otro lado de la puerta. No se viste. No se baña. Come y duerme. Los pelos crecidos del sobaco, de las piernas, como en defensa al marido sádico quien, sin embargo, no siente ni pizca de asco por el olor agrio de la carne velluda de su esposa. Mi Mujer. La piel pálida, la cara amoratada como en una mueca de silencio y ahogo. Desastrada o, mejor, en la plenitud del desastre.

Han sido unas semanas, como siempre, de tedio y de decepción. Sin reacción de ningún tipo, es decir, sin herviduras de sangre, emociones, y sólo con la seguridad de que *lo monstruoso es lo ordinario*. Pero al menos, me digo, ya come, mientras sorbo el café aguado preparado por la Rabona, y sin plan alguno. Tal vez llegue el día en que ella descienda las escaleras y le encuentre, y ella en mí, restos rescatables de vida. O tal vez pudiera ser yo, también, quien la violente. ¿Qué reacción podría tener? ¿Qué podría importarle? Sería como con su marido, pienso: tomarla por detrás, ensalivar con un lengüetazo mi mano para humedecer un poco su sexo antes de forzarla. Hacerlo así una, dos, tal vez diariamente antes del regreso de su esposo. Porque tengo necesidad. Amor, quizá. Y cargo su desnudez todavía en mi cabeza y en todo momento: sus muslos reventados, su sexo en ruinas. Tengo anudada, así, en mi cuerpo la fantasía desenredándose, cuando entra la vieja sirvienta, la de cara larga, colgante, lenguada. Se detiene frente a mí unos segundos. Todos los hombres tan iguales. Toma, luego, un cuchillo, unos huevos, jamón. Prepara el almuerzo a la criatura del piso de arriba. Yo la veo hacer, escrutando la impavidez de su rostro en contraste con los temblores de su cuerpo anciano: bajo el vestido negro, largo, unos senos sin sostén, aguados, que se revuelven al ritmo del cuchillo rebanando sobre la tabla. De tanto en tanto se gira a mirarme. Pasa la Rabona cerca de mí, con un balde de estiércol, sin decir nada, con prisas, sin darme un vistazo. Después, al fin, la otra sirvienta, vieja también, y vestida, también, de largo, en gris; mirándome fríamente. Cruza la cocina con una escoba en las manos, mirándome. Mirándonos. Y ya cuando nos han dejado solos otra vez, el almuerzo queda listo. Busca la bandeja. Llena un vaso de agua y, justo antes de que se decida a irse, la detengo. Le falta mucho por hacer, le digo. Permítame. Nuestras manos se rozan aferradas, las cuatro, a la bandeja. Nos miramos a los ojos, yo intentando ablandar mi mirada y ella endurecida, tosca, incriminándome de un delito que todavía no cometo. Y la suelta, casi como si dejara parte de su piel desprendida en el plástico. Sale, entonces, por la puerta de la cocina que da al patio dejándome solo. A mí, la bandeja y, más certeramente, a mí con la mujer de arriba para hacer a mis anchas lo que me plazca. Fue una suerte de bendición. Y a nadie importa.

Al pie de la escalera medito cómo debo actuar: pienso, primero, que la encontraré como el otro día: bajo la dureza del sol, dormida o desmayada. Despierta, quizá, pero soñando. Negro. Tan violento el cuadro como la vez última, o, mejor, desbordando su cuerpo de violencias, si bien yace pasiva. En el límite entre lo vivo y lo muerto, porque, habrá que decir, la muerte es la tranquilidad cargada de violencias. Un punto límbico. La hallaré, entonces, cadáver violento, desnuda. Desvirgada, deshumanizada, y después de acariciar su cuerpo, me montaré en la cama y, ella, indiferente, me recibirá. Ya sin convulsionarse. ¿Debería o no hacerlo? Ya apetente de ella, además de por amor, por mis imaginaciones, dudo, sin embargo. ¿No tendría que haber dudado antes? ¿O es que la duda nace del encuentro entre lo animal y lo humano? Y a medida que lo pienso, llego al último escalón, al umbral de la puerta; la decisión es irrevocable: voy a entrar. La puerta se desliza lentamente y el aire acalorado, viciado, de dentro, escapa hacia mis narices. Me inunda. El paisaje del cuarto se va abriendo ante mí: la pared, el estante, el camino a la cama, pelo colgando, grasoso, de un cráneo. La puerta, allí, se atranca, negándome lo que queda al otro lado, es decir, como protegiéndolo. Y me basta, por unos segundos, mirar solamente la redondez trasera del cráneo y el pelo que cuelga fuera de la cama. Empujo, entonces, suavemente, con la punta del pie la puerta para no dejar en el suelo la bandeja, cuando, como en desafío a la sutileza de mi acto, irrumpen en la entrada principal de la casa abriendo de par en par. En el momento me vuelvo exaltado por el ruido y porque la escalera que lleva a las habitaciones da de frente al acceso. Es el marido de Mi Mujer, quien me observa estupefacto al pie de la escalera. Sube, pesado, hundiendo en cada escalón la enormidad gorda de sus pies. Escupe rabietas ininteligibles. Se planta frente a mí que lo miro hacia arriba, sorteando las fosas velludas de sus narices para llegar hasta sus ojos. La bandeja aún en mis manos. Y me pregunta quién soy. Más allá de no saber con exactitud la respuesta, lo que ocurre es que mi cabeza está estancada en la sorpresa: ¿en plena mañana?, ¿a unos minutos siquiera de haberse ido? Vuelve a preguntarme: la cara reseca, mentón duro, barba incipiente, el ceño enfurecido. Gira hacia el cuarto donde se encuentra la mujer, el cráneo, el pelo colgante, y me arrebata la bandeja de las manos, la pone en el suelo, la desliza con el pie al interior, el agua se derrama, azota la puerta cerrándola y justo en ese momento le digo: Traigo la comida para la señora. Él gruñe. Trabajo aquí, agrego. Entra a una de las habitaciones contiguas, toma un paquete de cigarrillos y, sin decirme nada, pero embarrándome los ojos de arriba hacia abajo, se marcha. Con la cara de frente al cuarto clausurado de la mujer, escucho cómo cierra la puerta remarcando su gesto y mis límites: aquí puedes trabajar, pero no dar un paso más hacia donde ella se encuentra. Desvigorizado, me digo que ya estará despierta o comiendo, y desisto. No alcancé sino sólo a mirar una figura emborronada de carne descompuesta. La piel del color de una manzana pelada expuesta al aire. Pedazos de mierdas, se escucha desde fuera al hombre gritar mientras se aleja.

23 *(Afuera):* a la mañana siguiente, sin saber lo que hacía, fui a donde el burrero. La sombra. Desde allí alcanzaba a ver la casa de Mi Mujer cuya precariedad, a la luz del día tan notable, no parecía ser en absoluto distinta de aquella sobre la que se erguía la choza. Se desgajaba, como hoy, en pedazos y se mantenía apenas en pie, igual que el rancherío del burrero. Un monumento a la fragilidad es la casa de mi vieja…, y si aún soplara alguna corriente, pensé… Pero, estoy allí, entonces. Mis manos en la valla ridícula que protege la pobreza del hombre: su carne equina enferma. No se escucha nada ni se percibe movimiento alguno. Quizá no haya nadie en casa, me digo, y no encontraré ya luego mejor momento para entrar. Pedir prestado. Por lo que me resuelvo. Doy un paso apenas cruzando la cerca que se despedaza sola, cuando escucho un tiro. Me tumbo al suelo; no veo a nadie. No pudo ser a mí a quien se dirigía aquel disparo. Las manos cubriéndome la mollera. La precariedad, decía; los huesos que nos protegen. Me pongo en pie y truena un segundo disparo que me regresa al suelo. Andar a rastras, me digo; ya tan acostumbrado. Entonces, marchando así, con el pecho en tierra, con el sol solo de testigo y el aire quieto que nos envuelve, escucho un tercer disparo. Ya está, pienso, no es a mí a quien matan. Y, sin embargo, me sigo derecho llenándome la barbilla de tierra, preventivo. A mitad del terreno yermo, siento a un piojo que me pica como si fuera un pensamiento, algo de mí, un escalofrío. Es decir, lo único en mí vivo, naciendo desde dentro, revelándose.

Lo único que acontece, porque hasta mis campos de batallas y de tiros son aburridos, sin violencias ni emoción. Solitarios. Con la vida y las historias en otra parte. Casi llego ya a la choza y ya nada se escucha. El silencio es ahora más profundo y peligroso: angustia. Lo pienso dos veces antes de alzarme, pero, luego, me convenzo: si me matan, que me maten. Me acerco a la puerta y, al tiempo de querer abrirla, estalla un nuevo disparo. Me cubro contra el muro de lámina. Mi respiración agitada. Son fantasmas cazándome, me digo; una buena anécdota, al fin, que contar a los nietos nonatos. Y envalentonado, empujando mis espaldas contra la choza, camino hasta la orilla que da al establo para asomarme. Hay cuatro animales derrumbados en el suelo. Dos mulas. Dos burros. Estos dos últimos con los genitales tan hinchados como el de las otras noches; supuran un líquido blanquecino. El cuero repleto de chancros. Un agujero por encima del hocico rebosante de sangre quemada. Es de buena dote el hombre, pienso. Aunque sarnosa. Quedan un par en pie. Y no todos deben ser suyos, me digo acercándome a los cadáveres. Las dos bestias que restan, amarradas por el pescuezo, arman un escándalo, nerviosas, cuando veo aproximarse, desde el porche, al burrero cargando de más municiones su escopeta. Apunta al medio de los ojos, acomoda el hombro y se detiene. Me mira. No hay ninguna expresión en su rostro. Alza de nueva cuenta el rifle apuntándome ahora a mí. Si me matan, que me maten, pienso dando pasos en retaguardia y con las manos en alto. Está sin decir nada. Da un giro rápido y, más bien sin ver, revienta el ojo izquierdo del burro volándole los sesos. Están enfermos, me dice apenas pasado el ruido del cañón y del burro desplomándose. Ésta de aquí es la más sana, y ni siquiera vale ella la pena. Pronto le ocurrirá lo que a los otros, me cuenta: inflamaciones, hoyos en la piel. De súbito pienso en el niño leproso de la rata y las pústulas, hasta que menciona el siguiente síntoma: la parálisis. Los dos primeros que maté, continúa diciendo, ya no podían moverse. Apenas respiraban. Se toma un silencio largo para dar un trago a su aguardiente. La mula restante, ya apaciguada, vuelve su hocico al pasto esquivando la sangre derramada que le cruza por las patas. Antes de los míos, dice, fueron los burros de un amigo. Dos. Ya los habíamos vistos flacos, como los mira. Y un día él los encontró, uno juntito al otro, pegados al suelo. Un grupo de comadrejas se los estaban comiendo. Y lloraban, le digo, los burros. Estaban vivos. Mi amigo corrió para ahuyentar a las comadrejas, ¡malditas ratas!, pero al llegar ya no le vio caso. Gritaban, dijo, y me miraban suplicando. Esos fueron los que contagiaron a los míos. Los estuve llevando al pueblo para curarlos, pero nada se pudo. Ya nada se puede. Lanza un suspiro largo. Tanto trabajo desperdiciado, dice, y tanto se desperdicia uno en el trabajo. Hace un rato apenas mi amigo me trajo el resto de sus burros. Verá, es un hombre sensible, y me pidió hacerlo por él. ¿No le parece absurdo?, me pregunta, ¿que se nos muera un burro y que eso signifique quedarnos sin nada?… Pero, en fin, dice empuñando la escopeta. La mula lo mira mascando, como si ya se hubiera olvidado de lo que la escopeta y el individuo han hecho con los demás. Quizá ya resignada. Resignados todos. Y ay, de los hombres, pienso. La última, dice escupiendo al suelo, y está a punto de jalar cuando lo detengo. ¿Cuántos días le quedan?, le pregunto. Dos, quizá tres. Suficientes, digo. Démela. Me mira sorprendido. ¿Para qué la quiere? Tengo un par de trabajos pendientes y necesito algo de ayuda con las cargas. ¿Podría prestármela? Se vuelve hacia la mula que inclina la cabeza en reverencia, pellizca pasto seco y sigue tascando. No hay ni un viento ligero que le agite, aunque sea un poco, las orejas. No, responde. No me la devuelva. Y me suelta la escopeta en las manos. Y ésta de aquí tampoco, dice mientras me la entrega. Llévesela y, una vez que ya no le sea útil, mátela. Le hará un bien a la desgraciada.

Al cruzar la valla, otra vez en la carretera, y con la mula a cuestas, me pregunto qué será ahora del viejo. Qué será de él y de su amigo, el otro burrero. Las dos sombras, los dos fantasmas. Doy un jalón a la mula, negada a caminar lejos de su dueño. Miro la escopeta. ¿Cuándo comenzará la parálisis? Pienso en Mi Mujer. Rectifico: ¿cuándo se detendrá?

24 *(Afuera):* tomándome la palabra, me hice de una escoba, escombré, sacudí de los muebles el polvo: restos de hombres y heces de insectos. Y comencé, también, a hacerme cargo de las bestias de la casa: los perros, las vacas, las porquerizas; cualquier cosa que me mantuviese lejos de la Rabona era bienvenida. Y aunque en un principio me miraban las tres mujeres con extrañeza, pronto se acostumbraron a mi conducta. Nunca me preguntaron nada, y, de hacerlo, sólo tendría que responderles que el señor me había contratado, puesto que mi presencia significaba, para ellas, menos trabajo y no más. Por otra parte, de tanto en tanto, a pesar de mis intentos por huir y en pro de mi deseo de estar cerca de la mujer, tenía que cogerme a la Rabona: en la pocilga, en el establo, en el patio, en su alcoba; ya que suponíamos mantener una especie de relación que me significaba, además, tener dónde dormir. Trabajar entonces, y ensartar, de vez en cuando, a la Rabona eran la cuota de mi capricho. Y fue así que, pasada la tercera semana, ya prácticamente estaba instalado en su cuarto, ubicado en un recinto de concreto en la parte trasera de la casa. Las otras dos sirvientas, hermanas, compartían el otro cuarto de lo que llamábamos la casa de servicio, y al verlas en su camisón de noche pasaban, no sólo por gemelas, sino por idénticos fantasmas. Pensándolo bien, vivíamos mejor nosotros, sirvientes, que los vecinos de obra negra, dueños de sus tierras. Y, de igual forma, al poco tiempo, el marido de Mi Mujer se acostumbró a verme

desde temprano: su mirada siempre penetrándome antes de irse en las mañanas. Pero más allá de las otras actividades, la tarea más importante para mí, y a la que me encomendé sin aceptar objeción desde un inicio, fue la de hacerme cargo de subir la comida. Todavía hoy lo realizo sin haber intentado nunca, sin embargo, volver a entrar a la habitación: empujo la puerta sólo lo necesario para deslizar hacia adentro la bandeja. Y si bien, por momentos, mi deseo me traiciona... el olor..., sumiéndome entre el apetito y el asco, no hago nada. Es un embate diario entre el control y el instinto; la disciplina. Ya vendrá después la recompensa, me digo. Y ha sido así, también, como me he convertido en testigo permanente de las violaciones: él llega, ya muy entrada la noche, ya cuando las sirvientas y la Rabona están dormidas; casi siempre alrededor de las mismas horas. Yo me desenredo de la Rabona, quien, con el cuerpo extendido a lo largo de la yacija, invadiéndome, incluso, ronca. Me destrabo de debajo de una de sus piernas o brazos y salgo a la noche fría, profunda, callada. Empujo la puerta blanca de la cocina que chilla y cuyo ruido es tragado por el vacío de la casa en comunión con la oscuridad de la noche. Camino, sin temor, hasta las escaleras y, en el primer escalón, me siento a esperar. Espero, a veces, largo rato hasta que lo escucho; las coces del caballo, sus pies en la tierra. Entonces, sin mucha precipitación, me escondo en el hueco bajo las escaleras, desde donde lo miro subir y bambolearse. Cierra detrás de sí la puerta del cuarto y luego escucho sólo sus jadeos y la madera de la cama crujir, de nuevo desde mi asiento. Ella, sin embargo, no hace ningún ruido, sino sólo hasta el final del acto cuando derrama un gemido corto, ahogado, similar a aquel que escupe alguien cuando saca la parte última, la punta, de un vidrio enterrado en la palma del pie.

¿Qué tan complicado podría ser? Subir y rajarle como a los cerdos destripándolo o seguirlo, quizá, hasta la cantina del rancherío aquel donde se pasa las noches, alegar a una disputa de copas..., o, tal vez, mejor, tomarla a ella y fugarnos... Callo ahora mis pensamientos: el gemido.

Pasan así las noches, las semanas.

...ya sube, ya aprisiona a la mujer, ya restriega su lengua sobre su cuerpo, su cara, ya la invade, ya estrella su miembro en su humanidad profunda, apestados los dos, sudorosos, ya estruja los senos desvalidos y ruinosos, ya la rasguña... Silencio: otra vez y siempre, el gemido.

Todo sea por esa voz.

...jadea, jadea, jadea, su nariz gruñe como el hocico de los puercos, se astilla la madera, cruje, se azota, jadea, la cama, jadea, se quiebra, jadea, como el cuerpo flaco, jadea, pobre de la mujer, jadea...: el gemido.

Noche tras noche y pasando algunos meses, guardo envidia y me torturan las expresiones violentas del amor.

Voy directo a la cama, miro a la Rabona babosa durmiendo con la boca abierta; su cuerpo, destapado por el calor, suda; tiene el camisón alzado a la altura de la cintura y le miro el pelambre oscuro, abultado, transpirado, para imaginarme, ahora, a la mujer de arriba. La sensación de un cuerpo extraño penetrándola, la despierta. Se deja hacer, la Rabona, y está a punto de soltar el primer gemido pero lo evito. Le tapo la boca hasta que todo termina. En mi cabeza, atorada en mi memoria, la voz truncada de la mujer. Suelto yo un graznido ronco recordándola. Como si lo hiciéramos juntos y al mismo tiempo. Cansados y desenterrándonos lo que nos agobia.

Luego, un día, rompiendo la costumbre que ya nos cargábamos, el hombre desapareció. Lo esperé las primeras noches casi hasta despuntar el sol y podría decirse que lo extrañé. No. Extrañé, más bien, el resultado de nuestra rutina. Tan calculado tenía ya el tiempo que duraba..., el tiempo que tenía que esperar antes de escuchar ese pedazo de voz desahogándose. Pensé, muchas veces, en subir y hacer yo mismo que todo ocurriera. Tomarla al fin en mis brazos. Pero no me atreví. Llegaba sólo hasta el umbral de la puerta, donde pegaba la cara para alcanzar a escuchar lo que fuera: un respiro, una voz resignada a pronunciarse accidentalmente en una exhalación. Y nada. Pasaron los días, algunas semanas, y de no haber sido por la bandeja que siempre era devuelta con la comida sólo mordisqueada un poco y cuando nadie miraba, habría pensado, seguramente, por el silencio insondable, que ella ya estaba muerta. Sin duda, podría decirse que el abandono definitivo del hombre fue una sorpresa, pero no tanto como lo que miro ahora.

En la pocilga, sirvo el revoltijo a los puercos. Gruñen. Sin quererlo se mordisquean las trompas unos a otros, eufóricos. Y al verlos pienso en aquel tiempo en el que vivía con mi madre; en sus marranos, las gallinas, mi gato. Ella encerrada arriba agonizante y enferma. E, inevitablemente, se me llena el pecho de una sensación cálida, agradable, porque me siento como en casa; casi sonrío: tengo, otra vez, diez años. Escucho cómo tragan los cerdos, miro sus colas retorcidas, el jamón gordo de sus nalgas agitándose, mientras se dibuja ante mí mi infancia y la posibilidad de la renovación, de nacer de nuevo y mejor. La fantasía. Y me digo, entonces, que sólo me hace falta salir de la porqueriza donde está estancada mi vida; tener coraje, dejar atrás a los puercos, felices, enlodazarse en su fárrago, con sus cuerpos embarrados de su comida y sus desechos, entrar a la casa, subir las escaleras a paso firme, abrir de un golpe la puerta, tomar a la mujer en mis brazos y huir. Huir de lo que somos hasta vivir una vida propia. Alzarla, con sus brazos en mi cuello enredados, y no dejarla pudrir en la cama como mi madre. No se me presentará nunca otra oportunidad como ésta, pienso. Mis ojos todavía fijos en los puercos, en la carne que será rebanada, se pierden en ensoñaciones románticas; uno de ellos, entonces, resbala, haciendo más alegre el momento; su mondongo azota contra el suelo, mientras otro, el de junto, lo mira como ahogándose una carcajada para seguir tragando. A mí sí, sin embargo, se me escapa una risita inocente, la primera en mucho tiempo, cuando, por encima de las bestias, del ruido, y desvaneciéndose todo lo que venía figurando en mi cabeza, veo a la mujer, a la mujer de mis obsesiones, parada frente a la puerta, mirando al vacío, desnuda. Sin dar crédito a mis ojos, camino acercándome lentamente para observarla mejor y sin ahuyentarla: ¿un espejismo? No. Y es la primera vez que la veo desde hace meses... ¿y aquí afuera?... Y... Sí. Los brazos en huesos, la carne de la cara vuelta pellejo, los pómulos hundidos. Luego, las piernas en astillas, los codos y las rodillas envueltos en piel mórbida, delgada y a punto de rasgarse. Tan esquelética y chupada. Los senos fláccidos, desaparecidos y..., todavía así..., bajo esa carne deshinchada y colgante de los senos, y sobre esos muslos extenuados, un bulto. Un bulto enorme. El ombligo botado afuera. Y me sorprendo de no verla irse de bruces; la cara contra el suelo, la barriga, como la del cerdo, azotando. Mi boca abierta, mis pasos lentos. Un niño. No puede ser. Un niño. ¿Cómo engendra ese cuerpo destruido a otro? Más, tal vez, como un tumor sarnoso, como un enjambre de parásitos. Pero, ¿un niño?, ¿una criatura? Estoy cada vez más cerca, lo suficiente para ver bien, ahora, su vello y uñas largas; su suciedad, cuando de pronto, gira el cuello pausadamente, como si se atrancara el movimiento en los huesos tronantes, y me mira. Fijamente. Tal vez, reconociéndome. Pienso, entonces, que, si creíamos que *la diferencia entre los vivos y los muertos estaba en la mirada, aquí ya no hay distinción alguna.* Estamos tan cerca que la ligera brisa que corre me hace llegar sus humores. La pestilencia. Allí, todavía, sangre seca confundida con otras mugres, quizá con restos de carne, como en sus uñas. Estiro, hacia donde se encuentra, uno de mis brazos. Ella, todavía imperturbable, me observa. Tocarla, al fin tocarla, pienso. Pero, no. Ya llega una de las ancianas sirvientas, la envuelve en una manta, la lleva hacia adentro.

Nadie podría haberlo sabido. ¿Y qué podríamos haber hecho? Hacer es imposible. Está sentada en una de las sillas de la cocina. No dice nada, no hace nada. Las sirvientas corren, traen ropa, agua, comida. No saben cómo repararla. En el alboroto, a alguien se le ocurre traer una esponja. Se miran las tres a las caras. La llevan al baño, donde cierran, frente a mí, la puerta. Vuelvo a mi asiento en la escalera, escucho el agua correr. Entiendo, ahora, cuál fue el motivo de la desaparición del hombre. ¿Cuántos meses tendrá?, me pregunto y, sin quererlo, también: ¿Quién morirá primero, ella o el niño? Me levanto, empujo la puerta del cuarto. Están en el baño encerradas. El aire es grave. El olor. Me aplasta. ¿Por qué nunca abrió una ventana? Retiro de la cama las sábanas manchadas, dejo entrar al viento. El camisón, todavía, al costado de la cama, tieso. Subo la escoba, escombro. Habría que quemarlo todo, me digo, y me venzo, al fin después de un rato, sentándome en la orilla de la cama. Decido esperar, cuando me viene a la cabeza que es ya casi hora del almuerzo. Bajo a la cocina, lo preparo y subo, como siempre, con la bandeja en mis manos, cuando ya está recostada, otra vez, en la cama, sólo envuelta en una bata de baño. Y, ya quitada de toda la mugre, en su mayoría al menos, se percibe todavía más la demacración de su cuerpo y el exagerado bulto en su vientre. Una deformidad, eso es. La mujer está deforme. Deformados sus huesos, su espíritu. Y esa bola que se carga es como si ella, toda desde dentro, buscara la manera de salir; de romperse en mil pedazos y fugarse. La piel enferma allí tan tensa, se ha rasgado, ulcerado. Y, además, parece haber quedado imbécil. No habla, no se mueve, casi. El rostro endurecido. Y, mientras una de las ancianas la alimenta, me observa. No deja de mirarme. ¿Sabe quién soy?

Al día siguiente, pasada la euforia del acontecimiento, las caras de pez y la Rabona siguen con normalidad sus vidas. Mandaron a buscar a su madre, y allí está ahora, arriba, cuidándola. Ellas se desentienden rápidamente; es tarea de alguien más hacer de enfermera de la mujer, porque ellas no fueron contratadas para eso. Yo ayudo a preparar el almuerzo, cuando la Rabona, pasándome por detrás con el canasto apestado de ropa y telas sucias, me llama. Ahora no, me digo, pero salgo. ¿Qué quieres?, le pregunto, siguiéndola hasta el cuarto. Ya allí, se desnuda. Luego se viste con el camisón sucio de la mujer. Mirándome, sube a la cama, se da la vuelta, agacha la cabeza parando las nalgas, como los cerdos, ayer, que tragaban en la pocilga. Me suelto los pantalones, la tomo por el pelo. El olor, tan duro, del camisón… Jadeo. Ella aprieta la boca, no dice nada. Nos dejo gemir, juntos, al final.

87

Subo la comida. Está recostada y su madre, a un lado, la llena de arrumacos. Apenas entro, su mirada se clava en mí. Se pasa la lengua por los dientes amarillentos y alcanzo a mirarle las encías podridas. Mi Mujer, pienso. Le dejo la bandeja a la madre en las manos, y estoy por retirarme, cuando la mujer lanza un alarido que me hace volver. Me mira, otra vez aplacada. Me atraviesa. Me dirijo de nuevo a la puerta y, casi a tiempo que pongo un pie fuera del cuarto, chilla. Ahora con la voz más aguda. Su madre y yo nos miramos estupefactos. Ella, todavía, me observa. Y, a pesar del escalofrío que me da verla, la muerte en ella encarnada, jalo una silla y me siento junto con ellas, mientras come.

Así transcurren las semanas. Los tres allí callados. El vientre cada vez más pronunciado, y ella, todavía sin mejora alguna. Si no es su madre, soy yo el único a quien deja atenderla. Y aunque no lo comprendo, no podría ser mejor para mí.

Al fin juntos, pienso. Y no me iré a ninguna parte.

25 *(Refugio):* la carne jaloneada por las uñas, las mías, que se acaban mi piel a rasgones. ¿En búsqueda de encontrar qué cosa allí debajo? Dentro mío. Me veo los pellejos, las llagas, las heridas cada vez más abiertas. Las infecciones donde las liendres deshuevan. Los piojos viejos, ya muertos, enterrados en mis uñas que los jalan, que excavan, me dejan en herencia a sus hijos: la piel roída y blanda para sus dientecitos. Mi piel surcada por los piojos, por mis uñas, su mundo. Otro mundo deforme. Yo. Y en mí el círculo de la vida. A los pocos días de encerrarme en el sótano con Mi Mujer, sentí propagarse en mí la plaga. Más hambrientos, tal vez, los piojos o, quizá, sólo alentados por mi hacinamiento, mi suciedad, me han devorado todo. Así pues, me rasco ahora. Hago una pausa. Me rasco de nuevo. Escribo. Me rasco. Escribo. Me escarbo. Me escribo. Enardecido entero: mis brazos, el pliegue escondido detrás de la rodilla, la ingle, las axilas, el cuello, la cara, el borde de los párpados donde nacen las pestañas, mi cráneo. Me desgracian a sus anchas, siendo, más bien, si acaso, yo el que más daño se ocasiona. Soy yo el que, bajo su dirección, hace todo el trabajo y ellos, los piojos, los que lo gozan; me succionan. Dejo la pluma. Mi mano suda y justo allí donde recargo la pluma hay una herida y el sudor la quema. Muerdo mis uñas, intentando cortarlas para dejar de dañarme, pero nada funciona. Me miro la piel pellizcada de los dedos y..., me desespera. Ella, Mi Mujer, la mula, no puede sentirlos y, otra vez, la envidio. Mejor no

sentir. Nada. La ropa, las suturas, me escuecen. Me desnudo y así escribo, me paseo alrededor de Mi Mujer en el suelo que me mira las nalgas comidas, mi testículo por debajo, como los del burro, picado. Pero dormir así...; no he dormido desde hace días. De sólo pensar que la cucaracha que nos ronda pueda, a mitad de la noche, salir y posarse en mí, en mi carne abierta y despanzurrar, desovar..., siendo yo ya un criadero de alimañas, como los cadáveres, mi madre, mi gato. Dentro de mí el vacío, pero perforándome, haciendo por entrar, la vida de fuera: el mundo. Eso es, entre otras cosas, estar muerto. Y sin pasar por alto que esa vida que digo, la de afuera, es sólo aquella que se alimenta y vive de los muertos o moribundos. De los restos de los desastres, de las tragedias. Unas linduras, las liendres, dicen de sí, de sus criaturas, los piojos... Nos vamos a pudrir, Mujer, y ellos seguirán vivos. Y ella, también, la cucaracha. No morirá, lo sabemos, en el agujero encerrada. Ha pasado ya, antes, encierros más prolongados; como en la lata, pienso. Me alzo de mi silla. Tomo una de las latas, me hinco tronando, empujo la caja que cubre el agujero. Y espero. Allí agazapado al suelo, espero. La lata al aire.

Pasado el tiempo, me canso de estar de rodillas y me siento, estiradas las piernas, y con la espalda al muro a un lado del agujero. Ya vendrá. Hay que tener paciencia, pienso, cuando Mi Mujer comienza con sus quejidos de hambre. Pero, espérame, vieja, le digo. Estoy ocupado. Mis nalgas desnudas sobre el suelo frío, mi sexo, colgante y esmirriado a mitad de mis muslos en huesos, el resto de mis piernas, las escoriaciones a lo largo y ancho de toda mi piel. Esto tiene que terminar pronto. Necio. Hay que apurarse, mejor, por acabar, porque ya no se logró vivir. Ni nada. Lanzo un suspiro embarrado de flema y tos que me doblega y, justo al alzar la cabeza, la descubro: no saliendo del agujero, sino pegada a la caja de cartón del Intendente. Allí estuvo todo este tiempo. Y hay que ser astutos, ahora, y calmos. Me arrastro despacio hasta el archivo. Parece no mirarme. Me acuclillo, levanto la lata, y ella, maldita, corre hacia el interior de la caja. ¡No puede ser más listo que tú!, me grito, y en mi arrebato me pongo en pie, alzo la caja y vuelco su interior al suelo. Caen papeles, notas, cuadernos, libros gruesos de contaduría, pero no el insecto. Sostengo sobre mi cabeza la caja y busco en su interior: vacía. Y en el suelo también nada. Hago los papeles a un lado, la busco entre ellos enterrada, escondida cuando, finalmente, la encuentro: pegada al suelo, barriga al techo, bien aplastada por el peso del papel. En la carpeta que sostengo hay restos embarrados, pedazos de sus patas, quizá de su cara. Se acabo, hija de puta, digo apretando los dientes. Me inclino sobre su cuerpo y lo examino: despanzurrada ahora sí del todo. Enderezo mi cuerpo, empobrecido; mi espalda envarada, con una carga menos, siente el alivio. Dejo caer, otra vez, desde lo alto y sobre el cadáver, el peso entero de la carpeta sucia.

No hay mejor consuelo, me digo estirando el espinazo y respirando profundo, desconectado de mí. Luego, de nuevo, al exhalar, me truena la voz chillante, el gimoteo de mi vieja en los oídos. ¿Y tú?, ¿que será, acaso, Mujer, que no puedes morirte?, le digo en alta voz y pensando en la caja del Intendente. En llenarla otra vez de sus papeles, caminar hacia ella, detenerme sobre su cuerpo, con su cabeza entre mis piernas, y soltar, como martillo de juez, guillotina, la caja en su rostro y hundir, así, su nariz y mis pesares en el pavimento. Volver a respirar...

Acerco mi silla, sin embargo, como siempre. Tomo una lata. Me rasco. Le doy de tragar metiendo en su boca los dedos con los que acabo de despiojarme: repletas las uñas. Me rasco de nuevo. Y todo sigue: me escarbo. Me escarbo. Me escarbo.

26 *(Afuera)*: así la criatura, apenas mal engendrada, por mis brazos sostenida: si acaso, un aborto. El niño, ¿qué otra cosa podría esperarse?, un adefesio esmirriado. La piel, un colgajo azul, los ojos hinchados. La boca, como sellada, sin llanto. Pero, respirando. El engendro respira, cuando yo pienso que es imposible todo lo que transcurre dentro *de ese pequeño pedazo de carne*. Envuelto en los fluidos de su madre, en sus dolores, baboso, respira y vive. Tan condenado. Un milagro maldecido. Es decir, un hombre, al fin. Y a secas. Tan arruinado como su madre, como yo, como todos. El mundo, arruinado, deforme, que nos fecunda. Su cráneo, abollado, apenas cubre una parte de mi mano. Una de sus piernitas, torcida. Y quizá tendría que llamarlo mi hijo, al bastardo. La anciana sirvienta, sudorosa por la agitación, pero con la misma cara impávida de siempre, me lo arrebata, lo cubre con una manta, lo lleva lejos, porque no hemos terminado: la madre, Mi Mujer, en la cama ensangrentada, no se mueve. No responde.

Yace desgarrada. Desmayada por el dolor. El esfuerzo. La miro allí, tan frágil, tan derruida, aplastada por la panza enorme. El bebé, tan diminuto como es, ocupaba sólo un pequeño espacio en ese vientre; el resto, el fluido amniótico, la placenta, la orina del niño. Y ella como tragada, succionada; vaciado su cuerpo. ¿De qué vive? Su madre nos dice que la dejemos dormir, ya controlada la hemorragia. La tuve ya en mis brazos, sintiendo sus huesos, un saco liviano de papas desparramándose, mientras cambiaban las sábanas. Fue nuestro primer contacto y sentí como que la rompía. Salimos del cuarto, la abuela detrás de nosotros con el niño en brazos; ya anochece.

Estamos sentados a la mesa en la cocina. Bebemos café, guardamos silencio, porque estamos casi en luto: perseguidos por la imagen de la criatura, de la mujer, los dos, tan cadavéricamente vivos. Todos pensando, quizás, adivinando, apostando, más bien, el alma, por ver quién se muere primero. Es un crimen; nacer, así, vivir, es un crimen. Veo a las caras de pez, el gesto alargado y a la Rabona, indiferente. Luego a la madre de Mi Mujer, con el niño sobre su regazo durmiendo. Y no lo mira. La cara al frente, escrutando el vacío, rehuyendo a enfrentar la imagen de su nieto, cuando se da la primera alarma, antes de lo esperado: escuchamos, desde arriba, por vez primera la voz de la mujer corriendo al viento fuera de su boca. Son gritos. La madre suelta, como si de una piedra se tratara, al niño en los brazos de la Rabona y los demás subimos corriendo. No son gritos de dolor, sino de angustia. Miedo. Al cruzar la puerta, lo primero que su madre le dice para aplacarla es que el niño está bien, que está allá abajo. Pero, la mujer, sigue gritando. Sólo un alarido continuo y llanto. Gira los ojos solamente hacia nosotros y grita. El cuerpo quieto, las manos relajadas, los brazos, las piernas, inmóviles, reposadas. La tranquilidad de su cuerpo sumada a la expresión exagerada de sus ojos, de su mueca desesperada y sus gritos, nos aterran; un escalofrío nos recorre el cuerpo: un cadáver, es un cadáver despierto gritando. ¡¿Qué pasa, hija?!, le grita su madre. ¡Háblame! Nos sigue con los ojos, a mí, a su madre, a las sirvientas, mientras se desgarra la garganta. Se ha vuelto loca, pensamos, alucina, cuando de pronto se deshace su grito en gimoteos asmáticos y lágrimas. ¿Qué pasa?, le dice de nueva cuenta su madre, ahora con la voz en tono de consuelo. Le toma una mano, que sube a su cara, como para que desde el tacto la reconozca y se tranquilice. Sin embargo, al ver la mujer su brazo alzado, su mano en el rostro de su madre, se quiebra en sollozos. Hija, habla, le dice. No puedo, responde estremecida.

Entrecortada la voz que por primera vez desde hace tanto tiempo escucho hablar. No puedo, dice otra vez, ahogándose. ¿Qué? ¿Qué no puedes? No puedo, no puedo..., no puedo... moverme.

Y tampoco sentía nada: la mejilla de su madre, el calor de sus lágrimas, el viento, su sexo todavía hinchado. Nada. Quizá, sólo un dolor que quién sabe desde qué tan adentro, más allá de los nervios, le nacía. De allí de donde la angustia y el miedo provienen. En sus esfuerzos por sacarse al engendrado, tal vez, lo más rápido posible, como si de una roña se tratara, fue que sufrió la lesión en el cuello que le desgració los huesos de la columna. Sin olvidar, claro, la fragilidad de su cuerpo. Luego del desmayo, la sacudida preocupada de su madre habrá terminado por quebrantarle en virutas el poco resto de huesos que le quedaban. Lo que yo sentí, entonces, no fueron sino sólo los pedazos desperdigándose.

En ese momento tendría que haberme ido. Lo pensé, dejar al niño y a su madre tronada. No obstante, de inmediato, acallé mi pensamiento; consolé a la abuela, cuidé al bebé. Bien si, de cualquier forma, a los pocos días fallecería, el pobre. Y a nadie tomó desprevenido su muerte. Y, sin embargo, no es por esa razón que a nadie le haya causado dolor alguno.

27 *(Afuera):* no hay, en sus ojos, nada. Nada. Su cara yerma, vacía e indiferente. Como si fuese sólo el brazo estirado de un hombre y su muñón lo que la acaricia, y no así la boca negra de la escopeta que empuño, salpicada de otras sangres. Está, primero, el cañón en la punta de su cráneo recargado, allí donde reposa el cerebro; luego, se desliza sobre el hueso que se alarga hasta el hocico que tasca. Y en ella, en sus ojos, todavía nada. Y no obstante la escasa yerba no alcance ya para llenarle la carne, ella, ya tísica, sigue tascando. La escopeta, la mano amputada del hombre, la toca, así, como desde hace tiempo los hombres, todos, nos tocamos. Y nada: el gesto sin rostro le miro y el espinazo, el costillar casi desnudo, el cuero roído entre los huesos. Bajo el arma. La mirada bruta y su cuerpo me traen a cuenta a Mi Mujer, mientras derrama la orina sorda sobre la tierra y sin dejar de mascar y desinteresada de mí y del cañón, otra vez, sobre su cráneo. Tanteo la dureza de su hocico con la punta del rifle empujándolo, y el animal ni se inmuta; sólo roe la tierra. La escucho respirar como si no tuviese nada dentro. Y así termina todo, me digo: sin haber siquiera comenzado. La vida quieta. Y es que en ti todo lo comprendo: Mi Mujer, yo, los hombres como mulas, pero a sabiendas. ¿Qué dirías de ti si pudieras saber lo que eres?, porque, ¿cuánto dura para ti, mula, la vida? El tiempo te pasa desapercibido y el miedo a la muerte es sólo miedo a las violencias que la anteceden y no a morir. No a haber desperdiciado el cuerpo y

la sangre. Tú no te arrepientes, no te desesperas, no te angustias de ser apenas nada, de morir sin haber nacido. De envejecer sin experiencia alguna: la pasividad; donde el tiempo no corre, pero se agota. Mejor no pensar. No sentir, como han hecho los otros, los cuerpos demacrados, el gesto estático mientras se dirigen a la tumba. Me tiro al suelo, a la sombra roída del árbol deshojado que te atenaza por el pescuezo y *que se yergue al medio del brillante paraíso de dios.* Cambiemos lugares, te digo mirando la soga. Que sea yo otra rama torcida que cuelga al aire. Mientras tú, aquí debajo, buscas otro pasto que tascar hasta hundir, sin darte cuenta, el hocico en el mismo punto vacío de antes. Los hombres, dije, como mulas, y luego, *nadie. Nada. Nunca.*

¿Dónde Dios?, mula, te pregunto. Mi cuello hacia ti enroscado a mis espaldas, mis nalgas sobre la dura tierra, la escopeta a mi costado. Y enfrente, el campo, el paisaje destruido del pueblo, los largos páramos, la misma dura tierra estéril. Dije nada. Y nadie. El viento estancado en otra parte, y aquí todo en tanta calma y esperando: ¿lo ves? Ya vienen. Los veo marchar uno tras de otro, tullidos, cojeando, los brazos, como ahorcados, colgando. Caminan hasta acá, los hombres, *turba que en vida no fue nada,* y allá voy yo, también, jalando a cuestas, arrastrando detrás a Mi Mujer. Todavía respirando. Todavía quieta, mientras en procesión andamos, todos, ya cansados, urgidos, mandándonos a morir y manifestándonos ante dios, ¿dónde?, que nos mira. Ya hartos de esperar, bajo el sol, se arrojan los hombres al suelo sin postergar ya el juicio. Impacientes por reunirse con sus muertos. Y allí está el niño arrebatado, lánguido, el fiambre, nacido muerto, de Mi Mujer. Allí, también, mi suegra muerta, la vieja, tragada por las moscas tal y como la encontré en su último día: estaba sentada a la mesa, como siempre. La quijada desvencijada, la mirada perdida y un cúmulo de moscas sobre su rostro, buscando en su garganta el fresco entre tanto calor. Son mis relevaciones, mula. También allí la Rabona, echando rabietas, cogiendo con cadáveres y la coja y mi madre, ya cumplidos sus temores, porque yace tan destripada y podrida como mi gato. Me tiendo al suelo, entonces, como los otros, como Mi Mujer, enceguecido por el sol sobre nuestras cabezas y a mitad del campo baldío. Pero nada pasa. No nos vamos. Desde hace tiempo juzgados y no nos vamos. No nos terminamos de ir.

Son mis visiones, mula. El mundo, le digo poniéndome en pie. Anémico. Mierdoso. Del que te salvo ahora. Camino hasta donde entierra, como avergonzada, el hocico. Más en reverencia, tal vez. Corto el cartucho. Apunto sobre ella, en la sien, ahora sin tocarla, cuando de pronto, alza hacia mí la mirada; el moflete abultado de lo que cree que es yerba. Masca y por la boca se le derrama la tierra en moronas. Enlodazados los dientes, enormes. La cara imbécil, inocente, podría decirse. Tú tan estéril como todos, le digo. Te vas sin dejar de ti nada por detrás más que tu carne descompuesta. Es un favor que te hago, me dijo el burrero. No seas ingrata conmigo y baja los ojos. Vuelve tu hocico al suelo. Me tiembla el párpado cerrado mientras le apunto y ella, todavía, me mira. Ya sin la tierra en la boca que se desliza, más bien trabajosamente, por el gaznate. Luego sólo me observa, seria. Los ojos profundos. La boca atascada, como contracturada, bien hermética. Quizá rechine los dientes y me suelte una mordida, pienso. Al suelo, le repito sin dejar de apuntarle. Te lo ruego. Baja los ojos. Sin soltar el arma, mi dedo en el gatillo, la culata recargada en mi hombro, acerco a su jeta mi diestra. No temas, le digo acariciándola. Su cuero duro me raspa la palma de la mano que pasa, sin darme cuenta, sobre una llaga en la punta de su nariz que supura. Comienza a jadear, excitada, como asfixiándose. Escupe aire, espumarajos. Pela los ojos. Tose. Regurgita la flema que desde hace días envuelve sus pulmones. Pero me sigue mirando. ¿Qué esperas que haga?, le grito, cuando cae al suelo como derrumbada, como tajadas sus patas. Yace ya sobre su costado, ya inmóvil pero viva. Su ojo negro profundo, redondo, me ausculta de arriba abajo, me examina como preguntándose qué le he hecho. Quizá suplicándome la ayude. Resuella agotada porque intenta moverse. Hacer como antes, agitar las piernas, lanzar el cuello hacia arriba para encontrar el contrapeso, el equilibrio.

Ahora sí asustada, ¿de qué?, hace un esfuerzo descomunal más allá de los músculos y ligamentos inútiles. Eso es pensar, me digo. Ese esfuerzo inmóvil, esa pesada carga. Un trabajo que no ve realizada ninguna obra: pensar. Sólo pensar. Y nunca, mula, hasta hoy has llevado sobre ti carga más insoportable; y eres tú misma. Pasa el tiempo y ella todavía batalla, hiperventila desplomada en la tierra. Fatigada como nunca antes. Y yo sólo la miro, aunque quizá jamás se canse. Alzo el arma, le apunto al ojo desquiciado que me sigue en cada movimiento. Pensar es querer andar ya amputadas las piernas, construir con muñones. Pensar es estar vivo y no sólo vivir; saber ¿entiendes?, que no puedes moverte. Mejor no pensar, no sentir, le digo. Y luego no más respiración. El escopetazo todavía estalla en mis oídos. La sangre estancada en la tierra, como su orina.

Queda el silencio. El mundo indiferente. Mis botas, mis dedos ensangrentados. El cadáver allí, la lengua de fuera, otra quietud que a mi tacto, mientras la acaricio, me duele, ¿dónde? Todo enrarecido, y, sin embargo, todo igual. Aquí nada ha pasado. Nada cambia. Y así ha sido todo siempre. Y siempre lo he sabido: el hecho de que algo pueda existir es más improbable, imposible, que el hecho de que ese mismo algo muera; y la posibilidad de ser de la vida, se me ha hecho, al pasar el tiempo, cada vez más siniestra e insoportable.

28 *(Afuera):* en el cuarto, su madre le muestra al niño. Todavía vivo. Lo pone sobre su cara, como hiciera el mozo, en mi infancia, a mi madre con el gato destripado. Yo de pie al otro lado de la cama, idéntico a aquel entonces, lo miro todo, y en el niño, la misma muerte violenta de mi gato: descarnados los dos, tragados como de dentro por la parca. Y soy testigo, también, del rechazo de la madre, quien, al tener a su hijo enfrente, desvía la mirada lejos; el rostro endurecido, frío. Y no lo miró nunca. Nunca quiso hacerlo. Apenas y, sin importarle en lo más mínimo, llegó a enterarse de su muerte: la Rabona lo encuentra en su cuneta improvisada, ya sin respirar, ya concreto, el cadáver, una forma exacta, un objeto. La vemos bajar las escaleras, entrar a la cocina con el niño sujeto por el tobillo, colgando. Los brazos estirados al suelo. La abuela nos encomienda, apenas lo mira, la tarea de enterrarlo. Es lo mejor que pudo haber pasado, es todo lo que dice. Entonces, la Rabona y yo, ya en el patio, abrimos un agujero al pie de la casa. Ella vuelve a tomarlo por el mismo tobillo mientras se acerca a la tumba. Lo sostiene, después, un tiempo, ya acuclillada de frente al hoyo, como dudando; dudando la vida. La cara del bebé, los bracitos, ya más de medio cuerpo hundido en la tierra; este río de odio. Pero se mantiene indecisa, la Rabona. Es decir, ungido está ya gran parte de su cuerpo por el mundo de los muertos, por las profundidades ya tocado, empapado de ellas, y no se decide dejarlo ir, manteniendo ese tobillo atado al reino

de los mortales. Y a mi vista. Mirarlo colgar así, trapo descocido, me desespera. Ya, le digo, pero no atiende; está en el fondo del agujero pasmada. Que lo dejes, le repito, y nada. Le suelto, entonces, un manotazo al puño que sujeta al diminuto cadáver, para que luego, al fin, lo deje marcharse. El sonido de la caída es débil; como si se negara del todo que ese ser llegó, alguna vez, a existir. Y así tomó la noticia su madre. Callada y como si no le hubieran dicho más que un ruido. Pero quedará ella, pienso. Si los hijos son carne, evidencia, de que hubo una madre, una parturienta, si acaso, ella será la prueba, el vestigio desastrado, de su hijo malnacido.

Nada puede hacerse, es todo lo que el médico nos dice. Se quedará así para el resto de su vida: inmóvil, paralizada. Su madre, al oír las noticias, llora y ella, quizá ahogando el llanto, sólo gira los ojos lejos de las lamentaciones. También yo me lamento y, en respuesta, cada que salgo al patio a alimentar a los puercos, es decir, cada que cruzo por donde yace la tumba doy duras pisotadas, llenando de tierra la boca desvencijada del niño: no hay allí nada sagrado. Estoy fuera de mí, maldiciéndome, maldiciendo todo. No alcanzo hilar un pensamiento, trabajo apenas y descuidadamente. Ya nada importa. Nunca nada ha importado. Sólo me mantengo atento a las necesidades de la mujer. De Mi Mujer. Y es por eso que he dejado de revolcar a la Rabona en la tierra o en las sábanas. Me mira con desprecio y así mira a Mi Mujer. Pero ya no habiendo aquí otro hombre, y con la solicitud de la tetrapléjica de tenerme siempre cerca y dejarse sólo atender por mí, no tengo necesidad alguna de cogérmela. Por mí puede pudrírsete el sexo, pienso, mientras preparo la cena de la mujer y ella, la Rabona, pasa por mis espaldas empujándome y derramando al suelo todo lo que ya había preparado. La miro enfurecido y ella responde, sin titubear, mi mirada. Luego sale y yo tengo que volver a comenzar. Una vez ya arriba, alimento a la mujer. Su madre se ha ido por unos días para dar noticias a su padre, quien no se digna verla, y atenderlo. Volverá en una semana, dijo. Y mientras le doy de comer, callados los dos, pienso que debí haber aprovechado las oportunidades que tuve cuando su marido se marchaba, y cogerla. Sus muslos y sus brazos, todavía cálidos y no frígidos como ahora; cogerla, quiero decir, cuando aún, bien sin quererlo, podía sentirme. Me arrepiento. Sin embargo, mientras le doy de comer, su cuerpo, ya algo repuesto, pero aún desgraciado, todavía me llama. En mí la imagen de antes, sus senos firmes e hinchados, sus piernas redondeadas. Y la miro ahora, incluso si me duelen sus condiciones, todavía excitándome. Termino de lavar los trastos sucios y subo al cuarto de la mujer, donde pasaré la noche para cuidarla. Nuestra primera noche juntos. En el sillón, en la esquina, la veo dormir. La luz del baño encendida, por si necesita cualquier cosa yo pueda moverme, la presenta a mis ojos. Iluminada. Si tan sólo…, pienso, mientras recuerdo el día que la vi por vez primera, y aquel otro luego de haber salido de su cuarto, de su casa, apenas después de haber sido por primera vez violada: los pezones tiesos por el frío remarcados, los senos duros, firmes, los brazos desnudos, las piernas. Dudo que sea la misma mujer quien yace ahora en la cama; ella, ya es algo más. Pero, no para mí. Y eso, pienso yo, es el amor. Ya quitada de ternuras, ya sus voluptuosidades desgastadas hasta el hastío, ya su cuerpo fregado…, y aun así… La miro, y sin pensarlo, sin explicación alguna, tragado por la atmósfera permisible de la noche que deja asomar las rarezas escondidas, bajo mis pantalones. La miro. Y mirándola jadeo hasta derramarme. Luego duermo como sólo descansa un bebé en la cuna. Sólo en la cuna y en la tumba se duerme como yo he dormido. Fue una pequeña muerte reparadora.

Repetirme al día siguiente fue inevitable. Llegada la noche volví a hacerlo: sentado en el sillón, los pantalones a la altura de los tobillos, escuchándola respirar trabajosamente y, de nuevo, el sueño profundo. Aquellos momentos tendrían que ser lo más afortunado en mi triste vida, y nada sería comparable. Había que aprovechar nuestra soledad y seguí, por ello, haciéndolo los días siguientes, intentando, así, desahogarme. Hasta que tuve necesidad de más. Tenía que sentirla. La siguiente noche, entonces, apenas la escuché resollar dormida, me acerqué a ella, la saqué de debajo de las sábanas que la abrazaban destapándola. No debes sentirme, dije en voz baja. En teoría, no debes sentirme ni despertarte... quizás en sueños..., y sueñes ahora conmigo, con mi tacto y te guste. Los pantalones en el suelo, una de mis manos en sus senos, en su abdomen, sus costillas, el pelambre de su sexo bajo el camisón, y la otra mano en mí. Como unidos, los dos, a través de mi cuerpo. Si tan sólo escuchara tu voz, al final, gemir, como antes, como con él, se me escapa decir en voz alta y sin percatarme. Al terminar, mientras me agachaba para recoger los pantalones, me pareció mirarle los ojos abiertos fijos en mí. Me pasmé del espanto y casi tropiezo al dar un paso atrás. Una vez ya equilibrado mi cuerpo, miré sus ojos. Cerrados. Mis latidos destrozaban mi pecho, ¿me habrá visto?, pensé primero y luego... ¿me habrá sentido? Vacilante volví al sillón y pasé despierto toda la noche vigilando esos ojos. Como si, de pronto, pudiera alzarse y arremeter contra mí todas las furias guardadas. Me juré no repetirlo.

La tarde siguiente, sin embargo, después de haber lavado los trastos sucios de la comida, subo para revisarla; ver que todo se encuentre en orden. Lo que me hallo, no obstante, es algo inesperado. Algo improbable, imposible. Antes de bajar, había dejado yo a la mujer tapada con las sábanas y durmiendo. Ahora, sin embargo, que estoy de frente a ella, la puerta abierta y el sol sobre su cuerpo, yace destapada y, más todavía, con el camisón alzado a la cintura, el pelo al aire Y no lo comprendo. ¿Cómo pudo ser?, me pregunto, mientras me voy acercando. No hay nadie en la habitación ni en el piso de arriba. Me asomo por las escaleras y escucho a las mujeres trabajar abajo. ¿Será, acaso, que puede moverse?... ¿Me habrá sentido anoche, entonces? Camino hasta donde se encuentra, me detengo en la orilla de la cama: allí está, otra vez, su desnudez, llamándome. Sintiendo temor, la cubro rápidamente con las cobijas. Señora, le digo, ¿está despierta? Pero no responde. Los ojos bien cerrados. ¿Qué pudo haber ocurrido?, me pregunto cuando miro que uno de sus brazos cuelga fuera de la cama. ¿Estuvo siempre así? Señora, vuelvo a decirle. Pero, nada. Tomo su brazo por la muñeca, la mano vencida hacia mí, como ofreciéndose. Aprieto un poco para ver si reacciona. Y nada ocurre. Mi cabeza no encuentra rumbo ni sentido. Su muñeca, frágil, todavía en mis manos. Le miro los dedos, delgados, y no resisto: los beso a ojos cerrados, descubriéndolos sólo con mis labios y mi lengua. Un dedo suyo atorado en mi labio me abre la boca, y en ese momento me viene la sensación de estar sujetando el brazo rígido de una muerta que muevo a mis anchas. Me despierto del trance y giro a verla. ¿Sintió algo? Sus ojos todavía cerrados. Sin soltarla, bajo a la altura de su cara para oír su respiración, porque no ronca. Allí está, y sus narices me soplan aire cálido en el rostro, en la oreja. Me embriago. Cierro otra vez los ojos, respiro profundo, giro un poco la cara, su nariz da contra la mía, mis labios la rozan y comienzo a besar su boca, sus mejillas descarnadas, su cuello, su hombro, el brazo entero que sujeto en el aire. No me contengo más. Abro los ojos y me aseguro de que siga dormida. Cierro tras de mí la puerta asegurándola. Le quito las cobijas, veo sus piernas flacas, sus muslos, la maraña de su sexo. La felicidad, me digo, de verte a la luz dura del sol. Suelto mis pantalones, aturdido y descuidado, eufórico. La hebilla del cinturón choca contra el suelo y resuena agudo. Le miro la cara. Sigue igual, impávida. Subo más todavía el camisón, destapándola entera hasta el cuello. Y comienzo a besarla: las caderas, el ombligo, las tetas. Me saco por completo los pantalones para poder moverme a lo largo sin problemas, estrujarla, lamerla. No quiero terminar pronto. No quiero terminar nunca. Podría subir contigo, ahora, tocarte en lo profundo. Y sin pensar, lo hago. El sol calentándome las nalgas, mi cuerpo haciéndole sombra. Mi cara sobre la suya, quieta, su cuerpo bajo el mío, quieto, sus manos, quietas, sus piernas, abiertas, quietas, que me reciben. Lo hago despacio. Hundo mi cabeza entre sus senos malogrados, los muerdo, los pellizco. Podría morirme ahora, pienso. Que me maten ahora, me digo, jadeando, cuando alzo la cara y le miro los ojos pelados sobre mi rostro. Mirándome. Observándome.

En pánico, me lanzo a un lado en la cama y pido disculpas; le pido que me disculpe, que lo he hecho sin querer hacerlo. Me alzo, me pongo los pantalones, recojo mis zapatos y ella, todavía, me mira sin decir nada, sin gesto o mueca alguna. Me sigue con los ojos, pasiva, inmóvil, como un fantasma que observa desde el otro lado. Y salgo. Estoy en el patio, debatiéndome sobre lo que debo hacer ahora. Intranquilo, aterrado. Tan humano como nunca. Tan desagradable. No sé, no sé, es todo lo que alcanzo decirme, cuando me percato que estoy parado sobre la tumba del niño. ¿En qué nos diferenciamos los hombres?, me pregunto al pensar en su padre. Y decido marcharme. Entro a la habitación de la Rabona para recoger mis escasas cosas. No vuelvo nunca, me digo. Jamás. Cuando ella entra y, te vi, me dice. ¿Qué? Te vi, vuelve a decir. No has visto nada, le digo. Sí, te vi. ¿Cómo?, me pregunto, y lo comprendo. Ella ha sido. Ella preparó todo; el brazo, las cobijas. ¿Por qué? Podría golpearla, abofetearla, educarla así. Me ha arruinado. Todo mi trabajo arruinado. Podría matarla. Sí. Me acerco a ella, que parece estarme esperando fija. Sin temor. Te mato, le digo. No dice nada ni se mueve. Mis dientes apretados, mi puño cerrado, cuando entra una de las sirvientas cara de palo. La señora pregunta por ti, me dice. Te llama. Subo las escaleras sin saber qué esperar. La puerta cerrada. Entro. Termina, me dice.

La Rabona se fue al día siguiente. La madre volvió, y durmieron las dos juntas en la misma cama. Yo me quedé con el cuarto de la Rabona entero para mí solo. Y ella, la mujer, cada que veía la oportunidad, me pedía que me desnudase, que la montara: su gesto frío mientras lo hacía, su cuerpo rígido, en huesos, cada vez más ulcerado. Hacía el amor con la muerte. Y eso fue, quizá, la felicidad en mi vida. Me desesperó tan rápido. Luego vino la primera ocupación. Los aviones. Las bombas de gas cayendo del cielo. Los campos destruidos, yermos. Arruinados. Se peleaba una guerra civil que nos era ajena y que tuvo el mal tino de dejarnos con vida. Existía, quién sabe dónde, un mundo que nos era inaccesible. Se fueron los de uniformes con bandas azules y llegaron otros con bandas rojas que nunca se irían. Se fue la fortuna de Mi Mujer, económica, digo, con los campos enfermos de su padre quien, inevitablemente, o, mejor dicho, convenientemente, moriría pronto dejándomelo todo: a sus dos viejas maltrechas. Las sirvientas se fueron buscando otra vida o, más bien, buscando morirse. Yo entré al Ayuntamiento. Y la vida se detuvo. Todavía más.

Y así la recogí: en sobras. A mi Mujer, la vieja tetrapléjica.

29 *(Refugio):* ¿y luego que nos queda, Mujer, mi amor? El cuerpo en ruinas. Así construidos: destruyéndonos de a poco hasta quedar del todo deshechos. Una piltrafa, un desperdicio. Porque es eso lo que llamamos vivir, las experiencias: pequeños desastres que nos malogran y cuyos vestigios utilizamos de cimientos para ser. Pero la pasividad, Mujer, la pasividad ha sido mi único desastre; el aburrimiento, la nada. Tú. Y de alguna manera todo esto tiene que acabar. Y ahora: duermes. Agotada de veras, casi hasta tu última sustancia, y te resta no sino sólo aquella que, terca, se mantiene en ti vagando: un espíritu que es más una miasma y que, tan pronto logre destrancarse de entre tu cuerpo vacío, agusanado, se extenderá rancio por el aire hasta que, al fin, quedemos todos libres. El mundo. Sino es que envenenados y más bien muertos. Aunque lo digo, esto último, también con alivio, porque ya, Mujer, ya es tiempo. Y si tiene que ser ésta la única vez que emprenda algo, que tenga intenciones de algo y lo realice, que así sea. Estoy inspirado, vieja. El cadáver repugnante de la cucaracha me inspira. Los recuerdos, también repulsivos, me colman del ánimo necesario para reventar: al fin, sobre ti, vomitarme. Ya cansado, Mujer, vieja mula, de tragarme la víscera, la propia víscera. Y aquí se acaba. Despierta. Despierta, grito. Pero no respondes. Tu cara entre mis piernas, bajo mi desnudez, a la altura de la bolsa fláccida de mi testículo rasgado. Mis pies fríos de uñas largas tocando tus orejas. Despierta, Mujer,

despierta, repito mirándote. Mi cara justo sobre tu jeta embarrada de mugre. Pateo suavemente, más bien apenas empujando, tu cabeza para que me mires. Necesito que me mires, Mujer, porque te quiero. Y, sin embargo, tu insensibilidad, tu característica de cadáver, impide que te despiertes. Tu debilidad, quizá. Y tu cabeza sólo va a dar al otro costado. La pateo, entonces, de nuevo, pelota dura; tu cráneo disminuido, también. Y nada; el mismo resultado. Qué desesperante eres, vieja, digo trabajosamente. Saco de mi boca la escopeta sin dejar de mirarte. La pongo, ahora, sobre ti, en tu frente: una extensión de mí que te toca. Y empujo. Hurgo tu cara, tu boca abierta con el cañón, como hacen los niños con los cadáveres de pájaros que encuentran en el suelo: te pico, como con una vara y curioso, frío, te pico y te llamo: despierta, mula terca. Sé que respiras; no puedes morirte así y sin darme este pequeño placer. Insignificante. Y hasta humano. Presiono ahora sobre tu pecho, como hacen para reanimar a los del limbo: una, dos, tres veces. Duro. Y allí está, casi en milagro y escupiendo la flema. Buenos días, Mujer, te digo. Tus ojos, como siempre; sin expresión y mucho menos sorpresa y mucho menos dolor. Coloco otra vez la escopeta en mi boca mientras te miro. Mi cabeza colgando hacia ti; nuestras miradas encontradas. Tu rostro descascarado, transparente, vacío.

Ya no tienes nada dentro, ¿verdad, Mujer?

¿Y yo?

30 *(Refugio):* "es el mundo la creación de un degenerado. Y nosotros su obra. Tu hija, la niña, una criatura insoportable. Y también tú, mi vida. Nos estábamos volviendo locos. Íbamos enfermando y ya no hablabas. Eras como ella. Y yo no tenía intenciones, lo juro; desesperé. Perdí pronto la cabeza. Pero, soy un buen hombre, mi amor, y tú tienes que entenderlo y ser comprensiva; fue el pueblo, la situación, tu espalda, la carita larga de la niña..., siempre tu espalda, tu silencio... ya era como hablarle al... Ya ni siquiera discutíamos y ya ni nos dábamos motivos para odiarnos más, gritarnos. Nada. Yo volvía de la oficina y ella seguía allí, tirada al pasto, las piernitas cruzadas, las manitas entrelazadas. Tan linda. Tan triste. Y tú como viva, pero callada; lavando trastes, escombrando. Preparabas la comida, lavabas, nos metíamos en la cama, te torcías al otro lado, dormías en silencio. Los primeros manotazos me dolieron en el alma, mujer. Tu mejilla roja. Y ni así respondiste, como si algo en ti hubiera muerto. ¡Es la niña o nosotros!, te grité en amenaza. Pero te mantuviste en silencio. Luego salí todo el día, hasta la noche, y sólo volví para encontrarme la casa ya vacía. O así lo pensé".

Frente a este cuadro, uno no tiene otro camino que perder la fe, ¿verdad, Mujer, vieja mula? Tú lo viste: estamos condenados. Jalé una y otra vez el gatillo y nada. Allí las municiones y nada. Intenté en ti y nada. Ya lo dije, estamos condenados, sí, a vivir, muertos, a vivir siempre muriéndonos. Sin acabar, nunca, nadie, de morirse.

Aquí encerrados, en esta tumba. Y a sabiendas de que no existe nada más, mi amor. Que allá arriba ya está todo destruido desde hace tiempo. Los hombres ya se mataron. Que estamos aquí enterrados. Que no logramos salir. Que así será para siempre y que todo esto es real. Todo real. Es decir, que estamos condenados a esta clase, sólo a ésta, de eternidad. ¿No te da tristeza?, ¿no te da tristeza tener todo el tiempo del mundo para pensar, siempre pensar, en lo que eres y fuiste? ¿No sientes algo cercano a la vergüenza? Es la única historia que tenemos, Mujer, y nunca ha de abandonarnos. Por eso ya no me queda nada más que intentar hacer como tú; renunciarme. Morirme de veras. Sin pensar, sin sentir, porque mi vida no fue sino sólo *una agitación sin consistencia*. Sólo inquietud en la parálisis. Ya estoy a tu lado tendido, Mujer. Mi cuerpo destazado, habitado por otras plagas, además de ti y de mí y de todo, escupe pura basura mientras te tomo de la mano, te miro la mueca cadavérica de siempre. Tú a mi diestra y del otro lado el cuerpo reventado de la cucaracha, tan vacía como nosotros. Los tres con la panza hacia arriba, los tres aprisionados contra la tierra, inmóviles y tan vivos como siempre.

"¿Por qué no te la llevaste?, me dije una vez que la vi, recostada en su cama, la cara al techo. Luego lo supe, y puedo asegurarte que no sufrió. Estaba igual que siempre. Recogí el cojín del suelo, todavía algo húmedo por ambas partes. Y así supe que lloraste mientras la ahogabas. Es decir, mientras ella, quizá tan inerte e idiotizada como siempre, moría llenando de sus babas el otro costado de la almohada y que tú, también, todavía algo sentías. Llevé el cojín lleno de las dos al cuarto, y lo puse de tu lado de la cama para dormir juntos. A ella la dejé tal como la encontré y tal como siempre luego de apagar la luz: sus ojitos estancados en el vacío, como mirando un muro. Siempre el mismo muro. Siempre encerrada.

Quizá hayas llegado ya a alguna parte, mi amor. Si es posible. Y quizá leas todo lo que te escribo. Si es así, quiero que sepas que la niña sigue allí al día de hoy. Para cuando quieras volver. Y no nos iremos a ninguna parte".